Oh! 365 Nut-Free Recipes

(Oh! 365 Nut-Free Recipes - Volume 1)

Mary Rosado

Content

365 Awesome Nut-Free Recipes

***

---

1. 5 Ingredient Apple Pie

Serving: One 9-inch pie | Prep: | Cook: | Ready in: 1hours20mins

Ingredients

- ½ cup sugar, plus extra for sprinkling
- 2 tablespoons all-purpose flour
- 1 teaspoon ground cinnamon
- 6 apples, peeled and thinly sliced
- 2 store-bought pie crusts (I prefer the vegan brand Wholly Wholesome)
- Soy milk (optional, for brushing)

Direction

- Preheat oven to 375 degrees. Lightly grease a 9-inch pie pan.
- Whisk together sugar, flour and cinnamon in a large bowl. Add apples and mix with a large spoon until apples are evenly coated.
- On a lightly floured surface, roll out 1 dough until it is about 1/8 inch thick. Carefully lift the dough and fit it into the prepared pan, letting about 1 inch hang over the sides. Fill the pie shell with the apple filling.
- On a lightly floured surface, roll out the second disc of dough until it is about 1/8 inch thick and cut out eight 1-inch strips. My lattice technique does not require any weaving. Instead, lay four strips horizontally on top of the filling, leaving about 1/2 to 3/4 inch between strips. You may want to use a metal spatula to transfer the dough strips from your work surface to your pie. Lay the remaining four strips diagonally over the first four strips,

creating a diamond-like shape between strips. Fold the overhanging dough over the edges of the lattice top. Crimp the dough between your two index fingers to make a decorative border
- Brush the top and edges of the pie crust with nondairy milk and sprinkle with sugar for an extra sweet and crisp top. Bake for 50 to 55 minutes, until the crust is nicely browned.

---

2. Adi Giovanetti's Pasta Alla Checca (Linguine With Fresh Herbs)

Serving: 6 servings | Prep: | Cook: | Ready in: 20mins

Ingredients

- 2 tablespoons extravirgin olive oil
- ½ medium yellow onion, chopped
- 1 16-ounce can imported Italian tomatoes
- Salt and freshly ground black pepper
- 1 bunch arugula (see note)
- ½ pound grated pecorino Romano cheese
- 1 pound linguine or spaghettini or other thin pasta
- 1 tablespoon salt

Direction

- Over medium heat, saute the chopped onion in the olive oil until onion is just golden brown. Remove from heat and add the tomatoes, juice and all. Crush the tomatoes slightly with a fork. Return to low heat and simmer until the sauce has thickened. Taste for seasoning and add salt and freshly ground black pepper if desired.
- While the sauce is cooking, wash and dry the arugula, discarding thick stems. Cut into thin ribbons and set aside.
- Bring 4 quarts of water to a rolling boil. Add salt if desired and when water reboils, add pasta. Stir vigorously with a long-handled

wooden spoon or fork to separate pasta strands and bring water quickly back to a boil.

- When pasta is done, drain quickly and turn into a warm serving bowl. Remove sauce from fire and add the arugola, stirring to mix well. Pour sauce over pasta and sprinkle with half the pecorino cheese. Serve immediately, passing the rest of the cheese separately.

Nutrition Information

- 494: calories;
- 1 gram: polyunsaturated fat;
- 5 grams: sugars;
- 24 grams: protein;
- 7 grams: saturated fat;
- 6 grams: monounsaturated fat;
- 63 grams: carbohydrates;
- 644 milligrams: sodium;
- 16 grams: fat;

3. Alsatian Mussels In Riesling

Serving: 6 appetizers or 4 servings as a main dish | Prep: | Cook: | Ready in: 45mins

Ingredients

- 4 tablespoons unsalted butter
- 3 shallots, finely chopped
- ½ bottle Alsatian riesling
- 3 pounds medium-size mussels, scrubbed and debearded
- 1 ½ tablespoons finely chopped parsley
- 1 loaf crusty French bread

Direction

- Melt the butter in a heavy 6-quart saucepan. Add the shallots and saute over medium heat until they are tender but not brown.
- Add the wine and bring to a simmer. Add the mussels, cover and cook about 10 minutes,

until the mussels have opened. Discard any mussels that do not open.

- Spoon the mussels into soup plates and spoon the broth over them. Sprinkle with parsley and serve with crusty bread.

Nutrition Information

- 706: calories;
- 5 grams: monounsaturated fat;
- 7 grams: sugars;
- 50 grams: protein;
- 9 grams: saturated fat;
- 0 grams: trans fat;
- 1432 milligrams: sodium;
- 21 grams: fat;
- 3 grams: dietary fiber;
- 63 grams: carbohydrates;

4. Apple Compote

Serving: Makes about 3 1/2 cups, serving 6 | Prep: | Cook: | Ready in: 30mins

Ingredients

- 3 pounds tart apples, such as pippins, Gravensteins, Macintosh, Granny Smith, Pink Lady, peeled if desired, cored and cut in chunks
- 2 tablespoons water
- 2 tablespoons turbinado sugar
- 1 tablespoon fresh lemon or lime juice
- Sweet spices if desired (cinnamon, nutmeg, allspice, cloves)

Direction

- Place apples and water in a heavy saucepan and stir over medium-high heat until the mixture is bubbling. Reduce heat to low and cover. Cook, stirring often, until the apples have cooked down but still have some texture, 15 to 20 minutes. Add sugar, lemon or lime juice, and spices, cover and simmer for another 3 to 5 minutes. Remove from heat and allow to cool, or serve warm or hot.

Nutrition Information

- 151: calories;
- 36 grams: carbohydrates;
- 7 grams: dietary fiber;
- 26 grams: sugars;
- 1 gram: protein;
- 3 milligrams: sodium;
- 0 grams: polyunsaturated fat;

5. Apple Doughnuts

Serving: 18 doughnuts | Prep: | Cook: | Ready in: 45mins

Ingredients

- ½ cup brown sugar, firmly packed
- ¼ cup vegetable oil plus oil for frying
- ¼ cup buttermilk
- ¼ cup fresh apple cider
- 1 large egg
- 1 cup unsweetened applesauce
- 3 cups unbleached flour, approximately
- 1 teaspoon ground mace
- 1 teaspoon ground cinnamon
- 1 teaspoon baking powder
- ½ teaspoon baking soda
- Confectioners' sugar

Direction

- In a large bowl, combine the brown sugar, oil, buttermilk and cider. Whisk in the egg and applesauce (see recipe below).
- In a small bowl, sift two and a half cups of the flour with the mace, cinnamon, baking powder and baking soda. Add this mixture to the applesauce mixture and mix to make a soft dough, adding additional flour as needed.
- Turn the dough out onto a floured surface and dust liberally with flour. Flour your hands and knead the dough, adding additional flour as necessary, to make a soft dough that is no longer sticky. Roll the dough to one-half-inch thickness and cut with a doughnut cutter. Place the cut doughnuts on a baking sheet lined with parchment paper. Cover and place in the refrigerator. The cut doughnuts can be refrigerated for several hours, if desired.
- Pour at least two inches of oil into a deep pan and bring it to 375 degrees over moderate heat. Dip a spatula into the hot oil and slide the doughnuts into the oil three or four at a time and fry them a minute or so on each side, until golden brown. They should take about three minutes each to fry. If they brown in less time than that, your oil is too hot.
- Lift the fried doughnuts out of the oil with a slotted spoon and place them on several thicknesses of paper towel to drain. Dust them with sifted confectioners' sugar while they are still warm.

Nutrition Information

- 183: calories;
- 25 grams: carbohydrates;
- 5 grams: monounsaturated fat;
- 2 grams: polyunsaturated fat;
- 3 grams: protein;
- 68 milligrams: sodium;
- 8 grams: sugars;
- 1 gram: dietary fiber;
- 0 grams: trans fat;

6. Artichoke Fritters With Bearnaise Sauce

Serving: 4 appetizer servings | Prep: | Cook: | Ready in: 25mins

Ingredients

- 8 artichoke hearts (canned), drained and cut in half lengthwise

- ⅓ cup flour plus extra for dredging artichokes
- 1 egg
- 2 ½ cups milk
- 1 teaspoon salt
- 1 teaspoon baking powder
- 1 ounce water
- 1 ounce red-wine vinegar
- 1 teaspoon dried tarragon
- 1 teaspoon minced shallots
- 2 ounces dry white wine
- 2 egg yolks
- 8 ounces clarified butter
- Salt and white pepper to taste
- Juice of 1/2 lemon
- 1 1-pound can vegetable shortening

Direction

- Dredge the artichoke hearts lightly in flour, and set aside.
- In a bowl, mix the egg, milk and salt. In a separate bowl, combine 1/3 cup flour and baking powder. Gradually add this mixture to the egg mixture. It should have the consistency of light pancake batter.
- In a small saucepan, combine the water, vinegar, tarragon, shallots and white wine. Bring to a boil, and reduce until only about 2 tablespoons liquid remain in the pan. Remove from heat and let cool.
- In the top bowl of a double boiler over medium-low heat, whisk together the egg yolks and the reduced tarragon liquid. Remove from heat, and whip the butter very gradually into the mixture. When all the butter has been absorbed, season with salt, pepper and lemon juice. Keep warm until served.
- In a deep saucepan or wok, heat vegetable shortening to 375 degrees. There should be enough oil to cover the artichokes. Using up to six artichoke halves at a time, dip each in the batter, drain the excess and drop in the oil, frying until golden brown. Remove and drain well on paper towels, and keep warm. Repeat with remaining artichokes.
- Serve with bearnaise sauce.

7. Artichoke And Spinach Gratin

Serving: 6 servings | Prep: | Cook: | Ready in: 1hours15mins

Ingredients

- For the gratin
- 3 tablespoons plus 1 teaspoon unsalted butter
- 1 medium yellow onion, peeled and minced
- 1 ½ quarts cleaned fresh spinach
- 3 large, fresh globe artichokes, trimmed and cooked, then quartered lengthwise
- 3 soft-boiled eggs, peeled and cubed
- ½ teaspoon chopped fresh thyme
- 1 tablespoon chopped fresh flat-parsley
- 1 cup Leek Crema
- ¼ teaspoon grated nutmeg
- Pinch of kosher salt
- Freshly ground pepper
- ¼ cup grated vegetarian Parmesan
- ¼ cup freshly toasted breadcrumbs
- For the Leek Crema
- 1 teaspoon unsalted butter
- 1 leek, white only, cleaned and minced
- Pinch of kosher salt
- 1 cup heavy cream

Direction

-
-

Nutrition Information

- 405: calories;
- 20 grams: carbohydrates;
- 6 grams: dietary fiber;
- 5 grams: sugars;
- 33 grams: fat;
- 0 grams: trans fat;
- 9 grams: monounsaturated fat;
- 2 grams: polyunsaturated fat;
- 11 grams: protein;
- 307 milligrams: sodium;

8. Arugula And Corn Salad With Roasted Red Peppers And White Beans

Serving: Serves 4 | Prep: | Cook: | Ready in: 15mins

Ingredients

- 1 ear sweet corn
- 3 cups baby or wild arugula
- 2 red bell peppers, roasted
- 1 ½ cups (1 can) cooked white beans, such as cannellini or navy beans, rinsed if using canned beans
- 1 tablespoon chopped chives
- 1 tablespoon slivered fresh basil (more to taste)
- 2 tablespoons sherry vinegar or red wine vinegar
- 1 teaspoon balsamic vinegar
- Salt to taste
- 1 small garlic clove, pureed or put through a press
- ¼ teaspoon Dijon mustard
- 5 tablespoons extra-virgin olive oil
- Freshly ground pepper to taste
- ¼ cup shaved Parmesan

Direction

- Steam corn for 4 to 5 minutes, until just tender. Remove from heat, allow to cool, and cut kernels off cob. Combine with arugula in a large bowl.
- Remove seeds and membranes from roasted peppers and cut in 2-inch strips. Place in another bowl. Add beans, chives and basil and toss together.
- Whisk together vinegars, salt, garlic, mustard, and olive oil. Set aside 3 tablespoons of the dressing and toss the rest with beans and peppers. Season to taste with salt and pepper,

and allow to sit for at least 15 minutes and for up to 3 days (in the refrigerator).

- Toss remaining dressing with arugula and corn. Line salad plates or a platter with arugula and corn mixture. Top with peppers and beans. Garnish with shaved Parmesan, and serve.

Nutrition Information

- 339: calories;
- 0 grams: trans fat;
- 13 grams: monounsaturated fat;
- 2 grams: polyunsaturated fat;
- 31 grams: carbohydrates;
- 5 grams: sugars;
- 12 grams: protein;
- 20 grams: fat;
- 4 grams: saturated fat;
- 544 milligrams: sodium;
- 7 grams: dietary fiber;

9. Asparagus And Egg Sandwich

Serving: Two sandwiches | Prep: | Cook: | Ready in: 15mins

Ingredients

- ½ pound asparagus (preferably pencil-thin)
- 4 tablespoons olive oil
- Salt and freshly ground black pepper to taste
- 4 large eggs
- ½ 16-inch loaf Italian bread

Direction

- Wash the asparagus under cold running water. Snap off and discard the tough bottom portion. If using thicker asparagus, scrape each stalk to remove the skin, then cut it into thirds lengthwise, leaving the the asparagus head intact.

- In a medium-size saucepan, heat the oil until just warm. Add the asparagus and salt. Saute over medium heat, stirring, for about 2 minutes. Cover and cook for another 2 minutes, shaking the pan or stirring occasionally.
- Meanwhile, break the eggs into a bowl and beat, adding a pinch of salt and pepper. Cut the bread in half lengthwise. Remove the soft, doughy part and toast the loaf slightly.
- Uncover the asparagus, raise the heat slightly and add the eggs, stirring. Cook for 1 minute, or until the eggs are set. Scoop onto the bread and cut in half.

Nutrition Information

- 208: calories;
- 0 grams: trans fat;
- 8 grams: monounsaturated fat;
- 2 grams: dietary fiber;
- 15 grams: carbohydrates;
- 7 grams: protein;
- 13 grams: fat;
- 3 grams: saturated fat;
- 249 milligrams: sodium;
- 1 gram: sugars;

10. Aunt Phil's Brown Sugar Cake

Serving: 1 cake (6 to 8 servings) | Prep: | Cook: | Ready in: 50mins

Ingredients

- 4 eggs
- 1 pound brown sugar
- 1 ½ teaspoons vanilla
- 1 ¾ cups sifted flour
- ½ cup chopped dates
- ⅛ teaspoon salt

Direction

- Preheat oven to 350 degrees.
- Combine the eggs and sugar in the top of a double boiler and cook 20 minutes over low heat, stirring frequently with a wooden spoon until thick. Stir in the vanilla, flour, dates and salt. Pour into an ungreased 9-by-13-inch baking pan and bake 20 minutes. Cool, cut into squares and serve.

Nutrition Information

- 387: calories;
- 83 milligrams: sodium;
- 2 grams: dietary fiber;
- 1 gram: polyunsaturated fat;
- 0 grams: trans fat;
- 87 grams: carbohydrates;
- 65 grams: sugars;
- 6 grams: protein;

11. Austrian Marinated Fillet Of Beef With Asparagus Tips

Serving: 6 servings | Prep: | Cook: | Ready in: 1hours40mins

Ingredients

- 2 pounds asparagus
- 1 ½ tablespoons butter
- Salt and freshly ground pepper to taste
- ¾ pound fillet of beef (thinly sliced)
- 1 small bunch fresh cress
- 12 sprigs chervil
- Dressing (see recipe)

Direction

- Scrape the asparagus, bind together and trim to about 6 inches. Together with the butter, stand the asparagus in salted water and steam until tender. Cool. Sprinkle with salt and pepper to taste and marinate in part of the dressing.

- To serve, arrange the asparagus tips with the beef slices on a serving platter. Cover with the remaining dressing and garnish with cress and chervil.

- 4 grams: dietary fiber;
- 12 grams: sugars;
- 9 grams: protein;
- 765 milligrams: sodium;

12. Autumn Corn Chowder

Serving: 6 servings | Prep: | Cook: | Ready in: 1hours

Ingredients

- 1 tablespoon unsalted butter
- 1 cup finely chopped onion
- ½ cup finely chopped sweet red pepper
- 1 teaspoon ground cumin
- ¼ teaspoon cayenne pepper
- 1 pound boiling potatoes, peeled and diced
- 4 cups lowfat milk
- 2 cups fresh corn kernels
- Salt and freshly ground black pepper to taste
- 2 tablespoons chopped cilantro

Direction

- Heat the butter in a heavy saucepan. Add the onion and sweet pepper and cook slowly until the vegetables are tender. Stir in the cumin and cayenne pepper.
- Add the potatoes and milk to the saucepan. Bring to a simmer and cook, covered, until the potatoes are very tender, about 20 minutes. Coarsely mash the potatoes in the pot.
- Stir in the corn, bring to a simmer, and cook five minutes. Season to taste with salt and pepper. Stir in the cilantro and serve.

Nutrition Information

- 255: calories;
- 0 grams: trans fat;
- 2 grams: monounsaturated fat;
- 1 gram: polyunsaturated fat;
- 37 grams: carbohydrates;
- 8 grams: fat;

13. Baked Salmon Fillets With Goat Cheese And Cilantro

Serving: 4 servings | Prep: | Cook: | Ready in: 25mins

Ingredients

- 4 tablespoons olive oil
- ½ cup chopped onion
- 1 tablespoon finely chopped garlic
- ½ cup dry red wine
- 4 tablespoons capers
- 1 tablespoon chopped fresh rosemary or 1 teaspoon dried
- 1 teaspoon chopped fresh oregano or 1/2 teaspoon dried
- ⅛ teaspoon hot red pepper flakes
- ½ cup canned crushed tomatoes
- Salt and freshly ground pepper to taste
- 12 pitted black olives
- 4 boneless salmon fillets, about 6 ounces each
- ⅓ pound goat cheese, crumbled
- 2 tablespoons anise-flavored liquor, like Ricard
- 4 tablespoons chopped fresh cilantro

Direction

- Heat 2 tablespoons of the olive oil in a saucepan. Add the onion and garlic, and cook briefly while stirring. Add the wine, capers, rosemary, oregano, pepper flakes, tomatoes, salt, pepper and olives. Bring to a boil and simmer 5 minutes.
- Preheat the oven to 475 degrees.
- Pour 1 tablespoon of the oil in a baking dish large enough to hold the fish in one layer. Arrange the fish skin-side down, sprinkle with salt and pepper. Pour the tomato sauce around

the fish fillets, brush the top of the fillets with the remaining 1 tablespoon oil and the cheese.

- Bake for 5 minutes and sprinkle with Ricard. Switch to the broiler and broil for 5 minutes. Do not overcook the fish. Sprinkle with the cilantro and serve immediately

Nutrition Information

- 662: calories;
- 19 grams: monounsaturated fat;
- 8 grams: polyunsaturated fat;
- 2 grams: dietary fiber;
- 5 grams: sugars;
- 43 grams: protein;
- 46 grams: fat;
- 776 milligrams: sodium;
- 13 grams: saturated fat;
- 10 grams: carbohydrates;

14. Baked Stuffed Acorn Squash

Serving: 8 substantial main dish servings, 12 to 16 smaller servings | Prep: | Cook: |Ready in: 2hours

Ingredients

- 4 large or 6 smaller acorn squash
- 3 tablespoons extra virgin olive oil, plus additional for basting
- 1 medium onion, finely chopped
- 1 red pepper, diced
- 1 28-ounce can chopped tomatoes with juice, pulsed to a coarse purée in a food processor
- 2 tablespoons tomato paste
- 2 tablespoons mild honey, maple syrup or pomegranate molasses
- 2 tablespoons red wine vinegar, sherry vinegar or apple cider vinegar
- Salt to taste
- ½ teaspoon cayenne
- 3 cups cooked pintos, black beans or red beans, or 2 cans, drained and rinsed
- 1 cup corn kernels

- ⅔ cup breadcrumbs
- 2 ounces / 1/2 cup Gruyère, grated

Direction

- Heat oven to 375 degrees. Place squash on a baking sheet and bake 20 minutes, until soft enough to easily cut in half. Wait until cool enough to handle (about 15 minutes), then cut in half (stem to tip) and scoop out seeds and membranes.
- Meanwhile, heat 2 tablespoons of olive oil over medium heat in a large skillet and add onion. Cook, stirring often, until it begins to soften, about 3 minutes. Add red pepper and a generous pinch of salt and cook, stirring, until tender, about 5 minutes. Add tomatoes and tomato paste and cook, stirring often, until tomatoes have cooked down slightly, about 5 minutes. Add honey, maple syrup or pomegranate molasses, vinegar, salt and cayenne, and bring to a simmer. Simmer 8 to 10 minutes, until thick and fragrant. Taste and adjust seasonings. Stir in beans and corn and simmer another 5 minutes.
- Oil 1 or 2 baking dishes or a sheet pan that will accommodate all the squash. Season cavities and cut sides of the squash with salt and pepper and brush with olive oil or melted butter. Fill with bean mixture. Mix together bread crumbs, Gruyère and remaining olive oil and sprinkle over the filling. Brush exposed edges of squash with oil. Place in the baking dish or on baking sheet and cover tightly with foil. Bake large squash for 45 minutes, check smaller squash after 30 minutes. The flesh should be easy to penetrate with the tip of a knife. Uncover and return to oven for 5 to 10 minutes, or until breadcrumbs and cheese are lightly browned. Serve hot or warm.

Nutrition Information

- 513: calories;
- 10 grams: fat;
- 5 grams: monounsaturated fat;

- 90 grams: carbohydrates;
- 11 grams: sugars;
- 1088 milligrams: sodium;
- 3 grams: saturated fat;
- 2 grams: polyunsaturated fat;
- 18 grams: dietary fiber;
- 23 grams: protein;

15. Baked Ziti Or Penne Rigate With Cauliflower

Serving: 6 servings | Prep: | Cook: | Ready in: 1hours15mins

Ingredients

- 1 medium cauliflower, about 2 pounds, leaves and stem trimmed
- Salt to taste
- Pinch of saffron threads
- 2 tablespoons extra virgin olive oil
- 2 garlic cloves, minced
- 3 anchovy fillets, rinsed and chopped
- 1 14-ounce can chopped tomatoes, with juice
- Freshly ground pepper
- 2 tablespoons chopped flat leaf parsley
- ¾ pound ziti or penne rigata
- 2 ounces pecorino or Parmesan, grated (1/2 cup)

Direction

- Bring a large pot of water to a boil and salt generously. Add the cauliflower and boil gently until the florets are tender but the middle resists when poked with a skewer or knife, about 10 minutes. Using slotted spoons or tongs (or a pasta insert) remove the cauliflower from the water, transfer to a bowl of cold water and drain. Cover the pot and turn off the heat. You will cook the pasta in the cauliflower water. Cut the florets from the core of the cauliflower and cut them into small florets or crumble coarsely using a fork or your hands.
- Meanwhile, place the saffron in a small bowl and add 3 tablespoons warm water. Let steep for 10 to 15 minutes.
- Heat 1 tablespoon of the olive oil over medium heat in a large, heavy skillet and add the garlic. Cook, stirring, until it smells fragrant, about 30 seconds to a minute, and add the anchovies and tomatoes. Season to taste with salt (remembering that the anchovies will contribute a lot of salt) and freshly ground pepper. Turn the heat down to medium-low and cook, stirring often, until the tomatoes have cooked down and smell fragrant, about 10 minutes. Stir in the cauliflower, saffron with its soaking water, and parsley, cover and simmer for another 5 minutes. Remove from the heat. Taste and adjust seasonings.
- Bring the cauliflower water to a boil and add the pasta. Cook until just al dente, a few minutes less than you would cook it to serve. It will soften further when it bakes. Drain and transfer to a bowl.
- Heat the oven to 375 degrees. Oil a 3-quart baking dish. Toss the pasta with half the cauliflower mixture and half the cheese and spoon into the baking dish. Combine the remaining cauliflower mixture and remaining cheese and spoon over the pasta. Drizzle on the remaining tablespoon of oil. Place in the oven and bake for 20 to 25 minutes, until bubbling. Serve hot.

Nutrition Information

- 326: calories;
- 3 grams: saturated fat;
- 49 grams: carbohydrates;
- 5 grams: dietary fiber;
- 13 grams: protein;
- 685 milligrams: sodium;
- 9 grams: fat;
- 4 grams: sugars;
- 1 gram: polyunsaturated fat;

16. Baked And Loaded Acorn Squash

Serving: 8 servings | Prep: | Cook: |Ready in: 1hours30mins

Ingredients

- 4 acorn squash, halved, seeds and strings scooped out
- 3 tablespoons vegan margarine or extra virgin olive oil
- 8 pears, peeled, cored and diced
- 8 Granny Smith apples, peeled, cored and diced
- ¼ cup Calvados brandy (apple brandy) or apple liqueur
- Juice of 1 lemon
- 1 ½ teaspoons nutmeg
- 4 teaspoons cinnamon

Direction

- Preheat oven to 400 degrees. Place the halved squash on a sheet pan, skin side down. If necessary, cut a slice from the rounded side to make the squash level. Place 1 teaspoon (or so) of the margarine in each half, cover with foil and bake until squash has softened, about 45 minutes. Remove from the oven.
- Meanwhile, combine the diced pears and apples, and drizzle with the Calvados and lemon juice to prevent browning. Add nutmeg and cinnamon and stir until well mixed.
- Spoon the mixture into squash halves, dividing evenly. Cover with foil and return to the oven. Bake until fruit is warmed through, about 15 minutes. Uncover and bake watchfully until fruit is slightly browned, about 5 minutes.

Nutrition Information

- 368: calories;
- 15 grams: dietary fiber;
- 38 grams: sugars;
- 3 grams: protein;
- 50 milligrams: sodium;
- 5 grams: fat;
- 1 gram: polyunsaturated fat;
- 81 grams: carbohydrates;
- 2 grams: monounsaturated fat;

17. Banana Bread

Serving: 16 servings | Prep: | Cook: |Ready in: 55mins

Ingredients

- Oil for greasing pan
- 2 ½ cups cake flour
- 2 teaspoons baking powder
- 1 teaspoon baking soda
- 1 teaspoon ground cinnamon
- ½ cup applesauce
- 1 cup granulated sugar
- 1 ½ egg whites
- 2 cups very ripe bananas, peeled and mashed (abut 6 medium bananas)
- 1 teaspoon vanilla extract

Direction

- Preheat oven to 350 degrees. Lightly grease 9-by-5-inch loaf pan with oil.
- Combine flour, baking powder, baking soda and cinnamon.
- Whisk together applesauce, sugar, egg whites, bananas and vanilla. Add flour mixture all at once and stir gently to blend. Do not overbeat.
- Pour batter into prepared loaf pan and bake 45 to 50 minutes or until a knife inserted in center comes out clean. Cool bread completely before slicing.

Nutrition Information

- 166: calories;
- 1 gram: dietary fiber;
- 0 grams: polyunsaturated fat;
- 37 grams: carbohydrates;

- 17 grams: sugars;
- 2 grams: protein;
- 129 milligrams: sodium;

18. Barbecued Chicken

Serving: Twenty servings | Prep: | Cook: | Ready in:
1hours45mins

Ingredients

- 5 cups white vinegar
- 1 tablespoon whole cloves
- 2 teaspoons ground Salt and freshly ground pepper to taste
- 15 pounds chicken pieces
- ¼ cup vegetable oil
- 3 cloves garlic, minced
- 3 cups ketchup
- 1 cup dark brown sugar
- ½ cup mustard
- ¼ cup Worcestershire sauce
- Juice of 1 lemon
- 1 small onion, grated
- 1 tablespoon Tabasco sauce
- 3 teaspoons chili powder
- 1 teaspoon celery seeds

Direction

- The night before serving, combine the vinegar with 10 cups water, the whole cloves, salt and pepper. Add the chicken and marinate, refrigerated, overnight.
- To make the sauce, heat the oil in a large pan and saute the garlic until golden. Add all the remaining ingredients and a dash of salt, and bring to a simmer, stirring constantly. Cook over medium-low heat for 45 minutes, stirring occasionally. Remove and cool.
- Forty-five minutes before cooking, light the charcoal fire.
- Remove the chicken and discard the marinade. Cook the chicken over low heat for about 30 minutes, turning to cook evenly on each side.

Brush the pieces with the sauce and cook 30 minutes more, basting and turning occasionally. Serve the chicken hot or at room temperature, with the remaining sauce on the side.

Nutrition Information

- 843: calories;
- 12 grams: polyunsaturated fat;
- 64 grams: protein;
- 920 milligrams: sodium;
- 54 grams: fat;
- 0 grams: trans fat;
- 23 grams: monounsaturated fat;
- 1 gram: dietary fiber;
- 15 grams: sugars;
- 19 grams: carbohydrates;

19. Barley Risotto With Rabe

Serving: 8 cups | Prep: | Cook: | Ready in: 1hours10mins

Ingredients

- ½ cup olive oil
- 1 medium-size onion, minced
- 8 large garlic cloves, smashed, peeled and minced
- 2 cups medium-size pearl barley
- 5 ½ cups chicken broth or vegetarian broth (see Micro-Tip)
- 1 pound broccoli rabe, trimmed and cut in 1/2-inch pieces
- 2 teaspoons kosher salt
- Freshly ground black pepper to tast

Direction

- Place oil in an oval dish, 14 by 9 by 2 inches. Cook, uncovered, at 100 percent in a high-power oven for 2 minutes. Stir in onion and garlic. Cook for 4 minutes. Stir in barley. Cook for 2 minutes.

- Stir in broth. Cook for 15 minutes. Stir in rabe. Cook for 25 minutes.
- Remove from oven. Cover with a towel and let stand for 10 minutes. Stir in salt and pepper.

Nutrition Information

- 249: calories;
- 31 grams: carbohydrates;
- 1 gram: sugars;
- 7 grams: protein;
- 417 milligrams: sodium;
- 12 grams: fat;
- 2 grams: polyunsaturated fat;
- 8 grams: dietary fiber;

20. Barley, Corn And Lobster Salad

Serving: Four servings | Prep: | Cook: | Ready in: 15mins

Ingredients

- 2 1 1/2-pound lobsters
- 2 cups cooked barley, cooled
- 2 ears corn, cooked and kernels cut off cob
- 1 tablespoon fresh lemon juice
- 2 teaspoons olive oil
- 3 tablespoons chopped fresh basil
- 1 teaspoon salt, plus more to taste
- Freshly ground pepper to taste

Direction

- Steam the lobsters until they turn bright red, about 10 minutes. Set aside until cool enough to handle. Remove the meat and cut into large chunks.
- Toss the lobster, barley and corn together. Add the lemon juice, olive oil, basil, salt and pepper. Toss until well combined. Divide among 4 plates and serve.

Nutrition Information

- 427: calories;
- 1449 milligrams: sodium;
- 0 grams: trans fat;
- 33 grams: carbohydrates;
- 4 grams: sugars;
- 60 grams: protein;
- 6 grams: fat;
- 1 gram: saturated fat;
- 3 grams: monounsaturated fat;
- 2 grams: polyunsaturated fat;

21. Bass Steaks With Basil Pepper Compote

Serving: Four servings | Prep: | Cook: | Ready in: 1hours15mins

Ingredients

- 2 cloves garlic, peeled and crushed
- ¼ cup olive oil
- 2 tablespoons fresh lemon juice
- 2 teaspoons salt
- 1 teaspoon coarse ground black pepper
- ½ cup white wine
- 1 white onion, minced
- 2 red peppers, minced
- 2 yellow peppers, minced
- 2 tomatoes, coarsely chopped
- 1 cup fresh basil leaves, coarsely torn
- 4 bass steaks (about 6 to 8 ounces each)

Direction

- In a large bowl combine the garlic, olive oil and lemon juice. Add the salt and black pepper and whisk well to combine. Slowly drizzle in the white wine. Add the onions and peppers, stir well to combine and set aside for 1 hour. Add the tomatoes and basil, stir and adjust seasoning with more salt and pepper to taste. Place the bass in this mixture and marinate for 1 to 4 hours.
- If using a charcoal grill, prepare the coals. When they are hot, remove the bass from the

marinade and grill on each side for 5 to 8 minutes, depending on the thickness of the bass. After turning the fish, spoon the marinade over the bass and partially cover the grill so that the fish is allowed to smoke. Use a spatula to place each steak and its topping on plates and serve immediately. (If using a broiler, follow the same instructions, broiling the bass on one side, turning it, spooning on the marinade and broiling until done. Allow at least 4 inches between the fish and the flame to avoid burning.)

Nutrition Information

- 556: calories;
- 1164 milligrams: sodium;
- 21 grams: monounsaturated fat;
- 6 grams: sugars;
- 33 grams: protein;
- 1 gram: trans fat;
- 3 grams: polyunsaturated fat;
- 17 grams: carbohydrates;
- 4 grams: dietary fiber;
- 38 grams: fat;
- 12 grams: saturated fat;

22. Beet Greens And Rice Gratin

Serving: 4 to 6 servings. | Prep: | Cook: | Ready in: 1hours15mins

Ingredients

- 1 generous bunch beet greens, stemmed and washed
- 2 tablespoons extra virgin olive oil
- 1 medium onion, chopped
- 2 large garlic cloves, minced
- Salt to taste
- 1 teaspoon fresh thyme leaves or 1/2 teaspoon dried thyme
- 3 eggs
- ½ cup low-fat milk (2 percent)
- Freshly ground pepper
- 1 cup cooked brown rice, arborio rice or Calrose rice
- 2 ounces Gruyère cheese, grated (1/2 cup, tightly packed)
- 2 tablespoons freshly grated Parmesan
- ¼ cup bread crumbs (optional)

Direction

- Preheat the oven to 375 degrees. Oil a 2-quart gratin dish with olive oil. Either blanch the beet greens for 1 minute in a large pot of generously salted boiling water, or steam over an inch of boiling water for 2 to 5 minutes, until wilted and tender. Rinse with cold water, squeeze out water and chop medium-fine. Set aside.
- Heat 1 tablespoon of the oil over medium heat in a large, heavy skillet and add the onion. Cook, stirring, until tender, about 5 minutes, and add the garlic and a generous pinch of salt. Cook, stirring, until the garlic is fragrant, about 30 seconds. Stir in the cooked greens and the thyme and toss together. Season to taste with salt and pepper. Remove from the heat.
- In a large bowl, beat together the eggs and milk. Add 1/2 teaspoon salt and freshly ground pepper to taste. Stir in the greens mixture, the rice and the cheeses and mix together well. Scrape into the oiled baking dish. Sprinkle the bread crumbs over the top. Drizzle on the remaining tablespoon of oil.
- Bake 35 to 40 minutes, until sizzling and lightly browned on the top and sides. Remove from the heat and allow to sit for at least 10 minutes before serving.

Nutrition Information

- 269: calories;
- 0 grams: trans fat;
- 2 grams: sugars;
- 11 grams: protein;
- 4 grams: saturated fat;
- 6 grams: monounsaturated fat;

- 1 gram: dietary fiber;
- 31 grams: carbohydrates;
- 308 milligrams: sodium;

23. Beet, Potato, Carrot, Pickle And Apple Salad

Serving: 6 to 8 servings | Prep: | Cook: | Ready in: 30mins

Ingredients

- 2 medium beets
- 5 tablespoons olive oil
- Salt to taste
- 2 small (not tiny) potatoes
- 1 large carrot, peeled
- 2 tablespoons red or white wine vinegar
- 1 clove garlic, minced
- 1 teaspoon Dijon mustard
- Dash of sugar
- Freshly ground pepper to taste
- 1 large pickle, diced
- 1 tart green apple, diced
- 2 hard-boiled eggs, peeled and roughly chopped
- 1 tablespoon chopped fresh dill

Direction

- Preheat the oven to 350 degrees Fahrenheit and line a baking sheet with aluminum foil.
- Cut off the tops of the beets, scrub them, and place them on the baking sheet. Coat them with 1 tablespoon of the olive oil, and roast them in the oven for an hour. Remove from the oven, and when they are cool enough to handle, peel and cut them into 1/2-inch cubes.
- Bring a small pot of salted water to a boil, and cook the potatoes until they are tender, about 15 minutes. Remove from the water and allow to cool before peeling and cutting into 1/2-inch cubes. Cook the carrot for about 5 minutes in that same boiling salted water.

Remove with a slotted spoon, cool and cut into 1/2-inch rounds.
- Whisk together the vinegar, garlic, mustard, sugar and salt and freshly ground pepper to taste in a salad bowl. Stream in the remaining 4 tablespoons olive oil. Toss in the beets, the potatoes, the carrot, the pickle, the apple and the eggs. Stir until everything is just coated with the vinaigrette. Serve at room temperature garnished with fresh dill, or refrigerate and serve the next day.

Nutrition Information

- 159: calories;
- 1 gram: polyunsaturated fat;
- 16 grams: carbohydrates;
- 2 grams: saturated fat;
- 7 grams: monounsaturated fat;
- 0 grams: trans fat;
- 3 grams: protein;
- 5 grams: sugars;
- 299 milligrams: sodium;
- 10 grams: fat;

24. Beet, Rice And Goat Cheese Burgers

Serving: 6 burgers. | Prep: | Cook: | Ready in: 30mins

Ingredients

- 2 cups cooked brown or white rice
- 1 cup finely diced or grated roasted beets
- ¼ cup chopped fresh herbs, like a mixture of parsley and dill
- 1 15-ounce can white beans, drained and rinsed
- 1 tablespoon fresh lemon juice
- 1 egg
- 2 ounces goat cheese, crumbled
- Salt and freshly ground pepper
- 2 tablespoons extra virgin olive oil or canola oil, as needed

Direction

- Preheat the oven to 375 degrees. Combine the rice, beets and herbs in a large bowl.
- Purée the beans with the lemon juice and egg in a food processor fitted with the steel blade or with a fork. Scrape into the bowl with the rice and beets. Add the goat cheese, salt and pepper, and mix the ingredients together.
- Moisten your hands and form 6 patties.
- Working in batches, heat 1 tablespoon of the oil at a time in a heavy ovenproof skillet and brown the patties on one side for 2 minutes. Turn over onto the other side and place in the oven for 10 minutes. Serve with or without buns, ketchup and the works.

Nutrition Information

- 402: calories;
- 430 milligrams: sodium;
- 2 grams: sugars;
- 4 grams: dietary fiber;
- 1 gram: polyunsaturated fat;
- 69 grams: carbohydrates;
- 13 grams: protein;
- 8 grams: fat;
- 0 grams: trans fat;

25. Bibimbap With Clams, Kale, Daikon And Carrots

Serving: 4 servings. | Prep: | Cook: | Ready in: 1hours

Ingredients

- For the vegetables:
- 2 tablespoons rice vinegar
- 1 tablespoon sesame oil
- 2 large garlic cloves, minced or puréed
- 2 to 3 scallions, minced
- 1 tablespoon toasted sesame seeds
- Salt to taste
- Korean red pepper paste (kochujang) to taste (available at Korean markets)
- 1 daikon radish, grated
- 1 bunch kale, stemmed and washed in 2 changes of water
- ½ pound carrots, cut in matchsticks or grated
- Soy sauce to taste
- For the clams:
- 20 Manila clams
- ½ cup dry white wine
- ½ cup water
- 1 to 2 garlic cloves, to taste, crushed
- 1 tablespoon minced ginger
- 2 scallions, finely chopped
- 1 dried red chili pepper
- 1 teaspoon sugar
- 1 teaspoon soy sauce
- 1 teaspoon sesame oil
- For the rice and garnishes:
- 1 ½ to 2 cups brown rice, barley, quinoa or another grain of your choice, cooked (keep hot)
- 4 eggs (optional)
- Korean red pepper paste (kochujang) to taste (available at Korean markets)
- 2 sheets nori seaweed (kimgui), lightly toasted* and cut into thin strips (optional)
- 2 teaspoons toasted sesame seeds or black sesame seeds
- Toast nori sheets (if not toasted already) by quickly passing them over a gas flame (hold with tongs) until crisp.

Direction

- In a small bowl or measuring cup, mix together the rice vinegar, sesame oil, garlic, scallions, sesame seeds, chili paste and salt to taste for the vegetables. Set aside.
- In separate bowls, toss the prepared daikon and carrots with salt to taste and cover with cold water. Soak for 15 to 30 minutes. Drain and squeeze dry. Place in separate bowls and toss each with 1 tablespoon of the vinegar and sesame oil mixture. Add salt or soy sauce to taste. Set aside in the refrigerator.

- Blanch the kale for 2 to 3 minutes in salted boiling water. Transfer to a bowl of cold water, drain and squeeze out excess water. Remove from the heat and toss in a bowl with 1 tablespoon of the vinegar and sesame oil mixture. Add salt or soy sauce to taste.
- Rinse the clams in several changes of water and brush them to remove sand.
- Combine the wine, water, crushed garlic, ginger, scallions and dried chili pepper in a lidded pot or pan and bring to a boil. Add the clams, cover and steam until they open, about 3 minutes. Using tongs, remove the clams to a bowl, cover and keep warm. Strain the liquid in the pot through a cheesecloth-lined strainer set over a bowl and return to the pan. Add the sugar, soy sauce, sesame oil and any liquid that has accumulated in the bowl with the clams, and bring to a boil. Reduce to about 1/2 to 1/3 cup and remove from the heat.
- Fry the eggs in a nonstick skillet until the whites are set and the yolks are still runny. Season with salt and pepper.
- Heat 4 wide soup bowls. Place a mound of hot grains in the middle of each one and top with a spoonful of the broth from the clams. Surround with the clams and vegetables, as well as kimchi if desired, each ingredient in its own little pile. Place a fried egg and a small spoonful of chili paste on top of the rice and garnish with the toasted nori and sesame seeds. Serve at once. Diners should break the egg into the rice. Pass the chili paste and add more as desired.

26. Black Olive Paste

Serving: About 2 1/2 cups | Prep: | Cook: | Ready in: 15mins

Ingredients

- 2 cups oil-cured black olives, pitted and minced
- 2 cloves fresh garlic, minced
- 1 tablespoon lemon rind, minced
- ¼ teaspoon minced chili pepper
- 2 tablespoons fresh rosemary
- ¼ cup olive oil

Direction

- In a large bowl, combine the ingredients and blend with a fork. If using a food processor, be very careful not to over-process; a chunky texture is better. Store in a tightly sealed container in the refrigerator for up to one month.
- To use the olive paste as a marinade, slather chicken, fish, beef or veal well and marinate for up to 6 hours before cooking. The mixture can also be used as a sauce by spooning over meat, poultry or fish in the last five minutes of cooking.

Nutrition Information

- 192: calories;
- 20 grams: fat;
- 15 grams: monounsaturated fat;
- 0 grams: sugars;
- 442 milligrams: sodium;
- 3 grams: saturated fat;
- 2 grams: dietary fiber;
- 5 grams: carbohydrates;
- 1 gram: protein;

27. Black And Arborio Risotto With Beets And Beet Greens

Serving: 6 servings | Prep: | Cook: | Ready in: 2hours

Ingredients

- 1 cup black rice, like Lundberg Black Japonica or Forbidden Rice, cooked (3 cups cooked black rice)
- 1 quart chicken or vegetable stock, as needed
- 1 bunch beet greens, stemmed and washed

- 2 tablespoons extra virgin olive oil
- ½ cup finely chopped onion
- ⅔ cup arborio rice
- 2 garlic cloves, minced
- ½ cup dry white wine
- ¾ pound beets (1 bunch small), roasted, skinned and diced
- Salt
- Freshly ground pepper
- 1 to 2 ounces Parmesan cheese, grated (1/4 to 1/2 cup, to taste, optional)
- 2 tablespoons finely chopped flat-leaf parsley

Direction

- To cook the black rice, combine with 2 cups water in a saucepan, add salt to taste and bring to a boil. Reduce the heat, cover and simmer 30 to 40 minutes, until all of the liquid has been absorbed by the rice. Remove from the heat, remove the lid from the pan and place a dish towel over the pan, then return the lid. Let sit for 10 to 15 minutes.
- Bring the stock to a simmer in a saucepan. Season well and turn the heat to low. Stack the stemmed, washed greens and cut crosswise into 1-inch-wide strips.
- Heat the oil over medium heat in a large nonstick frying pan or wide, heavy saucepan and add the onion. Cook, stirring, until the onion begins to soften, about 3 minutes, and add the rice and garlic. Cook, stirring, until the grains of rice are separate and beginning to crackle, about 3 minutes.
- Stir in the wine and cook over medium heat, stirring constantly. The wine should bubble, but not too quickly. You want some of the flavor to cook into the rice before it evaporates. When the wine has just about evaporated, stir in a ladleful or two of the simmering stock (about 1/2 cup), enough to just cover the rice. The stock should bubble slowly (adjust heat accordingly). Cook, stirring often, until it is just about absorbed. Add another ladleful or two of the stock and continue to cook in this fashion, not too fast and not too slowly, stirring often and adding more stock when the rice is almost dry, for 10 minutes.
- Stir in the greens, the diced beets and black rice and continue adding more stock, enough to barely cover the rice, and stirring often, for another 10 to 15 minutes. The arborio rice should be chewy but not hard in the middle – and definitely not soft like steamed rice. If it is still hard in the middle, you need to continue adding stock and stirring for another 5 minutes or so. Now is the time to ascertain if there is enough salt. Add if necessary.
- When the rice is cooked through, add a generous amount of freshly ground pepper, and stir in another ladleful of stock, the Parmesan and the parsley. Remove from the heat. The risotto should be creamy; if it isn't, add a little more stock. Stir once, taste and adjust seasonings, and serve.

Nutrition Information

- 267: calories;
- 1 gram: polyunsaturated fat;
- 4 grams: dietary fiber;
- 40 grams: carbohydrates;
- 8 grams: protein;
- 768 milligrams: sodium;
- 7 grams: sugars;

28. Black Eyed Pea Soup Or Stew With Pomegranate And Chard

Serving: 4 to 6 servings | Prep: | Cook: |Ready in: 1hours15mins

Ingredients

- 1 bunch rainbow chard
- 2 tablespoons extra virgin olive oil
- ½ yellow onion, finely chopped
- 2 garlic cloves, minced
- 1 teaspoon ground turmeric
- 2 teaspoons ground cumin seeds

- ½ pound (1 1/8 cups) black-eyed peas, rinsed
- ½ cup barley
- 1 medium beet, peeled and cut in small dice
- 1 ½ to 2 quarts water (to taste)
- Salt to taste
- ¼ cup pomegranate molasses (more to taste)
- Freshly ground pepper to taste
- 1 generous bunch cilantro, chopped
- 1 cup thick yogurt
- Seeds of 1 ripe medium-size pomegranate

Direction

- Wash and stem the chard, and if the stems are wide and thick, cut the thickest parts of them into small dice (discard the thin parts). Heat the oil over medium heat in a large, heavy soup pot and add the onion and chard stems. Cook, stirring often, until the onion is very tender and lightly colored, about 10 minutes. Stir in the garlic, turmeric and cumin and cook, stirring, until fragrant, 30 seconds to a minute. Add the black-eyed peas, barley, beet and water and bring to a gentle boil. Add salt to taste and the molasses. Reduce the heat, cover and simmer 45 minutes to an hour, until the beans and barley are tender. Add freshly ground pepper, taste and adjust salt.
- Stir in the chard and the cilantro. Simmer for another 5 to 10 minutes, or until the chard is tender but still bright. Taste, adjust seasoning, and serve, garnishing each bowl with a spoonful of yogurt and pomegranate seeds.

Nutrition Information

- 229: calories;
- 7 grams: protein;
- 16 grams: sugars;
- 1159 milligrams: sodium;
- 2 grams: saturated fat;
- 0 grams: trans fat;
- 4 grams: monounsaturated fat;
- 1 gram: polyunsaturated fat;
- 38 grams: carbohydrates;

29. Blueberries Au Citron

Serving: 6 servings | Prep: | Cook: | Ready in: 5mins

Ingredients

- 3 tablespoons lemon juice
- ⅓ cup maple syrup
- 1 ½ pints (20 ounces) blueberries, preferably small wild ones

Direction

- Mix the lemon juice and maple syrup in a bowl large enough to hold the blueberries.
- Rinse the blueberries well in cool water, removing and discarding any damaged berries or foreign matter. Drain the berries well, and add them to the syrup mixture. Mix well, and refrigerate for at least 1 hour before serving.

Nutrition Information

- 101: calories;
- 3 milligrams: sodium;
- 0 grams: polyunsaturated fat;
- 26 grams: carbohydrates;
- 2 grams: dietary fiber;
- 20 grams: sugars;
- 1 gram: protein;

30. Blueberry Oatmeal

Serving: Serves two | Prep: | Cook: | Ready in: 15mins

Ingredients

- 1 ⅓ cups water
- ⅛ teaspoon salt (optional)
- ¼ teaspoon cinnamon
- 2 teaspoons mild honey
- ⅔ cup rolled oats or oatmeal
- ⅓ cup blueberries

- ½ teaspoon finely chopped or grated orange zest
- ½ cup low-fat milk, soy milk, almond beverage or rice beverage

Direction

- Bring the water to a boil in a medium-size saucepan. Add the salt, cinnamon, honey and oatmeal. Reduce the heat, and simmer uncovered for five minutes or until most of the water has been absorbed. Add the blueberries, orange zest and milk (or alternate beverage). Bring to a simmer, and simmer five more minutes or until the oatmeal is thick and creamy and the blueberries have begun to pop. Cover and let stand for five minutes, then serve.

Nutrition Information

- 311: calories;
- 2 grams: fat;
- 0 grams: saturated fat;
- 1 gram: polyunsaturated fat;
- 67 grams: carbohydrates;
- 9 grams: sugars;
- 7 grams: protein;
- 8 milligrams: sodium;
- 3 grams: dietary fiber;

31. Blueberry Pie Filling

Serving: 2 quarts | Prep: | Cook: | Ready in: 1hours

Ingredients

- 1 cup sugar
- ½ cup cornstarch
- Juice of two lemons
- 4 pints blueberries
- 1 teaspoon almond extract, optional
- 4 tablespoons Grand Marnier or other orange liqueur, optional

Direction

- Fit a large pot with a rack, or line with a folded kitchen towel. Fill 2/3 with water and bring to a boil. Add 2 one-quart canning jars and boil for 10 minutes. Jars may be left in the warm water in the pot until ready to be filled. (Alternatively, you can sterilize jars by running them through a dishwasher cycle, leaving them there until ready to fill.)
- Place canning rings in a small saucepan, cover with water and bring to a boil. Turn off heat and add lids to soften their rubber gaskets. Rings and lids may be left in the water until jars are filled.
- In a large heavy pot, combine 1 cup water with sugar, cornstarch and lemon juice, and whisk until smooth. Bring to a boil and add berries; the mixture will look gloppy. Smash some of the berries with a potato masher or the back of a spoon. Return mixture to a boil for 1 minute. Add extract and liqueur, if using, and stir well.
- Remove warm jars from pot and bring water back to a boil. Ladle hot filling into jars just up to the base of the neck, leaving 1 inch at the top. Wipe jar rims clean with a damp towel. Place lids on jars, screw on rings and lower jars back into the pot of boiling water. The water should cover the jars; if not, add more. Boil jars for 30 minutes. Transfer jars to a folded towel and allow to cool for 12 hours; you should hear them making a pinging sound as they seal.
- Test the seals by removing rings and lifting jars by the flat lid. If the lid releases, the seal has not formed. Unsealed jars should be refrigerated and used within a month, or reprocessed. (Rings and jars may be reused, but a new flat lid must be used each time jars are processed.) To reprocess, reheat filling to boiling point (as in Step 3), then continue as before.

Nutrition Information

- 108: calories;
- 0 grams: polyunsaturated fat;

- 28 grams: carbohydrates;
- 2 grams: dietary fiber;
- 20 grams: sugars;
- 1 gram: protein;
- 1 milligram: sodium;

32. Boiled Rice

Serving: 4 servings | Prep: | Cook: | Ready in: 20mins

Ingredients

- 3 cups remaining chicken broth (if not enough, add water)
- 1 cup converted or parboiled rice
- 1 tablespoon lemon juice

Direction

- Bring the chicken broth to a boil and add the rice. Return to a boil and stir. Simmer for 17 minutes over low flame, covered. Add the lemon juice, blend well and serve with the chicken.

Nutrition Information

- 117: calories;
- 1 gram: monounsaturated fat;
- 0 grams: dietary fiber;
- 18 grams: carbohydrates;
- 3 grams: sugars;
- 6 grams: protein;
- 258 milligrams: sodium;
- 2 grams: fat;

33. Braised Endive

Serving: 4 servings | Prep: | Cook: | Ready in: 35mins

Ingredients

- 8 heads of medium-size Belgian endive
- Salt and freshly ground white pepper to taste
- ¼ teaspoon ground cumin
- 1 tablespoon fresh lemon juice
- ½ cup water
- 1 tablespoon butter

Direction

- Wash endive and trim the stem ends.
- Put endive in one layer in a saucepan large enough to hold them in one layer. Sprinkle endive with salt and pepper, cumin and lemon juice. Add water and butter and cover tightly. Bring to a boil and simmer for about 25 minutes until water is evaporated. Uncover endive and brown lightly on both sides. Serve immediately.

Nutrition Information

- 45: calories;
- 3 grams: dietary fiber;
- 2 grams: saturated fat;
- 0 grams: sugars;
- 1 gram: protein;
- 5 grams: carbohydrates;
- 332 milligrams: sodium;

34. Bread And Onion Pancakes

Serving: 16 pancakes | Prep: | Cook: | Ready in: 40mins

Ingredients

- For the batter:
- 10 ounces bread, preferably coarse textured, cut into 1-inch cubes
- 2 cups chicken stock or broth
- 1 ½ cups chopped onion
- ⅓ cup, loose minced cilantro or parsley
- ½ teaspoon Tabasco sauce
- 4 eggs
- ½ teaspoon salt

- 8 tablespoons peanut or corn oil for cooking pancakes
- For the sauce:
- ¼ cup red wine vinegar
- ¼ cup soy sauce
- 1 teaspoon sugar
- ½ teaspoon ground ginger
- ½ teaspoon chili oil or Tabasco sauce
- 2 teaspoons chopped garlic
- 1 tablespoon corn oil

Direction

- To make the batter, crush the bread cubes into the chicken stock in a mixing bowl with the back of a spoon. Add the onion, cilantro, Tabasco, eggs and salt, and mix with your hands, kneading the mixture until it is well blended but not smooth; there should still be small visible lumps of wet bread.
- Heat 1 1/2 tablespoons of the oil in a large, nonstick skillet. When hot, add about 1/3 cup of the pancake mixture to the skillet, spreading it with a spoon to create a disk about 4 inches in diameter and about 3/8 inch thick. Repeat, working quickly. Have three or four pancakes cooking at a time (depending on the size of your skillet). Cook the pancakes over medium to high heat for about 4 minutes. Then turn and cook for 4 minutes on the other side.
- Transfer the pancakes to an ovenproof plate and set them aside in a warm oven while you continue making more with the remaining batter and oil. (Although the pancakes are best eaten immediately after cooking, they can be cooked ahead, cooled, and then reheated under a hot broiler just before serving.)
- To make the sauce, simply blend all the ingredients. Serve over the pancakes, or dip.

Nutrition Information

- 153: calories;
- 10 grams: fat;
- 2 grams: sugars;
- 12 grams: carbohydrates;
- 1 gram: dietary fiber;

- 370 milligrams: sodium;
- 0 grams: trans fat;
- 3 grams: monounsaturated fat;
- 5 grams: protein;

35. Broccoli, Carrot And Snow Pea Slaw

Serving: Four servings | Prep: | Cook: | Ready in: 1hours10mins

Ingredients

- 12 medium-size broccoli stems, trimmed, peeled and julienned
- 5 medium-size carrots, trimmed, peeled and julienned
- 2 cups snow peas, trimmed and julienned
- 1 teaspoon cracked coriander seeds
- ½ teaspoon ground cumin
- ⅛ teaspoon crushed red pepper flakes
- 2 tablespoons plus 1 teaspoon fresh lemon juice
- 1 teaspoon olive oil
- 1 ½ teaspoons salt

Direction

- Bring a large pot of water to a boil. Add the broccoli, carrots and snow peas and blanch for 30 seconds. Drain, refresh under cold running water and drain again. Place in a large bowl. Add the remaining ingredients and toss to coat. Let stand for 1 hour. Divide among 4 plates and serve.

Nutrition Information

- 111: calories;
- 6 grams: protein;
- 622 milligrams: sodium;
- 2 grams: fat;
- 21 grams: carbohydrates;
- 7 grams: dietary fiber;

- 0 grams: polyunsaturated fat;
- 1 gram: monounsaturated fat;
- 8 grams: sugars;

36. Broiled Calf's Liver

Serving: 2 servings | Prep: | Cook: | Ready in: 30mins

Ingredients

- 8 ounces sliced bacon
- 2 tablespoons olive oil
- 4 medium sweet onions, halved root-to-stem and thinly sliced
- ½ teaspoon paprika
- 1 pound calf's liver, sliced in half horizontally
- Salt
- freshly ground black pepper

Direction

- Preheat a broiler. In a large skillet over medium heat, sauté bacon, turning as needed, until crispy. Transfer to paper towels to drain. Discard excess bacon fat but do not wash pan.
- Return pan to medium heat. Add oil, onions and paprika. Sauté until onions are very soft and beginning to brown, 15 to 20 minutes. Toward the end of cooking, season liver with salt and pepper to taste, and broil as desired, 1 1/2 to 2 minutes a side for a medium (lightly pink) center.
- To serve, remove onions from heat and season with salt to taste. Place a slice of liver on each of two serving plates. Smother with onions and top with bacon. Serve hot.

37. Brown Rice Casserole

Serving: 8 to 10 servings | Prep: | Cook: | Ready in: 1hours30mins

Ingredients

- 4 cups water
- Salt
- 2 cups brown rice
- 4 tablespoons olive oil
- 2 ½ cups chopped onion
- Freshly ground black pepper
- 2 pounds ground beef or ground turkey
- 1 cup chopped green peppers
- 1 cup chopped red peppers
- 2 teaspoons ground cumin
- 3 cups crushed tomatoes
- 1 cup beef or chicken bouillon
- 2 ounces Parmesan cheese, in shavings
- 3 tablespoons bread crumbs

Direction

- Bring the water to a boil with a teaspoon of salt in a large saucepan. Add rice, cover and lower heat. Simmer until rice is tender and water has been absorbed, about 40 minutes.
- Meanwhile, heat two tablespoons of the oil in a heavy skillet. Add the onions and cook until lightly browned. When the rice has finished cooking, add it and mix with the onions. Season with salt and pepper.
- Mix about one-fourth of the rice mixture with the ground beef and set aside. Spread the remaining rice mixture in a baking dish at least two inches deep.
- Heat the remaining oil in a skillet. Saute the peppers until lightly browned, then spread them over the rice mixture in the casserole. Mix one teaspoon cumin and salt and pepper to taste with the meat and rice mixture, lightly brown in the pan and spread it over the peppers in the casserole.
- Add the tomatoes and bouillon to the pan. Bring to a simmer and season with remaining cumin and salt and pepper. Spoon over the meat. Cover with shaved Parmesan cheese and bread crumbs.
- Shortly before serving, preheat oven to 350 degrees. Place the casserole in the oven and bake about 20 minutes, until heated through.

Nutrition Information

- 516: calories;
- 27 grams: fat;
- 13 grams: monounsaturated fat;
- 2 grams: polyunsaturated fat;
- 24 grams: protein;
- 9 grams: saturated fat;
- 1 gram: trans fat;
- 44 grams: carbohydrates;
- 4 grams: dietary fiber;
- 6 grams: sugars;
- 2601 milligrams: sodium;

38. Buckwheat Crepes With Roasted Apricots

Serving: Yield: About 12 8-inch crepes, 15 7-inch crepes | Prep: | Cook: |Ready in: 1hours10mins

Ingredients

- For the Buckwheat Crepes:
- 3 large eggs
- 240 grams (1 cup) low-fat milk (2 percent)
- 80 grams (1/3 cup) water
- 1 tablespoon sugar (optional)
- 80 grams (2/3 cup) buckwheat flour
- 40 grams (1/2 cup) unbleached all-purpose flour
- ½ teaspoon salt
- 3 tablespoons melted butter, canola oil or grapeseed oil
- For the Roasted Apricots:
- 6 to 8 apricots, cut in half, pits removed (1 1/2 to 2 apricots per person, depending on the size)
- 1 tablespoon butter
- 1 tablespoon honey
- 1 drop almond extract
- 2 tablespoons chopped lightly toasted pistachios, plus additional for garnish
- 4 buckwheat crepes (above)

- Honey-sweetened plain yogurt or vanilla ice cream for serving (optional)

Direction

- In a medium bowl, whisk together the eggs, milk, water and sugar. Sift together the buckwheat and all-purpose flour and the salt and whisk into the liquid mixture. Add the melted butter or oil and whisk together. Insert a hand blender and blend for 1 minute. If you don't have a hand blender, blend the mixture in a regular blender for 1 minute and pour back into the bowl. Cover and let sit for 1 hour.
- Place a seasoned or nonstick 7- or 8-inch crepe pan over medium heat. Brush with butter or oil and when the pan is hot, remove from the heat and ladle in about 1/4 cup batter if using an 8-inch pan, 3 tablespoons for a 7-inch pan. Tilt or swirl the pan to distribute the batter evenly and return to the heat. Cook for about 1 minute, until you can easily loosen the edges with a spatula and the crepe is nicely browned. Turn and cook on the other side for 30 seconds. Turn onto a plate. Continue until all of the batter is used up.
- Preheat the oven to 400 degrees. Place the apricots in a baking dish large enough to accommodate them in a single layer, but not too large. Place the butter, honey and almond extract in a small saucepan or in a ramekin and heat until the butter melts, either on the stove or at 50 percent power for 25 seconds in the microwave. Pour over the apricots and toss together. Turn the apricots cut side down. Place in the oven and roast for 10 to 15 minutes, until the apricots are soft. Remove from the oven.
- Heat the crepes. Place 3 large or 4 small apricot halves on each crepe. Spoon a little of the juice in the pan over the apricots, but leave enough to spoon over the crepes. Sprinkle on some pistachios. Either roll up the crepe or simply fold over the apricots. Spoon juice from the pan over the crepe, garnish with more pistachios and serve. If you wish, serve these

with a little honey-sweetened yogurt or vanilla ice cream.

Nutrition Information

- 155: calories;
- 6 grams: sugars;
- 3 grams: saturated fat;
- 22 grams: carbohydrates;
- 5 grams: protein;
- 208 milligrams: sodium;
- 0 grams: trans fat;
- 2 grams: dietary fiber;
- 1 gram: polyunsaturated fat;

39. Buckwheat And Black Kale With Brussels Sprouts

Serving: 8 servings | Prep: | Cook: | Ready in: 30mins

Ingredients

- 3 medium onions, minced
- 3 cloves garlic, minced
- 1 tablespoon olive oil
- 3 cups buckwheat
- Salt
- Pepper
- 6 cups water
- 1 bunch black kale, blanched and finely chopped
- 2 parsnips, diced and blanched
- 1 tablespoon whipped cream
- 1 tablespoon chopped parsley
- 1 small red onion, sliced and sautéed
- 12 large shiitake mushrooms, quartered and sautéed
- 12 brussels sprouts, quartered or split into leaves (roasted in 375 degree oven until just tender).

Direction

- In a saucepan over medium heat, sweat the onions and garlic by cooking them in 1 tablespoon oil until they release some of their moisture and become slightly translucent, about 5 minutes
- Add buckwheat, and season with salt and pepper to taste. Cover with water and bring to a simmer for approximately 5 minutes. Remove from the heat and let buckwheat rest in water for approximately 10 minutes. Strain excess water. (Note: Do not let buckwheat rest too long or it will become too thick.)
- Once the buckwheat has been drained, immediately add kale and parsnips. Add whipped cream and parsley, and stir gently. Add vegetable stock as needed to reach desired consistency. Garnish by topping with shiitake mushrooms, onions and roasted brussels sprouts.

Nutrition Information

- 328: calories;
- 2 grams: monounsaturated fat;
- 66 grams: carbohydrates;
- 13 grams: protein;
- 6 grams: sugars;
- 1017 milligrams: sodium;
- 5 grams: fat;
- 1 gram: polyunsaturated fat;

40. Buttermilk Potato Salad

Serving: 8 servings | Prep: | Cook: | Ready in: 20mins

Ingredients

- 3 pounds new potatoes
- 1 cup low-fat buttermilk
- 1 medium red onion, about 6 ounces
- 1 tablespoon caraway seeds
- 4 teaspoons Dijon mustard
- 2 tablespoons lemon juice
- 2 tablespoons grated lemon rind

- ½ teaspoon salt
- Freshly ground black pepper to taste

Direction

- Scrub the potatoes, and boil until tender but firm. (For large potatoes, this will be about 45 minutes.) Drain. Do not peel.
- Combine the remaining ingredients in a bowl.
- Cool the potatoes slightly, and cut into 1-inch cubes. Stir gently into the buttermilk dressing. The salad can be eaten immediately but will be more flavorful if refrigerated for an hour or overnight.

Nutrition Information

- 158: calories;
- 243 milligrams: sodium;
- 1 gram: fat;
- 0 grams: polyunsaturated fat;
- 34 grams: carbohydrates;
- 5 grams: protein;
- 4 grams: sugars;

41. Butternut Squash And Purple Potato Latkes

Serving: About 20 to 24 latkes, serving 6 | Prep: | Cook: | Ready in: 15mins

Ingredients

- ½ medium onion, grated
- 3 cups grated butternut squash (1 small squash)
- 3 cups grated purple potatoes
- 3 tablespoons chopped or slivered fresh sage (more to taste)
- Salt and freshly ground pepper
- 1 teaspoon baking powder
- 3 tablespoons oat bran
- ¼ cup all-purpose flour or cornstarch
- 2 eggs, beaten

- About 1/4 cup canola, grape seed or rice bran oil

Direction

- Preheat the oven to 300 degrees. Place a rack over a sheet pan.
- Place the grated onion in a strainer set over a bowl while you prepare the other ingredients. Then wrap in a dishtowel and squeeze out excess water, or just take up by the handful to squeeze out excess water. Place in a large bowl and add the squash, potatoes, sage, baking powder, salt and pepper, oat bran, and flour or cornstarch. Add the eggs and stir together.
- Begin heating a large heavy skillet over medium-high heat. Add 2 to 3 tablespoons of the oil and when it is hot, take up heaped tablespoons of the latke mixture, press the mixture against the spoon to extract liquid (or squeeze in your hands), and place in the pan. Press down with the back of the spatula to flatten. Repeat with more spoonfuls, being careful not to crowd the pan. In my 10-inch pan I can cook 4 at a time without crowding; my 12-inch pan will accommodate 5. Cook on one side until golden brown, about 3 minutes. Slide the spatula underneath and flip the latkes over. Cook on the other side until golden brown, another 2 to 3 minutes. Transfer to the rack set over a baking sheet and place in the oven to keep warm. The mixture will continue to release liquid, which will accumulate in the bottom of the bowl. Stir from time to time, and remember to squeeze the heaped tablespoons of the mix before you add them to the pan.
- Serve hot topped with low-fat sour cream, Greek style yogurt or crème fraiche.

Nutrition Information

- 224: calories;
- 4 grams: polyunsaturated fat;
- 29 grams: carbohydrates;
- 11 grams: fat;
- 3 grams: saturated fat;

- 0 grams: trans fat;
- 5 grams: protein;
- 1 gram: sugars;
- 407 milligrams: sodium;

42. Cabbage And Basil Salad

Serving: 6 servings | Prep: | Cook: |Ready in: 10mins

Ingredients

- 1 small cabbage (about 1 1/4 pounds)
- 4 cloves garlic, peeled, crushed and chopped fine (1 tablespoon)
- ¾ teaspoon salt
- ½ teaspoon freshly ground black pepper
- 1 tablespoon mustard, preferably Dijon-style
- 2 tablespoons red-wine vinegar
- ¼ cup olive oil, preferably virgin
- ¼ cup shredded fresh basil leaves

Direction

- Cut the cabbage in half and remove the center rib. Shred as you would for coleslaw. You should have about 6 to 7 cups of lightly packed cabbage.
- For the dressing, combine the garlic, salt, pepper, mustard, vinegar and olive oil in a bowl, stirring with a whisk. Add the cabbage and stir. Just before serving, sprinkle the basil on top. The salad will develop more taste if made a few hours ahead.

Nutrition Information

- 104: calories;
- 2 grams: sugars;
- 264 milligrams: sodium;
- 9 grams: fat;
- 1 gram: protein;
- 0 grams: trans fat;
- 7 grams: monounsaturated fat;
- 5 grams: carbohydrates;

43. Caesar Salad

Serving: Six to eight servings | Prep: | Cook: |Ready in: 10mins

Ingredients

- The croutons:
- 1 cup cubed French bread pieces
- Olive oil
- The dressing:
- 2 ounces anchovy fillets
- 1 egg yolk (see note)
- 1 teaspoon finely chopped parsley
- 1 tablespoon finely chopped garlic (or less to taste)
- 1 cup extra-virgin olive oil
- ¼ cup grated Parmesan cheese
- ¼ cup red-wine vinegar
- The lettuce:
- 1 head romaine lettuce, cut, washed and drained

Direction

- Preheat the oven to 300 degrees. Spread the bread on a baking sheet, drizzle with olive oil and bake 4 to 5 minutes, stirring once or twice, until golden. Set aside.
- In a stainless-steel bowl, crush the anchovy fillets with a fork until they are well mashed. Add the egg yolk and stir with a wire whisk for 2 to 3 minutes. Stir in the parsley and garlic. Slowly add the olive oil in a steady stream while whisking to incorporate. Add the vinegar and 2 tablespoons of the Parmesan and stir briskly with the whisk.
- In a large bowl, toss the lettuce with the dressing and the croutons. Sprinkle remaining cheese on top.

Nutrition Information

- 322: calories;

- 0 grams: trans fat;
- 22 grams: monounsaturated fat;
- 3 grams: polyunsaturated fat;
- 6 grams: carbohydrates;
- 2 grams: dietary fiber;
- 1 gram: sugars;
- 355 milligrams: sodium;
- 31 grams: fat;
- 5 grams: protein;

- 1 gram: protein;
- 22 grams: sugars;

45. Cauliflower, Brussels Sprouts And Red Beans With Lemon And Mustard

Serving: 4 servings | Prep: | Cook: |Ready in: 30mins

Ingredients

- 1 medium cauliflower
- 2 teaspoons Dijon mustard
- 2 tablespoons fresh lemon juice
- ¼ cup water, stock or drained cooking liquid from the accompanying grain (optional)
- 2 tablespoons extra virgin olive oil
- ¾ pound brussels sprouts, trimmed and quartered
- Salt and freshly ground pepper to taste
- 1 can red beans, drained and rinsed
- 2 ½ tablespoons chopped fresh dill
- Suggested grain for serving: quinoa (1/2 to 3/4 cup per person)
- Optional: Lemon-flavored olive oil for drizzling

Direction

- Quarter and core the cauliflower, then slice thin so that it falls apart into small, thin pieces. Whisk together the Dijon mustard, lemon juice, 1 tablespoon of the olive oil, and water or stock in a small bowl and set aside.
- Heat the olive oil over medium-high heat in a well-seasoned wok or in a large, heavy nonstick skillet. Add the cauliflower and brussels sprouts and cook, stirring often, for 5 minutes, until the vegetables are seared and beginning to soften. Add salt and pepper and continue to cook, stirring or tossing (as you would a stir-fry), for another 5 minutes, or until the cauliflower and the brussels sprouts are just tender and flavorful.

44. Cantaloupe Star Anise Sorbet

Serving: about 1 1/2 quarts | Prep: | Cook: |Ready in: 30mins

Ingredients

- 2 very ripe cantaloupes, peeled, seeded and cut into large chunks
- 12 star anise
- ¾ cup sugar
- ¼ cup light corn syrup

Direction

- In a food processor, puree cantaloupe until smooth. This should yield at least 4 cups. In a large saucepan, combine 4 cups cantaloupe puree, star anise, sugar, corn syrup and 1 cup water. Place over medium-low heat and stir just until sugar is dissolved. Remove from heat and let rest for at least 2 hours at room temperature.
- Strain through a fine sieve, pressing out as much juice as possible. Pour liquid into an ice cream maker and follow manufacturer's instructions.

Nutrition Information

- 91: calories;
- 17 milligrams: sodium;
- 0 grams: polyunsaturated fat;
- 23 grams: carbohydrates;

- Add the beans, dill and lemon-mustard mixture and stir together for another minute or two. Taste, adjust seasonings, and remove from the heat. Serve with quinoa or another grain of your choice. If desired, add a drizzle of lemon-flavored olive oil to each serving.

46. Caviar Roulade

Serving: Eight to 10 servings | Prep: | Cook: | Ready in: 20mins

Ingredients

- 1 basic sponge roll for roulades (see recipe)
- 3 ounces cream cheese at room temperature
- 1 cup sour cream
- ¼ pound caviar

Direction

- Prepare the sponge roll and have it ready.
- Combine the cream cheese and three tablespoons of the sour cream. Blend well and spread this over the sponge roll. Roll the cake like a jellyroll, folding the small end over and over to make a roll about 10 inches long.
- Using a knife with a serrated blade, carefully slice off the bulky ends of the roll. Cut the remaining roll into neat, one-half-inch slices and top each serving with a spoonful or so of the remaining sour cream. Top each serving with a dollop of caviar. Serve lukewarm or cold.

Nutrition Information

- 120: calories;
- 10 grams: fat;
- 5 grams: saturated fat;
- 2 grams: monounsaturated fat;
- 1 gram: sugars;
- 4 grams: protein;
- 0 grams: dietary fiber;
- 243 milligrams: sodium;

47. Celery Root, Red Cabbage And Potato Colcannon

Serving: About 5 cups, serving 6 | Prep: | Cook: |Ready in: 35mins

Ingredients

- 1 ¼ pounds potatoes, scrubbed
- 1 ¼ pounds celery root (celeriac) (1 large), peeled and cut into chunks
- Salt to taste
- 1 tablespoon extra virgin olive oil
- ½ medium-size red cabbage, quartered, cored and shredded (about 4 cups shredded cabbage)
- ½ to 1 teaspoon caraway seeds, to taste
- 2 ½ tablespoons unsalted butter
- ¾ cup warm or hot milk
- Freshly ground pepper

Direction

- Place potatoes and celeriac in a saucepan and cover by an inch with water. Bring to a boil, add salt to taste, reduce heat to medium-low and cover partially. Boil gently until tender, 25 to 30 minutes. Drain, return to the pot and cover pot tightly. Let steam in the dry pot for 5 minutes.
- Meanwhile, heat olive oil over medium heat in a heavy skillet and add cabbage. Cook, stirring often, until it begins to wilt, about 5 minutes. Add caraway and salt to taste, and stir together. Cover and cook over medium-low heat, stirring often, until cabbage is very soft and fragrant, about 10 minutes. If cabbage begins to stick to the pan, add a little bit of water. Remove from heat. Taste and adjust seasoning.
- Heat milk and butter together until butter melts. Mash potatoes and celeriac with a potato masher or in a standing mixer fitted with the paddle, or put through a food mill.

Add milk and butter and mix until smooth. Stir in cabbage and caraway and mix until well blended. Season to taste with salt and pepper. Serve hot.

Nutrition Information

- 211: calories;
- 4 grams: saturated fat;
- 0 grams: trans fat;
- 3 grams: monounsaturated fat;
- 6 grams: sugars;
- 9 grams: fat;
- 1 gram: polyunsaturated fat;
- 31 grams: carbohydrates;
- 5 grams: protein;
- 670 milligrams: sodium;

48. Celery And Apple Salad

Serving: 6 servings | Prep: | Cook: | Ready in: 15mins

Ingredients

- 6 ribs celery (about 8 ounces), as white as possible
- 2 medium-size Red Delicious apples (12 ounces)
- 1 ½ tablespoons lemon juice
- ½ cup sour cream
- ¾ teaspoon freshly ground black pepper
- ½ teaspoon salt
- 1 teaspoon sugar
- 6 lettuce leaves, for garnish

Direction

- Trim celery ribs to remove leaves (reserving the trimmings for stock), and peel ribs with vegetable peeler if outer surface is tough or fibrous. Wash and cut the ribs into 2-inch pieces. Then press the pieces flat on the table and cut them lengthwise into thin strips. You should have about 2 1/2 cups. Place in a bowl.

- Since the apples are not peeled, wash them thoroughly in warm water, scraping lightly with a knife if necessary to remove any surface wax. Stand apples up and cut them lengthwise on all sides into slices 1/2-inch thick until you reach core. Discard it, pile apple slices together and cut into 1/2-inch strips. Add pieces to celery along with the all ingredients except lettuce leaves and mix well.
- To serve, arrange lettuce leaves on six individual plates and spoon the salad onto the leaves.

Nutrition Information

- 77: calories;
- 234 milligrams: sodium;
- 4 grams: fat;
- 2 grams: dietary fiber;
- 1 gram: protein;
- 0 grams: polyunsaturated fat;
- 10 grams: carbohydrates;
- 7 grams: sugars;

49. Chard And Sweet Corn Tacos

Serving: 8 tacos, serving 4 | Prep: | Cook: | Ready in: 15mins

Ingredients

- 1 generous bunch Swiss chard (about 3/4 pound)
- Salt to taste
- 1 medium white, red or yellow onion, sliced
- 3 large garlic cloves, minced
- Kernels from 2 ears sweet corn
- Freshly ground pepper
- 8 warm corn tortillas
- ½ cup crumbled queso fresco or feta (but not too salty a feta)
- Salsa of your choice

Direction

- Bring a large pot of water to a boil while you stem chard and wash leaves in 2 rinses of water. Rinse stalks and dice them if they are wide and not stringy.
- When water in pot comes to a boil, salt generously and add chard leaves. Blanch for a minute, then transfer to a bowl of cold water and drain. Take chard up by the handful and squeeze out excess water, then cut into 1/2-inch wide strips. Set aside.
- Heat oil over medium heat in a large, heavy skillet and add onion. Cook, stirring often, until onions are tender and beginning to color, about 8 minutes, and add a generous pinch of salt, the garlic, diced chard stalks and corn kernels. Continue to cook, stirring often, until corn is just tender, about 4 minutes. Stir in chard and cook, stirring, for another minute or two, until ingredients are combined nicely and chard is tender but still bright. Season to taste with salt and pepper. Remove from heat.
- Heat tortillas. Top with vegetables, a sprinkling of cheese and a spoonful of salsa.

50. Cherry Balsamic Iced Tea

Serving: One quart | Prep: | Cook: | Ready in: 15mins

Ingredients

- 1 cup dried cherries
- 4 cups boiling water
- 6 plain tea bags
- 2 teaspoons finely chopped ginger
- 1 teaspoon balsamic vinegar
- 12 pitted cherries

Direction

- Place the dried cherries in a food processor and process until finely chopped. Transfer to a bowl and add the boiling water, tea bags and ginger. After 4 minutes, remove the tea bags. Let stand until cool. Strain through a fine

sieve. Stir in vinegar and refrigerate until cold. Serve over ice, garnished with cherries.

Nutrition Information

- 50: calories;
- 0 grams: protein;
- 12 grams: carbohydrates;
- 1 gram: dietary fiber;
- 10 grams: sugars;
- 5 milligrams: sodium;

51. Cherry Clafouti

Serving: Six servings | Prep: | Cook: | Ready in: 1hours

Ingredients

- 1 quart Bing or Queen Anne cherries, about 1 pound, stemmed and pitted
- ¼ pound, plus 1 tablespoon, unsalted butter
- 3 eggs
- ¾ cup sugar
- ¾ cup all-purpose flour, sifted
- ½ teaspoon vanilla extract
- ½ pint heavy cream, lightly whipped (optional)

Direction

- Preheat the oven to 350 degrees.
- Evenly coat a glass or porcelain 10-inch pie pan with one tablespoon of butter. Melt the remaining butter in a saucepan and reserve.
- In a medium-sized bowl, beat the eggs with the sugar until the mixture is thickened and a light lemon color. Add the butter, flour and vanilla and beat until thoroughly blended. Set aside for 15 minutes.
- Place the cherries over the bottom of the buttered pan. Pour the batter evenly over the cherries and bake for 40 minutes or until golden and puffy. Serve warm with the lightly whipped cream.

Nutrition Information

- 248: calories;
- 37 grams: sugars;
- 5 grams: protein;
- 0 grams: trans fat;
- 52 grams: carbohydrates;
- 31 milligrams: sodium;
- 3 grams: fat;
- 1 gram: polyunsaturated fat;
- 2 grams: dietary fiber;

52. Cherry And Spring Onion Salsa

Serving: 4 to 8 servings | Prep: | Cook: | Ready in: 15mins

Ingredients

- 1 small red spring onion bulb and greens
- 3 tablespoons lemon juice, or more to taste
- 1 ½ cups pitted cherries, or about 8 ounces
- 1 teaspoon finely chopped chives
- 1 tablespoon finely chopped parsley
- 1 small jalapeño, seeded and finely chopped
- 5 tablespoons extra virgin olive oil
- ½ teaspoon kosher salt

Direction

- Finely dice spring onion bulb and greens. Place 3 tablespoons diced bulb and 1 tablespoon greens in a small bowl and pour lemon juice over them. Set aside for 10 minutes to macerate.
- Halve the cherries and slice into slivers. Place cherries, herbs, jalapeño, olive oil and salt in a medium-size bowl and stir to combine.
- Add onion and greens, taste and add more salt and lemon juice if needed.
- Let the salsa sit for at least 5 minutes to meld flavors.

Nutrition Information

- 124: calories;
- 131 milligrams: sodium;
- 11 grams: fat;
- 1 gram: dietary fiber;
- 6 grams: carbohydrates;
- 0 grams: protein;
- 2 grams: saturated fat;
- 8 grams: monounsaturated fat;
- 5 grams: sugars;

53. Chicken Breasts With Olives And Tomatoes

Serving: 6 servings | Prep: | Cook: | Ready in: 1hours

Ingredients

- 4 tablespoons extra-virgin olive oil
- 2 cloves garlic, minced
- Juice of 1 lemon
- Salt and freshly ground black pepper
- 2 ¼ pounds skinless and boneless chicken breasts
- 1 medium onion, chopped
- 1 pound canned plum tomatoes, very well drained and chopped
- 18 Nicoise olives, pitted and coarsely chopped
- 1 tablespoon chopped fresh parsley
- 1 teaspoon fresh thyme leaves or 1/2 teaspoon dried

Direction

- In a shallow baking dish combine two tablespoons of the olive oil with half the garlic, the lemon juice and salt and pepper to taste. Add chicken breasts, turning them in the dish so they are coated with the marinade. Arrange them in a single layer in the dish, cover with plastic wrap and allow them to marinate at room temperature for 30 minutes.
- Preheat oven to 375 degrees.

- Heat the remaining oil in a skillet. Add onion and remaining garlic and saute until tender but not brown. Add tomatoes and olives and allow to cook about 15 minutes, until the mixture begins to thicken. Stir in half the parsley and the thyme and season to taste with salt and pepper.
- Spread the tomato mixture over the marinated chicken breasts. Place in oven and bake about 20 minutes, until the chicken is done. Remove from oven and baste to combine juices in bottom of the pan with the tomato mixture on top. Sprinkle with the remaining parsley and serve.

Nutrition Information

- 411: calories;
- 37 grams: protein;
- 14 grams: monounsaturated fat;
- 7 grams: carbohydrates;
- 2 grams: dietary fiber;
- 3 grams: sugars;
- 4 grams: polyunsaturated fat;
- 686 milligrams: sodium;
- 26 grams: fat;
- 6 grams: saturated fat;
- 0 grams: trans fat;

54. Chicken With Carrots And Lemon Thyme Butter

Serving: Serves 4 | Prep: | Cook: | Ready in: 1hours25mins

Ingredients

- 2 whole chickens, 3 pounds or more each
- 8 tablespoons butter, soft
- ½ cup small celery cubes
- 1 cup white onions, chopped
- ¾ cups small carrot cubes
- 1 clove garlic, chopped
- ⅓ cup white wine
- 3 cups chicken broth (fresh or canned)
- 1 bay leaf
- 3 sprigs fresh thyme (or 1 1/2 teaspoons dried)
- ¼ teaspoon sugar
- 1 pound whole large carrots, scraped and sliced into very thin rounds
- Salt and freshly ground black pepper to taste
- Juice of 1 lemon
- 1 teaspoon grated lemon zest
- White pepper to taste
- 4 cups corn oil for frying
- 4 large carrots, peeled -- about 3/4 pound -- cut into long threads (it's best to use a mandoline or some other mechanical vegetable slicer), about 4 cups loosely packed
- 4 tablespoons chopped Italian parsley leaves for garnish

Direction

- Remove breasts from chickens, skin on, and include the first joint of the wing. (The legs will not be used.) Using a cleaver or heavy knife, hack the remaining carcasses into 1-inch pieces.
- Heat 1 tablespoon of butter in a saucepan over medium-heat until slightly brown. Add the pieces of chicken carcasses and cook, stirring, until well browned, about 10 minutes. Pour off all the fat. Lower heat to medium and add the celery, 1/2 cup of the onions, all the cubed carrots and the garlic. Cook, stirring, for 5 minutes.
- Add the wine. Then add the chicken broth, 1 cup water, bay leaf and 2 sprigs thyme (or 1 teaspoon dried). Bring to a boil, then reduce heat to low. Simmer uncovered for 45 minutes, occasionally skimming fat from the top. Strain. You should have about 1 3/4 cups of chicken broth. Set aside. (This broth can be made in advance and refrigerated.)
- In a pan, melt 1 tablespoon of butter over medium heat and add the remaining 1/2 cup of onions and the sugar. Cook the onions, stirring, until wilted, about 2 minutes. Add carrot rounds and chicken broth. Bring to a boil, reduce heat and simmer, covered, for

about 10 minutes, or until al dente. Remove from heat and set aside, with cooking liquid.

- Preheat oven to 400 degrees. Salt and pepper the chicken breasts. In a large, ovenproof skillet melt 1 tablespoon butter and add the chicken breasts, skin side down. Cook over medium-high heat for about 5 minutes, or until well browned. Flip the chicken. Reduce heat to medium and cook for about 6 minutes more. Remove from heat and place in oven for about 6 more minutes, or until done. Remove the breasts from the skillet and keep warm.
- Add 1 tablespoon butter to the chicken pan juices and stir.
- In a small mixing bowl, make the lemon butter by combining 4 tablespoons of soft butter, lemon juice, leaves from 1 sprig thyme (1/2 teaspoon dried), lemon zest, salt and white pepper.
- Gently remove the carrot rounds and set aside, keeping them warm. Stir lemon butter into the cooking liquid from the carrots. Keep warm.
- Place the corn oil in a large pot. Heat to 340 degrees, or until it is just beginning to smoke. Place a handful of carrot threads in the hot oil. Cook for about 30 to 40 seconds. Remove with slotted spoon to paper towels. When the carrots are cool enough to handle, mold into a loose ball. Repeat with the rest of the carrots for a total of four balls.
- Divide the carrot rounds into the middle of 4 large warmed plates. Slice each chicken breast into 3 pieces, on a slight angle, and arrange the slices over the carrot rounds. The wing joint should be facing tip up. Ladle some of the chicken-pan juices over the chicken, and then some of the lemon-butter sauce. Place a deep-fried carrot ball on top of the chicken. Garnish all with parsley leaves and serve.

55. Chicken And Pepper Stew

Serving: 4 servings | Prep: | Cook: | Ready in: 50mins

Ingredients

- 6 to 8 chicken legs and/or thighs, skinned
- Salt and freshly ground pepper
- 1 tablespoon canola or vegetable oil
- 1 tablespoon extra virgin olive oil
- 1 large onion, cut in half lengthwise and then sliced across the grain
- 2 mildly hot chilies, like Anaheim or New Mexico chilies, cored, seeded and cut in very thin strips, or 1/4 to 1/2 teaspoon hot red pepper flakes (optional)
- 3 to 4 garlic cloves, thinly sliced
- 1 ½ pounds (4 large) mixed green and red bell peppers, cored, seeded and thinly sliced
- 1 28-ounce can chopped tomatoes with juice, pulsed in a food processor
- Pinch of sugar

Direction

- Rinse the chicken pieces and pat dry. Season with salt and pepper. Heat the canola or vegetable oil in a large, heavy skillet over medium-high heat, and brown the chicken pieces, in batches, on each side for about 5 minutes. Transfer to a bowl or plate. Pour off the fat from the pan and discard.
- Turn the heat down to medium. Add the olive oil and the onion with a pinch of salt. Cook, stirring and scraping the bottom of the pan to deglaze, until the onions begin to soften. Continue to cook, stirring occasionally, until the onions are tender, about 5 minutes. Add the hot and sweet peppers, a bit of salt and the garlic, and cook, stirring, until the peppers begin to soften, about 5 minutes. Add the tomatoes and sugar and stir together until the tomatoes begin to bubble and smell fragrant, about 5 minutes.
- Return the chicken pieces to the pan. Cover and cook 25 to 30 minutes over medium-low heat, stirring at regular intervals and turning the chicken pieces over so that the ingredients don't scorch and the chicken cooks evenly. The peppers should be very soft and the chicken quite tender. Add freshly ground pepper, taste

and adjust the salt, and serve with rice, other grains of your choice or noodles.

Nutrition Information

- 746: calories;
- 23 grams: monounsaturated fat;
- 10 grams: polyunsaturated fat;
- 24 grams: carbohydrates;
- 14 grams: sugars;
- 51 grams: fat;
- 13 grams: saturated fat;
- 0 grams: trans fat;
- 1578 milligrams: sodium;
- 9 grams: dietary fiber;
- 47 grams: protein;

56. Chicken, Greek Style

Serving: 2 servings | Prep: | Cook: | Ready in: 35mins

Ingredients

- 16 ounces whole onion or 14 ounces chopped ready-cut onion (about 3 1/3 cups)
- 1 tablespoon olive oil
- 2 cloves garlic
- 8 ounces skinless, boneless chicken breast
- 1 lemon to yield 1 teaspoon grated lemon rind
- ¼ cup dry vermouth
- ½ teaspoon cinnamon
- ¼ cup no-salt-added chicken broth plus 1 tablespoon
- 1 tablespoon cornstarch
- ½ cup nonfat plain yogurt
- ⅛ teaspoon salt
- Freshly ground black pepper to taste

Direction

- Chop the onion for this recipe along with the onion for the rice dish.
- Heat a nonstick skillet until it is very hot. Reduce the heat to medium high, and add oil.

- Add all the onion, and saute until the onion begins to brown.
- Mince garlic; remove1/3 of onion from pan, and add to rice (see rice recipe). Add garlic to remaining onion, and stir.
- Wash, dry and cut chicken into bite-size chunks, and add to onion; brown chicken on both sides.
- Grate lemon rind, and add to pan with the vermouth and cinnamon and 1/4 cup chicken broth. Cover, and cook over low heat until the chicken is cooked through.
- Stir the remaining tablespoon of chicken broth into the cornstarch, and mix to a smooth paste; stir into pan. Then, add the yogurt, and stir to mix well. Season with salt and pepper.

Nutrition Information

- 443: calories;
- 3 grams: polyunsaturated fat;
- 5 grams: dietary fiber;
- 15 grams: sugars;
- 330 milligrams: sodium;
- 18 grams: fat;
- 4 grams: saturated fat;
- 0 grams: trans fat;
- 31 grams: protein;
- 10 grams: monounsaturated fat;
- 34 grams: carbohydrates;

57. Chipotle Chili Sauce

Serving: about 2 1/4 cups | Prep: | Cook: | Ready in: 30mins

Ingredients

- 2 cups partly drained canned tomatoes, preferably imported
- 2 or 3 chipotle chilies with sauce that clings to each (see note)
- 1 ½ tablespoons corn, peanut or vegetable oil
- ½ cup quartered, thinly sliced onion

Direction

- Combine the tomatoes and chilies in the container of a food processor or electric blender. Blend as finely as possible.
- Heat the oil in a skillet, and add the onion. Cook, stirring, until wilted, and add the tomato and chili mixture. Let simmer, stirring often, about 20 minutes.

Nutrition Information

- 74: calories;
- 1 gram: protein;
- 7 grams: carbohydrates;
- 599 milligrams: sodium;
- 5 grams: sugars;
- 0 grams: trans fat;
- 3 grams: dietary fiber;

58. Chive Blossom Salad With Mushrooms

Serving: 4 servings | Prep: | Cook: | Ready in: 10mins

Ingredients

- 1 pound raw white mushrooms
- ½ cup extra-virgin olive oil
- About 12 chive blossoms
- ⅓ cup chopped chives
- Coarse salt and freshly ground pepper to taste

Direction

- Wipe the dirt off the mushrooms with paper towels. Slice the mushrooms and arrange them on a serving platter. Sprinkle the oil over the top (because the mushrooms absorb oil like a sponge, you may find it easier to brush them with the oil so that it is more evenly distributed).
- Sprinkle the mushrooms with blossoms and chives and season with salt and pepper.

Nutrition Information

- 268: calories;
- 3 grams: polyunsaturated fat;
- 1 gram: dietary fiber;
- 2 grams: sugars;
- 351 milligrams: sodium;
- 27 grams: fat;
- 4 grams: protein;
- 20 grams: monounsaturated fat;

59. Chocolate Cake

Serving: 8 servings | Prep: | Cook: | Ready in: 1hours45mins

Ingredients

- ½ cup unsalted butter, cut into small pieces, plus additional for greasing pan
- 8 ounces bittersweet chocolate, cut into small pieces
- 5 large eggs, separated
- ⅛ teaspoon salt
- ⅔ cup sugar
- Powdered sugar, for garnish
- ½ cup unsweetened whipped cream

Direction

- Preheat oven to 325 degrees. Butter and flour a 10-inch-round cake pan with 3-inch sides. Place butter and chocolate in a double boiler over simmering water until melted, stirring occasionally. Whisk together the egg yolks, salt and all but 3 tablespoons of the sugar in a large bowl. Stir the melted chocolate mixture into the yolk mixture.
- With an electric mixer, beat the egg whites on medium speed until soft peaks form. Gradually beat in the remaining sugar and beat until whites are stiff but not dry. Stir 1/4 of the whites into the chocolate mixture. Fold in the remaining whites. Pour into the prepared pan.

- Bake until a toothpick inserted into cake's center comes out clean, about 1 hour, 15 minutes. Immediately turn the cake out onto a rack. As the cake cools, the center will sink and crack, don't worry. Dust the cake with powdered sugar and serve with unsweetened whipped cream.

Nutrition Information

- 357: calories;
- 14 grams: saturated fat;
- 0 grams: trans fat;
- 35 grams: carbohydrates;
- 5 grams: protein;
- 24 grams: fat;
- 7 grams: monounsaturated fat;
- 1 gram: polyunsaturated fat;
- 2 grams: dietary fiber;
- 33 grams: sugars;
- 86 milligrams: sodium;

60. Chopped Herb Salad With Farro

Serving: Serves 6 | Prep: | Cook: | Ready in: 30mins

Ingredients

- 2 cups chopped fresh flat-leaf parsley (from 2 large bunches)
- ¼ cup chopped fresh mint
- 1 cup chopped arugula or a mix of arugula and other herbs
- ¾ pound (2 large) ripe tomatoes, very finely chopped
- 1 bunch scallions, finely chopped
- 1 cup cooked farro or spelt
- 1 teaspoon ground sumac
- Juice of 1 to 2 large lemons, to taste
- Salt to taste
- ¼ cup extra-virgin olive oil
- Small leaves from 1 romaine lettuce heart, leaves separated, washed and dried (optional)

Direction

- In a large bowl, combine parsley, mint, arugula and/or other herbs, tomatoes, scallions, farro, sumac, lemon juice and salt to taste. Refrigerate for 2 to 3 hours so the farro marinates in the lemon juice.
- Add olive oil, toss together, taste and adjust seasonings. The salad should taste lemony. Add more lemon juice if it doesn't. Serve with lettuce leaves if desired.

Nutrition Information

- 157: calories;
- 5 grams: dietary fiber;
- 10 grams: fat;
- 17 grams: carbohydrates;
- 4 grams: protein;
- 381 milligrams: sodium;
- 1 gram: polyunsaturated fat;
- 7 grams: monounsaturated fat;
- 3 grams: sugars;

61. Chowchow

Serving: 8 pint jars | Prep: | Cook: | Ready in: 45mins

Ingredients

- 4 cups string beans, trimmed and cut into 1-inch lengths
- ½ head cauliflower, broken into small flowerets
- 1 ½ cups fresh corn kernels
- 1 ½ cups fresh or frozen lima beans
- 6 cups cider vinegar
- 1 cup sugar
- ⅓ cup kosher salt
- 5 tablespoons dry mustard
- 1 tablespoon celery seeds
- 1 tablespoon mustard seeds
- 1 ½ teaspoons turmeric
- 4 cups green tomatoes, cut into 1-inch chunks

- 2 green bell peppers, stemmed, seeded and cut into 1/2-inch dice
- 1 red bell pepper, stemmed, seeded and cut into 1/2-inch dice
- 2 red onions, peeled and cut into 1/2-inch dice

Direction

- Bring a large kettle 1/4 full of salted water to a boil. Add the string beans, cauliflower, corn and fresh limas (if using frozen limas, do not add yet) and cook until just tender, about 5 minutes. Drain and plunge the vegetables into cold water to stop the cooking. When cool, drain again and set aside.
- Return kettle to the stove and add the vinegar, sugar, salt, dry mustard, celery seeds, mustard seeds and turmeric. Bring just to a boil. Add the tomatoes, red and green bell peppers and onions. (If you are using frozen limas, add them now.) Simmer for 10 minutes. Add the cooled vegetables to the pot and cook another 10 minutes.
- Have ready 8 hot, sterilized pint (2-cup) canning jars and lids. (See pickled peppers for sterilizing instructions.) Pour chowchow into the jars, leaving about 1/4inch of space below the lip. Wipe rims with a clean, damp towel and screw lids on securely but not too tightly.
- Fill a large kettle fitted with a rack halfway with water and bring to a boil. Meanwhile, bring a teapot full of water to a boil. Place the filled jars on the rack (do not let them touch -- work in batches if necessary) and pour in boiling water from the teapot until jar tops are covered by 2 inches. Bring to a boil and boil 10 minutes.
- Using tongs, remove jars from kettle. Using potholders, tighten lids. Allow to cool. Store in a cool, dark place.

Nutrition Information

- 299: calories;
- 7 grams: dietary fiber;
- 8 grams: protein;
- 3 grams: fat;

- 0 grams: trans fat;
- 1 gram: polyunsaturated fat;
- 56 grams: carbohydrates;
- 36 grams: sugars;
- 1197 milligrams: sodium;

62. Chunky Avocado Papaya Salsa

Serving: Serves 6 to 8 | Prep: | Cook: | Ready in: 20mins

Ingredients

- 2 medium-size ripe Hass avocados, halved, pitted and cut in small dice
- 1 small ripe papaya, halved, seeded, peeled and cut in small dice (about 2 cups dice)
- 1 tart apple, unpeeled, or Asian pear, peeled if desired, cored and cut in small dice
- ¼ cup freshly squeezed lime juice
- 1 fresh red or green serrano chile, seeded and thinly sliced or minced, or more to taste
- ¼ cup chopped cilantro
- 2 tablespoons chopped fresh mint
- ½ small red onion, diced small, soaked for 5 minutes in water to cover, drained and rinsed (optional)
- Salt to taste

Direction

- Combine diced avocados and papaya in a medium bowl. Add remaining ingredients and toss together. Season to taste with salt. Serve as a salad or a salsa.

Nutrition Information

- 105: calories;
- 7 grams: fat;
- 1 gram: protein;
- 5 grams: dietary fiber;
- 11 grams: carbohydrates;
- 4 grams: sugars;
- 241 milligrams: sodium;

63. Classic Irish Salad

Serving: 6 servings | Prep: | Cook: | Ready in: 1hours10mins

Ingredients

- 2 medium beets
- 2 small heads bibb lettuce
- 2 bunches watercress
- 2 tablespoons creme fraiche
- 1 tablespoon chopped parsley
- 5 tablespoons extra-virgin olive oil
- 3 tablespoons herb infused white vinegar (or to taste)
- Coarse salt and freshly ground pepper to taste
- 1 dozen quail eggs, boiled for two minutes
- ½ cup chopped chervil leaves

Direction

- Place the beets in a saucepan with water to cover and simmer for one hour or until tender. Remove from heat and allow to cool in the liquid. Peel and julienne.
- Break up the heads of bibb lettuce, leaving the leaves whole. Wash and dry. Cut the stems from the watercress; wash and dry the leaves.
- Make the dressing. Mix the creme fraiche, parsley, olive oil and vinegar together and season to taste with salt and pepper.
- To assemble, put whole leaves of lettuce around the outer edges of six individual plates. Place watercress in the middle of the plate and sprinkle the beets on top. Peel the quail eggs and cut them in half. Place the eggs on top and sprinkle with chervil. Drizzle dressing over and serve.

Nutrition Information

- 162: calories;
- 2 grams: dietary fiber;
- 5 grams: carbohydrates;
- 4 grams: protein;
- 346 milligrams: sodium;
- 14 grams: fat;
- 3 grams: sugars;
- 9 grams: monounsaturated fat;

64. Coconut Bread Pudding

Serving: 8 servings | Prep: | Cook: | Ready in: 45mins

Ingredients

- 6 large eggs
- 1 ⅛ cups sugar, more for topping dish
- 2 cups heavy cream
- 1 13 1/2-ounce can coconut milk
- 2 tablespoons dark rum
- 10 slices challah or brioche, 1/3.-inch thick

Direction

- In bowl of an electric mixer fitted with a whisk attachment, combine eggs and 1 1/8 cups sugar. Mix until smooth. In a small pan, bring cream to a boil. With mixer running at medium-low speed, slowly add hot cream. Add coconut milk and rum, and mix again just until smooth. Allow mixture to rest at room temperature for one hour.
- Heat oven to 350 degrees. Fill a kettle with water and place over high heat to bring to a boil. In an 8 1/2-by-12-inch baking dish, arrange challah slices so they overlap in two columns. Pour custard evenly over top, and press down lightly with a spatula. Place dish in a large, deep pan, like a roasting pan. Carefully pour in boiling water so that it comes about halfway up the sides of baking dish. Bake until custard is set but not too firm, 30 to 35 minutes.
- Sprinkle liberally with sugar, and caramelize it with a kitchen torch or by placing it under a broiler for 2 to 3 minutes. Serve, scooping out individual portions.

Nutrition Information

- 614: calories;
- 39 grams: fat;
- 25 grams: saturated fat;
- 0 grams: trans fat;
- 9 grams: monounsaturated fat;
- 2 grams: polyunsaturated fat;
- 31 grams: sugars;
- 272 milligrams: sodium;
- 55 grams: carbohydrates;
- 1 gram: dietary fiber;
- 12 grams: protein;

65. Cold Spinach Soup

Serving: 8 to 12 servings | Prep: | Cook: | Ready in: 25mins

Ingredients

- 2 pounds spinach, stemmed
- ¼ cup loosely packed fresh dill
- 1 scallion, white and light green parts trimmed and thinly sliced
- ½ pound good-quality dill pickles, cut in 1/4-inch dice (or substitute peeled and seeded cucumbers)
- 12 ounces beer
- ¼ teaspoon peeled, freshly grated horseradish
- 1 ½ cups water
- Kosher salt to taste
- 6 bunches sorrel (about 1 1/2 pounds), stemmed and cut horizontally into 1/8-inch-wide strips (optional)
- Scant 1 tablespoon unsalted butter (if adding sorrel)
- ½ cup sour cream (1 1/2 cups if adding sorrel)
- ½ cup plain yogurt (1 1/2 cups heavy cream if adding sorrel)
- 1 tablespoon apple-cider vinegar

Direction

- Wash spinach and place in a large skillet with the adhering water. Cover. Cook over medium heat for 10 minutes, stirring once or twice, just until wilted. Drain. Place the spinach and the dill in a food processor and process until finely chopped.
- Scrape mixture into a metal bowl. Stir in scallion, pickles, beer, horseradish, water and salt.
- If using sorrel, heat the butter in a large skillet over medium heat until just melted. Add the sorrel and cook 4 to 5 minutes, or until color turns. Remove from heat. Stir sorrel, 1 1/2 cups sour cream and 1 1/2 cups heavy cream into spinach mixture. If not using sorrel, stir in 1/2 cup yogurt instead of heavy cream and 1/2 cup sour cream. Refrigerate until cold. Just before serving, stir in vinegar. Add more salt if needed.

Nutrition Information

- 80: calories;
- 4 grams: protein;
- 2 grams: sugars;
- 0 grams: polyunsaturated fat;
- 1 gram: monounsaturated fat;
- 6 grams: carbohydrates;
- 492 milligrams: sodium;

66. Cold Tomato Soup With Rosemary

Serving: 4 servings | Prep: | Cook: | Ready in: 15mins

Ingredients

- 2 slices stale French or Italian white bread, crusts removed
- 3 pounds ripe tomatoes, peeled, seeded and roughly chopped
- 1 teaspoon fresh rosemary leaves
- 1 small clove garlic, peeled
- 1 cup chicken stock or ice cubes

- Salt and freshly ground black pepper to taste
- The juice of 1 lemon, or more to taste

Direction

- Soak bread in cold water briefly; squeeze dry, and combine in a blender with tomatoes, rosemary and garlic (you may have to do this in two batches). If using stock, turn on machine and drizzle in the stock; blend until smooth. If using ice cubes, place them in the blender and blend until mixture is smooth. Pour the mixture into a bowl.
- Season with salt and pepper, then add lemon juice to taste. Chill and serve.

Nutrition Information

- 130: calories;
- 0 grams: trans fat;
- 25 grams: carbohydrates;
- 11 grams: sugars;
- 6 grams: protein;
- 1003 milligrams: sodium;
- 2 grams: fat;
- 1 gram: polyunsaturated fat;
- 5 grams: dietary fiber;

67. Cold Tomato Soup With Farro

Serving: Serves 4 | Prep: | Cook: | Ready in:

Ingredients

- 1 long European or Japanese cucumber
- 1 ½ pounds ripe tomatoes, quartered
- 2 slices red onion, soaked for 5 minutes in cold water, drained and rinsed
- 2 large garlic cloves, halved, green germs removed
- 2 tablespoons sherry vinegar
- 2 tablespoons extra-virgin olive oil
- Salt to taste
- ¼ cup broth from the farro (optional)

- 2 to 4 ice cubes (optional)
- 1 cup cooked farro or spelt (see below)
- Slivered fresh basil leaves or very small whole basil leaves and additional olive oil if desired for garnish

Direction

- Cut cucumber into 2 equal pieces. Peel and roughly chop one piece, and cut the other piece into 1/4-inch dice, for garnish.
- Working in 2 batches, blend roughly chopped cucumber, tomatoes, onion, garlic, vinegar, olive oil, salt, farro broth and ice cubes (if using) in a blender for 2 minutes or longer, until smooth and frothy. Taste and adjust salt. Transfer to a bowl or container (a metal bowl is the most efficient for chilling) and chill for 1 to 2 hours.
- Place about 1/4 cup cooked farro (or spelt) in each soup bowl. Ladle in the soup. Garnish with diced cucumber and basil. Drizzle on olive oil if desired and serve.

Nutrition Information

- 172: calories;
- 8 grams: fat;
- 1 gram: polyunsaturated fat;
- 5 grams: protein;
- 24 grams: carbohydrates;
- 6 grams: sugars;
- 746 milligrams: sodium;

68. Coleslaw With Yogurt Dressing

Serving: 8 servings | Prep: | Cook: | Ready in: 25mins

Ingredients

- 1 small head green cabbage, about one pound
- 1 bunch scallions, finely chopped
- 1 carrot, peeled and coarsely grated
- 1 cup plain low-fat or non-fat yogurt

- ½ cup mayonnaise
- Salt and freshly ground black pepper
- A pinch of sugar, or more, to taste
- 3 tablespoons finely chopped Italian parsley

Direction

- Remove any wilted outer leaves from the cabbage. Quarter the cabbage and slice off the cores. Shred the cabbage into a large bowl. Fold in the scallions and carrot.
- Mix the yogurt and mayonnaise together and season to taste with salt, pepper and sugar. Pour the dressing over the vegetables and mix. Refrigerate for at least an hour and up to 24 hours.
- Check seasonings and add the parsley just before serving.

Nutrition Information

- 149: calories;
- 3 grams: protein;
- 7 grams: polyunsaturated fat;
- 10 grams: carbohydrates;
- 6 grams: sugars;
- 367 milligrams: sodium;
- 11 grams: fat;
- 2 grams: saturated fat;

69. Cooked Tomatillo Salsa

Serving: 2 cups | Prep: | Cook: | Ready in: 40mins

Ingredients

- 1 pound fresh tomatillos, husked and rinsed, or 2 13-ounce cans, drained
- 2 or 3 jalapeño or serrano chiles, stemmed, seeded for a milder salsa
- ¼ cup chopped white onion, soaked for 5 minutes in cold water, then drained and rinsed
- 2 large garlic cloves, peeled
- ½ cup chopped cilantro

- 1 tablespoon grapeseed oil, sunflower oil or canola oil
- 2 cups chicken stock or vegetable stock
- Salt to taste (1/2 to 1 teaspoon)

Direction

- Place the tomatillos in a saucepan, cover with water and bring to a boil. Reduce the heat and simmer for 8 to 10 minutes, flipping them over halfway through, until softened and olive green. Drain and place in a blender. Add the chiles, chopped onion, garlic, salt, and cilantro sprigs. Blend until smooth.
- Heat the oil in a large, heavy saucepan or skillet over medium-high heat until it ripples. Drizzle in a drop of tomatillo purée to test the heat. If it makes a lot of noise and sputters immediately, the oil is hot enough. Add the tomatillo purée, and stir constantly until it thickens and begins to stick to the pan, about 5 minutes. When you run your spoon down the middle of the pan it should leave a canal. Stir in the stock, bring to a simmer, and simmer 10 to 15 minutes, stirring often. The sauce should coat the front and back of your spoon. Taste and adjust seasoning. Remove from the heat. Serve warm or at room temperature.

Nutrition Information

- 119: calories;
- 3 grams: dietary fiber;
- 13 grams: carbohydrates;
- 7 grams: sugars;
- 5 grams: protein;
- 597 milligrams: sodium;
- 6 grams: fat;
- 1 gram: monounsaturated fat;

70. Corn Off The Cob

Serving: 6 servings | Prep: | Cook: | Ready in: 15mins

Ingredients

- 6 ears corn
- ½ cup water
- 1 tablespoon vegetable (canola) oil
- 2 tablespoons unsalted butter
- ½ teaspoon salt

Direction

- Remove the husks from the corn and cut the kernels off the cobs with a sharp knife. You should get 5 to 6 cups of kernels. Place in a saucepan with the water, oil, butter and salt. Bring to a boil over high heat, stirring. Cover and continue to boil over high heat for 2 to 3 minutes. Serve as soon as possible.

Nutrition Information

- 142: calories;
- 3 grams: protein;
- 1 gram: polyunsaturated fat;
- 6 grams: sugars;
- 210 milligrams: sodium;
- 8 grams: fat;
- 0 grams: trans fat;
- 19 grams: carbohydrates;
- 2 grams: dietary fiber;

71. Corn And Black Bean Salad

Serving: 3 cups | Prep: | Cook: | Ready in: 15mins

Ingredients

- 1 cup cooked corn kernels (see Micro-Tips)
- 1 cup canned black beans, thoroughly rinsed and drained, or 1 cup dried beans cooked
- 8 to 9 ounces ripe tomato, cored and cut 1/4-inch dice (1 cup)
- 1 ½ ounces peeled onion, finely diced
- 1 cup lightly packed cilantro leaves, coarsely chopped

- 1 to 2 jalapeno peppers, fresh or canned, seeded and very finely chopped
- 2 tablespoons lime juice
- 2 tablespoons olive oil
- 1 teaspoon kosher salt, or more if using home-cooked beans
- Freshly ground pepper to taste

Direction

- Combine all ingredients. Allow to stand for 1/2 hour. Taste for salt and pepper.

Nutrition Information

- 185: calories;
- 4 grams: sugars;
- 6 grams: protein;
- 90 milligrams: sodium;
- 8 grams: fat;
- 1 gram: polyunsaturated fat;
- 25 grams: carbohydrates;
- 5 grams: monounsaturated fat;
- 7 grams: dietary fiber;

72. Corn And Lobster Pie In A Chili Polenta Crust

Serving: Six servings | Prep: | Cook: | Ready in: 2hours30mins

Ingredients

- The polenta:
- 2 ⅔ cups water
- ⅔ cup yellow cornmeal
- 1 teaspoon chili powder
- ¾ teaspoon salt
- Freshly ground pepper to taste
- Olive oil spray
- The custard:
- 3 large cloves garlic, unpeeled
- 2 eggs
- 1 cup milk

- 1 teaspoon salt
- Freshly ground pepper to taste
- Kernels from 2 large ears of corn
- The lobster mix:
- Kernels from 1 large ear of corn
- 2 lobsters, steamed, tail and claw meat removed and cut into 1/2-inch dice
- 1 red and 1 yellow bell pepper, stemmed, cored, deribbed and cut into 1/4-inch dice
- 1 jalapeno pepper, seeded and minced
- 1 tablespoon chopped cilantro
- 2 scallions, chopped
- 1 tablespoon fresh lime juice
- ½ teaspoon salt, plus more to taste
- Freshly ground pepper to taste

Direction

-
-
-

Nutrition Information

- 178: calories;
- 2 grams: dietary fiber;
- 0 grams: trans fat;
- 640 milligrams: sodium;
- 4 grams: fat;
- 1 gram: polyunsaturated fat;
- 21 grams: carbohydrates;
- 3 grams: sugars;
- 14 grams: protein;

73. Corn And Vegetable Gratin With Cumin

Serving: Serves six | Prep: | Cook: | Ready in: 1hours

Ingredients

- 1 tablespoon extra virgin olive oil
- 1 medium onion, finely chopped
- 1 medium red bell pepper, diced

- Salt to taste
- 1 large garlic clove, minced
- ½ pound zucchini, thinly sliced or diced
- Freshly ground pepper to taste
- Kernels from 2 ears sweet corn (about 2 cups)
- 3 large eggs
- ½ cup milk
- 1 teaspoon cumin seeds, lightly toasted and coarsely ground in a spice mill, or slightly crushed in a mortar and pestle
- 2 ounces Gruyère cheese, grated (1/2 cup, tightly packed)

Direction

- Preheat the oven to 375 degrees. Oil a 2-quart gratin or baking dish. Set aside the kernels from one of the ears of corn. Heat the olive oil in a large, nonstick skillet over medium heat and add the onion. Cook, stirring often, until it begins to soften, about three minutes, and add the red pepper and a generous pinch of salt. Cook, stirring often, until the onions and peppers are tender, about five minutes. Add the garlic and the zucchini, stir together and add another generous pinch of salt and some pepper. Cook, stirring often, until the zucchini is just beginning to look bright green and some of the slices are translucent. Stir in the kernels from one of the ears of corn. Stir together for a minute or two, and remove from the heat. Scrape into a large bowl.
- Place the remaining corn kernels in a blender jar, and add the eggs, milk and 1/2 teaspoon salt. Blend until smooth. Pour into the bowl with the vegetables. Add the cumin and the cheese, and stir everything together. Scrape into the gratin dish.
- Bake 35 to 40 minutes, until the top is browned and the gratin is firm to the touch. Serve hot or warm.

Nutrition Information

- 131: calories;
- 9 grams: fat;
- 3 grams: saturated fat;

- 0 grams: trans fat;
- 4 grams: sugars;
- 1 gram: dietary fiber;
- 6 grams: carbohydrates;
- 8 grams: protein;
- 313 milligrams: sodium;

74. Cornmeal And Buckwheat Blueberry Muffins

Serving: 12 muffins (1/3 cup tins) or 18 mini muffins | Prep: | Cook: | Ready in: 40mins

Ingredients

- 65 grams whole- wheat flour (1/2 cup, approximately)
- 125 grams buckwheat flour (1 cup, approximately)
- 4 grams salt (rounded 1/2 teaspoon)
- 15 grams baking powder (1 tablespoon)
- 2 grams baking soda (1/2 teaspoon)
- 85 grams cornmeal (1/2 cup, approximately)
- 2 eggs
- 360 grams buttermilk (1 1/2 cups) or kefir
- 75 grams mild honey, such as clover (3 tablespoons)
- 50 grams canola or grape seed oil (1/4 cup)
- 250 grams blueberries, or a mix of blueberries and blackberries (1 3/4 cups, approximately)

Direction

- Preheat oven to 375 degrees. Oil or butter muffin tins. Sift together whole wheat flour, buckwheat flour, salt, baking powder and baking soda into a medium bowl. Stir in cornmeal.
- In a separate large bowl whisk eggs with buttermilk or kefir, honey, and oil. Quickly stir in flour mixture. Fold in berries.
- Using a spoon, measuring cup or ice cream scoop, fill muffin cups to the top. Bake 25 minutes, or until lightly browned and well risen. Remove from the oven and if muffins

come out of the tins easily, remove from tins and allow to cool on a rack. If they don't release easily, allow to cool in tins, then remove from tins.

Nutrition Information

- 174: calories;
- 25 grams: carbohydrates;
- 3 grams: dietary fiber;
- 0 grams: trans fat;
- 4 grams: polyunsaturated fat;
- 1 gram: monounsaturated fat;
- 5 grams: protein;
- 214 milligrams: sodium;
- 7 grams: sugars;

75. Couscous With Eggplant

Serving: 4 servings | Prep: | Cook: | Ready in: 15mins

Ingredients

- 1 tablespoon olive oil
- 1 tablespoon finely chopped shallots or scallions
- 2 tablespoons finely chopped onions
- ¼ teaspoon turmeric
- ¼ teaspoon ground coriander
- 1 cup diced eggplant cut into 1/4-inch cubes
- Salt and freshly ground pepper to taste
- 1 cup water
- 1 cup precooked couscous
- 1 tablespoon butter
- 1 tablespoon fresh lemon juice

Direction

- Heat the oil in a saucepan, add the shallots, onions, turmeric, coriander, eggplant, salt and pepper. Cook over medium-high heat, stirring, until wilted, but do not brown.

- Add the water, bring to a boil, add the couscous and blend well. Cover tightly, remove from the heat and let stand 5 minutes.
- Add the butter and lemon juice, stir and blend with a fork to separate the grains. Keep warm.

Nutrition Information

- 230: calories;
- 2 grams: saturated fat;
- 3 grams: dietary fiber;
- 36 grams: carbohydrates;
- 7 grams: fat;
- 0 grams: trans fat;
- 1 gram: sugars;
- 6 grams: protein;
- 329 milligrams: sodium;

76. Couscous With Tomatoes, Okra And Chickpeas

Serving: 6 to 8 servings | Prep: | Cook: | Ready in: 30mins

Ingredients

- 1 pound okra
- Salt to taste
- ½ cup red wine vinegar or cider vinegar
- 2 tablespoons olive oil
- 1 large onion, chopped
- 2 to 4 large garlic cloves (to taste), minced
- Salt, preferably kosher, to taste
- 1 ½ teaspoons paprika
- ½ teaspoon cayenne (more to taste)
- 1 pound tomatoes, grated, or peeled, seeded and chopped
- 2 cups chickpeas, soaked for 6 hours or overnight and drained
- A bouquet garni consisting of 8 sprigs each parsley
- A bouquet garni consisting of 8 sprigs cilantro
- 1 large sweet red pepper, seeded and cut in large dice

- 2 tablespoons tomato paste
- 1 tablespoon harissa (more to taste), plus additional for serving (optional)
- ½ cup chopped fresh parsley, or a mixture of parsley and cilantro or mint
- 2 to 2 ⅔ cups couscous (1/3 cup per serving)

Direction

- Heat 1 tablespoon of the olive oil in a large, heavy soup pot or Dutch oven over medium heat and add the onion. Cook, stirring, until it is tender, about 5 minutes, and stir in the garlic, 1/2 teaspoon salt and the spices. Stir together for about 1 minute and add the tomatoes. Cook, stirring often, until the tomatoes have cooked down slightly, 5 to 10 minutes. Add the chickpeas, 2 quarts water and the bouquet garni. Bring to a gentle boil, reduce the heat, cover and simmer 1 1/2 hours.
- Meanwhile, trim the stems off the okra and place in a large bowl. Salt generously, douse with the vinegar and let sit for 30 minutes to an hour. Drain the okra and rinse thoroughly. Set aside.
- After 1 1/2 hours, season the chickpeas with salt to taste and add the harissa, tomato paste, red pepper and okra. Bring back to a simmer and simmer 30 to 45 minutes, or until okra and beans are tender. Remove a cup of broth to use for flavoring the couscous. Stir in the chopped fresh herbs and simmer another few minutes. Taste and adjust salt. The stew should be spicy and flavorful.
- Reconstitute and steam the couscous (see recipe). Serve the couscous in wide bowls or mound onto plates and top with the stew. Pass more harissa at the table.

Nutrition Information

- 463: calories;
- 7 grams: fat;
- 3 grams: monounsaturated fat;
- 2 grams: polyunsaturated fat;
- 10 grams: sugars;

- 655 milligrams: sodium;
- 1 gram: saturated fat;
- 82 grams: carbohydrates;
- 12 grams: dietary fiber;
- 19 grams: protein;

77. Cranberry Beans With Tomatoes And Herbs

Serving: 10 to 12 servings | Prep: | Cook: | Ready in: 1hours15mins

Ingredients

- ¼ cup olive oil
- 1 large onion, halved lengthwise and cut across in thin slices
- 3 ½ pounds cranberry beans, shelled and soaked in water at least 1 hour, or 3 19-ounce cans cannellini beans, drained and rinsed (see note)
- 2 ¼ pounds tomatoes, cored and cut in 1 1/4-inch chunks
- 6 to 8 fresh sage leaves, chopped fine
- 1 large sprig summer savory or 1 teaspoon dried
- Kosher salt and freshly ground black pepper to taste

Direction

- Place olive oil in a 5-quart casserole with a tight-fitting lid. Cook, uncovered, at 100 percent power in a high-power oven for 2 minutes. Add onions and stir to coat with oil. Cook, uncovered, for 4 minutes.
- Drain beans and stir them in. Cook, uncovered, for 3 minutes. Stir in tomatoes, sage and savory. Cook, covered, for 45 minutes, stirring twice.
- Remove from oven and uncover. Season with salt and pepper. Cook, covered, for 7 minutes to reheat.

Nutrition Information

- 174: calories;
- 8 grams: protein;
- 548 milligrams: sodium;
- 5 grams: fat;
- 1 gram: polyunsaturated fat;
- 3 grams: sugars;
- 25 grams: carbohydrates;
- 10 grams: dietary fiber;

78. Cream Of Raspberries And Yogurt

Serving: 6 servings | Prep: | Cook: | Ready in: 10mins

Ingredients

- 2 pints (about 1 1/2 pounds) ripe raspberries (4 cups), washed and patted dry with with paper towel
- 1 cup plain yogurt
- ⅓ cup sugar

Direction

- Place half the berries (2 cups) in a food processor with the yogurt and sugar. Process until very smooth. (If desired, push mixture through a fine-screened sieve or food mill to remove small seeds.)
- Combine remaining berries with sauce, and refrigerate (for up to 6 hours) until serving time. Divide among 6 dessert dishes, and serve.

Nutrition Information

- 111: calories;
- 23 grams: carbohydrates;
- 5 grams: dietary fiber;
- 17 grams: sugars;
- 20 milligrams: sodium;
- 2 grams: protein;

- 1 gram: saturated fat;
- 0 grams: polyunsaturated fat;

79. Creamed Mushrooms

Serving: 4 servings | Prep: | Cook: | Ready in: 10mins

Ingredients

- ¾ pound fresh mushrooms, about 4 cups
- 1 tablespoon butter
- 1 tablespoon freshly squeezed lemon juice
- Salt to taste if desired
- Freshly ground pepper to taste
- 3 tablespoons shallots, finely chopped
- ½ cup heavy cream
- ⅛ teaspoon cayenne pepperpepper

Direction

- Rinse mushrooms and pat dry.
- Heat butter in a skillet and add mushrooms, lemon juice, salt, pepper and shallots. Stir and cook about 2 minutes and add cream. Sprinkle cayenne pepper on top. Cover closely and cook 5 minutes. Uncover and reduce the liquid briefly.

Nutrition Information

- 154: calories;
- 302 milligrams: sodium;
- 3 grams: sugars;
- 0 grams: trans fat;
- 4 grams: protein;
- 1 gram: dietary fiber;
- 5 grams: carbohydrates;
- 14 grams: fat;
- 9 grams: saturated fat;

80. Creamed Spinach

Serving: Six or more servings | Prep: | Cook: | Ready in: 20mins

Ingredients

- 2 pounds fresh spinach
- 1 tablespoon butter
- 2 tablespoons flour
- 1 ½ cups milk
- ½ cup heavy cream
- Salt to taste, if desired
- Freshly ground pepper to taste
- ⅛ teaspoon cayenne pepper
- ⅛ teaspoon nutmeg

Direction

- Pick over the spinach and remove and discard any tough stems or blemished leaves. Rinse and drain the spinach well.
- Bring enough water to the boil to cover the spinach when added. Add the spinach and cook, stirring occasionally, about three minutes. Drain thoroughly and press to extract any excess liquid. Put the spinach into the container of a food processor or electric blender and blend briefly.
- Heat the butter in a saucepan and add the flour, stirring with a wire whisk. When blended and smooth, add one cup of the milk, stirring rapidly with the whisk. Stir in the cream and add salt, pepper, cayenne and nutmeg. Stir in the remaining one-half cup of milk.
- Add the spinach and blend. There should be about three cups. Heat thoroughly and serve.

Nutrition Information

- 169: calories;
- 1 gram: polyunsaturated fat;
- 11 grams: carbohydrates;
- 553 milligrams: sodium;
- 12 grams: fat;
- 7 grams: protein;

- 0 grams: trans fat;
- 3 grams: monounsaturated fat;
- 4 grams: sugars;

81. Creamy Corn And Poblano Soup

Serving: 4 to 6 servings | Prep: | Cook: |Ready in: 2hours

Ingredients

- 6 ears of corn (5 cups kernels)
- 6 cups water
- Salt to taste
- 1 tablespoon extra virgin olive oil
- 1 medium white onion, chopped
- 2 garlic cloves, minced
- 2 poblano chilies
- ¼ cup chopped fresh cilantro or 2 tablespoons minced chives (optional)

Direction

- Take the corn off the cobs. You should have about 5 cups kernels. Set aside 1 cup of the kernels.
- Place the corn cobs in a large soup pot and add the water. Make sure they are covered or at least floating in the water; you can break them in half if they are very large. Bring to a boil, reduce the heat, partly cover and simmer 30 minutes. Season to taste with salt. Remove and discard the cobs. Line a strainer with cheesecloth and set it over a bowl. Strain the broth and measure out 5 cups. Freeze any leftover broth.
- Heat the oil over medium heat in a heavy soup pot and add the onion. Cook, stirring, until it is tender, about 5 minutes. Add the garlic and stir until fragrant, about 30 seconds, and then add the 4 cups of corn kernels and salt to taste. Cook, stirring often, for 4 to 5 minutes, until the corn is just tender. Add the corn broth and bring to a simmer. Cover and simmer for 30 minutes.

- Meanwhile roast the chilies, either directly over a gas flame or under a broiler, turning often until they are uniformly charred. Transfer to a plastic bag and seal, or transfer to a bowl and cover tightly. Allow the peppers to cool, then remove the charred skin, rinse and past dry. Remove the seeds and veins (I recommend that you wear plastic gloves for this) and cut in thin strips or dice.
- Steam the kernels set aside for the garnish for 5 minutes, until tender. Set aside.
- Working in batches, purée the soup in a blender, taking care to remove the insert from the top and cover tightly with a kitchen towel to avoid splashes. Return to the heat, taste and adjust salt, and heat through.
- Ladle the soup into bowls. Combine the steamed corn kernels and diced chilies and place a spoonful in the middle of each bowl of soup. Garnish with a sprinkling of cilantro or chives if desired, and serve.

Nutrition Information

- 109: calories;
- 956 milligrams: sodium;
- 3 grams: protein;
- 0 grams: saturated fat;
- 2 grams: monounsaturated fat;
- 1 gram: polyunsaturated fat;
- 21 grams: carbohydrates;
- 4 grams: sugars;

82. Crespéu

Serving: Serves 8 to 10 | Prep: | Cook: |Ready in: 1hours

Ingredients

- Ingredients for Onion and Zucchini Frittata to Go, using 3 eggs instead of 4 if desired
- Ingredients for Tomato Frittata to Go, using 3 eggs instead of 4 if desired

- Ingredients for Greens and Garlic Frittata to Go, using 3 eggs instead of 4 if desired
- Ingredients for Frittata to Go with Peas, Herbs and Feta or Parmesan, using 3 eggs instead of 4 if desired

Direction

-
-

83. Crispy Polenta Medallions

Serving: Serves 8 to 12 as an hors d'oeuvre | Prep: | Cook: | Ready in: 50mins

Ingredients

- 1 recipe Soft Anson Mills Polenta
- 2 to 3 tablespoons olive oil, as needed
- Toppings
- Blue cheese or gorgonzola (about 1 ounce)
- Romesco Sauce (about 1/4 cup)
- Marinara Sauce (about 1/4 cup)
- Green Pipian (about 1/4 cup)

Direction

- Cover a baking sheet with plastic or lightly oil a baking dish. Make polenta and when done, pour onto plastic or into lightly oiled baking dish. Spread to a thickness of about 1/3 inch using an offset spatula. If you are using a baking dish and can't spread the polenta that thin, you can always slice the rounds after they are cut to make thinner medallions. Cover with plastic and allow to stiffen completely, preferably in the refrigerator overnight.
- Cut the stiff polenta into 1 1/2 to 2-inch rounds with a cookie cutter. If the rounds are thick, cut crosswise into 1/3 inch thick rounds.
- Heat 2 tablespoons olive oil over medium-high heat in a heavy nonstick or cast iron skillet. The polenta should sizzle as soon as you place the medallion in the oil. Cook the rounds in

batches until nicely browned on each side, about 3 minutes per side. Turn them carefully with a spatula, and do not crowd the pan. Drain on paper towels. Transfer to a platter while warm and place a pinch – about 1/4 teaspoon – of blue cheese on each round. It should soften and melt a little bit on the hot surface of the polenta. Or top with small dollops of the other toppings of your choice. Serve warm (they are also good when they cool down).

84. Cucumber And Israeli Couscous Salad

Serving: 6 to 8 servings | Prep: | Cook: | Ready in: 30mins

Ingredients

- ¼ cup extra virgin olive oil
- 1 cup Israeli couscous
- 6 to 8 tablespoons fresh lemon juice, to taste
- 3 cups chopped fresh flat-leaf parsley (from 3 large bunches)
- ¼ cup chopped fresh mint
- ½ pound ripe tomatoes, very finely chopped
- ¾ pound cucumbers (1 European or 4 Persian), seeded if using regular cucumbers, cut in fine dice
- 1 bunch scallions, finely chopped, or 1/4 cup chopped chives
- Salt to taste
- 1 romaine lettuce heart, leaves separated, washed and dried

Direction

- Heat one tablespoon of the olive oil over medium-high heat in a medium saucepan and add the couscous. Stir until the couscous begins to color and smell toasty, 4 to 5 minutes. Add 2 cups water and salt to taste and bring to a boil. Reduce the heat, cover and simmer 15 minutes, or until the couscous is tender. Drain if any liquid remains in the pan.

- Transfer the couscous to a large bowl and toss with the lemon juice, parsley, mint, tomatoes, cucumbers, scallions or chives and salt to taste. Add the olive oil, toss together, taste and adjust seasonings. Serve with lettuce leaves.

Nutrition Information

- 174: calories;
- 424 milligrams: sodium;
- 7 grams: fat;
- 1 gram: polyunsaturated fat;
- 5 grams: protein;
- 24 grams: carbohydrates;
- 4 grams: dietary fiber;
- 3 grams: sugars;

85. Cucumber And Radish Raita

Serving: 3 cups (6 servings) | Prep: | Cook: | Ready in: 5mins

Ingredients

- 2 cups plain low-fat yogurt (not fat-free)
- ¾ pound cucumber (1 European or 4 Persian), peeled if waxed, seeded if necessary, and finely diced or shredded
- 4 to 6 radishes, finely diced
- 1 teaspoon cumin seeds, lightly toasted and ground
- ½ teaspoon coriander seeds, lightly toasted and ground
- Salt to taste
- 2 to 3 tablespoons finely chopped cilantro, to taste
- 1 to 2 serrano or bird chilies, finely chopped (optional)

Direction

- Combine all the ingredients. Taste and adjust salt and other seasonings. Refrigerate until ready to serve.

Nutrition Information

- 64: calories;
- 5 grams: protein;
- 349 milligrams: sodium;
- 1 gram: dietary fiber;
- 0 grams: polyunsaturated fat;
- 8 grams: carbohydrates;
- 7 grams: sugars;

86. Cumin Chicken With Black Bean Sauce

Serving: 2 servings | Prep: | Cook: | Ready in: 30mins

Ingredients

- 8 ounces boneless, skinless chicken breasts
- 1 teaspoon ground cumin
- ½ teaspoon ground coriander
- 1 15-ounce can no-salt-added black beans
- 1 large clove garlic
- ½ to 1 Serrano chili
- 2 tomatillos, to yield 3 tablespoons chopped
- Few sprigs cilantro, to yield 2 tablespoons chopped
- 1 small onion, to yield 1 tablespoon chopped
- 1 small green pepper, to yield 4 teaspoons chopped
- 2 teaspoons lime juice
- ⅛ teaspoon salt
- Freshly ground black pepper to taste

Direction

- Preheat broiler, if using. Wash and dry the chicken, and rub the breasts on both sides with cumin and coriander.
- Rinse and drain the beans.

- Turn on the food processor, and put garlic through feed tube. Wash, trim and seed the chili, add as much as you like to the food processor and process until finely chopped. Chop the tomatillos. Wash and chop the cilantro. Chop the onion and the green pepper.
- To the garlic and chili in the food processor add the beans, tomatillos, cilantro, onion, green pepper, lime juice, salt and pepper, and process until mixture is pureed.
- Prepare stove-top grill, if using. Broil or grill chicken, browning on both sides and cooking until chicken is no longer pink, about 10 minutes.
- Heat the bean puree in a pot slowly until warm.
- Place the bean puree in the middle of each of two dinner plates. Place the chicken on top, and top with mango salsa.

Nutrition Information

- 376: calories;
- 45 grams: carbohydrates;
- 17 grams: dietary fiber;
- 40 grams: protein;
- 496 milligrams: sodium;
- 4 grams: sugars;
- 1 gram: polyunsaturated fat;
- 0 grams: trans fat;

87. Cumin Orange Tomato Sauce

Serving: One and one-quarter cups | Prep: | Cook: | Ready in: 35mins

Ingredients

- 4 tomatoes, cored and halved
- 1 teaspoon olive oil
- 1 ½ teaspoons cumin seeds
- 1 teaspoon orange zest
- Pinch saffron
- ½ teaspoon salt, plus more to taste

Direction

- Preheat oven to 425 degrees. Place tomatoes on a lightly oiled baking sheet, skin side up. Brush with olive oil. Sprinkle cumin seeds over tomatoes. Roast until tomatoes are very soft, about 25 minutes.
- Place roasted tomatoes with orange zest, saffron and salt in a blender. Process until smooth. Taste and adjust seasoning.

Nutrition Information

- 57: calories;
- 8 grams: carbohydrates;
- 3 grams: dietary fiber;
- 5 grams: sugars;
- 467 milligrams: sodium;
- 2 grams: protein;
- 0 grams: polyunsaturated fat;

88. Cumin Tomato Relish

Serving: 4 to 6 servings | Prep: | Cook: | Ready in: 10mins

Ingredients

- 2 teaspoons cumin seeds, or 1 1/2 teaspoons ground cumin
- 1 ½ pounds plum or other tomatoes, cored and roughly chopped
- ½ red bell pepper, seeded, stemmed and minced (optional)
- 1 tablespoon minced onion
- Salt and cayenne pepper to taste
- Juice of one lime
- 2 tablespoons chopped cilantro

Direction

- If you're using cumin seeds, place them in a small skillet and toast over medium heat, shaking the pan occasionally, just a minute or two, until they are fragrant. Finely grind all but 1/2 teaspoon.

- Combine the ground cumin, the tomatoes, the optional pepper, the onion, the salt, the cayenne and the lime juice; taste and adjust seasoning if necessary. Just before serving, toss with the cilantro and reserved cumin seeds.

Nutrition Information

- 59: calories;
- 2 grams: dietary fiber;
- 12 grams: sugars;
- 298 milligrams: sodium;
- 1 gram: protein;
- 0 grams: polyunsaturated fat;
- 15 grams: carbohydrates;

89. Curried Lamb

Serving: 2 servings | Prep: | Cook: | Ready in: 40mins

Ingredients

- ¾ cup long-grain rice
- 8 ounces boneless leg of lamb
- 12 ounces whole onion, or 11 ounces chopped ready-cut onion (2 1/4 to 2 1/2 cups)
- 1 teaspoon canola oil
- 1 medium head cauliflower, or 16 ounces cauliflower florets (6 cups)
- 1 teaspoon ground cumin
- ½ teaspoon ground coriander
- ½ teaspoon fennel seeds
- ½ teaspoon turmeric
- ⅛ to ¼ teaspoon hot-pepper flakes
- 1 cup frozen peas
- 5 sprigs cilantro (1 tablespoon chopped)
- ⅛ teaspoon salt
- Freshly ground black pepper

Direction

- Combine rice with 1 1/2 cups water, and bring to boil in heavy-bottomed pot. Reduce heat, cover and simmer for 17 minutes.
- Trim fat from meat, wash and dry. Cut into bite-size pieces. Chop whole onion.
- Heat large nonstick pan until it is very hot. Reduce heat to medium-high, and heat oil. Add lamb and onion, and saute until meat is brown on all sides and onion begins to soften.
- Wash cauliflower, and trim and discard core if using whole cauliflower. Break into bite-size pieces, and add to pan along with cumin, coriander, fennel seeds, turmeric and hot-pepper flakes. Stir to mix thoroughly. Add 1/4 cup water, cover and simmer for 3 or 4 minutes, until cauliflower is almost tender.
- Add the peas, and cook another minute or two.
- Wash, dry and chop cilantro.
- Season with salt and pepper, top with cilantro and serve with the rice.

Nutrition Information

- 728: calories;
- 17 grams: sugars;
- 387 milligrams: sodium;
- 21 grams: fat;
- 8 grams: saturated fat;
- 9 grams: monounsaturated fat;
- 2 grams: polyunsaturated fat;
- 100 grams: carbohydrates;
- 14 grams: dietary fiber;
- 38 grams: protein;
- 0 grams: trans fat;

90. Dessert Galette Pastry

Serving: Makes enough for 2 9 -inch galettes | Prep: | Cook: | Ready in: 1hours30mins

Ingredients

- 5 grams (1 1/2 teaspoons) active dry yeast

- 115 grams (1/2 cup) lukewarm water
- 2 tablespoons plus 1/4 teaspoon sugar
- 1 large egg, at room temperature, beaten
- 135 grams (1 cup) whole-wheat flour
- 155 grams (1 1/4 cups) unbleached flour
- 25 grams (1/4 cup) almond flour (optional)
- ½ teaspoon salt
- 60 grams (4 tablespoons) unsalted butter at room temperature

Direction

- Dissolve the yeast in the water. Add 1/4 teaspoon of the sugar, and allow the mixture to sit until it is creamy, about 5 minutes. Beat in the egg.
- Sift together the flours, 2 tablespoons sugar, and salt into a large bowl or into the bowl of a standing mixer fitted with the paddle or a large bowl. Add the butter and work with your fingers or beat at low speed until the mixture is crumbly. Add the yeast mixture and stir or beat at low speed until the ingredients come together. Turn out onto a lightly floured surface and knead gently just until the dough is smooth, about a minute. Shape into a ball. Place in a lightly buttered bowl, cover the bowl with plastic wrap, and allow the dough to rise in a draft-free spot until it has doubled in size, about 1 hour.
- Turn the dough out onto a lightly floured surface and divide into 2 equal pieces. Gently shape each piece into a ball without kneading it, cover the dough loosely with plastic wrap and let it rest for 5 minutes.
- Roll out into very thin rounds, about 12 to 13 inches in diameter. If you have a Silpat silicone mat, roll the dough out on the mat; otherwise, use a lightly floured surface and dust regularly with flour to prevent the dough from sticking.
- Cover a pizza pan or a baking sheet with plastic wrap and place the rolled-out dough on top. Wrap the edges of the plastic wrap over the dough and place plastic wrap on top. Roll out the other round, wrap in plastic and place

on top of the first round. Freeze until ready to use.

Nutrition Information

- 821: calories;
- 1 gram: trans fat;
- 8 grams: monounsaturated fat;
- 21 grams: protein;
- 627 milligrams: sodium;
- 29 grams: fat;
- 17 grams: saturated fat;
- 122 grams: carbohydrates;
- 10 grams: dietary fiber;
- 14 grams: sugars;
- 2 grams: polyunsaturated fat;

91. Easter Lamb From Sicily

Serving: 8 servings | Prep: | Cook: | Ready in: 1hours

Ingredients

- 2 tablespoons olive oil
- 1 onion, minced
- 4 pounds well-trimmed boneless lamb shoulder for stew, in chunks
- 2 ½ cups lamb, chicken or beef stock, approximately
- 2 tablespoons potato starch
- 2 cups heavy cream
- 6 egg yolks
- Juice of 4 lemons
- Salt and freshly ground black pepper
- 1 tablespoon chopped fresh mint

Direction

- Heat the oil in a large, heavy casserole, add the onion and saute until it is translucent. Stir in the lamb and add the stock, using enough to cover the lamb. Bring to a simmer; cover and cook over medium-low heat until the lamb is tender, about 45 minutes.

- Remove the lamb from the broth. Strain the broth and remove as much of the fat as possible. You can do this by starting the preparation the night before and refrigerating the lamb, covered, overnight and also refrigerating the stock. When the stock has chilled sufficiently, the fat can be lifted off and discarded.
- Shortly before serving, measure the stock. You should have about two cups. Add a little water if there is less. If there is more you should plan to increase the amount of potato starch proportionately.
- Slowly beat some of the cream into the potato starch, beating to blend the cream and the starch together. When the starch is liquefied stir in any remaining cream.
- Bring the stock to a simmer in a casserole. Whisk the egg yolks and lemon juice together in a bowl. With the stock barely simmering, slowly whisk in the egg-yolk mixture. Then slowly beat the cream mixture into the stock mixture. Cook slowly, about five minutes, until the stock thickens and becomes sauce, then return the lamb to the sauce. When the lamb has been sufficiently reheated, season the sauce to taste with salt and pepper. Transfer the stew to a warm serving dish, sprinkle with the mint, then serve.

Nutrition Information

- 902: calories;
- 77 grams: fat;
- 30 grams: monounsaturated fat;
- 10 grams: carbohydrates;
- 36 grams: saturated fat;
- 6 grams: polyunsaturated fat;
- 1 gram: dietary fiber;
- 4 grams: sugars;
- 43 grams: protein;
- 985 milligrams: sodium;

92. Easy Roast Duck

Serving: 2 to 4 servings | Prep: | Cook: | Ready in: 1hours

Ingredients

- 1 4- to 5-pound duck
- Freshly ground black pepper
- ¼ cup soy sauce, more or less

Direction

- Preheat oven to 450 degrees. Remove giblets and neck from duck cavity and discard or reserve for another use. Cut off excess fat from duck cavity.
- Place duck, breast side down (wings up), on a rack in a roasting pan; add water to come just below the rack. Sprinkle duck with pepper and brush with a little soy sauce.
- Roast 30 minutes, undisturbed. Prick the back all over with point of a sharp knife, then flip bird onto its back. Sprinkle with pepper and brush with soy sauce again. Add a little more water to the pan if the juices are spattering (carefully--you don't want to get water on the duck).
- Roast 20 minutes, then prick the breast all over , and brush with soy sauce. Roast 10 minutes; brush with soy sauce. Roast 5 or 10 minutes more if necessary, or until duck is a glorious brown all over and an instant-read thermometer inserted into the thigh measures at least 155 degrees. Let rest 5 minutes before carving and serving.

93. Endive Leaves With Crab Rillettes

Serving: Serves 6 to 8 | Prep: | Cook: | Ready in: 20mins

Ingredients

- 8 ounces lump crabmeat
- 2 tablespoons extra virgin olive oil

- 2 tablespoons plain Greek yogurt
- 2 tablespoons crème fraîche (or omit and use 4 tablespoons yogurt)
- 1 to 2 tablespoons fresh lime juice (to taste)
- 1 to 2 tablespoons minced chives (to taste)
- 1 to 2 tablespoons finely chopped mint (to taste)
- 1 serrano pepper, finely chopped
- Salt to taste
- 4 endives

Direction

- Drain crabmeat and place in a medium bowl. Mash with a fork. Add olive oil, yogurt and crème fraîche and mash together until mixture is spreadable. Add lime juice, chives, mint and chile and work in. Season to taste with salt. You should have about 1 1/3 cups.
- Break off endive leaves at the base. The easiest way to do this is to cut base away, break off a round of leaves, then keep slicing away the base so that the leaves will easily break off at the bottom. Spoon crab rillettes onto leaves and arrange on a platter. Serve at once, or refrigerate until ready to serve.

Nutrition Information

- 70: calories;
- 0 grams: sugars;
- 3 grams: monounsaturated fat;
- 2 grams: carbohydrates;
- 6 grams: protein;
- 166 milligrams: sodium;
- 5 grams: fat;
- 1 gram: dietary fiber;

94. Endive And Radicchio Salad With Caramelized Pear

Serving: 4 servings | Prep: | Cook: | Ready in: 1hours

Ingredients

- Roasted Pears
- 3 Comice pears
- Olive oil, for drizzle
- Honey, for drizzle
- 1 tablespoon allspice
- Butter, one pat
- Blue Cheese Fritters
- 3 ounces Roquefort style blue cheese
- 5 ounces butter, softened
- 1 teaspoon Worcestershire sauce
- Salt
- Pepper
- 3 tablespoons flour
- 2 eggs, beaten
- 3 tablespoons Panko style bread crumbs
- Cooking oil for deep frying (such as olive or peanut oil)
- Walnut-Ice Wine Vinegar Dressing
- 2 ounces walnuts, chopped
- 1 shallot, minced
- 2 tablespoons walnut oil
- Salt
- Pepper
- 3 endives

Direction

- Peel the pears, cut them in half and trim to remove the seeds. Reserve one uncooked pear to finish the salad, and roast the remaining two. Preheat oven to 400 degrees Fahrenheit. Place the two pears cut side down on a baking sheet lined with parchment paper. Drizzle pears with olive oil, honey and allspice and top with a small pat of butter. Cover with aluminum foil and bake for 20 minutes. Set aside.
- Make the blue cheese fritters. Combine cheese and butter in a mixing bowl until soft and fully incorporated. Add Worcestershire sauce and salt and pepper to taste. Form into small balls and refrigerate for 15 minutes, or until firm. Once firm, roll the balls between your palms to obtain a perfectly round shape. Dredge balls in flour, then beaten egg, then bread crumbs. The uncooked fritters can be reserved in the refrigerator until ready to fry.

To fry, heat enough oil to cover the fritters in a fryer to 375 degrees. Add fritters to the pan and fry until golden brown.

- Make the walnut dressing. Toast walnuts in sauté pan for five minutes. Allow to cool, then chop. In a separate bowl, combine honey and ice wine vinegar and mix well. Add minced shallot and walnut oil. Mix with chopped walnuts and salt and pepper to taste.
- Make the salad. Cut radicchio in half and drizzle with olive oil and season with salt and pepper. Cook on hot grill for a couple of minutes on each side. Slice washed and dried endive into long strips.
- To assemble the salad, lay roasted radicchio on large plate. Season endive with walnut dressing and arrange around the radicchio. Top with roasted pear and freshly fried fritters. Finish with raw pear shavings.

95. Enfrijoladas

Serving: Serves 4 | Prep: | Cook: | Ready in: 2hours30mins

Ingredients

- ½ pound (1 1/8 cups) black beans, washed, picked over and soaked for 4 to 6 hours or overnight in 1 quart water
- 1 onion, cut in half
- 2 plump garlic cloves, minced
- 1 to 2 sprigs epazote or 2 tablespoons chopped cilantro, plus additional for garnish (optional)
- 1 to 2 teaspoons ground cumin, to taste
- ½ to 1 teaspoon ground mild chili powder (more to taste)
- Salt to taste
- 12 corn tortillas
- ¼ cup chopped walnuts (optional)

Direction

- In a large soup pot or Dutch oven combine the black beans with their soaking water (they

should be submerged by at least 1 1/2 inches of water; add if necessary), one half of the onion, and half the garlic and bring to a boil. Reduce the heat, cover and simmer gently for 1 hour. Add the remaining garlic, epazote or cilantro if using, cumin, chili powder, and salt to taste and simmer for another hour, until the beans are very soft and the broth thick, soupy and aromatic. Remove from the heat. Remove and discard the onion.

- Using an immersion blender or a food processor fitted with the steel blade coarsely puree the beans. The mixture should retain some texture and the consistency should be thick and creamy. Heat through, stirring the bottom of the pot so the beans don't stick. Taste and adjust salt. Keep warm.
- Slice the remaining onion half crosswise into thin half-moons and cover with cold water while you assemble the enfrijoladas. Heat the corn tortillas: either wrap them in a damp dish towel and heat them, 4 at a time, in the microwave for about 30 seconds at 100 percent power, or wrap in a dish towel and steam for 1 minute, then let rest for 5 minutes.
- Assemble the enfrijoladas just before serving them. Spoon about 1/2 cup of the hot, thick beans over the bottom of a large lightly oiled baking dish or serving platter. Using tongs, dip a softened tortilla into the beans and flip over to coat both sides with black beans. Remove from the beans and place on the baking dish or platter (this is messy; have the serving dish right next to the pot.) Fold into quarters. Use the tongs to do this, and if you find that the tortilla tears too much, then just coat one side with the black beans, transfer to the baking dish and spoon some of the black beans over the other side, then fold into quarters. Continue with the remaining tortillas, arranging the quartered bean-coated tortillas in overlapping rows. When all of the tortillas are in the dish, spoon the remaining black bean sauce over the top. Drain and rinse the onions, dry briefly on paper towels and sprinkle over the bean sauce. Garnish with

cilantro and chopped walnuts if desired and serve at once.

Nutrition Information

- 369: calories;
- 3 grams: sugars;
- 1 gram: polyunsaturated fat;
- 72 grams: carbohydrates;
- 14 grams: dietary fiber;
- 17 grams: protein;
- 378 milligrams: sodium;

96. Extra Rich Chocolate Cake

Serving: 10 to 12 servings | Prep: | Cook: | Ready in: 1hours

Ingredients

- Butter for greasing
- 10 ounces semisweet chocolate, broken into pieces
- 2 tablespoons strong coffee
- ½ pound unsalted butter
- ½ cup granulated sugar
- 5 large eggs, separated
- ¼ cup flour
- 2 teaspoons confectioners' sugar

Direction

- Preheat the oven to 350 degrees. Butter a nine-and-a-half-inch springform pan or nonstick cake pan.
- Melt the chocolate with the coffee, butter and granulated sugar in the top of a double boiler over gently simmering water. Stir until blended. Set the mixture aside, uncovered, to cool.
- When the mixture has cooled, whisk the egg yolks into the chocolate one at a time. Add the flour and whisk until smooth.

- In a separate bowl, beat the egg whites until they stand up in stiff peaks. Add one-third of the egg white to the chocolate mixture. Fold them in carefully until blended. Fold in the remaining whites gently until there are no streaks left.
- Pour the mixture into the prepared pan and bake for about 35 minutes, or until the cake is firm. A toothpick or skewer inserted into the cake about three inches from the center of the pan should come out clean (the cake should not be too dry). Cool on a rack before unmolding. Dust with confectioners' sugar before serving.

Nutrition Information

- 330: calories;
- 7 grams: monounsaturated fat;
- 22 grams: sugars;
- 15 grams: saturated fat;
- 26 grams: carbohydrates;
- 4 grams: protein;
- 35 milligrams: sodium;
- 25 grams: fat;
- 1 gram: dietary fiber;

97. Farofias (Poached Meringues In Lemon Custard With Cinnamon)

Serving: 4 to 6 servings | Prep: | Cook: | Ready in: 45mins

Ingredients

- 3 ¼ cups milk
- Zest of 1 lemon, cut in long strips
- 4 extra-large eggs, separated
- 1 cup sugar
- 1 tablespoon cornstarch
- ¼ teaspoon ground cinnamon

Direction

- In a deep 10- or 11-inch skillet set over moderately low heat, bring 3 cups of the milk and the lemon zest to a simmer; remove from the heat and let steep 5 minutes. Strain the milk and return to the skillet.
- Beat the egg whites to soft peaks, then add 1/2 cup of the sugar, 1 tablespoon at a time, beating all the while; continue until stiff glossy peaks form.
- Return the milk to low heat and when steam rises from the surface, drop meringue in by rounded tablespoons. (To keep meringue from sticking, dip the spoon often in hot water).
- Poach the meringues about 2 minutes in the milk, turn and poach the other side 2 minutes. With a slotted spoon, carefully transfer them to a large wet plate and reserve.
- As soon as all meringues are poached, strain the milk into a medium-size heavy saucepan and mix in the remaining sugar. Combine the remaining 1/4 cup milk with the cornstarch, whisk a little of the hot milk into this mixture, then blend into the pan and cook, stirring constantly, over moderately low heat 3 minutes or until slightly thickened.
- Beat the egg yolks lightly, whisk in a little of the hot sauce, stir back into pan and cook, stirring constantly, over low heat 2 to 3 minutes until no raw egg taste remains (do not boil or the mixture may curdle).
- Pour the hot custard into a large shallow heatproof bowl, cool 10 minutes, then float the meringues on top.
- Serve warm or well chilled, dusting the meringues with cinnamon at the last minute.

Nutrition Information

- 271: calories;
- 0 grams: dietary fiber;
- 42 grams: carbohydrates;
- 40 grams: sugars;
- 9 grams: protein;
- 4 grams: saturated fat;
- 8 grams: fat;
- 2 grams: monounsaturated fat;
- 1 gram: polyunsaturated fat;
- 111 milligrams: sodium;

98. Farro With Mushrooms

Serving: 6 servings | Prep: | Cook: | Ready in: 2hours

Ingredients

- ½ ounce (1/2 cup, approximately) dried porcini mushrooms
- 1 quart chicken stock or vegetable stock
- 1 ½ cups farro
- 2 tablespoons extra virgin olive oil
- ½ cup finely chopped onion
- 1 pound cremini mushrooms or wild mushrooms (or a mixture of the two), cleaned, trimmed and sliced
- Salt to taste
- 2 large garlic cloves, green shoots removed, minced
- 2 teaspoons chopped fresh rosemary
- ½ cup dry white wine
- Freshly ground pepper to taste
- 1 to 2 ounces Parmesan cheese, grated (1/4 to 1/2 cup)
- ¼ cup chopped fresh parsley

Direction

- Place the farro in a bowl, and pour on enough hot water to cover by an inch. Let soak while you prepare the remaining ingredients. Drain.
- Place the dried mushrooms in a large Pyrex measuring cup or bowl, and pour in 2 cups boiling water. Let sit 30 minutes.
- Drain the mushrooms through a strainer set over a bowl and lined with cheesecloth or a paper towel. Squeeze the mushrooms over the strainer, then rinse in several changes of water to remove grit. Chop coarsely if the pieces are large and set aside. Add the broth from the mushrooms to the stock. You should have 6 cups (add water if necessary). Place in a

saucepan, and bring to a simmer. Season with salt to taste.

- Heat the oil over medium heat in a large, heavy nonstick skillet. Add the onion. Cook, stirring, until it begins to soften, about three minutes. Add the fresh mushrooms. Cook, stirring, until they begin to soften and sweat. Add salt to taste, the garlic and rosemary. Continue to cook, stirring often, until the mushrooms are tender, about five minutes. Add the farro and reconstituted dried mushrooms. Cook, stirring, until the grains of farro are separate and beginning to crackle, about two minutes. Stir in the wine and cook, stirring until the wine has been absorbed. Add all but about 1 cup of the stock, and bring to a simmer. Cover and simmer 50 minutes or until the farro is tender; some of the grains will be beginning to splay. Remove the lid, and stir vigorously from time to time. Taste and adjust seasoning. There should be some liquid remaining in the pot but not too much. If the farro is submerged in stock, raise the heat and cook until there is just enough to moisten the grains, like a sauce. If there is not, stir in the remaining stock. If not serving right away, cover and let stand. Just before serving, bring back to a simmer, add the Parmesan, parsley and pepper, and stir together. Remove from the heat and serve.

Nutrition Information

- 323: calories;
- 3 grams: saturated fat;
- 5 grams: monounsaturated fat;
- 1 gram: polyunsaturated fat;
- 45 grams: carbohydrates;
- 6 grams: dietary fiber;
- 8 grams: sugars;
- 15 grams: protein;
- 769 milligrams: sodium;
- 9 grams: fat;

99. Fennel And Black Olives

Serving: 2 servings | Prep: | Cook: | Ready in: 20mins

Ingredients

- 6 ounces fennel (1 1/2 cups)
- 6 large Italian, French or Greek black olives
- 1 teaspoon olive oil

Direction

- Wash fennel bulb and trim off leaves and stems. Slice off bottom of bulb; then, thinly slice the remainder of it and separate into rings. Arrange on two salad plates.
- Pit olives, and sprinkle over fennel. Dribble olive oil on top.

Nutrition Information

- 51: calories;
- 3 grams: sugars;
- 1 gram: protein;
- 2 grams: dietary fiber;
- 0 grams: polyunsaturated fat;
- 5 grams: carbohydrates;
- 105 milligrams: sodium;

100. Fettuccine With Morels

Serving: 4 servings | Prep: | Cook: | Ready in: 35mins

Ingredients

- 2 ounces dried morels, soaked in warm water for 30 minutes
- ½ pound fresh morels
- 2 shallots, chopped fine
- 2 tablespoons unsalted butter
- ¾ cup chicken stock, preferably homemade
- ½ cup heavy cream
- Coarse salt and freshly ground pepper to taste
- ½ pound fettuccine
- 3 tablespoons Italian parsley, chopped

- Freshly grated Parmesan

Direction

- Bring six to eight quarts of water to boil for the fettuccine.
- Scoop the dry morels up from their soaking liquid and squeeze them, letting them drain back into the bowl. Strain the soaking liquid through several layers of cheesecloth. Rinse the morels under running water and slice them.
- Prepare the fresh morels. Rinse them quickly under running water and dry them with paper towels. Slice the tops and stems.
- Soften the shallots in the butter in a skillet. Add the morels and the dried morels with their soaking liquid with the chicken stock and simmer for 10 to 15 minutes, stirring occasionally. Add the cream and reduce until thickened enough to coat a spoon. Season to taste with salt and pepper.
- Cook the fettuccine in the boiling water until al dente. Drain and combine in a heated bowl with the morels and the parsley. Toss immediately and serve, passing the Parmesan cheese separately.

Nutrition Information

- 426: calories;
- 11 grams: saturated fat;
- 0 grams: trans fat;
- 5 grams: dietary fiber;
- 54 grams: carbohydrates;
- 12 grams: protein;
- 1 gram: polyunsaturated fat;
- 6 grams: sugars;
- 564 milligrams: sodium;
- 19 grams: fat;

---

101. Fettuccine With Ham And Asparagus

Serving: 4 servings | Prep: | Cook: | Ready in: 20mins

Ingredients

- 1 ¼ pounds fresh asparagus
- Salt and freshly ground pepper to taste
- ¾ pound dry fettuccine
- 2 tablespoons olive oil
- 1 cup diced, boiled ham (about 1/3 pound)
- 4 ripe plum tomatoes, peeled, seeded and diced
- 2 teaspoons finely chopped garlic
- ¼ pound soft goat cheese, crumbled
- ¼ cup heavy cream
- 4 tablespoons coarsely chopped fresh basil leaves or Italian parsley
- Grated Asiago or Parmesan cheese to taste

Direction

- Scrape and trim the asparagus; discard the tough ends. Slice the spears on the bias into 1-inch lengths.
- In a kettle or large saucepan, bring 2 quarts of water to a boil. Add salt and the fettuccine. Boil gently for 9 minutes, or until al dente. Reserve 1/4 cup of the cooking water and drain the pasta.
- Heat the olive oil in a large saucepan and add the asparagus, ham, tomatoes and garlic. Cook, stirring, over medium heat for 3 minutes. Do not overcook. Add the drained fettuccine, goat cheese, cream, basil leaves, the reserved water and salt and pepper to taste. Toss well over medium heat until blended well. Serve immediately with grated Asiago or Parmesan cheese on the side.

Nutrition Information

- 615: calories;
- 75 grams: carbohydrates;
- 7 grams: sugars;
- 27 grams: protein;

- 890 milligrams: sodium;
- 24 grams: fat;
- 10 grams: monounsaturated fat;
- 2 grams: polyunsaturated fat;

---

102. Figs And Blueberries In Citrus Broth

Serving: Four servings | Prep: | Cook: | Ready in: 15mins

Ingredients

- 1 ½ cups fresh orange juice
- 1 cup fresh grapefruit juice
- 3 tablespoons fresh lemon juice
- ½ teaspoon grated ginger
- 2 tablespoons honey
- 1 tablespoon rum
- 16 ripe black figs, pricked a few times with a fork
- 4 tablespoons fresh blueberries
- 1 banana, peeled and cut into 1/4-inch slices
- 8 fresh mint leaves

Direction

- Combine the juices in a nonreactive saucepan. Add the ginger, honey and rum and bring to a boil. Gently place the figs, blueberries and banana in the liquid. Cover, remove from heat and set aside to cool. Refrigerate until cold. Take the figs out of the liquid, cut them in half lengthwise and return them to the liquid. Divide among 4 shallow rimmed soup plates, garnish with the mint leaves and serve.

Nutrition Information

- 292: calories;
- 5 milligrams: sodium;
- 1 gram: fat;
- 0 grams: polyunsaturated fat;
- 72 grams: carbohydrates;
- 7 grams: dietary fiber;

- 60 grams: sugars;
- 3 grams: protein;

103. Filet Mignon Of Beef With Roganjosh Spices

Serving: Four servings | Prep: | Cook: | Ready in: 6hours15mins

Ingredients

- The meat:
- 2 teaspoons ground coriander
- ½ teaspoon ground cumin
- ½ teaspoon ground turmeric
- ¼ teaspoon ground fenugreek
- 1 teaspoon red chili-powder
- 1 large clove garlic, peeled and smashed to a paste
- 2 tablespoons fresh grated ginger
- 2 tablespoons grape-seed oil
- 4 6-ounce tournedos
- 1 teaspoon vegetable oil
- The salad:
- ½ cup fresh lime juice
- 1 tablespoon apple-cider vinegar
- ½ teaspoon salt
- 1 teaspoon minced jalapeno chili pepper
- 2 tablespoons olive oil
- 1 medium celery root, peeled and grated
- 1 large red delicious apple, peeled and grated
- 1 small jicama, peeled and grated
- ½ cup minced mint leaves
- ½ cup minced coriander leaves
- The vinaigrette:
- ¼ cup fresh lime juice
- 1 teaspoon grated orange rind
- ¼ teaspoon salt
- ½ teaspoon freshly ground pepper
- 1 tablespoon olive oil

Direction

- Combine all of the spices, garlic, ginger and grape-seed oil in a blender. Puree until smooth. Place tournedos with marinade in a large glass or ceramic bowl. Marinate in the refrigerator for 6 hours.
- To make the salad: Combine lime juice, cider vinegar, salt and minced jalapeno in a large glass or ceramic bowl. Whisk in 2 tablespoons of olive oil. Add celery root, apple and jicama. Toss. Refrigerate for 4 hours.
- To make the vinaigrette: Combine lime juice, orange rind, salt and pepper in a small glass or ceramic bowl. Whisk in 1 tablespoon olive oil. Set aside.
- Heat the vegetable oil in a seasoned cast-iron skillet. Add the tournedos and cook over medium-high heat until medium rare, about 5 minutes per side. Set aside to rest for 5 minutes.
- Add mint and coriander to the salad and toss. Divide among four plates. Cut the meat into thin strips. Drape the meat around the salad. Drizzle with the vinaigrette. Serve immediately.

---

104.   Fluke Crudo With Lime, Sea Salt And Olive Oil

Serving: 4 appetizer servings | Prep: | Cook: | Ready in: 10mins

Ingredients

- 1 pound fresh fluke fillet, skinned and chilled
- 1 to 2 limes
- Coarse sea salt
- Extra virgin olive oil

Direction

- Slice the fillet in half lengthwise at its natural seam. Then slice the fillet horizontally from end to end at an angle like lox. The slices should be about 1/8-inch thick and 2 inches

wide. Divide among 4 small plates. Cover and chill for at least 10 minutes.
- When ready to serve, juice the lime over the fish; be generous. Season with sea salt and sprinkle with olive oil. Serve.

Nutrition Information

- 104: calories;
- 4 grams: fat;
- 1 gram: dietary fiber;
- 0 grams: sugars;
- 2 grams: monounsaturated fat;
- 3 grams: carbohydrates;
- 14 grams: protein;
- 336 milligrams: sodium;

---

105.   Focaccia With Cauliflower And Sage

Serving: 12 to 15 servings | Prep: | Cook: | Ready in: 1hours15mins

Ingredients

- 1 recipe Whole-Wheat Focaccia
- 1 pound cauliflower (1 small head or 1/2 large), cut into florets, stems trimmed
- Salt and freshly ground pepper to taste
- 2 tablespoons extra virgin olive oil
- 30 to 40 fresh sage leaves (depending on the size)

Direction

- Mix up the focaccia dough as directed and set in a warm spot to rise.
- Meanwhile, bring a large pot of water to a boil and salt generously. Add the cauliflower and blanch for 2 minutes. Transfer to a bowl of cold water, then drain and pat dry. Cut the florets into small pieces and toss in a large bowl with 2 tablespoons olive oil and salt and freshly ground pepper.

- When the focaccia dough has risen, shape as directed into 1 large focaccia or 2 smaller focacce. Cover with a damp cloth and let rise in a warm spot for 30 minutes while you preheat the oven to 425 degrees, preferably with a baking stone in it.
- Dimple the dough with your fingertips and arrange the sage leaves, then the cauliflower on top. Drizzle with olive oil. Bake, setting the pan on top of the baking stone (if using), for 25 minutes, until the bread is deep golden brown and the cauliflower lightly colored in spots. Let rest for at least 10 minutes before serving, or allow to cool completely.

Nutrition Information

- 98: calories;
- 2 grams: dietary fiber;
- 154 milligrams: sodium;
- 4 grams: fat;
- 1 gram: sugars;
- 3 grams: protein;
- 12 grams: carbohydrates;

106. Focaccia With Sweet Onion And Caper Topping

Serving: 12 to 15 servings | Prep: | Cook: | Ready in: 2hours

Ingredients

- 1 recipe Whole-Wheat Focaccia
- 2 tablespoons extra virgin olive oil
- 2 large spring onions or white onions (1 1/2 pounds)
- Salt to taste
- 2 tablespoons capers, rinsed and coarsely chopped
- 2 teaspoons fresh thyme leaves
- 2 garlic cloves, minced (optional)
- Freshly ground pepper

Direction

- Mix the focaccia dough as directed and set in a warm spot to rise.
- Meanwhile, prepare the onion filling. Heat the olive oil over medium heat in a large, heavy lidded skillet. Add the onions and cook, stirring, until they soften, about 5 minutes. Add a generous pinch of salt, the capers, thyme and garlic, and turn the heat to low. Cover and simmer gently, stirring often, for 30 to 40 minutes, until the onions have cooked down and are very soft and lightly colored but not browned. They should taste sweet. Season to taste with salt and pepper and remove from the heat.
- When the focaccia dough has risen, shape as directed into 1 large focaccia or 2 smaller focacce. Cover with a damp cloth and let rise in a warm spot for 30 minutes while you preheat the oven to 425 degrees, preferably with a baking stone in it.
- Dimple the dough with your fingertips and spread the onion mixture over the top in an even layer. Drizzle with olive oil. Bake, setting the pan on top of the baking stone (if using), for 20 to 25 minutes, until the bread is deep golden brown and bits of the onion topping are browned. Let rest for at least 10 minutes before serving, or allow to cool completely.

Nutrition Information

- 97: calories;
- 181 milligrams: sodium;
- 4 grams: fat;
- 1 gram: saturated fat;
- 3 grams: protein;
- 0 grams: polyunsaturated fat;
- 13 grams: carbohydrates;
- 2 grams: sugars;

107. Fried Plantains With Herbs

Serving: 4 servings | Prep: | Cook: | Ready in: 40mins

Ingredients

- 2 green plantains
- Salt to taste
- 2 cups vegetable oil
- 3 tablespoons olive oil
- 2 garlic cloves
- ⅛ teaspoon red hot pepper flakes
- 4 tablespoons freshly chopped coriander or parsley

Direction

- Peel the plantains by making four incisions lengthwise in the skin. Peel the skin off with your fingers.
- Cut the plantains into 1-inch diagonal slices. Place in salted water to soak for 15 minutes. Drain well.
- Heat the 2 cups vegetable oil to 350 degrees in a fryer or skillet. Add the plantains and fry at 300 degrees for about 15 minutes or until done but not brown. Remove and drain on paper towels.
- In the container of a food processor, add the plantains, 2 tablespoons of the olive oil, garlic and pepper flakes. Blend to a semicoarse texture.
- To serve hot, add the remaining 1 tablespoon olive oil to a nonstick skillet. Add the plantains and coriander. Toss and cook 1 minute. Serve immediately.

Nutrition Information

- 345: calories;
- 4 grams: dietary fiber;
- 19 grams: monounsaturated fat;
- 26 grams: fat;
- 3 grams: saturated fat;
- 0 grams: trans fat;
- 32 grams: carbohydrates;
- 13 grams: sugars;
- 2 grams: protein;
- 281 milligrams: sodium;

108. Fried Winter Squash With Mint

Serving: 4 to 6 servings | Prep: | Cook: | Ready in: 15mins

Ingredients

- ¼ cup extra virgin olive oil
- 2 garlic cloves, peeled and crushed
- 1 ½ pounds peeled, seeded winter squash, like kabocha or butternut, cut in slices 1/4 inch thick by 2 or 3 inches long
- Salt
- freshly ground pepper
- 2 to 3 tablespoons chopped fresh mint, plus additional leaves for garnish
- Pomegranate seeds for garnish

Direction

- Heat the oil over medium-high heat in a large heavy skillet, preferably cast iron. Add the garlic cloves and cook, stirring, until golden brown. Remove the garlic from the oil and discard.
- Cook the squash slices in the hot oil, adding only 1 layer of slices at a time to the pan. Cook for about 3 minutes, or until squash is lightly browned on the first side, and flip over using a spatula or tongs. Cook until squash is lightly browned on the other side and tender all the way through. Season to taste with salt and pepper and transfer first to paper towels to drain, then to a platter. Repeat until all of the squash is used up. Sprinkle with chopped fresh mint, garnish with whole mint leaves and pomegranate seeds, and serve.

Nutrition Information

- 121: calories;
- 1 gram: protein;
- 7 grams: monounsaturated fat;
- 10 grams: carbohydrates;
- 2 grams: dietary fiber;
- 3 grams: sugars;
- 288 milligrams: sodium;
- 9 grams: fat;

109. Frittata With Turnips And Olives

Serving: 6 servings. | Prep: | Cook: | Ready in: 1hours15mins

Ingredients

- 1 pound firm medium-size or small turnips
- Salt
- 2 tablespoons extra virgin olive oil
- 2 teaspoons fresh thyme leaves, chopped
- 6 eggs
- 1 tablespoon milk
- Freshly ground pepper
- ½ cup chopped flat-leaf parsley
- 1 ounce imported black olives, pitted and chopped, about 1/3 cup (optional)
- 1 or 2 garlic cloves, minced or puréed (optional)

Direction

- Peel the turnips and grate on the large holes of a box grater or with a food processor. Salt generously and leave to drain in a colander for 30 minutes. Take up handfuls and squeeze tightly to rid the turnips of excess water.
- Heat 1 tablespoon of the olive oil over medium-low heat in a wide saucepan or skillet and add the turnips and the thyme. When the turnips are sizzling, cover and cook gently, stirring often, for about 15 minutes, until they are tender. If they begin to stick to the pan or brown, add a tablespoon of water. Season to taste with salt and pepper. Remove from the heat and allow to cool slightly.
- Beat the eggs and milk in a bowl and season to taste with salt and pepper. Stir in the parsley, chopped olives and garlic. Add the turnips and mix together.
- Heat the remaining olive oil over medium-high heat in a heavy 10-inch skillet, preferably nonstick. Hold your hand above it; it should feel hot. Drop a bit of egg into the pan, and if it sizzles and cooks at once, the pan is ready. Pour in the egg mixture. Swirl the pan to distribute the eggs and filling evenly over the surface. Shake the pan gently, tilting it slightly with one hand while lifting up the edges of the frittata with a spatula in your other hand, to let the eggs run underneath during the first few minutes of cooking. Once a few layers of egg have cooked during the first couple of minutes of cooking, turn the heat down to very low, cover (use a pizza pan if you don't have a lid that will fit your skillet) and cook 10 minutes, shaking the pan gently every once in a while. From time to time, remove the lid and loosen the bottom of the frittata with a spatula, tilting the pan, so that the bottom doesn't burn.
- Meanwhile, heat the broiler. Uncover the pan and place under the broiler, not too close to the heat, for 1 to 3 minutes, watching very carefully to make sure the top doesn't burn (at most, it should brown very slightly and puff under the broiler). Remove from the heat, shake the pan to make sure the frittata isn't sticking and allow it to cool for at least 5 minutes (the frittata is traditionally eaten warm or at room temperature). Loosen the edges with a spatula. Carefully slide from the pan onto a large round platter. Cut into wedges or into smaller bite-size diamonds. Serve warm, at room temperature or cold.

Nutrition Information

- 127: calories;
- 1 gram: polyunsaturated fat;

- 9 grams: fat;
- 2 grams: dietary fiber;
- 3 grams: sugars;
- 305 milligrams: sodium;
- 0 grams: trans fat;
- 5 grams: monounsaturated fat;
- 6 grams: protein;

110. Game Chips

Serving: Eight to 10 servings | Prep: | Cook: | Ready in: 20mins

Ingredients

- 4 cups vegetable oil
- 12 medium baking potatoes, peeled and sliced 1/16 inch thick, submerged in cold water
- 2 teaspoons salt
- 1 tablespoon dried basil
- 1 tablespoon dried parsley
- 1 tablespoon dried rosemary
- 1 teaspoon saffron

Direction

- Heat the oil in a heavy skillet to 360 degrees or until the oil begins to ripple on the surface.
- When ready, drain the potatoes and pat thoroughly dry.
- Place approximately a half cup of potatoes at a time into hot oil. Fry for two to three minutes, or until golden.
- Remove the potatoes from the oil with a slotted spoon and drain in a single layer on a paper bag.
- Sprinkle with salt and herbs.

Nutrition Information

- 996: calories;
- 6 grams: protein;
- 4 grams: dietary fiber;
- 2 grams: sugars;

- 479 milligrams: sodium;
- 90 grams: fat;
- 1 gram: trans fat;
- 65 grams: monounsaturated fat;
- 15 grams: polyunsaturated fat;
- 47 grams: carbohydrates;

111. Garlic Soup With Spinach

Serving: Serves 4 | Prep: | Cook: | Ready in: 30mins

Ingredients

- 1 ½ quarts chicken stock, turkey stock, vegetable stock, or water
- A bouquet garni made with a bay leaf and a couple of sprigs each thyme and parsley
- Salt and freshly ground pepper to taste
- 2 to 3 large garlic cloves (to taste), minced
- ½ cup elbow macaroni
- 2 eggs
- 1 6-ounce bag baby spinach, or 12 ounces of bunch spinach, stemmed, washed, dried and coarsely chopped
- ¼ cup freshly grated Parmesan (1 ounce)

Direction

- Place the stock or water in a large saucepan or soup pot with the bouquet garni. Season to taste with salt and freshly ground pepper. Bring to a simmer and add the garlic. Cover and simmer 15 minutes. Add the pasta and simmer 5 minutes, until cooked al dente. Remove the bouquet garni.
- Beat the eggs in a bowl and stir in 1/3 cup of stock, making sure that it is not boiling, and the cheese.
- Stir the spinach into the simmering stock and simmer for 1 minute. Drizzle in the egg mixture, scraping all of it in with a rubber spatula. Turn off the heat and stir very slowly with the spatula, paddling it back and forth until the eggs have set. Taste, adjust seasoning, and serve at once.

Nutrition Information

- 255: calories;
- 0 grams: trans fat;
- 26 grams: carbohydrates;
- 18 grams: protein;
- 1043 milligrams: sodium;
- 9 grams: fat;
- 3 grams: monounsaturated fat;
- 1 gram: polyunsaturated fat;
- 2 grams: dietary fiber;
- 6 grams: sugars;

112.   Garlic Spiedies

Serving: 6 to 8 servings | Prep: | Cook: | Ready in: 1hours

Ingredients

- 3 pounds lean beef, pork, lamb or venison suitable for grilling
- ½ cup red-wine vinegar
- 4 large cloves garlic, peeled
- ¾ cup olive oil
- ¼ cup brown sugar
- 1 teaspoon Dijon-style mustard
- 1 teaspoon Worcestershire sauce
- Salt and freshly ground black pepper
- 12 to 14 sprigs fresh herbs: parsley, oregano, dill, tarragon, and/ or thyme parsley, oregano, dill, tarragon, and/ or thyme (about 1/4 cup)
- ½ cup minced fresh chives
- 1 teaspoon plus 1 tablespoon lemon juice
- 1 large red bell pepper, seeded and cut in squares
- 1 large green bell pepper, seeded and cut in squares
- 1 pound small white onions, peeled and blanched
- 1 head elephant garlic, peeled and blanched
- 2 tablespoons finely chopped garlic
- 1 cup plain yogurt
- 12 pita breads, split and warmed (optional)

- :
- 2 tablespoons plus 1/4 cup minced fresh mint

Direction

- Trim meat of excess fat. Cut in 1- to 1 1/2-inch cubes so it can be threaded on skewers. Put meat in single layer in glass baking dish.
- Combine vinegar, garlic, oil, sugar, mustard and Worcestershire sauce in a food processor and process until smooth. Season to taste with salt and pepper. Add mixed herbs, chives, 2 tablespoons of the mint and 1 teaspoon of the lemon juice, and process briefly.
- Pour marinade over meat. Turn meat to coat it well, cover and refrigerate 24 hours to 3 days. Stir at least once every day.
- Preheat grill or broiler to hot. Thread meat on skewers, alternating the cubes with pieces of pepper, onions and elephant garlic.
- Puree the chopped garlic, the remaining tablespoon of lemon juice and a half cup of the yogurt together in a food processor. Stir into the remaining yogurt and add the remaining 1/4 cup of mint. Set aside.
- Grill or broil skewers, turning once, until meat is cooked to desired degree of doneness, 10 to 20 minutes.
- Remove meat and vegetables from skewers and serve with yogurt sauce, in pita bread if desired.

Nutrition Information

- 485: calories;
- 6 grams: saturated fat;
- 3 grams: dietary fiber;
- 10 grams: sugars;
- 840 milligrams: sodium;
- 28 grams: fat;
- 0 grams: trans fat;
- 19 grams: carbohydrates;
- 40 grams: protein;

113. Gazpacho Sans Bread

Serving: Serves 4 | Prep: | Cook: | Ready in: 15mins

Ingredients

- 2 slices red or white onion
- 2 pounds ripe tomatoes
- 2 to 3 garlic cloves, to taste, halved, green germ removed
- 2 tablespoons olive oil
- 1 to 2 tablespoons sherry vinegar or wine vinegar (to taste)
- ½ to 1 teaspoon sweet paprika (to taste)
- ½ to 1 cup ice water, depending on how thick you want your soup to be
- Salt and freshly ground pepper
- ½ cup finely chopped cucumber (more to taste)
- ½ cup finely chopped tomato (more to taste)
- ½ cup finely chopped green or yellow pepper
- ½ cup finely chopped celery
- Slivered fresh basil or chopped fresh parsley for garnish

Direction

- Put the onion slices in a bowl, cover with cold water and add a few drops of vinegar. Let sit for 5 minutes while you prepare the remaining ingredients. Drain and rinse with cold water. Cut in half or into smaller pieces.
- Combine the tomatoes, garlic, onion, olive oil, vinegar, paprika, and salt in a blender and blend until smooth. Taste and adjust seasonings. Pour into a bowl or pitcher, thin out as desired with water, cover and chill for several hours.
- Meanwhile, prepare the remaining ingredients and toss together in a large bowl. Season to taste with salt and pepper.
- Spoon the chopped vegetables into soup bowls and pour or ladle in the gazpacho. Garnish with basil chiffonade or chopped fresh parsley, and serve.

Nutrition Information

- 123: calories;
- 1 gram: polyunsaturated fat;
- 5 grams: monounsaturated fat;
- 14 grams: carbohydrates;
- 4 grams: dietary fiber;
- 3 grams: protein;
- 821 milligrams: sodium;
- 7 grams: sugars;

114. Giant Limas With Winter Squash

Serving: 4 to 6 servings. | Prep: | Cook: | Ready in: 2hours

Ingredients

- 2 tablespoons extra virgin olive oil
- 1 medium onion, chopped
- 4 garlic cloves, minced
- 1 pound (about 2 1/2 cups) dried giant lima beans, rinsed
- 2 quarts plus 1 cup water
- A bouquet garni made with a bay leaf, a Parmesan rind and a sprig each of sage, thyme and parsley
- 1 pound winter squash, peeled and cut in small dice
- Salt to taste
- Freshly ground pepper
- 2 tablespoons slivered fresh sage leaves
- Freshly grated Parmesan for serving (optional)

Direction

- Preheat the oven to 325 degrees. Heat the olive oil over medium heat in a large, heavy ovenproof casserole or Dutch oven and add the onion. Cook, stirring often, until it is tender, about 5 minutes. Stir in half the garlic and cook, stirring, until it is fragrant, 30 seconds to a minute. Add the beans, water and bouquet garni and bring to a simmer. Cover and place in the oven for 45 minutes.

- Remove the casserole from the oven and stir in the remaining garlic, the winter squash, and salt to taste. If the mixture seems dry, add a little more water. Return to the oven and bake an hour longer, or until the beans and squash are very tender. Remove from the heat and remove the bouquet garni. Adjust salt, add pepper to taste and stir in the slivered sage.

Nutrition Information

- 344: calories;
- 18 grams: protein;
- 1 gram: polyunsaturated fat;
- 3 grams: monounsaturated fat;
- 59 grams: carbohydrates;
- 17 grams: dietary fiber;
- 9 grams: sugars;
- 6 grams: fat;
- 1245 milligrams: sodium;

---

115.   Ginger Peach Soup

Serving: Four servings | Prep: | Cook: | Ready in: 10mins

Ingredients

- 1 ½ pounds peaches
- 2 tablespoons plus 1 teaspoon fresh lemon juice
- 1 ½ cups buttermilk
- ⅔ cup apple juice
- ½ teaspoon peeled, freshly grated ginger
- 1 teaspoon honey
- Scant 1 teaspoon kosher salt
- The garnish for each serving:
- 1 aromatic geranium leaf or 1 unsprayed rose petal or 3 to 4 slices peeled, pitted peach

Direction

- Peel and pit the peaches, rubbing them with 2 tablespoons of the lemon juice to prevent

discoloration as you work. Place peaches in a food processor and process until smooth.
- Scrape peach puree into a medium bowl. Stir in remaining ingredients. Refrigerate until cold. Serve garnished as desired.

Nutrition Information

- 144: calories;
- 0 grams: polyunsaturated fat;
- 31 grams: carbohydrates;
- 3 grams: dietary fiber;
- 28 grams: sugars;
- 5 grams: protein;
- 647 milligrams: sodium;
- 1 gram: saturated fat;

---

116.   Ginger Pear Sauce

Serving: Eight cups | Prep: | Cook: | Ready in: 2hours

Ingredients

- 6 pounds firm pears, peeled
- ½ cup grated fresh ginger
- ⅔ cup sugar

Direction

- Combine the pears, ginger and sugar in a large pot over low heat, stirring frequently until the sugar melts and the pear juices begin to accumulate. Cover and cook, stirring occasionally, until pears are soft, about 45 minutes. Pass the pear mixture through a food mill and place in a clean saucepan. Simmer over medium heat, stirring frequently, until reduced to 8 cups, about 1 hour. Refrigerate in an airtight container.

Nutrition Information

- 132: calories;
- 1 gram: protein;

- 2 milligrams: sodium;
- 0 grams: polyunsaturated fat;
- 35 grams: carbohydrates;
- 5 grams: dietary fiber;
- 25 grams: sugars;

117.   Giuliano Bugialli's Spaghetti Con Broccoli (Spaghetti With Broccoli)

Serving: 4 to 6 servings | Prep: | Cook: | Ready in: 1hours

Ingredients

- Coarse-grained salt
- 1 bunch fresh broccoli
- 1 pound spaghetti or linguine
- 5 whole anchovies in salt, or 10 fillets in oil, drained
- ¾ cup extravirgin olive oil
- Pinch of red pepper flakes
- Freshly ground black pepper to taste

Direction

- Remove and discard large tough stems from broccoli and cut the remainder into thick julienne strips, about 1 1/2 inches long and 1/4 to 1/2 inch thick. Soak the pieces in a bowl of cold water for about 30 minutes.
- Bring 4 quarts water to the boil. Add salt to taste. Add broccoli pieces to boiling water and cook for about 5 minutes. Drain broccoli, saving the cooking water. Place broccoli in a large warmed serving dish and set aside, covered, in a warm place.
- Bring the broccoli water back to a boil, add pasta and stir with a long- handled wooden fork or spoon to separate pasta and bring water rapidly back to the boil. Cover and cook pasta until done.
- While pasta is cooking, prepare the sauce. If using salted anchovies, fillet them and wash well, draining on paper towels. Heat olive oil in a heavy enamel or aluminum saucepan over low heat. When the oil is hot, remove the pan from the heat and quickly add the filleted anchovies and the red pepper flakes. Use a fork to mash them into the oil until amalgamated.
- Drain pasta and place in serving dish on top of the broccoli. Pour the anchovy sauce over the pasta. Sprinkle with freshly ground black pepper and toss gently but very well. Serve immediately.

Nutrition Information

- 562: calories;
- 29 grams: fat;
- 4 grams: sugars;
- 3 grams: polyunsaturated fat;
- 5 grams: dietary fiber;
- 14 grams: protein;
- 64 grams: carbohydrates;
- 483 milligrams: sodium;
- 20 grams: monounsaturated fat;

118.   Glazed Parsley Carrots

Serving: 4 servings | Prep: | Cook: | Ready in: 15mins

Ingredients

- 1 ¼ pounds carrots, trimmed and scraped
- Salt and freshly ground pepper to taste
- ½ teaspoon sugar
- ¼ cup water
- 1 tablespoon fresh lemon juice
- 2 tablespoons butter
- 2 tablespoons finely chopped parsley

Direction

- Cut the carrot into very thin slices. There should be about 4 cups. Place in a saucepan. Add salt, pepper, sugar, water, lemon juice and butter.

- Cover tightly. Cook over moderately high heat, shaking pan occasionally. Cook about 7 minutes until carrots are tender, the liquid has evaporated and the carrots are lightly glazed. Take care they do not burn. Sprinkle with parsley and serve.

Nutrition Information

- 114: calories;
- 7 grams: sugars;
- 396 milligrams: sodium;
- 6 grams: fat;
- 4 grams: dietary fiber;
- 0 grams: polyunsaturated fat;
- 2 grams: protein;
- 15 grams: carbohydrates;

---

119.   Gluten Free Pumpkin Muffins With Crumble Topping

Serving: 12 muffins | Prep: | Cook: | Ready in: 45mins

Ingredients

- Topping
- ¼ cup store-bought gluten-free flour blend
- ¼ cup packed light brown sugar
- ¼ cup granulated sugar
- ½ teaspoon pumpkin pie spice
- 4 tablespoons all-vegetable shortening
- Confectioners' sugar, for sprinkling
- Muffins
- 1 ¾ cups store-bought gluten-free flour blend
- 2 teaspoons baking powder
- 2 teaspoons pumpkin pie spice
- ¾ teaspoon salt
- 2 large eggs, at room temperature
- 1 cup canned pure pumpkin puree
- 1 cup granulated sugar
- ½ cup vegetable oil
- 1 tablespoon pure vanilla extract

Direction

- Preheat oven to 350 degrees Fahrenheit. Line a 12-cup muffin pan with paper liners.
- Prepare the crumble topping. Whisk together the flour, brown sugar, granulated sugar and pumpkin pie spice in a medium bowl. Add the shortening and, using your fingers or a fork, blend together until coarse crumbs form.
- To make the muffins: Whisk together the flour, baking powder, pumpkin pie spice and salt in a large bowl.
- In a medium bowl, whisk together the eggs, pumpkin puree, granulated sugar, oil and vanilla until smooth. Add to the flour mixture; stir until just combined.
- Fill each muffin cup almost full; top each with crumble topping. Bake until the muffins are springy to the touch and a toothpick inserted into the center comes out clean, 20 to 25 minutes. Let cool in the pan, set on a wire rack. Using a sieve, sprinkle with confectioners' sugar.

---

120.   Goat Cheese Salad With Pancetta, Garlic And Figs

Serving: Four servings | Prep: | Cook: | Ready in: 15mins

Ingredients

- ½ pound pancetta, cut into small dice
- 4 tablespoons olive oil
- 4 teaspoons minced garlic
- 2 teaspoons minced fresh thyme
- ¾ cup sherry vinegar
- ½ pound goat cheese
- 8 cups mixed wild greens, washed and stemmed
- 12 fresh or dried figs, stemmed and halved
- Salt and freshly ground pepper to taste

Direction

- Place the pancetta in a large skillet over low heat and cook until it has browned and released half of its fat. Remove the pancetta from the skillet with a slotted spoon. Add the olive oil to the skillet and increase the heat to medium. When the pancetta is hot but not smoking, return it to the pan and cook for a few seconds.

- Add the garlic and cook until lightly browned. Add the thyme and cook just until it makes a popping sound. Stir in the vinegar and simmer until reduced to 1/4 cup, about 5 minutes. Crumble the goat cheese into the skillet and cook just until it begins to weep. Toss in the greens and immediately remove the pan from the heat. Toss in the figs and season with salt and pepper to taste. Place the salad in a bowl and serve warm.

---

121. Goat Cheese, Chard And Herb Pie In A Phyllo Crust

Serving: Serves 6 to 8 | Prep: | Cook: |Ready in: 1hours15mins

Ingredients

- 1 generous bunch Swiss chard (about 3/4 pound), stemmed and washed
- Salt to taste
- 8 sheets phyllo (4 ounces)
- 3 eggs
- 6 ounces goat cheese
- ¾ cup low-fat milk
- 2 garlic cloves, pureed or put through a press
- ½ cup chopped fresh herbs, such as parsley, dill, chives, tarragon, marjoramSalt and freshly ground pepper
- 2 tablespoons extra virgin olive oil, or 1 tablespoon olive oil and 1 tablespoon melted unsalted butter

Direction

- Bring a large pot of water to a boil while you stem and wash the Swiss chard. If the stems are wide and meaty set them aside for another purpose. If they are thin and sinewy, discard.

When the water comes to a boil salt generously and add the chard leaves. Fill a bowl with cold water. Blanch the chard for 1 minute, just until tender, and transfer to the bowl of cold water. Drain, take up the chard by the handful and squeeze out excess water. Chop medium-fine. You should have about 1 cup chopped cooked chard.

- Preheat the oven to 350 degrees. Blend together the eggs and goat cheese, either in an electric mixer or in a food processor fitted with the steel blade. Add the milk and the garlic and blend until smooth. If using a processor, scrape into a bowl. Stir in the blanched chopped chard, the herbs, and salt and pepper to taste.

- Brush a 9- or 10-inch tart pan or cake pan with olive oil and place on a baking sheet for easier handling. Open up the package of phyllo and unfold the sheets of dough. Remove 8 sheets of phyllo and fold the remaining dough back up. Wrap tightly in plastic, return to the box if you wish and either refrigerate or freeze. Lay a sheet of phyllo in the pan, tucking it into the seam of the pan, with the edges overhanging the rim. Brush it lightly with olive oil (or melted butter and oil) and turn the pan slightly, then place another sheet on top, positioning it so that the edges overlap another section of the pan's rim. Continue to layer in 6 more sheets of phyllo, brushing each one with oil – both the bottom and the sides and edges that overhang the pan -- and staggering them so that the overhang on the rim of the pan is evenly distributed and covers the entire pan.

- Pour the goat cheese and chard filling into the phyllo-lined pan, scraping all of it out of the bowl with a rubber spatula. Scrunch the overhanging phyllo in around the edges of the pan to form an attractive lip. Brush the scrunched rim with olive oil. Place in the oven and bake 40 minutes, until the filling is puffed, set and lightly colored on the surface. Remove from the heat (if it puffed up it will settle) and allow to sit for at least 10 minutes before cutting. Serve hot, warm or at room temperature.

Nutrition Information

- 190: calories;
- 2 grams: sugars;
- 9 grams: protein;
- 292 milligrams: sodium;
- 12 grams: carbohydrates;
- 5 grams: monounsaturated fat;
- 0 grams: trans fat;
- 1 gram: dietary fiber;

122. Grand Marnier Soufflé

Serving: 4 servings | Prep: | Cook: | Ready in: 20mins

Ingredients

- 1 tablespoon soft butter
- ½ cup plus 3 tablespoons granulated sugar
- 5 eggs, separated
- ⅓ cup grated orange rind
- 2 tablespoons Grand Marnier

Direction

- Preheat oven to 450 degrees.
- Rub the butter on the bottom and sides of four 1-cup souffle dishes. Sprinkle 1 tablespoon of sugar over the insides of the souffle dishes.
- Place the egg yolks in a bowl and add 1/2 cup sugar, the orange rind and the Grand Marnier. Beat briskly until well blended.
- In a large, deep bowl, preferably copper, beat the egg whites until stiff. Toward the end, beat in the remaining 2 tablespoons sugar. (You can use an electric stand mixer, but keep an eye on the egg whites. They should not be too stiff.)
- Spoon the egg-yolk mixture into the whites, folding in rapidly. Place equal portions of the mixture in the prepared souffle dishes.

- Put the dishes on a baking sheet, and place on the bottom of the oven. Bake for 10 to 12 minutes, and serve immediately.

Nutrition Information

- 257: calories;
- 4 grams: saturated fat;
- 0 grams: trans fat;
- 35 grams: sugars;
- 77 milligrams: sodium;
- 8 grams: fat;
- 37 grams: carbohydrates;
- 7 grams: protein;
- 3 grams: monounsaturated fat;
- 1 gram: dietary fiber;

123. Grated Carrot Salad With Dates And Oranges

Serving: Serves 4 | Prep: | Cook: | Ready in: 10mins

Ingredients

- 1 pound carrots, grated on the medium blade of your grater
- 8 dates, pitted and quartered lengthwise
- 2 tablespoons fresh lemon juice
- ¼ cup fresh orange juice
- Salt to taste
- ¼ teaspoon ground cinnamon, plus additional for sprinkling
- 2 tablespoons olive oil
- 2 to 3 oranges (as needed)

Direction

- In a large bowl combine the carrots and dates.
- Whisk together the lemon juice, orange juice, salt, cinnamon and olive oil. Toss with the carrots.
- Remove the peel and pith from one of the oranges. Cut the sections away from between the membranes, holding the orange above the

bowl to catch juice. Cut the orange sections into halves or thirds, depending on the size, and toss with the carrots. Transfer to a platter or a wide bowl.

- Slice the remaining orange or oranges into thin rounds. Cut the rounds in half, and arrange in an overlapping ring around the carrots. Sprinkle a little more cinnamon over the carrots and oranges, and serve.

Nutrition Information

- 286: calories;
- 46 grams: sugars;
- 3 grams: protein;
- 634 milligrams: sodium;
- 5 grams: monounsaturated fat;
- 59 grams: carbohydrates;
- 7 grams: fat;
- 1 gram: polyunsaturated fat;
- 8 grams: dietary fiber;

---

124. Greek Chicken Stew With Cauliflower And Olives

Serving: 4 to 6 servings | Prep: | Cook: |Ready in: 1hours15mins

Ingredients

- 2 tablespoons extra virgin olive oil
- 1 large red onion, chopped
- 2 to 4 garlic cloves (to taste), minced
- 6 to 8 chicken legs and/or thighs, skinned
- 2 tablespoons red wine vinegar
- 1 28-ounce can chopped tomatoes, with juice, pulsed in a food processor
- ½ teaspoon cinnamon
- Salt and freshly ground pepper
- ½ teaspoon dried thyme, or 1 teaspoon fresh thyme leaves
- 1 small or 1/2 large cauliflower, cored, broken into florets, and sliced about 1/2 inch thick

- 12 kalamata olives (about 45 grams), rinsed, pitted and cut in half (optional)
- 1 to 2 tablespoons chopped flat-leaf parsley
- 1 to 2 ounces feta cheese, crumbled (optional)

Direction

- Heat 1 tablespoon of the oil over medium-high heat in a large, deep, heavy lidded skillet or casserole and brown the chicken, in batches if necessary, about 5 minutes on each side. Remove the pieces to a plate or bowl as they're browned. Pour off the fat from the pan. Add the vinegar to the pan and scrape up all the bits from the bottom of the pan.
- Add the remaining tablespoon of the olive oil to the pan, and turn the heat down to medium. Add the onion and a generous pinch of salt and cook, stirring often and scraping the bottom of the pan, until it begins to soften, about 5 minutes. Turn the heat to low, cover and let the onion cook for 10 minutes, stirring from time to time, until it is lightly browned and very soft.
- Add the garlic and stir together for a minute or two more, until the garlic is fragrant, then add the tomatoes and their juice, the cinnamon, thyme, and salt and pepper to taste. Bring to a simmer and simmer 10 minutes, stirring from time to time, until the mixture is reduced slightly and fragrant.
- Return the chicken pieces to the pot, along with any juices that have accumulated in the bowl. If necessary, add enough water to barely cover the chicken. Bring to a simmer, reduce the heat, cover and simmer 20 minutes.
- Add the cauliflower and kalamata olives and simmer for another 20 minutes, or until the cauliflower is tender and the chicken is just about falling off the bone. Stir in the parsley, taste and adjust seasonings. Serve with grains, with the feta sprinkled on top if desired.

Nutrition Information

- 498: calories;
- 15 grams: monounsaturated fat;

- 6 grams: dietary fiber;
- 33 grams: protein;
- 1127 milligrams: sodium;
- 9 grams: saturated fat;
- 0 grams: trans fat;
- 7 grams: sugars;
- 16 grams: carbohydrates;
- 34 grams: fat;

125. Green Beans With Mustard Oil And Black Mustard Seeds

Serving: Four servings | Prep: | Cook: | Ready in: 15mins

Ingredients

- Salt to taste
- 1 pound green beans, washed, ends snipped off
- 1 to 2 tablespoons mustard oil (see note)
- ½ teaspoon black mustard seeds (see note; if unavailable, use yellow mustard seeds)
- 1 bunch scallions, white and pale green parts, sliced
- 1 tablespoon chopped cilantro

Direction

- Fill a large saucepan with water and bring to a boil. Add salt to taste and the beans. Cook until the beans are tender but still firm, about 4 minutes. Drain and set aside.
- In large skillet, heat the oil with the mustard seeds. As soon as seeds begin to pop, about 2 to 3 minutes, add the scallions. Saute for 20 seconds, then add the beans, tossing them until the oil is evenly distributed.
- Add the cilantro and toss again. Taste for salt and serve.

Nutrition Information

- 92: calories;

- 1 gram: polyunsaturated fat;
- 3 grams: protein;
- 10 grams: carbohydrates;
- 4 grams: sugars;
- 344 milligrams: sodium;
- 6 grams: fat;

126. Green Soup With Baby Shrimp And Basil

Serving: Four servings | Prep: | Cook: | Ready in: 30mins

Ingredients

- 4 medium-size cucumbers, peeled, halved, seeded and coarsely chopped
- 2 large scallions, green part only, coarsely chopped
- 1 jalapeno, seeded and coarsely chopped
- ½ cup fresh cilantro
- 2 cups buttermilk
- 1 ½ teaspoons fresh lemon juice
- ½ teaspoon salt, plus more to taste
- Freshly ground pepper to taste
- ½ lemon
- ½ pound baby shrimp, in the shell
- 8 large basil leaves, cut across into thin strips

Direction

- Place the cucumbers, scallions, jalapeno, cilantro and buttermilk in a blender and blend until smooth. Stir in lemon juice, 1/2 teaspoon salt and pepper to taste. Chill in refrigerator.
- Place the 1/2 lemon and 1 1/2 cups water in a medium saucepan and bring to a boil. Reduce to a simmer, add the shrimp, cover and cook until the shrimp turn pink, about 3 minutes. Drain. When the shrimp are cool enough to handle, peel them. Season with salt and pepper to taste.
- Taste the soup and adjust seasoning. Divide among 4 bowls and top with shrimp. Garnish with the basil and serve immediately.

Nutrition Information

- 137: calories;
- 1 gram: saturated fat;
- 0 grams: polyunsaturated fat;
- 18 grams: carbohydrates;
- 11 grams: sugars;
- 14 grams: protein;
- 853 milligrams: sodium;
- 2 grams: dietary fiber;

127. Green Tomato And Swiss Chard Gratin

Serving: Serves six | Prep: | Cook: | Ready in: 1hours

Ingredients

- 1 bunch Swiss chard
- 1 pound green tomatoes, sliced a little less than 1/2 inch thick
- Cornmeal for dredging (about 1/2 cup)
- Salt
- freshly ground pepper to taste
- 3 tablespoons extra virgin olive oil
- 1 medium onion, chopped
- 2 garlic cloves, green shoots removed, minced
- 2 teaspoons fresh thyme leaves, chopped
- 3 large eggs, beaten
- ½ cup low-fat milk
- 3 ounces gruyere cheese, grated (1/2 cup, tightly packed)

Direction

- Preheat the oven to 375 degrees. Oil a 2-quart baking dish or gratin with olive oil. Bring a large pot of generously salted water to a boil, and fill a bowl with ice water. Stem the chard and wash the leaves in two changes of water. Rinse the stems if wide and dice. Set them aside. When the water comes to a boil, add the chard leaves and blanch for about one minute. Transfer to the ice water, cool for a minute and drain. Squeeze out excess water and chop. Set aside.
- Season the sliced tomatoes and the cornmeal lightly with salt and pepper. Dredge the tomatoes in the cornmeal. Heat 2 tablespoons of the olive oil in a heavy nonstick skillet over medium-high heat, and fry the sliced tomatoes for two minutes on each side, just until lightly colored. Remove from the heat and set aside.
- Heat the remaining tablespoon of olive oil over medium heat in the skillet in which you cooked the tomatoes, and add the onion and the chopped chard stems. Cook, stirring, until tender, about five minutes. Add a generous pinch of salt and the garlic, and cook together for another minute, until the garlic is fragrant. Add the thyme and the chopped chard, and stir together for minute over medium heat. Season to taste with salt and pepper.
- Beat the eggs in a large bowl with 1/2 teaspoon salt and freshly ground pepper to taste. Whisk in the milk. Stir in the cheese and the chard mixture. Transfer to the gratin dish. Layer the tomatoes over the top. Place in the oven, and bake 30 to 40 minutes, until set and beginning to brown.

Nutrition Information

- 254: calories;
- 2 grams: polyunsaturated fat;
- 21 grams: carbohydrates;
- 6 grams: sugars;
- 5 grams: saturated fat;
- 0 grams: trans fat;
- 7 grams: monounsaturated fat;
- 14 grams: fat;
- 3 grams: dietary fiber;
- 12 grams: protein;
- 583 milligrams: sodium;

128. Grillades And Grits (Rosalie's)

Serving: 4 servings | Prep: | Cook: |Ready in: 13mins

Ingredients

- 2 tablespoons minced fresh thyme
- ¼ to ½ teaspoon cayenne pepper
- 1 teaspoon ground black pepper
- Salt to taste
- 1 pound loin of veal, completely trimmed
- 1 tablespoon olive oil plus oil for brushing the meat
- Sauce (see recipe)
- Grits (see recipe)

Direction

- Combine thyme, peppers and salt.
- Brush veal with oil and coat with pepper mixture on both sides. Set aside while making sauce and grits.
- To serve, preheat oven to 500 degrees.
- Heat heavy pan and add 1 tablespoon oil.
- Sear meat quickly on all sides over high heat, about 4 minutes.
- Place veal in pan in oven and roast quickly, 7 to 10 minutes for rare. Slice meat thinly and place on heated plates with warm grits. Spoon sauce over.

129. Grilled Figs With Pomegranate Molasses

Serving: 6 servings | Prep: | Cook: |Ready in: 30mins

Ingredients

- 12 large or 18 medium-size ripe but firm fresh figs (1 pound)
- 1 tablespoon balsamic vinegar
- 2 tablespoons extra-virgin olive oil
- 1 tablespoon pomegranate molasses (available at Middle Eastern markets)

- 12 1/2-inch thick slices goat cheese from a log, about 6 ounces (see variations that follow)
- Fresh mint leaves for garnish

Direction

- Prepare a hot or medium-hot grill or heat a grill pan to medium-hot. Cut figs in half.
- In a large bowl, whisk together balsamic vinegar and olive oil. Add figs to the bowl and gently toss until they are thoroughly coated.
- Place on grill or grill pan flat side down. Grill for 2 to 3 minutes (depending on the heat), until grill marks appear. Turn over using tongs or a spatula and grill for another 2 to 3 minutes on the other side.
- Remove to a platter or sheet pan and brush each fig on the cut side with pomegranate molasses (you don't need much).
- Arrange 2 slices of goat cheese and 2 to 3 whole figs (4 to 6 halves, to taste) on each of 6 serving plates, garnish with mint leaves, and serve.

Nutrition Information

- 257: calories;
- 17 grams: carbohydrates;
- 9 grams: saturated fat;
- 15 grams: sugars;
- 263 milligrams: sodium;
- 6 grams: monounsaturated fat;
- 1 gram: polyunsaturated fat;
- 2 grams: dietary fiber;
- 11 grams: protein;

130. Grilled Potatoes

Serving: 2 servings | Prep: | Cook: |Ready in: 20mins

Ingredients

- 1 pound new potatoes
- 2 teaspoons olive oil

- 1 teaspoon ground cumin

Direction

- Scrub potatoes; do not peel. If potatoes are large, slice 1/8-inch thick. If potatoes are very small, cut in quarters.
- Mix oil and cumin, and stir potatoes into mixture, coating well.
- Prepare stove-top grill. Arrange potatoes on grill; cook over medium heat, turning when potatoes brown on one side, and cook through.

Nutrition Information

- 218: calories;
- 5 grams: protein;
- 1 gram: polyunsaturated fat;
- 3 grams: monounsaturated fat;
- 40 grams: carbohydrates;
- 2 grams: sugars;
- 15 milligrams: sodium;

131.   Grilled Sardines

Serving: Serves four | Prep: | Cook: | Ready in: 15mins

Ingredients

- 24 medium or large sardines, cleaned
- 2 tablespoons extra virgin olive oil
- Salt
- freshly ground pepper
- A handful of fresh rosemary sprigs
- Lemon wedges

Direction

- Prepare a hot grill, making sure the grill is oiled. Rinse the sardines, and dry with paper towels. Toss with the olive oil, and season with salt and pepper.
- When the grill is ready, toss the rosemary sprigs directly on the fire. Wait for the flames

to die down, then place the sardines directly over the heat, in batches if necessary. Grill for a minute or two on each side, depending on the size. Transfer from the grill to a platter using tongs or a wide metal spatula, and serve with lemon wedges.

Nutrition Information

- 160: calories;
- 15 grams: protein;
- 197 milligrams: sodium;
- 10 grams: fat;
- 2 grams: polyunsaturated fat;
- 6 grams: monounsaturated fat;
- 1 gram: carbohydrates;
- 0 grams: sugars;

132.   Grilled Swordfish With Tomatillo Sauce

Serving: 4 servings | Prep: | Cook: | Ready in: 35mins

Ingredients

- 2 swordfish steaks about 1-inch thick (about 1 1/2 to 2 pounds)
- 2 tablespoons olive oil
- For the sauce:
- 3 cloves garlic, unpeeled
- 1 pound tomatillos
- 2 jalapeno chilies, seeded and sliced
- 1 to 2 teaspoons sugar (or to taste)
- ⅓ cup dry white wine
- 1 tablespoon white-wine vinegar
- 2 tablespoons unsalted butter
- Coarse salt and freshly ground pepper to taste
- ⅓ cup fresh coriander leaves
- Coriander sprigs to garnish

Direction

- Cut the swordfish steaks in half. Wipe them dry with paper towels and coat them on both sides with the olive oil. Set aside.
- Make the sauce. Boil the garlic for 10 minutes. Peel the cloves, mash them and set aside. Chop the tomatillos coarsely and put them in a saucepan with the chilies, sugar, wine and vinegar. Cook until soft, stirring frequently. Add the garlic. Taste to see if more sugar or vinegar is needed and season with salt and pepper. Add the butter to thicken the sauce.
- Pour the sauce into a food processor with the garlic cloves and add the coriander leaves. Puree, taste and correct seasoning. Set aside.
- Preheat broiler or coals. Broil the fish steaks six inches from the heat for about five minutes on each side or until cooked. Meanwhile, reheat the sauce.
- To serve, pour some sauce on each of four individual plates. Put the steaks on top and sprinkle with coriander leaves.

Nutrition Information

- 463: calories;
- 0 grams: trans fat;
- 4 grams: polyunsaturated fat;
- 7 grams: sugars;
- 41 grams: protein;
- 841 milligrams: sodium;
- 27 grams: fat;
- 8 grams: saturated fat;
- 11 grams: carbohydrates;
- 3 grams: dietary fiber;
- 13 grams: monounsaturated fat;

---

133. Grilled Turkey Breast With Chive Butter

Serving: 4 servings | Prep: | Cook: | Ready in: 20mins

Ingredients

- 4 turkey breast steaks, about 1 1/2 pounds
- Salt and freshly ground pepper to taste
- 2 tablespoons olive oil
- 2 tablespoons chopped fresh sage or 2 teaspoons dried
- 4 tablespoons butter
- 1 tablespoon lemon juice
- ¼ teaspoon ground cumin
- 1 teaspoon Worcestershire sauce
- 4 tablespoons finely chopped chives

Direction

- Preheat a charcoal grill until quite hot. The coals should be placed quite close to the grill because the meat will only be seared.
- Place each turkey steak between sheets of clear plastic wrap. Pound lightly and evenly with a flat mallet or meat pounder to make slices about 1/4-inch thick.
- Season the turkey with salt and pepper. Brush both sides with olive oil and sprinkle both sides with sage.
- Heat the butter until melted. Add the lemon juice, cumin, Worcestershire, salt, pepper and chives. Blend well. Keep warm.
- Place the steaks on the grill and cook on both sides for about 2 minutes to a side or until done. Do not overcook. Transfer the steaks to a serving dish. Pour the chive butter over them and serve.

Nutrition Information

- 419: calories;
- 30 grams: fat;
- 12 grams: monounsaturated fat;
- 4 grams: carbohydrates;
- 34 grams: protein;
- 11 grams: saturated fat;
- 0 grams: sugars;
- 2 grams: dietary fiber;
- 474 milligrams: sodium;

134. Grits

Serving: | Prep: | Cook: | Ready in: 8mins

Ingredients

- 4 cups water
- 1 cup yellow stone-ground cornmeal
- Salt and pepper to taste

Direction

- Bring water and salt to boil. Slowly add cornmeal, stirring to prevent lumping. Cook over low heat until grits are cooked and mixture is thick. Season with pepper.
- Either serve grits from the pot or pour into 10-inch pie plate and chill.
- If chilled, cut into triangles and reheat in oven at 350 degrees for 10 minutes before serving.

Nutrition Information

- 112: calories;
- 1 gram: polyunsaturated fat;
- 0 grams: sugars;
- 24 grams: carbohydrates;
- 2 grams: dietary fiber;
- 3 grams: protein;
- 624 milligrams: sodium;

135. Hake In Vegetable And Lemon Broth

Serving: 6 servings | Prep: | Cook: | Ready in: 30mins

Ingredients

- 2 carrots (6 ounces)
- 1 lemon
- 12 scallions, trimmed (leaving most of the green), cleaned and minced (1 1/4 cups)
- 1 red onion (8 ounces), peeled and coarsely chopped (2 cups)
- ¾ cup dry white wine
- 2 teaspoons salt
- 1 teaspoon thyme leaves
- 1 teaspoon freshly ground black pepper
- 6 hake fillets (each about 6 ounces and 3/4 inch thick)
- ¼ cup olive oil
- 2 tablespoons unsalted butter

Direction

- Peel the carrots, and cut them into 3-inch pieces. Then, cut each piece into 1/8-inch slices. Stack the slices together, and cut them into 1/8-inch strips (julienne). You should have about 2 cups of julienned carrot.
- Peel the lemon with a vegetable peeler, removing the peel in long strips. Pile the strips together, and cut them into a fine julienne, making about 1 tablespoon. Cut the lemon in half, and press the halves to extract 2 tablespoons of juice.
- In a large saucepan (preferably stainless steel), combine the carrots, lemon peel, lemon juice, scallions, red onion, white wine, salt, thyme leaves and pepper with 3/4 cup water. Bring the mixture to a boil over high heat, cover, reduce the heat to low, and boil gently for 10 minutes.
- Fold each of the hake fillets in half and arrange them carefully on top of the vegetables in the saucepan. Cover, return the mixture to a boil, reduce the heat and boil gently for 5 minutes. The hake should be barely cooked through. Lift the fish from the saucepan and arrange it on a platter.
- Add the olive oil and butter to the vegetable mixture in the pan, and bring it to a strong boil over high heat. Continue to boil for about 20 to 30 seconds, until the mixture is emulsified. Pour over the fish, and serve immediately.

Nutrition Information

- 366: calories;
- 15 grams: fat;
- 0 grams: trans fat;
- 8 grams: monounsaturated fat;

- 2 grams: dietary fiber;
- 897 milligrams: sodium;
- 4 grams: sugars;
- 10 grams: carbohydrates;
- 42 grams: protein;

136. Herbed And Butterflied Leg Of Lamb

Serving: 6 servings | Prep: | Cook: |Ready in: 1hours

Ingredients

- 1 teaspoon black peppercorns
- 1 teaspoon whole coriander seed
- ⅓ cup olive oil (not extra-virgin)
- 1 teaspoon salt
- 2 to 3 unpeeled cloves garlic, slightly crushed
- 1 lemon
- 2 9-inch sprigs fresh rosemary (or the equivalent in shorter lengths)
- 1 4-pound leg of lamb, boned and butterflied (opened with meat scored slightly to flatten it)

Direction

- With a mortar and pestle, lightly crush peppercorns and coriander seeds. Transfer to a small bowl, and add olive oil, salt and garlic. Finely grate lemon peel, and add to mixture. Cut lemon into quarters, and squeeze juice into mixture, then add leftover lemon as well.
- Place lamb skin side down in a shallow dish, and press whole rosemary sprigs into scored meat. Pour marinade over meat, pressing lemon pieces into meat. Cover dish with plastic wrap; refrigerate overnight.
- When ready to cook, remove lamb from refrigerator, and allow to sit at room temperature while oven heats to 425 degrees. Place lamb skin side up in a roasting pan, keeping lemon pieces and rosemary pressed into underside.
- Roast 35 to 40 minutes, until an instant-read thermometer inserted into thickest part of

lamb registers 145 degrees (for medium-well lamb), or adjust cooking time as desired. When cooked to taste, remove lamb from oven, and allow to rest in pan for 10 to 15 minutes before carving.

Nutrition Information

- 608: calories;
- 1 gram: dietary fiber;
- 44 grams: protein;
- 523 milligrams: sodium;
- 23 grams: monounsaturated fat;
- 4 grams: polyunsaturated fat;
- 2 grams: carbohydrates;
- 0 grams: sugars;
- 46 grams: fat;
- 16 grams: saturated fat;

137. Homemade Oreos

Serving: 24 two-inch sandwich cookies. | Prep: | Cook: |Ready in: 2hours

Ingredients

- FOR THE COOKIES
- 6 tablespoons unsalted butter, at room temperature
- 105 grams (1/2 cup) sugar
- 45 grams (3 tablespoons) brown sugar
- 1 ½ teaspoons salt
- ¼ teaspoon plus 1/8 teaspoon baking powder
- ¼ teaspoon baking soda
- 1 teaspoon instant coffee powder
- 1 ½ teaspoons vanilla extract
- 2 large egg yolks
- 15 grams (3/4 cup) sifted all-purpose flour or rice flour
- 85 grams (1 cup) sifted cocoa powder, plus more as needed
- FOR THE FILLING:
- 4 tablespoons shortening or unsalted butter, at room temperature

- 145 grams (1 1/4 cups) sifted confectioner's sugar
- 1 teaspoon vanilla extract
- ⅛ teaspoon salt.

Direction

- For the cookies: Using a mixer, cream together butter, sugar, brown sugar, salt, baking powder, baking soda, coffee powder and vanilla extract. With mixer still running, add egg yolks one at a time.
- Stop mixer and scrape bowl with a rubber spatula. Add flour and 1 cup cocoa, and resume mixing at low speed until the mixture is crumbly and uniformly blended. Scrape the bowl and knead the dough lightly to form a smooth ball. Transfer to a work surface and flatten into a disk. The dough may be rolled right away or wrapped in plastic and refrigerated for up to a week; bring to room temperature before rolling.
- Heat oven to 350 degrees. Lightly sift some cocoa powder onto a work surface, and roll the dough to .125-inch thickness. Slide a metal spatula under the dough to prevent it from sticking. Using a 2-inch round cookie cutter, cut out cookies and transfer to an ungreased baking sheet. The cookies will not spread during baking so may be placed close together. Knead and reroll the dough scraps to make more cookies.
- To add texture to the cookies, place any remaining dough in a mixing bowl. Mix with enough hot water until the dough has thinned into a paste. Transfer to a piping bag fitted with a very small tip, or a heavy duty Ziploc bag with a tiny hole poked in the corner. Pipe a design on each cookie; a tight cornelli lace design gives the impression of an Oreo.
- Bake the cookies until firm, about 12 minutes. Remove from heat and cool completely on a rack.
- For the filling: Using a mixer, cream together shortening or butter, confectioner's sugar, vanilla and salt. Beat on medium speed for 5 minutes, scraping the bowl periodically. The long mixing time smoothes, whitens and aerates the filling.
- For assembly: Using a pastry bag fitted with a plain tip or a spoon, place 1 teaspoon (or more if desired) of filling directly onto the center of the undersides of half the cookies. To finish, top with remaining wafers and press down with your fingers, applying very even pressure so the filling will spread uniformly across the cookie. Place cookies in an airtight container and refrigerate for several hours before serving.

Nutrition Information

- 106: calories;
- 6 grams: fat;
- 2 grams: monounsaturated fat;
- 1 gram: protein;
- 12 grams: sugars;
- 0 grams: polyunsaturated fat;
- 15 grams: carbohydrates;
- 57 milligrams: sodium;
- 3 grams: saturated fat;

---

138.   Honeycrisp Apple And Parsnip Soup

Serving: 4 servings | Prep: | Cook: | Ready in: 20mins

Ingredients

- 1 ½ cups diced white onion (1 medium)
- 1 tablespoon butter
- 1 cup sparkling wine
- 2 large parsnips, peeled and roughly chopped, about 2 cups
- 2 large Honeycrisp apples, peeled and roughly chopped, about 2 cups
- 1 russet potato or white sweet potato, peeled and roughly chopped, about 1 1/2 cups
- 1 teaspoon rubbed sage
- 2 cups vegetable stock
- 1 cup half-and-half

- Sea salt and cracked black pepper (to taste)
- ½ cup sliced green onions (to garnish)

Direction

- In a soup pot or Dutch oven, sauté onions in butter over medium heat until translucent, and then add wine. Allow the mixture to reduce until most of the liquid has evaporated, and then add parsnip, apple, potato and sage to the mixture.
- Cover and cook for about 10 minutes, or until vegetables have softened and have taken on a slight color. Add the stock and reduce heat to medium-low. Bring the stock up to temperature. Slowly add the half-and-half to the warm mixture. Do not allow soup to boil after adding the half-and-half as it could curdle.
- Using an immersion blender, blend the mixture smooth. Add enough stock or water to achieve the consistency you desire up to another full cup. Garnish with sliced green onion.

Nutrition Information

- 325: calories;
- 1202 milligrams: sodium;
- 6 grams: saturated fat;
- 1 gram: polyunsaturated fat;
- 47 grams: carbohydrates;
- 9 grams: dietary fiber;
- 11 grams: fat;
- 0 grams: trans fat;
- 3 grams: monounsaturated fat;
- 22 grams: sugars;
- 5 grams: protein;

139.   Hot Cajun Style Crab Boil

Serving: 6 servings | Prep: | Cook: |Ready in: 1hours15mins

Ingredients

- 2 bags (3 ounces each) commercial crab-boil seasoning, or equivalent amount of your own spice mixture (see article)
- Salt, to taste
- 2 pounds medium onions (about 8), peeled
- 3 pounds small potatoes (about 24), washed but not peeled
- 24 live medium blue crabs
- 2 pounds kielbasa, cut into 3-inch pieces
- 35 to 40 cloves garlic (3 heads), unpeeled
- 12 ears sweet corn, hulled

Direction

- Place 2 gallons of water and the crab-boil seasoning in a large stockpot, cover and bring to a boil. (Note: This can be done a few hours ahead, set aside and brought back to a boil at serving time to intensify the stock flavor.) Add salt to taste.
- Add the onions and potatoes to the boiling stock, cover and bring the stock back to a boil. Boil gently for 10 minutes.
- Meanwhile, rinse the crabs well in a sink filled with cold water. Using metal tongs, lift the crabs from the sink, and after discarding any dead or smelly crabs, add them to the stockpot with the sausage and garlic. Bring the mixture back to a boil, and boil gently for 5 minutes.
- Add the corn, and bring the mixture back to a boil. Then, turn off the heat, and let the pot sit (up to 1 hour) until serving time.
- At serving time, drain off the stock, and arrange crab boil ingredients separately on a large platter. Serve with the hot mayonnaise (see following recipe), if desired.

Nutrition Information

- 1075: calories;
- 8 grams: polyunsaturated fat;
- 123 grams: carbohydrates;
- 15 grams: dietary fiber;
- 24 grams: sugars;
- 2024 milligrams: sodium;

- 19 grams: monounsaturated fat;
- 48 grams: fat;
- 16 grams: saturated fat;
- 1 gram: trans fat;
- 51 grams: protein;

---

140. I Trulli's White Anchovy And Orange Salad

Serving: 6 servings | Prep: | Cook: | Ready in: 15mins

Ingredients

- 6 oranges
- 48 marinated anchovy fillets
- Juice of 1 lemon
- ⅓ cup extra-virgin olive oil
- Salt and freshly ground black pepper
- 6 ounces mesclun
- 2 tablespoons minced flat-leaf parsley

Direction

- Use a sharp knife to cut peel from oranges, removing all the white pith. Cut sections out, slicing close to membrane. On 6 salad plates, arrange orange sections like spokes of a wheel, alternating with anchovy fillets, leaving a space in the center of each plate.
- Beat lemon juice and olive oil together and season. Toss with mesclun and put in center of each plate. Scatter parsley over anchovies and oranges. Season with pepper.

Nutrition Information

- 244: calories;
- 2 grams: polyunsaturated fat;
- 10 grams: monounsaturated fat;
- 18 grams: carbohydrates;
- 13 grams: sugars;
- 15 grams: fat;
- 4 grams: dietary fiber;
- 11 grams: protein;

- 1183 milligrams: sodium;

---

141. Indian Broiled Marinated Fish

Serving: 4 servings | Prep: | Cook: | Ready in: 1hours15mins

Ingredients

- 4 white fleshed fish steaks (or a large fish, split, head removed), about 2 to 2 1/2 pounds, 1 1/2 inches thick
- 2 tablespoons coriander seed
- 4 cardomom seeds, peeled
- 1 small onion, coarsely chopped
- 1 clove garlic, coarsely chopped
- ½ teaspoon paprika
- ½ teaspoon aniseed
- 1 long green chili, seeded and coarsely chopped
- 1 cup lowfat yogurt
- 2 tablespoons fresh mint leaves
- Freshly ground pepper to taste
- Juice of 1 lemon
- 1 tablespoon safflower oil

Direction

- Wipe the fish steaks dry with paper towels.
- Combine the remaining ingredients in the jar of a blender and puree until smooth. Coat the fish steaks with the mixture and leave for an hour.
- Preheat broiler. Broil fish about 6 to 7 minutes on each side, basting with the marinade.

Nutrition Information

- 290: calories;
- 8 grams: fat;
- 2 grams: monounsaturated fat;
- 3 grams: dietary fiber;
- 11 grams: carbohydrates;

- 6 grams: sugars;
- 45 grams: protein;
- 151 milligrams: sodium;

142. Italian Meat Sauce With Half The Meat

Serving: 3 cups, or enough for 9 pasta servings | Prep: | Cook: | Ready in: 35mins

Ingredients

- 1 tablespoon extra virgin olive oil
- ½ yellow or red onion, finely chopped
- 2 plump garlic cloves, minced
- ¼ pound ground beef or veal
- Pinch of ground cinnamon
- Salt to taste
- freshly ground black pepper to taste
- ¼ pound (about 2/3 cups) roasted mushroom mix
- 1 28-ounce can plus 1 14.5-ounce can chopped tomatoes in juice, pulsed in a food processor
- ¼ teaspoon sugar
- 1 teaspoon oregano
- 1 teaspoon fresh thyme leaves or 1/2 teaspoon dried thyme

Direction

- In a large, deep skillet or casserole heat olive oil over medium heat and add onion. Cook, stirring often, until tender, about 5 minutes, and add garlic. Cook, stirring, until fragrant, about 30 seconds, and turn heat up to medium-high. Add ground beef or veal and brown for about 5 minutes, stirring. Add cinnamon and season to taste with salt and pepper.
- Stir in roasted mushroom mix, tomatoes, sugar, oregano and thyme. Season with salt and pepper and bring to a rapid bubble over medium-high heat. Turn heat down to medium, cover partially if sauce is spluttering too much, and simmer, stirring often, until

thick and fragrant, 15 to 20 minutes. Taste and adjust seasonings. Serve with pasta, figuring on 1/3 cup per 3-ounce serving.

Nutrition Information

- 113: calories;
- 2 grams: saturated fat;
- 1 gram: polyunsaturated fat;
- 5 grams: dietary fiber;
- 6 grams: protein;
- 590 milligrams: sodium;
- 7 grams: fat;
- 0 grams: trans fat;
- 3 grams: monounsaturated fat;
- 10 grams: carbohydrates;

143. Jalapeño Spoonbread

Serving: 6 to 8 servings | Prep: | Cook: | Ready in: 1hours

Ingredients

- 1 cup water
- ¾ teaspoon salt
- 130 grams (1 cup) cornmeal, fine or medium, but not coarse
- 2 cups milk (1 percent or 2 percent)
- 2 tablespoons unsalted butter
- 3 eggs, separated
- Kernels from 1 ear of corn or 3/4 cup frozen corn (optional)
- 2 jalapeños, seeded if desired and minced
- 2 ounces Gruyère cheese, grated (1/2 cup) (optional)

Direction

- Preheat the oven to 350 degrees. Oil or butter a 9- or 10-inch cast iron skillet or a 2-quart soufflé dish or baking dish.
- Combine the water, milk and salt in a heavy medium saucepan and bring to a boil over medium heat. Slowly add the cornmeal in a

very thin stream while stirring all the time with a whisk or a wooden spoon. Turn the heat to low and stir for 10 to 15 minutes, until the mixture is smooth and thick. Remove from the heat and stir in the butter.

- One at a time, stir in the egg yolks, then add the optional cheese and corn kernels, and the jalapeños.
- In a medium bowl or in the bowl of an electric mixer, beat the egg whites on medium until they form stiff but not dry peaks. Stir 1/4 of the egg whites into the cornmeal mixture and gently fold in the rest. Scrape into the prepared baking dish. Place in the oven and bake for 30 minutes until spoonbread is puffed and beginning to brown. Serve at once. Chill leftovers.

Nutrition Information

- 147: calories;
- 4 grams: sugars;
- 0 grams: trans fat;
- 2 grams: monounsaturated fat;
- 1 gram: dietary fiber;
- 16 grams: carbohydrates;
- 5 grams: protein;
- 7 grams: fat;
- 270 milligrams: sodium;

144. Jerusalem Artichoke Soup With Crispy Sage Leaves

Serving: 4 to 6 servings | Prep: | Cook: | Ready in: 45mins

Ingredients

- ¼ cup extra-virgin olive oil
- 1 leek, white and pale green parts, rinsed and finely chopped
- ½ cup finely chopped white onion
- 2 pounds Jerusalem artichokes, peeled and rinsed

- 5 cups water or vegetable stock
- 1 teaspoon sea salt
- Crispy Sage Leaves
- 1 tablespoon extra-virgin olive oil
- 8 to 12 fresh sage leaves

Direction

- Heat the olive oil in a soup pot over medium heat. Add the leek and onion and sauté until softened, about 5 minutes. Add the Jerusalem artichokes, water and salt and bring to a boil. Decrease the heat, cover and simmer until the artichokes are tender, about 30 minutes.
- Remove from the heat and let cool. Transfer the mixture to a blender and process until smooth. Taste and adjust the seasonings if necessary. Gently reheat before serving.
- To crisp the sage leaves, heat the olive oil in a small sauté pan over medium heat. Add the sage leaves and sauté until just crisp, about 2 minutes. Drain on paper towels. Garnish each serving with a couple of the sage leaves.

Nutrition Information

- 232: calories;
- 8 grams: monounsaturated fat;
- 1 gram: polyunsaturated fat;
- 16 grams: sugars;
- 4 grams: protein;
- 353 milligrams: sodium;
- 12 grams: fat;
- 2 grams: saturated fat;
- 31 grams: carbohydrates;

145. Kale And Quinoa Salad With Plums And Herbs

Serving: Serves 4 to 6 | Prep: | Cook: | Ready in: 45mins

Ingredients

- ½ cup quinoa

- Salt to taste
- 3 cups stemmed, slivered kale
- 1 serrano or Thai chiles, minced (optional)
- 1 to 2 ripe but firm plums or pluots, cut in thin slices
- ½ cup basil leaves, chopped, torn or cut in slivers
- 2 to 4 tablespoons chopped chives
- 1 tablespoon chopped cilantro (optional)
- 2 tablespoons seasoned rice vinegar
- Grated zest of 1 lime
- 2 tablespoons fresh lime juice
- 1 garlic clove, minced or puréed
- 3 tablespoons sunflower or grapeseed oil

Direction

- Rinse the quinoa and cook in a pot of rapidly boiling, generously salted water for 15 minutes. Drain, return to pot, place a towel across the top and replace the lid. Let sit for 15 minutes. Transfer to a sheet pan lined with paper towels and allow to cool completely.
- To cut the kale, stem, wash and spin dry the leaves, then stack several at a time and cut crosswise into thin slivers. Toss in a large bowl with the quinoa, chile, herbs, and half the plums.
- Whisk together the vinegar, lime zest and juice, salt to taste, garlic and sunflower or grapeseed oil. Toss with the salad. Garnish with the remaining plums and serve.

Nutrition Information

- 131: calories;
- 14 grams: carbohydrates;
- 2 grams: sugars;
- 3 grams: protein;
- 164 milligrams: sodium;
- 8 grams: fat;
- 1 gram: monounsaturated fat;
- 5 grams: polyunsaturated fat;

146. Key Lime Pie

Serving: One 9-inch pie | Prep: | Cook: | Ready in: 3hours30mins

Ingredients

- 4 egg yolks
- 1 14-ounce can sweetened condensed milk
- ½ cup Key lime juice (see note)
- ½ teaspoon cream of tartar
- 1 9-inch graham cracker crust
- Whipped cream

Direction

- Heat the oven to 325 degrees. With an electric mixer, beat the egg yolks on high speed until thick and light in color. Add the condensed milk and mix on low speed. Still on low speed, add half the lime juice, cream of tartar and then the remaining lime juice, mixing after each addition. Mix well until blended.
- Pour into pie crust and bake for 10 to 15 minutes, or until the center is firm and dry to the touch. Freeze for at least 3 hours. Serve with whipped cream.

147. King Arthur Flour's Banana Crumb Muffins

Serving: 12 muffins | Prep: | Cook: | Ready in: 40mins

Ingredients

- TOPPING
- ½ cup King Arthur unbleached all-purpose flour
- ¼ cup sugar
- 1 teaspoon cinnamon
- 4 tablespoons (1/2 stick) butter or margarine, room temperature
- MUFFINS
- 1 ½ cups King Arthur unbleached all-purpose flour

- 1 teaspoon baking soda
- 1 teaspoon baking powder
- ½ teaspoon salt
- 3 large, ripe bananas, mashed
- ¾ cup sugar
- 1 egg, slightly beaten
- ⅓ cup butter or margarine, melted

Direction

- For the topping, in a medium bowl, mix flour, sugar and cinnamon. Add butter or margarine and mix with a fork or pastry cutter until crumbly. Put aside while preparing muffin batter.
- For the muffins, in large bowl, combine dry ingredients. Set aside.
- In another bowl, combine mashed bananas, sugar, slightly beaten egg and melted butter or margarine. Mix well. Stir into dry ingredients just until moistened.
- Fill greased muffin cups two-thirds full. (Do not use paper muffin cups!) Using hands, arrange coarse, pea-sized crumbs over muffin batter.
- Bake at 375 degrees for 18 to 20 minutes or until muffins test done with a cake tester. Cool in pan 10 minutes before removing to a wire rack.

---

148.   Lamb Chops, Yellow Pepper Tarragon Sauce

Serving: 2 servings | Prep: | Cook: | Ready in: 40mins

Ingredients

- 4 spring loin lamb chops
- 3 tablespoons olive oil
- 3 yellow peppers
- 1 tablespoon tarragon vinegar
- 1 medium onion, coarsely chopped
- 1 clove garlic, crushed
- Coarse salt and freshly ground white pepper to taste

- 2 tablespoons fresh tarragon leaves

Direction

- Wipe the lamb chops dry with paper towels. Sprinkle with one-and-a-half tablespoons olive oil and set aside.
- Seed the peppers and cut into quarters. Cut the quarters in half.
- Place the peppers in a small heavy saucepan with the remaining olive oil, vinegar, onion and garlic. Season with salt and pepper. Cover and cook over low heat for about 20 minutes, or until the onions and peppers are soft.
- Puree the pepper mixture in a food processor and pass the mixture through a strainer. Keep warm. Meanwhile, preheat broiler.
- Broil the lamb chops until browned on the outside and pink in the middle. Place two chops on two heated plates and pour small pool of yellow pepper sauce next to them. Sprinkle the sauce with tarragon leaves and serve.

Nutrition Information

- 1133: calories;
- 8 grams: polyunsaturated fat;
- 37 grams: protein;
- 99 grams: fat;
- 24 grams: carbohydrates;
- 4 grams: dietary fiber;
- 2 grams: sugars;
- 1379 milligrams: sodium;
- 38 grams: saturated fat;
- 47 grams: monounsaturated fat;

---

149.   Lamb Patties Moroccan Style With Harissa Sauce

Serving: 4 servings | Prep: | Cook: | Ready in: 25mins

Ingredients

- 1 ½ pounds ground lean lamb
- 1 teaspoon paprika
- ¼ teaspoon crushed dried red hot pepper flakes
- ¼ teaspoon freshly ground black pepper
- 1 teaspoon ground cumin
- 2 teaspoons finely chopped garlic
- 2 tablespoons grated onion
- 4 tablespoons finely chopped parsley
- Salt to taste
- 1 tablespoon vegetable oil
- Harissa sauce (see recipe)

Direction

- Put the lamb in a mixing bowl and add all of the ingredients except the vegetable oil and harissa sauce. Blend the mixture thoroughly by hand.
- Shape the mixture into 8 equal-size patties similar to hamburgers.
- Heat the oil in a nonstick skillet large enough to hold all of the patties. Two pans may be necessary.
- Add the patties to the skillet. Cook them over medium-high heat about 3 to 4 minutes on each side, depending on the degree of doneness desired. Drain on paper towels and serve with the harissa sauce on the side.

Nutrition Information

- 1143: calories;
- 121 grams: fat;
- 60 grams: saturated fat;
- 2 grams: carbohydrates;
- 11 grams: protein;
- 431 milligrams: sodium;
- 0 grams: sugars;
- 50 grams: monounsaturated fat;
- 6 grams: polyunsaturated fat;
- 1 gram: dietary fiber;

150.   Lamb Stew With Funghi Porcini

Serving: 6 servings | Prep: | Cook: | Ready in: 2hours30mins

Ingredients

- 1 ounce dried mushrooms (funghi porcini, also called cepes)
- 3 pounds boned shoulder of lamb cut in 2-inch cubes
- 1 tablespoon sugar
- 2 tablespoons peanut or vegetable oil
- 1 large onion, chopped
- 2 cloves garlic, minced
- 1 cup canned peeled tomatoes, chopped
- 1 tablespoon tomato paste
- 1 cup dry white wine
- 4 carrots, sliced
- 3 strips orange peel
- ½ teaspoon thyme
- Coarse salt and freshly ground pepper to taste

Direction

- Soak the mushrooms in one cup of warm water for 20 minutes. Meanwhile, trim the fat from the lamb and sprinkle the cubes with the sugar (this helps them to brown). Heat the oil in a large heavy casserole and brown the lamb pieces a few at a time, on all sides, turning them with tongs. Remove the browned pieces to a bowl.
- Pour off excess fat from the casserole. Add the onion and garlic and cook slowly until soft. Add the tomatoes, tomato paste, white wine and carrots. Scrape up the cooking juices with a spoon, stir well and return the lamb pieces to the casserole.
- Drain the mushrooms through a paper towel and add the liquid to the casserole. Rinse the mushrooms, chop them and add, along with the orange peel, thyme, salt and pepper. Simmer, covered, for two hours or until the meat is tender. Correct seasoning and serve.

Nutrition Information

- 734: calories;
- 54 grams: fat;
- 0 grams: trans fat;
- 23 grams: monounsaturated fat;
- 5 grams: polyunsaturated fat;
- 7 grams: sugars;
- 21 grams: saturated fat;
- 16 grams: carbohydrates;
- 3 grams: dietary fiber;
- 39 grams: protein;
- 901 milligrams: sodium;

151. Lapin Saute Aux Pruneaux (Sauteed Rabbit With Prunes)

Serving: Four servings | Prep: | Cook: | Ready in: 1hours

Ingredients

- 1 young rabbit, about 2 1/2 pounds, cleaned weight, cut into serving pieces
- ½ cup coarsely chopped carrots
- ½ cup coarsely chopped onions
- ½ cup coarsely chopped celery
- ¼ cup red-wine vinegar
- 2 cups dry red wine
- 4 sprigs fresh parsley
- 2 sprigs fresh thyme or 1/2 teaspoon dried
- 1 bay leaf
- Salt to taste, if desired
- Freshly ground pepper to taste
- 2 tablespoons olive oil
- 1 tablespoon butter
- 2 tablespoons flour
- ½ cup fresh or canned chicken broth
- ¾ pound packaged pitted prunes, about 30

Direction

- In a mixing bowl, combine the rabbit pieces, carrots, onions, celery, vinegar, wine, parsley, thyme, bay leaf, salt and pepper. Cover and refrigerate. Let stand overnight or up to 24 hours, turning the pieces occasionally.
- Drain and reserve the strained liquid. Reserve the rabbit pieces and vegetables, but discard the parsley, thyme and bay leaf.
- Heat the oil and butter in a heavy casserole and add the rabbit pieces. Cook until nicely browned on one side, about four or five minutes. Turn the pieces and cook until browned on the second side.
- Scatter the reserved vegetables in the casserole and stir. Cook briefly and pour off all fat.
- Sprinkle the rabbit pieces with flour and stir. Add the reserved marinating liquid and stir. Add the broth. Bring to the boil and cover. Cook about 20 minutes and add the prunes. Cover and cook 20 minutes. Serve.

Nutrition Information

- 967: calories;
- 0 grams: trans fat;
- 5 grams: polyunsaturated fat;
- 66 grams: carbohydrates;
- 83 grams: protein;
- 32 grams: fat;
- 9 grams: saturated fat;
- 12 grams: monounsaturated fat;
- 8 grams: dietary fiber;
- 35 grams: sugars;
- 1646 milligrams: sodium;

152. Lasagna With Collard Greens

Serving: 6 servings | Prep: | Cook: | Ready in: 1hours20mins

Ingredients

- ½ pound collard greens, preferably large leaves, stemmed and washed, leaves left intact
- Salt to taste

- Extra virgin olive oil for the pan
- 2 cups marinara sauce, preferably homemade from fresh or canned tomatoes
- ½ pound no-boil lasagna noodles
- ½ pound ricotta
- 4 ounces freshly grated Parmesan

Direction

- Steam the collard greens for 5 minutes above an inch of boiling water, or blanch in boiling salted water for 2 minutes. Transfer to a bowl of cold water, drain and pat dry with paper towels.
- Preheat the oven to 350 degrees. Oil a 2- or 3-quart rectangular baking dish with olive oil. Spread a small amount of tomato sauce over the bottom and top with a layer of lasagna noodles. Top the noodles with a thin layer of ricotta. Lay collard green leaves over the ricotta in a single layer. Top the leaves with a layer of tomato sauce, followed by a thin layer of Parmesan.
- Set aside enough tomato sauce and Parmesan to top the lasagna and repeat the layers until all of the ingredients are used up. Spread the tomato sauce you set aside over the top, and sprinkle on the Parmesan. Make sure the noodles are covered, and cover the baking dish tightly with foil.
- Place in the oven and bake 30 minutes. Remove from the oven and uncover. Check to be sure that the noodles are soft and the mixture is bubbly. Return to the oven for another 5 to 10 minutes if desired, to brown the top. Allow to sit for 10 minutes before serving.

Nutrition Information

- 331: calories;
- 14 grams: fat;
- 35 grams: carbohydrates;
- 4 grams: dietary fiber;
- 3 grams: sugars;
- 18 grams: protein;
- 500 milligrams: sodium;

- 7 grams: saturated fat;
- 5 grams: monounsaturated fat;
- 1 gram: polyunsaturated fat;

153.   Lasagna With Pistou And Mushrooms

Serving: Serves 6 | Prep: | Cook: |Ready in: 1hours15mins

Ingredients

- For the pistou
- 1 cup, tightly packed, basil leaves (1 ounce)
- 1 large garlic clove, peeled, halved green shoot removed if there is one
- Salt to taste
- 3 tablespoons extra virgin olive oil
- 1 ounce Parmesan, grated (1/4 cup, tightly packed)
- For the lasagna
- 1 egg
- ½ pound fresh ricotta
- Salt and freshly ground pepper
- 2 tablespoons extra virgin olive oil
- 1 pound mushrooms, sliced
- 1 garlic clove, minced
- 2 tablespoons dry white wine (optional)
- 6 to 8 ounces no-boil lasagna noodles (depending on the size of your baking dish)
- 2 ounces freshly grated Parmesan (1/2 cup, tightly packed)

Direction

- Grind the basil leaves and garlic in a food processor fitted with the steel blade, or in a mortar and pestle. Add salt to taste and slowly drizzle in the olive oil. Blend or grind until smooth. Blend in the Parmesan (1/4 cup) and set aside.
- In a medium size bowl whisk the egg and add the ricotta and the pistou. Whisk to blend well.
- Heat 1 tablespoon of the olive oil over medium-high heat in a large, heavy skillet and

add the mushrooms. Do not stir for about 1 minute, then shake the pan and cook, stirring occasionally, until the mushrooms are moist and beginning to soften. Add a generous pinch of salt and the garlic and cook, stirring, for another minute or two. Add the wine if using, or a couple of tablespoons of water or stock and cook, stirring, until the mushrooms are tender and fragrant, another couple of minutes. Season to taste with salt and pepper. Remove from the heat.

- Preheat the oven to 350 degrees. Lightly oil a rectangular baking dish with olive oil. Spread a small spoonful of the ricotta mixture in a thin layer over the bottom of the baking dish. Top with a layer of lasagna noodles. Top the noodles with a thin layer of ricotta, spooning on a few dollops then spreading it with an offset or a rubber spatula. Top the ricotta with half the mushrooms, and sprinkle Parmesan over the mushrooms. Repeat the layers, then add a final layer of lasagna noodles topped with ricotta and Parmesan. Make sure that the noodles are covered with ricotta and that there are no dry exposed edges. Drizzle a little bit of olive oil over the top.

- Cover the baking dish tightly with foil and place in the oven. Bake 35 to 40 minutes, until the noodles are tender and the mixture is bubbling. Remove from the heat and allow to sit for 5 to 10 minutes before serving.

Nutrition Information

- 375: calories;
- 21 grams: fat;
- 7 grams: saturated fat;
- 2 grams: dietary fiber;
- 17 grams: protein;
- 0 grams: trans fat;
- 11 grams: monounsaturated fat;
- 30 grams: carbohydrates;
- 3 grams: sugars;
- 432 milligrams: sodium;

154. Lasagna With Roasted Brussels Sprouts And Carrots

Serving: 6 servings | Prep: | Cook: | Ready in: 1hours20mins

Ingredients

- ¾ pound brussels sprouts, trimmed at base and sliced (not much thicker than 1/4 inch; I get about 3 slices out of a small brussels sprout, 4 out of a larger one)
- ½ pound carrots, peeled and sliced on the diagonal
- Salt and freshly ground pepper
- 3 tablespoons extra virgin olive oil, plus additional for oiling baking dish
- 8 ounces ricotta cheese
- 1 egg
- 1 tablespoon water
- Very small pinch of cinnamon
- Salt and freshly ground pepper
- 2 ⅓ to 2 ½ cups marinara sauce (more to taste)
- 7 to 8 ounces no-boil lasagna (depends on the size and shape of your dish)
- 4 ounces (1 cup) freshly grated Parmesan

Direction

- Heat oven to 425 degrees. Line a sheet pan with parchment. Place brussels sprouts and carrots on the parchment and season with salt and pepper. Toss with 2 tablespoons olive oil until evenly coated. Place in oven and roast 15 to 20 minutes, stirring every 5 to 10 minutes, until tender and lightly colored. Remove from oven and turn heat down to 350 degrees.
- Lightly oil a rectangular baking dish.
- Blend ricotta cheese with egg, water, cinnamon, and salt and pepper to taste.
- Spread a small spoonful of tomato sauce in a thin layer over the bottom of the baking dish. Top with a layer of lasagna noodles. Top the noodles with a thin layer of ricotta. Spoon on a few dollops then spread with an offset or a rubber spatula. Top ricotta with half the

brussels sprouts and carrots, and top vegetables with a layer of tomato sauce and a layer of Parmesan. Repeat layers, then add a final layer of lasagna noodles topped with tomato sauce and Parmesan. Drizzle remaining tablespoon of oil over the top.

- Cover baking dish tightly with foil and place in the oven. Bake 40 minutes, until the noodles are tender and the mixture is bubbling. Remove from the heat and allow to sit for 5 to 10 minutes before serving.

Nutrition Information

- 438: calories;
- 20 grams: protein;
- 8 grams: monounsaturated fat;
- 0 grams: trans fat;
- 7 grams: dietary fiber;
- 10 grams: sugars;
- 2 grams: polyunsaturated fat;
- 46 grams: carbohydrates;
- 791 milligrams: sodium;

155. Lemon And Blood Orange Gelée Parfaits

Serving: Serves 6 | Prep: | Cook: | Ready in: 1hours30mins

Ingredients

- For the lemon layer
- 1 tablespoon powdered unflavored gelatin (1 envelope plus 1/2 teaspoon)
- 1 ¼ cups water
- 6 to 7 tablespoons sugar (to taste; I like to use organic sugar, which is coarser than regular granulated sugar and has an off-white color)
- ⅔ cup strained freshly squeezed lemon or Meyer lemon juice
- For the blood orange layer
- 2 tablespoons powdered unflavored gelatin (2 envelopes plus 1 teaspoon)

- ½ cup water
- ¼ cup sugar
- 3 ½ cups freshly squeezed blood orange juice, all but 1/2 cup of it strained of pulp

Direction

- Get out six 6- or 8-ounce glasses (I use 6-ounce tumblers that taper out from the bottom).
- Make the lemon layer. Place the gelatin in a medium bowl and pour in 1/4 cup of the water. Allow the gelatin to sit and "bloom" for 10 minutes. Combine the remaining water and the sugar in a saucepan and bring to a bare simmer. Simmer until the sugar has dissolved and remove from the heat. Pour over the gelatin mixture and stir until the gelatin has dissolved. Stir in the lemon juice. Pour about an inch into each of the glasses. Place in the refrigerator until set, about 1 hour.
- Make the blood orange gelée. Juice all but one of the oranges and strain. Juice the remaining orange, strain out the seeds but not the pulp, and add to the strained juice. Place the gelatin in a medium bowl and pour in 1/4 cup of the water. Allow the gelatin to sit and "bloom" for 10 minutes. Combine the remaining water and the sugar in a saucepan and bring to a bare simmer. Simmer until the sugar has dissolved and remove from the heat. Pour over the gelatin mixture and stir until the gelatin has dissolved. Stir in the orange juice. Make sure that the lemon layers are set and fill the tumblers with the orange juice mixture. If you want, you can make different patterns, alternating stripes of orange and yellow, but you will have to allow each layer to set before you add the next one. Refrigerate for several hours, until set.

Nutrition Information

- 170: calories;
- 0 grams: dietary fiber;
- 39 grams: carbohydrates;
- 35 grams: sugars;
- 5 grams: protein;

- 13 milligrams: sodium;

156. Lentils, Potatoes And Peas In Indian Style Tomato Sauce

Serving: 2 servings | Prep: | Cook: |Ready in: 30mins

Ingredients

- 12 ounces new potatoes
- ½ cup red lentils
- 8 ounces whole onion or 7 ounces chopped, ready-cut onion (1 2/3 cups)
- 2 teaspoons olive oil
- 1 clove garlic
- 1 teaspoon ground cumin
- ½ teaspoon ground coriander
- ⅛ to ¼ teaspoon hot-pepper flakes
- 1 15- or 16-ounce can tomato puree, no salt added
- 1 teaspoon sun-dried-tomato paste
- ½ cup dry red wine
- 1 cup frozen peas
- 1 tablespoon balsamic vinegar
- 3 tablespoons raisins
- Freshly ground black pepper

Direction

- Scrub potatoes, and cut into 1-inch pieces. Place in pot with lentils and 3 cups of water. Cover, and bring to a boil. Cook over medium-high heat for about 10 minutes, until lentils and potatoes are cooked.
- Chop whole onion, and saute in hot oil in a nonstick skillet.
- Mince garlic, and add to onion; stir in cumin, coriander and hot-pepper flakes, cooking until onion is soft.
- Stir in tomato puree, tomato paste and wine, and simmer.
- When lentils and potatoes are cooked, drain well and stir into tomato mixture. Then, add

peas, vinegar and raisins. Continue cooking about 3 minutes.

Nutrition Information

- 555: calories;
- 167 milligrams: sodium;
- 6 grams: fat;
- 1 gram: polyunsaturated fat;
- 4 grams: monounsaturated fat;
- 98 grams: carbohydrates;
- 16 grams: dietary fiber;
- 22 grams: protein;

157. Light Lentil Soup With Smoked Trout

Serving: 4 servings. | Prep: | Cook: |Ready in: 1hours

Ingredients

- 1 cup (6 ounces) lentils, rinsed
- 1 onion, cut in half
- 2 garlic cloves, minced
- A bouquet garni made with a Parmesan rind, a bay leaf and a sprig of parsley
- 7 cups water
- Salt to taste
- Freshly ground pepper
- 4 ounces smoked trout, drained and rinsed if canned
- 2 tablespoons chopped fresh parsley

Direction

- Combine the lentils, onion, garlic, bouquet garni, water, and salt to taste in a soup pot or a large saucepan and bring to a boil. Reduce the heat, cover and simmer 45 minutes, or until the lentils are tender. Add pepper, taste and adjust salt. Remove the onion halves and bouquet garni and discard. Stir in the parsley.
- Divide the smoked trout among 4 bowls. Ladle in the soup and serve.

Nutrition Information

- 202: calories;
- 6 grams: dietary fiber;
- 16 grams: protein;
- 1214 milligrams: sodium;
- 2 grams: sugars;
- 0 grams: saturated fat;
- 1 gram: polyunsaturated fat;
- 31 grams: carbohydrates;

---

158. Linguine Puttanesca

Serving: 4 servings | Prep: | Cook: | Ready in: 35mins

Ingredients

- Salt
- 3 tablespoons extra-virgin olive oil
- 4 cloves garlic, sliced thin
- 2 pounds ripe plum tomatoes, chopped fine, or a 35-ounce can plum tomatoes drained and chopped fine
- 8 anchovy fillets, chopped
- 1 ½ tablespoons capers
- 12 black Italian or Greek olives, pitted and chopped
- Hot red pepper flakes to taste
- 1 pound linguine
- 2 tablespoons minced fresh basil
- 1 tablespoon minced flat parsley

Direction

- Bring a large pot of salted water to a boil for the linguine.
- While the water is heating, place 2 tablespoons of the olive oil in a large skillet, add the garlic and cook over low heat for five minutes, until the garlic softens and becomes fragrant but does not brown. Add the tomatoes.
- Increase heat to medium high and cook for 10 minutes, until the tomatoes give off their juices

and the sauce begins to thicken. Add the anchovies, capers, olives and red pepper flakes, lower heat to medium and cook about 5 minutes longer.
- As soon as the water comes to a boil, add the linguine and cook it until it is al dente, about 7 minutes. Drain and place in a warm serving bowl.
- Add the basil, parsley and remaining tablespoon of olive oil to the sauce. Taste it and add a pinch of salt if necessary. Spoon the sauce over the pasta, toss it well and serve at once.

Nutrition Information

- 582: calories;
- 14 grams: fat;
- 2 grams: polyunsaturated fat;
- 9 grams: sugars;
- 95 grams: carbohydrates;
- 7 grams: dietary fiber;
- 19 grams: protein;
- 872 milligrams: sodium;

---

159. Linguine With Creamy Arugula And Goat Cheese

Serving: 2 servings | Prep: | Cook: | Ready in: 20mins

Ingredients

- 1 cup arugula, about one bunch or less
- ½ cup nonfat plain yogurt
- ½ cup reduced-fat ricotta
- 3 tablespoons reduced-fat goat cheese
- ⅛ teaspoon salt
- Freshly ground black pepper to taste
- 8 ounces fresh eggless linguine

Direction

- Bring water to boil in covered pot for linguine.

- Trim and wash arugula thoroughly. Dry thoroughly.
- In food processor, blend yogurt, ricotta and goat cheese until creamy.
- Add arugula to ricotta mixture and blend until arugula is thoroughly blended. Season with salt and pepper.
- Cook linguine according to package directions.
- When linguine is cooked, drain and top immediately with sauce.

Nutrition Information

- 612: calories;
- 1 gram: polyunsaturated fat;
- 4 grams: dietary fiber;
- 8 grams: sugars;
- 3 grams: monounsaturated fat;
- 92 grams: carbohydrates;
- 29 grams: protein;
- 332 milligrams: sodium;
- 14 grams: fat;

160. Linguine With Lentils And Prosciutto

Serving: 6 servings | Prep: | Cook: | Ready in: 35mins

Ingredients

- 1 stalk celery, chopped
- 1 carrot, chopped
- 4 or 5 ounces onion, diced
- 1 tablespoon minced garlic
- 1 jalapeno, chopped
- ¼ teaspoon hot red pepper flakes
- 3 ounces prosciutto, diced
- 2 tablespoons olive oil
- 1 heaping cup red lentils
- Salt to taste
- 1 ½ pounds linguine
- 1 red onion, chopped

Direction

- Saute celery, carrot, onion, garlic, jalapeno, pepper flakes and prosciutto in the oil in a large, deep skillet for about 10 minutes, until very soft and fragrant.
- Add lentils and 5 cups water, and bring to a boil. Reduce heat, and boil gently until lentils are soft but not mushy, about 10 minutes. Season with salt.
- Cook the pasta according to the package directions. Drain, and add to the lentil mixture; toss well. Serve topped with chopped red onion.

Nutrition Information

- 626: calories;
- 527 milligrams: sodium;
- 8 grams: dietary fiber;
- 1 gram: polyunsaturated fat;
- 4 grams: monounsaturated fat;
- 111 grams: carbohydrates;
- 6 grams: sugars;
- 27 grams: protein;

161. Little Birds In A Nest

Serving: Four servings | Prep: | Cook: | Ready in: 1hours

Ingredients

- 8 slices filet mignon, each 1/3-inch thick, approximately 1 pound
- 8 paper-thin slices prosciutto
- 8 large leaves fresh sage
- 1 large eggplant, about 1 1/4 pounds
- 2 medium-sized zucchini, about 10 ounces
- About 3 tablespoons olive oil
- ½ teaspoon salt
- 1 large clove garlic, minced fine
- 2 teaspoons orange zest, shredded on the 1/8-inch holes of the grater
- ¼ cup fresh orange juice
- 1 ½ cups peeled, seeded, ripe fresh tomatoes, chopped fine (or use canned tomatoes)

- 1 tablespoon butter
- ¼ cup dry vermouth

Direction

- Pound the meat into sheets about an eighth-inch-thick. Place a slice of prosciutto on each, lay a sage leaf in the center and roll tightly, pressing constantly, tucking in the sides to make compact cylinders roughly three-and-a-half-inches long. Set aside, uncovered.
- Peel the eggplant and cut the flesh into large julienned strips - about the size of big french fries. Set aside.
- Cut the zucchini into julienned strips slightly smaller than the eggplant. Set aside.
- Put two tablespoons of the oil in a large, nonreactive saucepan over medium-high heat and heat until it almost smokes. Add the julienned eggplant, zucchini and salt, stirring well. Continue to cook, stirring often, until the eggplant is thoroughly soft and the zucchini barely translucent, about 15 minutes. The mixture may stick at first but will loosen as cooking proceeds. Remove the vegetables with a slotted spoon and keep them covered in a warm place. Reduce the heat to low.
- If necessary, add just enough additional oil to the pan to film the bottom. Add the garlic and orange zest and cook, stirring, for three minutes. Stir in the orange juice and tomatoes and simmer over medium heat for about 12 minutes, or until the sauce is thick.
- After the sauce has cooked five minutes, warm four large serving plates. Put the remaining tablespoon of oil in a wide, nonstick skillet over medium-high heat. When it shimmers, add the butter. Put in the beef rolls seam side down and cook until they are seared. Turn with tongs and continue cooking, shaking the pan, for about five minutes, or just until meat is nicely browned. Interior should remain pink. Remove the rolls, keeping them warm.
- Pour the vermouth into the skillet and boil, stirring to get up all browned bits, until reduced to about two tablespoons. Stir in the tomato sauce and any juices collected under the vegetables.
- Spread the sauce evenly over the plates. Make nests of the mixed vegetables and arrange two beef rolls on each. Serve at once.

Nutrition Information

- 1129: calories;
- 36 grams: monounsaturated fat;
- 16 grams: carbohydrates;
- 7 grams: dietary fiber;
- 82 grams: protein;
- 30 grams: saturated fat;
- 80 grams: fat;
- 0 grams: trans fat;
- 4 grams: polyunsaturated fat;
- 10 grams: sugars;
- 1389 milligrams: sodium;

---

162. Mango And Scotch Bonnet Barbecue Sauce

Serving: 6 cups | Prep: | Cook: | Ready in: 2hours

Ingredients

- 2 green bell peppers, halved, cored and seeded
- 2 red bell peppers, halved, cored and seeded
- 4 ripe tomatoes, peeled, seeded and halved
- 3 ripe mangoes, peeled, seeded and chopped
- 1 large sweet onion, chopped
- 2 tablespoons minced garlic
- 2 Scotch bonnet chilies, halved
- ¾ cup cider vinegar
- 1 ¼ cups, packed, light-brown sugar
- ¼ cup molasses
- ¼ cup Dijon mustard
- ¼ cup tamarind paste
- 2 tablespoons cinnamon
- 1 tablespoon ground cumin
- 1 tablespoon fresh thyme leaves
- 1 tablespoon fresh marjoram leaves

- Salt and freshly ground black pepper

Direction

- Light a home smoker, and smoke bell peppers and tomatoes 30 minutes, preferably over oak chips. Alternatively, a smoker can be made by completely lining bottom and cover of a wok with foil and placing two tablespoons each of rice, brown sugar and black tea leaves in bottom of wok. Place wok, covered, over medium heat. When smoke starts rising, put peppers and tomatoes on a rack in wok, cover, and smoke vegetables 30 minutes. Chop vegetables and transfer them to a 5-quart saucepan. (Without a smoker, peppers and tomatoes can be chopped and placed in saucepan.)
- Add remaining ingredients to saucepan with 1 cup water. Bring to a boil, reduce heat and simmer, stirring occasionally, 1 hour. Allow to cool briefly.
- Puree mixture in a food processor. You may have to do this in two shifts. Pass puree through a medium-mesh strainer. Check seasoning. Refrigerate until ready to use.

Nutrition Information

- 209: calories;
- 1 gram: fat;
- 0 grams: polyunsaturated fat;
- 51 grams: carbohydrates;
- 4 grams: dietary fiber;
- 44 grams: sugars;
- 2 grams: protein;
- 598 milligrams: sodium;

163. Marinated Brochettes Of Lamb With Honey

Serving: 4 servings | Prep: | Cook: | Ready in: 30mins

Ingredients

- 1 ½ pounds skinless, boneless loin or leg of lamb meat
- 4 tablespoons fresh lemon juice
- 4 tablespoons olive oil
- ½ cup dry red wine
- ⅓ cup honey
- 1 tablespoon chopped fresh rosemary or 2 teaspoons dried
- 1 tablespoon finely chopped garlic
- 2 teaspoons ground cumin
- Salt and freshly ground pepper to taste
- 2 large red peppers, cut into 16 2-inch squares
- 2 large white onions, cut into 16 2-inch squares
- 1 medium-size eggplant, cut into 16 2-inch squares 1/2-inch thick
- 8 tablespoons coarsely chopped fresh coriander or parsley

Direction

- Cut the lamb into 16 2-inch cubes.
- Combine the lamb with lemon juice, olive oil, wine, honey, rosemary, garlic, cumin, salt and pepper. Blend well, cover with plastic wrap and marinate for 15 minutes.
- Preheat the oven broiler or a charcoal grill. If wooden skewers are used, soak them in cold water until ready to use.
- Drain the meat, reserving the marinade, and arrange the meat on four skewers, alternating with red pepper, onion and eggplant squares.
- Broil under high heat 3 minutes for rare on each side, brushing with the reserved marinade.

Nutrition Information

- 784: calories;
- 25 grams: monounsaturated fat;
- 5 grams: polyunsaturated fat;
- 32 grams: protein;
- 51 grams: fat;
- 18 grams: saturated fat;
- 48 grams: carbohydrates;
- 8 grams: dietary fiber;
- 35 grams: sugars;

- 1301 milligrams: sodium;

164.   Marinated Pork

Serving: 2 servings | Prep: | Cook: | Ready in: 20mins

Ingredients

- 8 ounces pork tenderloin
- Fresh or frozen ginger to yield 1 tablespoon coarsely grated
- 1 teaspoon toasted sesame oil
- 2 tablespoons dry red or white wine
- 1 tablespoon hoisin sauce

Direction

- Turn on broiler, and cover pan with aluminum foil.
- Wash, dry and trim fat from tenderloin. Cut in half crosswise.
- Grate ginger, and combine with sesame oil, wine and hoisin sauce. Marinate pork in the mixture until it is time to broil.
- Broil pork two or three inches from source of heat 10 to 15 minutes, until meat is slightly pink inside, turning once. Slice and serve.

Nutrition Information

- 188: calories;
- 0 grams: dietary fiber;
- 3 grams: monounsaturated fat;
- 4 grams: carbohydrates;
- 24 grams: protein;
- 189 milligrams: sodium;
- 7 grams: fat;
- 2 grams: sugars;

165.   Mark Strausman's Grilled Mushrooms

Serving: 4 servings | Prep: | Cook: | Ready in: 20mins

Ingredients

- 1 anchovy mashed, or 1 1/2 teaspoons anchovy paste
- 2 cloves garlic, minced
- ¼ cup lemon juice
- ⅓ cup extra-virgin olive oil
- Salt and freshly ground black pepper to taste
- 1 pound mushrooms with large caps (portobello, cremini, oyster, shiitake or a mixture)
- ¼ cup vegetable oil
- 1 tablespoon chopped Italian parsley

Direction

- Preheat the grill.
- Mash the anchovy or anchovy paste with the garlic in a mortar. Blend in the lemon juice and olive oil. Season to taste with salt and pepper, and set aside.
- Wipe any soil from the mushrooms with a damp paper towel. Remove stems from the mushrooms, and discard or set aside for another use, like making stock. (It is not necessary to do this with oyster mushrooms.) Brush the caps with the vegetable oil, and sprinkle with salt and pepper.
- Place the caps on the grill, top side down, and grill for a minute or two. Give each cap a quarter turn to set crisscross grill marks, and continue grilling another minute. Turn the caps over, and grill another minute or two, until a knife can easily pierce the cap.
- Remove the mushrooms from the grill, and arrange them on a plate. Beat the dressing to reblend it, and sprinkle it over the warm mushrooms. Scatter the parsley on top, and serve.

Nutrition Information

- 317: calories;
- 33 grams: fat;
- 5 grams: polyunsaturated fat;
- 383 milligrams: sodium;
- 3 grams: sugars;
- 0 grams: trans fat;
- 23 grams: monounsaturated fat;
- 6 grams: carbohydrates;
- 1 gram: dietary fiber;
- 4 grams: protein;

166.   Mashed Potatoes With Scallions

Serving: 4 servings | Prep: | Cook: | Ready in: 25mins

Ingredients

- 5 Idaho or Washington potatoes, about 1 1/2 pounds
- Salt to taste
- 2 tablespoons unsalted butter
- 1 ⅓ cups milk
- ⅓ cup finely chopped scallions
- Freshly ground white pepper to taste
- ⅛ teaspoon freshly grated nutmeg

Direction

- Peel the potatoes and cut them into 2-inch cubes. Place the cubes in a saucepan. Add water to cover and salt.
- Bring to a boil and simmer 15 minutes, or until tender. Drain and put the potatoes through a food mill or mash them well with a potato masher. Add the butter and beat to blend. Stir in the milk, scallions, salt, pepper and nutmeg. Serve piping hot.

Nutrition Information

- 311: calories;
- 8 grams: protein;
- 9 grams: fat;

- 5 grams: saturated fat;
- 2 grams: monounsaturated fat;
- 1 gram: polyunsaturated fat;
- 52 grams: carbohydrates;
- 6 grams: sugars;
- 0 grams: trans fat;
- 847 milligrams: sodium;

167.   Melon And Lime Parfait

Serving: Serves 6 | Prep: | Cook: | Ready in: 1hours20mins

Ingredients

- 1 small Cavaillon melon or cantaloupe, seeded and flesh cut into chunks
- ½ cup plain full-fat yogurt
- Grated zest of 1 lime
- ½ cup 2-percent milk
- ½ teaspoon Banyuls or other flavorful white-wine vinegar

Direction

- Purée the melon in a food processor, then refrigerate for at least 1 hour. Combine the yogurt and lime zest. Divide the yogurt mixture among six glasses. Chill.
- Just before serving, carefully pour the melon purée atop the yogurt in each glass.
- In a food processor, combine the milk and vinegar and pulse until solidly foamy on top. Place a spoonful of the foam in each glass and serve immediately.

Nutrition Information

- 60: calories;
- 0 grams: polyunsaturated fat;
- 11 grams: carbohydrates;
- 10 grams: sugars;
- 2 grams: protein;
- 35 milligrams: sodium;

- 1 gram: dietary fiber;

- 374 milligrams: sodium;
- 21 grams: fat;
- 12 grams: monounsaturated fat;
- 3 grams: dietary fiber;
- 45 grams: protein;

168. Mexican Mako

Serving: 6 servings | Prep: | Cook: | Ready in: 13mins

Ingredients

- 1 teaspoon chili powder
- 1 teaspoon ground cumin
- 3 tablespoons extra-virgin olive oil
- Juice of 2 limes
- 2 ½ to 3 pounds mako shark, 1 inch thick
- ½ teaspoon salt or to taste
- 1 ripe avocado
- Fresh coriander leaves for garnish

Direction

- Mix chili powder, cumin, oil and the juice of one lime together in a shallow dish that will hold the fish in a single layer. Season with salt.
- Trim the skin from the fish and cut the fish into six pieces of uniform size. Place the fish in the dish, turn it to coat both sides with the marinade, then cover and refrigerate for two hours, turning it once during this time.
- Preheat grill. While the grill is preheating, peel and pit the avocado and cut it into thin slices. Mix the avocado slices with the remaining lime juice.
- Grill the fish over very hot coals until seared on the outside and still slightly pink in the middle. Brush with the marinade while grilling.
- Serve garnished with avocado slices and fresh coriander leaves.

Nutrition Information

- 393: calories;
- 4 grams: polyunsaturated fat;
- 6 grams: carbohydrates;
- 1 gram: sugars;

169. Middle Eastern Salad

Serving: Six servings | Prep: | Cook: | Ready in: 30mins

Ingredients

- 2 cups small French lentils
- 4 tablespoons fresh lemon juice
- ¼ cup extra-virgin olive oil
- 1 teaspoon ground cumin, toasted
- ½ teaspoon ground turmeric
- ¼ teaspoon Tabasco sauce
- ½ teaspoon salt, plus more to taste
- Freshly ground black pepper to taste
- 2 tablespoons finely chopped mint
- 2 tablespoons finely chopped dill
- 3 scallions, chopped

Direction

- Simmer the lentils in 4 cups of water until barely tender, about 20 minutes. Drain and cool. Add half the lemon juice. Toss well and set aside.
- Put the olive oil in a skillet over high heat. Add the cumin and the turmeric, stirring constantly, for 1 minute. Remove from heat. Add the Tabasco, the salt and the remaining lemon juice and stir this into the lentils. Stir carefully to avoid getting a big mushy mess. Taste and adjust seasoning with additional salt and some pepper if you choose. Gently stir in the mint, dill and scallions, arrange on a large platter and serve at room temperature buffet style.

Nutrition Information

- 313: calories;
- 0 grams: trans fat;
- 7 grams: dietary fiber;
- 2 grams: sugars;
- 16 grams: protein;
- 10 grams: fat;
- 1 gram: polyunsaturated fat;
- 42 grams: carbohydrates;
- 202 milligrams: sodium;

170.   Minted Rice Pilaf

Serving: 5 cups; 8 servings as a side dish | Prep: | Cook:
| Ready in: 43mins

Ingredients

- 10 sprigs mint, stems reserved and leaves chopped (about 1/4 cup)
- 1 ½ cups chicken or vegetarian broth
- 1 ½ cups water
- 1 medium-size onion (about 6 ounces), peeled and finely chopped
- 2 tablespoons olive oil
- 1 ½ cups converted white rice, or basmati
- ½ teaspoon kosher salt
- Freshly ground black pepper to taste

Direction

- Place mint stems, chicken broth and water in a 2 1/2-quart souffle dish or casserole with tight-fitting lid. Cook, covered, at 100 percent power in a 650- to 700-watt oven for 10 minutes. If using plastic, prick to release steam.
- Remove from oven and uncover. Strain liquid and allow liquid to cool to room temperature. Reserve.
- Place onion and oil in the 2 1/2-quart souffle dish or casserole. Cover and cook at 100 percent power for 4 minutes.
- Remove from oven and uncover. Stir in rice. Cook, uncovered, at 100 percent power for 1 minute 30 seconds.

- Remove from oven. Stir in reserved liquid. Recover and cook at 100 percent power for 10 minutes.
- Remove from oven and uncover. Stir in 2 tablespoons of the chopped mint leaves. Recover and cook for 8 minutes longer.
- Remove from oven and uncover. Stir in remaining chopped mint, salt and pepper. Serve hot.

Nutrition Information

- 172: calories;
- 3 grams: protein;
- 0 grams: polyunsaturated fat;
- 31 grams: carbohydrates;
- 128 milligrams: sodium;
- 4 grams: fat;
- 1 gram: sugars;

171.   Miso Glazed Eggplant

Serving: Serves 4 as an appetizer or side dish | Prep: |
Cook: | Ready in: 45mins

Ingredients

- 2 long Japanese eggplants or 4 small Italian eggplants (about 3/4 pound)
- Salt to taste
- 1 teaspoon sesame oil, plus additional for the baking sheet
- 1 tablespoon mirin
- 1 tablespoon sake
- 2 tablespoons white or yellow miso
- 1 tablespoon sugar

Direction

- Cut the eggplants in half lengthwise and cut off the stem and calyx. Using the tip of a paring knife, cut an incision down the middle of each half, making sure not to cut through the skin, but cutting down to it. Salt the eggplant lightly and let sit for 10 minutes. Meanwhile preheat the oven to 425 degrees. Line a baking sheet with foil or parchment and brush with sesame oil.

- Blot the eggplants with paper towels and place, cut side down, on the baking sheets. Roast for 15 to 20 minutes, until the skin is beginning to shrivel and the flesh is soft. Remove from the oven, carefully turn the eggplants over, and preheat the broiler.
- To make the glaze, combine the mirin and sake in the smallest saucepan you have and bring to a boil over high heat. Boil 20 seconds, taking care not to boil off much of the liquid, then turn the heat to low and stir in the miso and the sugar. Whisk over medium-low heat without letting the mixture boil, until the sugar has dissolved. Remove from the heat and whisk in the sesame oil.
- Brush the eggplants with the miso glaze, using up all of the glaze. Place under the broiler, about 2 inches from the heat, and broil for about 1 minute, until the glaze begins to bubble and looks shiny. Remove from the heat. Allow to cool if desired or serve hot. To serve, cut the eggplant halves on the diagonal into 1- to 1-1/2-inch slices.

Nutrition Information

- 117: calories;
- 2 grams: fat;
- 0 grams: saturated fat;
- 1 gram: polyunsaturated fat;
- 9 grams: dietary fiber;
- 13 grams: sugars;
- 684 milligrams: sodium;
- 22 grams: carbohydrates;
- 4 grams: protein;

---

172.   Miso Glazed Fish

Serving: 4 servings | Prep: | Cook: | Ready in: 3hours30mins

Ingredients

- ¼ cup mirin
- ¼ cup sake
- 3 tablespoons white or yellow miso paste
- 1 tablespoon sugar
- 2 teaspoons dark sesame oil
- 4 salmon, trout, Arctic char, mahi mahi or black cod fillets, about 6 ounces each

Direction

- Combine the mirin and sake in the smallest saucepan you have and bring to a boil over high heat. Boil 20 seconds, taking care not to boil off much of the liquid, then turn the heat to low and stir in the miso and the sugar. Whisk over medium heat without letting the mixture boil until the sugar has dissolved. Remove from the heat and whisk in the sesame oil. Allow to cool. Transfer to a wide glass or stainless steel bowl or baking dish.
- Pat the fish fillets dry and brush or rub on both sides with the marinade, then place them in the baking dish and turn them over a few times in the marinade remaining in the dish. Cover with plastic wrap and marinate for 2 to 3 hours, or for up to a day.
- Light the broiler or prepare a grill. Line a sheet pan with foil and oil the foil. Tap each fillet against the sides of the bowl or dish so excess marinade will slide off. Place skin side up on the baking sheet if broiling.
- Place the fish skin side down on the grill, or skin side up under the broiler, about 6 inches from the heat. Broil or grill for 2 to 3 minutes on each side, until the surface browns and blackens in spots. If necessary (this will depend on the thickness of the fillets) finish in a 400-degree oven, for about 5 minutes, until the fish is opaque and can be pulled apart easily with a fork.

Nutrition Information

- 450: calories;
- 36 grams: protein;

- 576 milligrams: sodium;
- 7 grams: monounsaturated fat;
- 4 grams: sugars;
- 1 gram: dietary fiber;
- 26 grams: fat;
- 6 grams: saturated fat;
- 8 grams: carbohydrates;

173.   Mississippi Mud Pie

Serving: 16 servings | Prep: | Cook: |Ready in: 1hours30mins

Ingredients

- For the graham cracker crust:
- About 15 whole graham crackers
- ¼ cup/50 grams granulated sugar
- ½ teaspoon kosher salt
- 8 tablespoons/114 grams (1 stick) unsalted butter, melted
- For the Brownie Cake:
- 8 tablespoons/114 grams (1 stick) unsalted butter, cut into pieces
- 6 ounces/170 grams bittersweet chocolate, chopped
- ⅓ cup/67 grams dark brown sugar
- ⅓ cup/33 grams Dutch-processed cocoa powder, plus more for dusting
- 1 teaspoon pure vanilla extract
- ¾ teaspoon kosher salt
- 3 large eggs, separated
- ½ cup/100 grams granulated sugar
- ¼ cup/32 grams all-purpose flour
- For the chocolate custard:
- 4 ounces/113 grams bittersweet chocolate, chopped
- 2 tablespoons/29 grams unsalted butter, cut into pieces
- ½ cup/100 grams granulated sugar
- ¼ teaspoon kosher salt
- ¼ cup/25 grams Dutch-processed cocoa powder
- ¼ cup/28 grams cornstarch

- 2 cups/480 milliliters whole milk
- 4 large egg yolks
- To Finish:
- 1 ½ cups/360 milliliters cold heavy cream

Direction

- Heat the oven to 325 degrees. In a food processor, grind the graham crackers to fine crumbs — you should have about 2 1/4 cups crumbs — and tip into a bowl. Add sugar, salt and butter, and toss until evenly moistened. Tip the crumb mixture into a 9-inch springform pan. Use your fingers to press the crumbs into a thin, even layer on the bottom of the pan and at least 2 1/4 inches up its sides. Bake the crust until just set, about 10 minutes. (The crust will continue to cook in the next step.) Increase heat to 350 degrees.
- Prepare the cake: In a bowl set over a pot of barely simmering water but not touching it, melt together the butter and chocolate. (Alternatively, do this in short bursts in the microwave but be careful not to scorch the chocolate.) Remove the bowl from the heat and whisk in the dark brown sugar, cocoa powder, vanilla extract and salt. Let cool slightly, then whisk in the 3 large egg yolks.
- In large bowl, beat the remaining 3 large egg whites with an electric mixer on medium until foamy, about 30 seconds. While mixing, gradually add the granulated sugar in a steady stream. Increase the mixer speed to high and continue to beat until you have stiff peaks, about 3 minutes. Using a large rubber spatula, fold the egg-white mixture evenly into the chocolate mixture. Sift the flour evenly over the chocolate mixture and fold it in. Transfer the batter to the prepared crust and smooth the top. Bake until a crust has formed over the top, the center is just set and a toothpick inserted 1 inch from the edges comes out with moist crumbs attached, 30 to 35 minutes. The center of the cake, under the crust, should still be very moist and fudgy. (Peek under the crust if necessary.) Do not overbake. The cake will

sink slightly as it cools. Let the cake cool completely, at least 90 minutes.

- Prepare the custard: Set the chocolate and butter in a medium bowl. Place a fine-mesh sieve over the bowl and set it aside. In a medium saucepan, whisk together the sugar, salt, cocoa powder, and cornstarch. Add the milk, little by little, while whisking to incorporate it fully. Whisk in the egg yolks. Heat the mixture over medium heat, stirring constantly, until it has thickened and just come to a low boil. Continue to cook the custard, whisking, for another minute, then immediately pour it into the sieve, pushing it through with a small spatula. Let the custard stand for 1 minute, then whisk it together with the butter and chocolate until smooth. Pour the custard over the cooled cake. Cover the custard with plastic wrap or wax paper, making sure to press it gently into the surface of the custard. Chill until the custard has set completely, at least 4 hours and up to overnight.
- Just before serving, remove the ring from springform pan base and transfer pie to a serving plate. Whip the cream to soft peaks and spoon high dollops over the top of the pie, leaving about a 1-inch border. Dust with cocoa powder.

---

174. Mixed Greens Galette With Onions And Chickpeas

Serving: Serves 8 to 10 | Prep: | Cook: |Ready in: 2hours30mins

Ingredients

- 1 whole wheat Mediterranean pie crust
- 1 large onion
- 1 1-pound bag washed, stemmed greens, such as a Southern greens mix (kale, collards, turnip greens and spinach)
- Salt to taste
- 1 tablespoon extra virgin olive oil

- 2 plump garlic cloves, minced
- Freshly ground pepper
- 1 ½ teaspoons za'atar (see below)
- 1 can chickpeas, drained and rinsed
- 2 eggs
- 3 ounces feta
- 1 tablespoon egg wash (1 egg beaten with 1 teaspoon milk) for brushing the crust

Direction

- Mix together the dough for the crust and set it in a warm spot to rise. Meanwhile prepare the filling.
- Bring a large pot of water to a boil. Fill a bowl with cold water. Cut the onion into quarters, cutting from root to stem end, then cut thin slices across the grain.
- When the water in the pot reaches a boil, salt generously and add the greens. Boil for about 3 minutes, until tender. Use a skimmer to transfer the greens to the bowl of cold water, then drain. Take the greens up by the handful and squeeze out excess water. You can squeeze out the water most effectively if you take up small handfuls. Then coarsely chop (they are already chopped but the stems can be big). Set aside.
- Heat the olive oil over medium heat in a wide saucepan or a large skillet and add the onions. Cook, stirring often, until soft and golden, about 10 minutes. After the first couple of minutes of cooking add a generous pinch of salt so they don't brown too quickly or stick to the pan. When the onions are nicely colored and soft add the garlic and continue to cook for another 30 seconds to a minute, until fragrant. Stir in the greens and combine well with the onions. Add the za'atar and season to taste with salt and pepper. Stir in the chickpeas, taste and adjust seasonings, and set aside.
- Beat the eggs in a large bowl. Crumble in the feta and stir in the greens mixture. Stir well to combine.
- Dust a large work surface with flour and turn out the dough. Shape into a ball and let rest for

5 minutes. Then roll out into a thin round, 16 to 18 inches in diameter. Line a sheet pan with parchment and place the round in the middle, with the edges overlapping the pan (this will eliminate the need to lift the galette once it is filled). Place the filling in the middle of the rolled out pastry and spread it to a circle, leaving a 3 or 4-inch margin all the way around the pastry. Fold the edges in over the filling, pleating them to cover the filling and drawing them up to the middle of the galette, so that the filling is enclosed. The finished galette should be about 10 to 11 inches in diameter. There can be a small circle of exposed filling in the middle but it shouldn't be more than an inch in diameter. Cover with plastic wrap and place in the freezer for 45 minutes to an hour.

- Meanwhile, heat the oven to 375 degrees. Remove the galette from the freezer, brush with egg wash, and place in the oven. Bake 50 minutes, or until golden brown. Remove from the oven and let sit for at least 15 minutes before serving.

Nutrition Information

- 231: calories;
- 3 grams: sugars;
- 0 grams: trans fat;
- 2 grams: polyunsaturated fat;
- 5 grams: dietary fiber;
- 27 grams: carbohydrates;
- 7 grams: protein;
- 340 milligrams: sodium;
- 11 grams: fat;
- 4 grams: monounsaturated fat;

---

175. Monkfish With Tomatoes And Olive Oil

Serving: 4 servings | Prep: | Cook: | Ready in: 25mins

Ingredients

- 1 ½ pounds monkfish
- Juice of 1 lemon
- Salt and freshly ground pepper
- 6 tablespoons extra-virgin olive oil
- 2 tablespoons fresh bread crumbs
- 1 small onion, chopped
- 2 cloves garlic, minced
- 2 medium-sized ripe tomatoes, chopped
- 1 tablespoon minced fresh basil

Direction

- Slice monkfish into medallions about one-inch thick. Place in a dish, sprinkle with lemon juice and season with salt and pepper.
- Heat one tablespoon of oil in heavy skillet, add bread crumbs and saute until they are golden. Remove from pan and wipe out pan.
- Heat another two tablespoons of the olive oil in the skillet. Add onion and saute over medium heat until tender. Add garlic and saute briefly, then add tomatoes. Stir tomatoes in with other ingredients for a minute or two, just enough to warm them without cooking them through. Remove vegetables from pan.
- Add one more tablespoon of the oil to pan and cook the monkfish over medium heat, about three minutes on each side, until just cooked through. The monkfish will probably not take on any color. Arrange monkfish medallions on a warm platter or on individual plates.
- Return tomato mixture to skillet, add remaining two tablespoons of oil, stir, season with salt and pepper and add basil. Pour this mixture around the medallions of fish. Sprinkle the fish with the bread crumbs and serve.

Nutrition Information

- 348: calories;
- 2 grams: dietary fiber;
- 26 grams: protein;
- 675 milligrams: sodium;
- 23 grams: fat;

- 3 grams: sugars;
- 15 grams: monounsaturated fat;
- 9 grams: carbohydrates;

---

176. Mousse Au Chocolat

Serving: | Prep: | Cook: | Ready in: 15mins

Ingredients

- ½ pound sweet chocolate
- 3 tablespoons water
- ¼ cup sugar
- 4 eggs, separated
- 1 inch scraped vanilla bean
- 1 cup heavy cream, whipped

Direction

- In top of double boiler over hot water, melt the chocolate with the water and the sugar. Remove and cool.
- Add the yolks, one at a time, mixing well after each addition. Add the vanilla bean.
- Beat the whites until stiff. Fold into chocolate mixture. Spoon into six or eight individual pots, souffle dishes or ramekins. Refrigerate.
- To serve, top with whipped cream.

Nutrition Information

- 252: calories;
- 0 grams: trans fat;
- 24 grams: carbohydrates;
- 21 grams: sugars;
- 4 grams: protein;
- 41 milligrams: sodium;
- 17 grams: fat;
- 10 grams: saturated fat;
- 6 grams: monounsaturated fat;
- 1 gram: polyunsaturated fat;
- 2 grams: dietary fiber;

177. Mushroom Omelet With Chives

Serving: 2 servings | Prep: | Cook: | Ready in: 15mins

Ingredients

- For the mushroom omelet with chives
- 2 tablespoons plus 1 teaspoon extra-virgin olive oil
- 1 shallot, minced
- ¼ pound white or cremini mushrooms, rinsed briefly and wiped dry
- Salt
- freshly ground pepper to taste
- 1 to 2 garlic cloves (to taste), minced
- 2 teaspoons minced flat-leaf parsley
- 4 eggs
- 1 tablespoon minced chives
- 2 teaspoons low-fat milk
- 3 tablespoons grated Gruyère cheese

Direction

- Trim off the ends of the mushrooms, and cut into thick slices. Heat a large, heavy frying pan over medium-high heat, and add 1 tablespoon of the olive oil. Add the shallot, and cook, stirring, until it begins to soften, two or three minutes. Add the mushrooms, and cook, stirring or tossing in the pan, for a few minutes, until they begin to soften and sweat. Add salt to taste and the garlic, and cook, stirring often, until the mushrooms are tender, about five minutes. Stir in the parsley, season to taste with salt and pepper, and remove from the heat.
- If making individual omelets: Heat an 8-inch nonstick omelet pan over medium-high heat. Break 2 eggs into a bowl, and beat with a fork or a whisk until frothy. Add salt and freshly ground pepper to taste, and 2 teaspoons milk. Whisk in half the chives. Add 2 teaspoons of the olive oil to the pan. When the pan feels hot as you hold your hand above it, pour in the eggs, scraping every last bit into the pan. Tilt

the pan to distribute the eggs evenly over the surface. Tilt it slightly again, and gently shake with one hand while lifting up the edges of the omelet with the spatula in your other hand so as to let the eggs run underneath during the first few minutes of cooking. Spread half the mushrooms down the middle of the eggs. Top with half the cheese. As soon as the eggs are set on the bottom (the top will still be runny), jerk the pan quickly away from you then back towards you so that the omelet folds over on itself. Shake in the pan for another minute if you don't like the omelet soft on the inside; for a moist omelet, tilt the pan at once and roll out onto a plate. Keep warm in a low oven while you repeat with the remaining eggs and herbs, and serve.

- If making 1 large omelet, heat a 10-inch nonstick pan over medium-high heat. Beat all 4 eggs in a bowl with the milk, salt and pepper, and the chives. Heat the remaining tablespoon of olive oil in the pan, and follow the instructions for the 2-egg omelet, pouring all of the eggs into the pan. The eggs will take longer to set, and you may want to flip the omelet in the pan again after it's rolled, if the middle seems too runny. Roll the finished omelet onto a platter, or cut in half in the pan, and serve.

- Add 2 teaspoons of the olive oil to the pan. When the pan feels hot as you hold your hand above it, pour in the eggs, scraping every last bit into the pan. Tilt the pan to distribute the eggs evenly over the surface. Tilt it slightly again, and gently shake with one hand while lifting up the edges of the omelet with the spatula in your other hand so as to let the eggs run underneath during the first few minutes of cooking.

- Spread half the mushrooms down the middle of the eggs. Top with half the cheese. As soon as the eggs are set on the bottom (the top will still be runny), jerk the pan quickly away from you then back towards you so that the omelet folds over on itself. Shake in the pan for another minute if you don't like the omelet soft on the inside; for a moist omelet, tilt the

pan at once and roll out onto a plate. Keep warm in a low oven while you repeat with the remaining eggs and herbs, and serve.

Nutrition Information

- 388: calories;
- 509 milligrams: sodium;
- 0 grams: trans fat;
- 17 grams: monounsaturated fat;
- 4 grams: sugars;
- 2 grams: dietary fiber;
- 19 grams: protein;
- 31 grams: fat;
- 9 grams: saturated fat;
- 10 grams: carbohydrates;

---

178.   Mushroom And Beef Meatballs

Serving: 22 to 24 meatballs, serving 5 to 6 | Prep: | Cook: | Ready in: 2hours45mins

Ingredients

- 1 cup cubed Italian bread (2 ounces)
- ¼ cup milk
- 1 medium carrot (about 4 ounces), cut in 1/4 inch dice
- 2 teaspoons extra virgin olive oil
- ½ pound lean ground beef
- ½ pound roasted mushroom base (just under 1/2 recipe, about 1 1/3 cups)
- ¼ cup finely chopped onion
- 3 tablespoons beaten egg (1/2 extra large egg)
- 2 tablespoons finely chopped flat-leaf parsley
- Salt to taste (about 3/4 teaspoon)
- Freshly ground pepper

Direction

- Preheat the oven to 400 degrees. Put the bread in a bowl, toss with the milk (add a little more milk if 1/4 cup isn't enough to moisten all the bread) and let soak for 20 minutes.

- Meanwhile toss the carrots with 2 teaspoons olive oil on a parchment-covered sheet pan and roast for 15 to 20 minutes, stirring every 5 minutes, until tender and lightly browned (you can also make the mushroom base at this time).
- Squeeze the milk out of the bread and crumble the bread into a large bowl. Add the beef, mushrooms, carrots, onion, egg, parsley, salt, and pepper and mix together well.
- Turn the oven down to 300 degrees. Line a sheet pan with parchment. Working in batches, pulse the meat and vegetable mixture in a food processor fitted with the steel blade until pasty. Return to the bowl. Fill a small bowl with water for dipping your hands, then with wet hands form 1-ounce balls, which will be about the size of a golf ball, and place them on the parchment-lined baking sheet. You will need to keep wetting your hands.
- Bake 40 minutes, or until the meatballs are nicely browned. Remove from the oven and if desired, simmer for up to an hour in tomato sauce. I like to serve these with spaghetti.

Nutrition Information

- 161: calories;
- 10 grams: fat;
- 3 grams: saturated fat;
- 5 grams: monounsaturated fat;
- 2 grams: sugars;
- 289 milligrams: sodium;
- 0 grams: trans fat;
- 1 gram: dietary fiber;
- 9 grams: protein;

---

179.   Mussel Pizza

Serving: 1 14-inch pizza, serving 3. | Prep: | Cook: | Ready in: 45mins

Ingredients

- 16 to 20 black mussels (about 10 to 12 ounces)
- 1 whole-wheat pizza dough (1/2 batch, see recipe)
- 3 tablespoons extra virgin olive oil
- 2 large garlic cloves, minced or puréed
- ¾ cup canned crushed or puréed tomatoes
- Salt and freshly ground pepper
- ¼ cup chopped fresh parsley
- Dried red pepper flakes
- Dried oregano
- ½ ounce Parmesan, freshly grated (2 tablespoons)

Direction

- Clean the mussels. Inspect each one carefully and discard any that have opened (if some are partly opened, tap them with your finger, and if they close back up they are O.K.) or have cracked shells. Place in a large bowl, fill the bowl with cold water and rinse several times, swishing the mussels around in the water, pouring out the water and refilling. Clean the shells, if necessary, with a brush or the end of one of the mussels, and pull out the beards – the hairy attachments emerging from the shells. Do not do this until just before cooking, or the mussels will die and spoil.
- Preheat the oven to 450 degrees, preferably with a pizza stone in it. Roll out the pizza dough and place on a peel or on a lightly oiled pan.
- Bring 1 cup water or white wine to a boil in a large saucepan, pot or lidded skillet, and add the mussels. Cover and steam until they open, 3 to 4 minutes, stirring the mussels after the first 2 minutes. Using tongs, transfer the mussels to a bowl and discard the water or wine from the pan. When the mussels are cool enough to handle, remove them from their shells and toss with 2 tablespoons of the olive oil, 1 of the garlic cloves, a pinch of red pepper flakes and half of the parsley.
- Stir the remaining garlic into the tomatoes and season to taste with salt and pepper. Brush the

pizza dough, but not the rim, with the remaining tablespoon of olive oil. Spread the tomato sauce on the pizza and sprinkle with chili flakes and oregano or marjoram. Place in the hot oven and bake 10 minutes. Remove from the heat and arrange the mussels over the pizza. Pour on any marinade and return to the oven. Bake for another 10 minutes, or until the crust is brown and crispy on the edges. Remove from the heat, sprinkle with the remaining parsley and the Parmesan, and serve.

180. Mustardy Veal Stew

Serving: 4 to 6 servings | Prep: | Cook: | Ready in: 2hours

Ingredients

- 2 tablespoons extra-virgin olive oil
- ½ pound small fresh mushrooms
- 2 pounds stewing veal, in 1-inch cubes
- ½ cup chopped onion
- 2 cloves garlic, minced
- ½ cup veal or chicken stock
- ½ cup dry white wine
- 1 teaspoon fresh rosemary leaves
- ½ teaspoon dry thyme
- 3 tablespoons Dijon mustard
- 3 tablespoons heavy cream
- 1 ½ tablespoons drained capers
- Salt and freshly ground black pepper to taste
- 2 tablespoons minced fresh parsley

Direction

- Heat the oil in a heavy casserole. Brown mushrooms over high heat, then remove from casserole.
- Add the veal to the casserole, brown it lightly, then stir in the onion and garlic. Saute another couple of minutes, then add the stock, wine, rosemary and thyme. Return the mushrooms to the casserole.

- Cover and cook over low heat until the veal is tender, about one-and-a-half hours. Mix the mustard and cream together and stir it in. Cook uncovered about 10 minutes, until the sauce has thickened somewhat. Stir in the capers, then season with salt and pepper. Cook a few minutes longer, transfer to a serving dish and sprinkle with parsley.

Nutrition Information

- 276: calories;
- 5 grams: carbohydrates;
- 12 grams: fat;
- 4 grams: saturated fat;
- 0 grams: trans fat;
- 6 grams: monounsaturated fat;
- 1 gram: dietary fiber;
- 2 grams: sugars;
- 33 grams: protein;
- 619 milligrams: sodium;

181. Not Too Sweet Wok Popped Coconut Kettle Corn

Serving: About 12 cups popcorn | Prep: | Cook: | Ready in: 5mins

Ingredients

- 2 tablespoons coconut oil
- 6 tablespoons popcorn
- 2 tablespoons raw brown sugar
- Kosher salt to taste

Direction

- Place the coconut oil in a 14-inch lidded wok over medium heat. When the coconut oil melts add a few kernels of popcorn and cover. When you hear a kernel pop, quickly lift the lid and pour in all of the popcorn. Cover, turn the heat to medium-low, and cook, shaking the wok constantly, until you no longer hear the kernels popping against the lid. Turn off the heat, uncover and add the sugar and salt. Cover again and shake the wok vigorously for 30 seconds to a minute. Transfer the popcorn to a bowl, and if there is any caramelized sugar on the bottom of the wok scrape it out. Stir or toss the popcorn to distribute the caramelized bits throughout, and serve.

Nutrition Information

- 159: calories;
- 1 gram: monounsaturated fat;
- 0 grams: protein;
- 10 grams: carbohydrates;
- 9 grams: sugars;
- 56 milligrams: sodium;
- 14 grams: fat;
- 12 grams: saturated fat;

182.   Omelets With Roasted Vegetables And Feta

Serving: Serves 1 | Prep: | Cook: | Ready in: 2mins

Ingredients

- For each omelet
- 2 eggs
- Salt and freshly ground pepper to taste
- 2 to 3 teaspoons milk
- 2 teaspoons unsalted butter or extra virgin olive oil
- ⅓ cup Roasted Winter Vegetable Medley
- 1 tablespoon crumbled feta

Direction

- Break eggs into a bowl and beat with a fork or a whisk until frothy. Whisk in salt and pepper to taste and 2 to 3 teaspoons milk.
- Heat an 8-inch nonstick omelet pan over medium-high heat. Add 2 teaspoons unsalted butter or olive oil. When butter stops foaming

or oil feels hot when you hold your hand above it, pour eggs right into the middle of the pan, scraping every last bit into the pan with a rubber spatula. Swirl pan to distribute eggs evenly over the surface. Shake pan gently, tilting it slightly with one hand while lifting up edges of the omelet with the spatula in your other hand, to let eggs run underneath during first few minutes of cooking.

- As soon as eggs are set on the bottom, spoon roasted vegetables over the middle of the egg "pancake" and sprinkle feta over vegetables. Jerk pan quickly away from you then back towards you so that the omelet folds over onto itself. If you don't like your omelet runny in the middle, jerk pan again so that omelet folds over once more. Cook for 30 seconds to a minute longer. Tilt pan and roll omelet out onto a plate.

183.   Onion Gruyere Tart

Serving: 10 servings | Prep: | Cook: | Ready in: 1hours40mins

Ingredients

- 2 pounds yellow onions, peeled
- 4 tablespoons butter
- 1 teaspoon vegetable oil
- Pinch sugar
- ½ cup gewurztraminer
- Salt to taste
- Dash nutmeg
- ½ cup heavy cream
- 1 egg
- ¾ pound Gruyere cheese
- 1 11-inch tart crust, chilled (see recipe)

Direction

- Cut onions into slices about 1/4 inch thick. Chop coarsely.
- Heat butter and oil in heavy skillet. Add onions and cook, covered, over medium heat

about 10 minutes, or until onions are limp and begin to render liquid. Add pinch of sugar.

- Uncover onions and cook over medium-high heat 30 to 45 minutes. Stir frequently with a wooden spoon or spatula to scrape up brownings in pan. The onions should be a deep brown and reduced to a small mass. They must be watched carefully and stirred to prevent scorching and to ensure even browning.
- Transfer onions to a bowl. Add wine to skillet and boil, scraping up pan brownings, until liquid is reduced to a thick glaze. Add glaze to onions, along with salt, nutmeg, cream and egg. Adjust seasoning. (Dish may be prepared to this point a day in advance and refrigerated.)
- Preheat oven to 375 degrees.
- Grate cheese and distribute half of it on bottom of chilled pastry shell in pastry tin. Distribute onion mixture evenly over cheese; top with remaining cheese.
- Bake 40 to 45 minutes. If top browns too much, reduce heat slightly toward the end. Serve as a first course, warm or at room temperature. Tart can be made a few hours ahead, but do not refrigerate.

Nutrition Information

- 381: calories;
- 27 grams: fat;
- 0 grams: trans fat;
- 9 grams: monounsaturated fat;
- 15 grams: saturated fat;
- 2 grams: dietary fiber;
- 21 grams: carbohydrates;
- 4 grams: sugars;
- 13 grams: protein;
- 423 milligrams: sodium;

---

184. Orange Muscat Pears

Serving: 6 servings | Prep: | Cook: | Ready in: 35mins

Ingredients

- 1 ½ cups (1/2 bottle) sweet Muscat wine such as Muscat de Beaumes de Venise
- 3 tablespoons honey
- ½ cup orange juice
- ½ teaspoon ground coriander
- 6 firm ripe pears, peeled, cored and halved
- 3 tablespoons orange marmalade

Direction

- Combine the wine, honey, orange juice and coriander in a non-reactive three-quart sauce pan. Bring to a simmer and simmer for five minutes.
- Add pears and cook until they are just tender, about 15 minutes. Remove pears to a serving dish with a slotted spoon, draining them well.
- Boil cooking liquid until reduced by half. Stir in marmalade. Pour syrup over pears. Serve warm or cool.

Nutrition Information

- 222: calories;
- 8 milligrams: sodium;
- 0 grams: polyunsaturated fat;
- 49 grams: carbohydrates;
- 6 grams: dietary fiber;
- 35 grams: sugars;
- 1 gram: protein;

---

185. Orecchiette With Fresh And Dried Beans And Tomatoes

Serving: Serves 4 | Prep: | Cook: | Ready in: 2hours30mins

Ingredients

- ½ pound (about 1 1/2 cups) Good Mother Stallard Beans, pintos, or borlottis, rinsed and soaked for 4 hours or overnight in 1 quart water
- ½ large onion, or 1 small onion, cut in half or quartered
- 2 to 3 large garlic cloves, minced
- Salt to taste
- 1 cup marinara sauce (using fresh or canned tomatoes), or 1 cup finely chopped fresh tomatoes
- ½ pound orecchiette
- ½ pound green beans, broken into 2- or 3-inch lengths
- Slivered fresh basil leaves (about 2 tablespoons)
- Freshly grated Parmesan for serving

Direction

- To cook dried beans, transfer with their soaking water to a heavy pot. Add more water as necessary to cover the beans with 1 1/2 to 2 inches of water. Over medium-high heat, bring to a gentle boil and skim away foam. Add onion and garlic, cover, reduce heat to low and simmer 30 minutes. Add salt to taste (I use at least a rounded teaspoon), cover and continue to simmer very gently for 1 to 1 1/2 hours, until the beans are tender all the way through and their texture is plush and velvety. Taste the bean broth and add more salt as necessary. Remove from heat. Let beans cool in the broth if not using right away.
- Place a strainer over a bowl and drain beans. Measure out 1 cup of the broth and combine with the tomato sauce or tomatoes in a wide pan or a pasta bowl.
- Bring a large pot of water to a boil, salt generously and add orecchiette. Boil 5 minutes and add green beans. Boil another 5 minutes, until pasta is cooked al dente. Drain and toss green beans and pasta with the cooked beans and tomato sauce or tomatoes. Add half the basil and toss again.
- Serve in wide bowls, garnishing each serving with fresh basil and Parmesan.

Nutrition Information

- 290: calories;
- 2 grams: fat;
- 0 grams: monounsaturated fat;
- 1 gram: polyunsaturated fat;
- 58 grams: carbohydrates;
- 6 grams: dietary fiber;
- 10 grams: sugars;
- 11 grams: protein;
- 603 milligrams: sodium;

---

186.   Orecchiette With Raw And Cooked Tomatoes

Serving: Serves four | Prep: | Cook: | Ready in: 50mins

Ingredients

- 2 tablespoons extra virgin olive oil
- 1 small onion, chopped
- 2 large garlic cloves, green shoots removed, minced or thinly sliced, plus 1 small clove, green shoots removed, minced or pureed
- ¼ teaspoon crushed red pepper flakes (optional; more to taste)
- 2 pounds ripe tomatoes
- Pinch of sugar
- A few sprigs of fresh basil
- Salt to taste
- ¾ pound orecchiette
- Parmesan, Pecorino or ricotta salata for serving

Direction

- Set aside 1/2 pound of the tomatoes. Quarter the remaining tomatoes, or cut into wedges if very large. Heat 1 tablespoon of the olive oil in a wide, nonstick frying pan or in a 3-quart saucepan over medium heat. Add the onion. Cook, stirring often, until the onion is tender and golden, about eight minutes. Add the two large garlic cloves. Cook, stirring, until fragrant, 30 seconds to a minute. Add the quartered tomatoes, the sugar, basil sprigs and salt, and bring to a simmer. Simmer, stirring often, until the tomatoes have cooked down and the sauce is thick. Taste and adjust seasonings. Remove the basil sprigs, and put through the medium blade of a food mill. Return to the pan.

- Meanwhile, finely chop the tomatoes you set aside. Add the remaining small clove of garlic, salt to taste, 1 tablespoon extra virgin olive oil and a couple of leaves of basil, chopped or slivered. Allow to sit for 15 minutes.

- Bring a large pot of water to a boil, and salt generously. Add the pasta, and cook al dente, 10 to 12 minutes, following the cooking time suggestion on the package. If desired, stir 1/4 to 1/2 cup of the cooking water into the tomato sauce. Drain the pasta, and toss with both the warm tomato sauce and the uncooked tomato concassée. Serve with Parmesan, Pecorino or ricotta salata.

Nutrition Information

- 427: calories;
- 6 grams: dietary fiber;
- 13 grams: protein;
- 1 gram: polyunsaturated fat;
- 5 grams: monounsaturated fat;
- 789 milligrams: sodium;
- 9 grams: sugars;
- 0 grams: trans fat;
- 75 grams: carbohydrates;

187. Orzo With Fresh Tomato

Serving: Four servings | Prep: | Cook: | Ready in: 30mins

Ingredients

- 4 cups water
- Salt to taste

- 3 cups fresh orzo
- 2 tablespoons olive oil
- 4 tablespoons finely chopped onions
- ¾ pound ripe fresh tomatoes, peeled and cut into 1/2-inch cubes
- Freshly ground pepper to taste
- ¼ teaspoon hot red-pepper flakes

Direction

- Bring the water to a boil in a saucepan. Add salt. Cook the orzo according to package directions. Drain.

- Meanwhile, heat the oil in a saucepan. Cook the onions until they are wilted. Add the tomatoes, sprinkle with salt and pepper and the pepper flakes. Stir gently and bring the pan juices to a boil.

- Add the orzo and stir gently to blend.

Nutrition Information

- 385: calories;
- 5 grams: monounsaturated fat;
- 2 grams: dietary fiber;
- 3 grams: sugars;
- 1035 milligrams: sodium;
- 13 grams: protein;
- 9 grams: fat;
- 1 gram: saturated fat;
- 63 grams: carbohydrates;

188. Oustau De Baumaniere's Warm Oysters With Zucchini

Serving: Four to six servings as a first course | Prep: | Cook: | Ready in: 25mins

Ingredients

- 4 small zucchini, about 5 inches long, skins removed and reserved
- 3 ¾ cups fish stock
- 24 oysters

- 1 diced shallot
- 5 tablespoons unsalted butter
- ½ cup white wine
- 3 tablespoons creme fraiche

Direction

- Cut each zucchini into six rounds and each round in fourths. Bring three cups of the fish stock to a boil and add the zucchini, cooking for about four minutes until the zucchini is crunchy. Plunge the zucchini into cold water. Prepare a julienne with the skin of the zucchini, blanch rapidly in the fish stock and place in cold water. Drain and dry, saving the stock to reheat later.
- Shuck the oysters, reserving the oyster water.
- Saute the shallot in one tablespoon of the butter in a two-quart pan. Add the white wine, the remaining three-quarters cup of fish stock, the creme fraiche and reduce by half. Add the oyster water, then the remaining butter, then put through a chinoise or other strainer and return to the pan.
- Heat the oysters in the sauce without letting the sauce boil.
- Reheat the zucchini rounds in the reserved fish stock.
- On each serving plate, arrange zucchini rounds into four to six circles per plate. Top each zucchini round with an oyster and decorate with zucchini julienne. Surround with the sauce.

Nutrition Information

- 320: calories;
- 17 grams: fat;
- 0 grams: trans fat;
- 1 gram: dietary fiber;
- 24 grams: protein;
- 452 milligrams: sodium;
- 8 grams: saturated fat;
- 4 grams: monounsaturated fat;
- 2 grams: polyunsaturated fat;
- 15 grams: carbohydrates;

- 3 grams: sugars;

189.   Panna Cotta With Dulce De Leche

Serving: Serves 8 | Prep: | Cook: | Ready in: 4hours

Ingredients

- 3 cups heavy cream
- ⅓ cup sugar
- 1 vanilla bean, seeds scraped, pod and seeds reserved
- 1 (1/4-ounce) envelope gelatin (about 2 1/2 teaspoons)
- 1 cup dulce de leche or goat's-milk dulce de leche (see note)

Direction

- Combine the cream and sugar in a large saucepan, set over medium heat and bring to a boil. Whisk in the vanilla pod and seeds, breaking up the seed clumps. Lower the heat and gently simmer for 1 minute. Remove from the heat and let sit for 10 minutes.
- Pour the gelatin into a small saucepan. Add 2 tablespoons cold water and let sit for a few minutes. Put the saucepan over the lowest heat possible and warm it until the gelatin has dissolved, making sure it doesn't boil. Transfer the gelatin mixture to the vanilla-infused cream and whisk to combine. Remove the vanilla pod.
- Set out 8 (1/2-cup) glasses. Place 2 tablespoons of dulce de leche in each. (Avoid using a wet spoon: water will discolor the dulce de leche.)
- Divide the warm cream mixture between the glasses. Let cool to room temperature, then place in the refrigerator for at least 3 hours. If left for more than a day, the water in the panna cotta will discolor the dulce de leche, so do not prepare too far in advance.

Nutrition Information

- 464: calories;
- 36 grams: fat;
- 0 grams: trans fat;
- 10 grams: monounsaturated fat;
- 1 gram: polyunsaturated fat;
- 5 grams: protein;
- 84 milligrams: sodium;
- 22 grams: saturated fat;
- 32 grams: carbohydrates;
- 30 grams: sugars;

190.   Pappa Al Pomodoro

Serving: 5 to 6 servings as first course; 3 as main course | Prep: | Cook: | Ready in: 30mins

Ingredients

- ½ pound loaf stale Tuscan or other peasant bread
- 3 pounds very ripe tomatoes
- 6 tablespoons extra-virgin olive oil
- 1 large garlic clove, sliced
- 12 large basil leaves
- Freshly ground black pepper to taste
- Freshly grated Parmigiano Reggiano to taste (optional)

Direction

- Cut bread into large chunks. If any of the center is soft, discard it.
- Cut tomatoes in half. Squeeze out the seeds and discard. Cut tomatoes into large chunks.
- Heat oil in a large pot and saute garlic until it begins to brown.
- Stir in the tomatoes and cook for about 5 minutes, until they soften.
- Add bread and continue cooking, stirring occasionally, until bread has absorbed most of the liquid.
- Shred basil and stir in along with the pepper. Allow mixture to stand for about 15 minutes

or longer. Serve lukewarm or at room temperature. If desired, serve with grated Parmigiano, about one tablespoon a serving.

Nutrition Information

- 265: calories;
- 10 grams: monounsaturated fat;
- 4 grams: dietary fiber;
- 8 grams: sugars;
- 6 grams: protein;
- 204 milligrams: sodium;
- 15 grams: fat;
- 2 grams: polyunsaturated fat;
- 0 grams: trans fat;
- 28 grams: carbohydrates;

191.   Pasta E Fagioli

Serving: 8 servings | Prep: | Cook: | Ready in: 1hours50mins

Ingredients

- 1 recipe Simmered Pintos using only 1/2 pound (about 1 1/8 cups) beans
- 1 tablespoon extra virgin olive oil
- 1 medium or large onion, chopped
- 1 ½ teaspoons chopped fresh rosemary
- 2 large garlic cloves, minced
- 1 28-ounce can chopped tomatoes with juice
- Pinch of sugar
- Salt and freshly ground pepper
- 1 tablespoon tomato paste
- 1 small dried red pepper, or 1/4 to 1/2 teaspoon red pepper flakes (optional)
- A bouquet garni made with a bay leaf, 1 or 2 Parmesan rinds, and a few sprigs of thyme and parsley
- 6 ounces elbow macaroni or small shells (1 cup)
- 2 to 3 tablespoons chopped fresh parsley
- 2 ounces Parmesan cheese, grated (1/2 cup), optional

Direction

- Make the simmered beans as directed, changing only the amount of beans (use 2 quarts water). Remove onion and bay leaf, using tongs or a slotted spoon, as directed. Place a strainer over a bowl and drain beans. Measure broth and top up with enough water to make 6 cups.
- Heat oil over medium heat in a large, heavy casserole or Dutch oven and add chopped onion. Cook, stirring, until just tender, about 5 minutes. Add rosemary and garlic and stir together for another minute, until garlic is fragrant. Stir in tomatoes, add sugar, salt and pepper, and cook, stirring often, until tomatoes have cooked down and the mixture is very fragrant, 10 to 15 minutes.
- Add broth from the beans, tomato paste, hot pepper, bouquet garni, and salt to taste and bring to a boil. Reduce heat, cover and simmer 30 minutes. Stir in beans and heat through. Taste and adjust salt.
- 10 to 15 minutes before serving, stir in pasta. When it is cooked al dente, taste and adjust seasonings, stir in parsley, and serve, passing Parmesan in a bowl.

Nutrition Information

- 92: calories;
- 0 grams: polyunsaturated fat;
- 1 gram: monounsaturated fat;
- 16 grams: carbohydrates;
- 3 grams: protein;
- 4 grams: sugars;
- 322 milligrams: sodium;
- 2 grams: fat;

192.   Pate Sucree

Serving: | Prep: | Cook: | Ready in: 30mins

Ingredients

- For a 9-inch pan:
- 1 cup all-purpose flour
- 2 tablespoons sugar
- ¼ teaspoon kosher salt
- 6 ½ tablespoons cold unsalted butter, cut into 1/2-inch pieces
- 2 ½ tablespoons cold water
- For a 10-inch pan:
- 1 ½ cups all-purpose flour
- 3 tablespoons sugar
- ¼ teaspoon kosher salt
- 9 ¼ tablespoons cold unsalted butter, cut into 9 pieces
- 3 tablespoons plus 2 teaspoons cold water

Direction

- In a food processor, pulse to combine the flour, sugar and salt. Add the butter, and process until the mixture resembles coarse meal. With the machine running, pour in the water. Process until the mixture just begins to come together and form large clumps.
- Remove the dough from the food processor, and place on a board. Shape dough into a disk about 4 inches in diameter (5 inches for a 10-inch crust). Wrap in plastic and refrigerate for 1 hour.
- Place a rack in the middle of the oven, and heat to 425 degrees.
- Remove the dough from the refrigerator, and unwrap. Roll it out to fit a 9-inch tart pan (or a 10-inch pan). Place the dough in the pan. Trim the excess dough, leaving 1/2inch to fold under so the rim is thicker than the rest of the crust. If using a pie plate or a tart pan with high edges, trim just below the edge and fold the edges under in the same manner. For the grapefruit tart, trim the edge to within 1/2 inch of the rim.
- Prick the bottom of the crust with the tines of a fork. Cover the dough with a double thickness of aluminum foil. Fill the foil with rice, beans or pie weights.
- To bake the crust partially, bake for 15 to 20 minutes, or until the dough is set. Remove from the oven. Remove weights and

aluminum foil. To bake fully, bake for an additional 3 to 5 minutes, or until lightly golden. Remove from oven, and cool.

Nutrition Information

- 249: calories;
- 81 milligrams: sodium;
- 15 grams: fat;
- 4 grams: monounsaturated fat;
- 5 grams: sugars;
- 10 grams: saturated fat;
- 1 gram: dietary fiber;
- 25 grams: carbohydrates;
- 3 grams: protein;

---

193. Paupiettes Of Sole With Spinach And Mushroom Stuffing

Serving: Four servings | Prep: | Cook: | Ready in: 30mins

Ingredients

- 4 skinless, boneless fillets of sole (or use any nonoily white-fleshed fish such as fluke or flounder), about 1/4 pound each
- Salt to taste, if desired
- Freshly ground pepper to taste
- ¾ pound fresh spinach
- 2 tablespoons butter
- 2 tablespoons finely chopped shallots
- ½ pound fresh mushrooms, thinly sliced, about 3 cups
- ⅛ teaspoon freshly grated nutmeg
- 1 egg yolk
- Ginger butter sauce (see recipe)

Direction

- Sprinkle the fillets with salt and pepper and set aside.
- Pick over the spinach. Remove and discard any tough stems and blemished leaves. Rinse

and drain the spinach well. There should be about 8 cups loosely packed. Set aside.

- Heat the butter in a skillet and add the shallots. Cook briefly, stirring, and add the mushrooms, salt, pepper and nutmeg. Cook, stirring, until the mushrooms are wilted. Add the spinach and cook until wilted. Continue cooking until all the moisture evaporates.
- Scrape the mixture into a bowl and add the egg yolk. Let stand until cool.
- Place the fillets of fish on a flat surface, skinned side up. Spoon an equal portion of the spinach and mushroom mixture onto the center of each fillet. Roll the fillets jellyroll style to enclose the filling.
- Bring a quantity of water to the boil in the bottom of a steamer. Arrange the rolled fillets, seam side down, on a steamer rack. Set the rack over the steamer bottom. Steam five minutes. Serve hot with a ginger butter sauce (see recipe).

Nutrition Information

- 219: calories;
- 5 grams: saturated fat;
- 0 grams: trans fat;
- 1 gram: polyunsaturated fat;
- 8 grams: carbohydrates;
- 2 grams: sugars;
- 25 grams: protein;
- 762 milligrams: sodium;
- 10 grams: fat;
- 3 grams: dietary fiber;

---

194. Pear Cake

Serving: One 9-inch cake | Prep: | Cook: | Ready in: 1hours

Ingredients

- 2 tablespoons butter, plus additional butter for the pan

- ½ cup dry, fine, unflavored bread crumbs
- 2 eggs
- ¼ cup milk
- 1 cup granulated sugar
- Tiny pinch salt
- 1 ½ cups flour
- 2 pounds ripe pears

Direction

- Preheat the oven to 350 degrees. Grease a 9-inch-round layer-cake pan with butter and sprinkle with the bread crumbs. Turn the pan upside down and tap it or shake it lightly to get rid of all the loose crumbs.
- In a bowl, beat together the eggs and milk. Add the sugar and salt and continue beating until well combined. Add the flour, mixing thoroughly with the other ingredients.
- Peel the pears, slice in half and scoop out the seeds and core. Cut lengthwise into thin slices. Add to the bowl, mixing them well with the other ingredients; the batter will be very thick.
- Spoon the batter into the pan, leveling it off with the back of a spoon or a spatula. Dot the surface with the butter.
- Bake in the top rack of the preheated oven for 45 minutes, or until the top is lightly golden.
- Remove it from the pan as soon as it is cool and firm enough to handle. It may be served lukewarm or cold.

195. Peas With Garam Masala

Serving: 4 servings | Prep: | Cook: | Ready in: 10mins

Ingredients

- 1 tablespoon olive oil
- ½ medium onion, chopped
- ½ teaspoon garam masala
- 4 cups frozen small peas
- ½ cup whole-milk yogurt, preferably sheep's milk
- Salt to taste

Direction

- Pour the oil into a medium saucepan and place over medium-high heat. When it shimmers, add the onion and garum masala and saute until the onion is translucent but not browned, about 5 minutes.
- Pour in the peas and cook, stirring, until the peas are warmed through. Remove from heat, fold in the yogurt and season with salt.

Nutrition Information

- 157: calories;
- 3 grams: monounsaturated fat;
- 8 grams: protein;
- 364 milligrams: sodium;
- 6 grams: dietary fiber;
- 2 grams: saturated fat;
- 1 gram: polyunsaturated fat;
- 19 grams: carbohydrates;
- 7 grams: sugars;

196. Penne With Tomatoes Basil And Garlic

Serving: 4 servings | Prep: | Cook: | Ready in: 15mins

Ingredients

- 1 pound penne
- 2 tablespoons extra-virgin olive oil
- 3 to 4 ripe tomatoes, seeded and chopped
- ½ cup basil leaves, coarsely chopped
- 1 clove garlic, green part removed, minced
- Coarse salt and freshly ground pepper to taste

Direction

- Cook the penne in boiling salted water and drain when al dente.
- Pour the oil into a large serving bowl and add the penne. Toss and add the tomatoes, basil

and garlic. Season to taste with salt and pepper and serve.

Nutrition Information

- 503: calories;
- 9 grams: fat;
- 1 gram: polyunsaturated fat;
- 5 grams: dietary fiber;
- 90 grams: carbohydrates;
- 6 grams: sugars;
- 16 grams: protein;
- 540 milligrams: sodium;

197. Pepper Shrimp

Serving: Eight servings | Prep: | Cook: | Ready in: 35mins

Ingredients

- ½ cup fruity red wine, such as Beaujolais or red zinfandel
- 1 8-ounce can tomato sauce
- 1 teaspoon dried chervil
- 1 tablespoon lemon juice
- 1 teaspoon dry mustard
- 1 teaspoon dried oregano
- Salt to taste
- 2 teaspoons pepper
- ½ cup olive oil
- 2 cloves garlic, minced
- ½ cup loosely packed flat-leaved parsley, chopped
- 2 pounds medium shrimps, peeled and deveined

Direction

- In a bowl, whisk together the wine, tomato sauce, chervil, lemon juice, mustard, oregano, salt and pepper.
- Heat the oil in a skillet and cook the minced garlic over medium heat for 1 minute. Add the

tomato-sauce mixture and bring to a boil, then lower the heat and simmer the mixture, stirring occasionally, for 10 minutes.

- Remove from heat and set aside to cool for 5 minutes. Stir in chopped parsley.
- Place the shrimp in a single layer in a nonmetal baking dish. Pour the sauce over the shrimp and marinate, covered, for 3 hours at room temperature, or overnight in the refrigerator.
- Preheat the broiler. Broil the shrimps about 6 inches from the heat for 10 minutes or until cooked through, turning once.

Nutrition Information

- 226: calories;
- 0 grams: trans fat;
- 10 grams: monounsaturated fat;
- 4 grams: carbohydrates;
- 16 grams: protein;
- 2 grams: polyunsaturated fat;
- 779 milligrams: sodium;
- 15 grams: fat;
- 1 gram: sugars;

198. Perciatelli With Broccoli, Tomatoes And Anchovies

Serving: Serves 4 | Prep: | Cook: | Ready in: 1hours

Ingredients

- ¼ cup golden raisins or currants (optional)
- 1 pound baby broccoli
- Salt to taste
- 2 tablespoons extra virgin olive oil
- 2 garlic cloves, minced
- 2 anchovy fillets, rinsed and chopped
- 2 teaspoons fresh thyme leaves
- 1 pound tomatoes, grated, or 1 14-ounce can chopped tomatoes, with juice
- 8 imported black olives, pitted and chopped
- Freshly ground pepper to taste

- ¾ pound perciatelli (also sold as bucatini) or spaghetti
- 2 to 4 tablespoons grated pecorino or Parmesan cheese

Direction

- Place the raisins in a small bowl and cover with warm water. Let sit for 20 minutes while you prepare the other ingredients.
- Bring a large pot of water to a boil, salt generously and add the baby broccoli. Blanch for 4 minutes and, using a skimmer or tongs, transfer to a bowl of cold water. Drain and shake out excess water. If the stems are thick and hard, peel. Chop coarsely.
- Heat the olive oil over medium heat in a large, heavy skillet and add the garlic. Cook, stirring, until it smells fragrant, about 30 seconds to a minute, and add the anchovies, thyme and tomatoes. Turn the heat down to medium-low and cook, stirring often, until the tomatoes have cooked down and smell fragrant, about 10 minutes. Stir in the olives. Drain the raisins or currants and add, along with the broccoli and about 1/4 cup of the cooking water from the broccoli. Season to taste with salt and pepper. Cover, turn the heat to low and simmer 5 to 10 minutes, stirring occasionally, until the broccoli is very tender and the sauce is fragrant. Keep warm while you cook the pasta.
- Bring the water back to a boil and cook the pasta al dente, following the timing instructions on the package. Check the sauce and if it seems dry add another 1/4 to 1/2 cup of the pasta cooking water. Drain the pasta and transfer to the pan with the sauce. Toss together and serve, sprinkled with pecorino or Parmesan. If desired, drizzle a little olive oil over each serving.

Nutrition Information

- 490: calories;
- 7 grams: sugars;
- 2 grams: polyunsaturated fat;

- 77 grams: carbohydrates;
- 792 milligrams: sodium;
- 12 grams: fat;
- 3 grams: saturated fat;
- 20 grams: protein;
- 8 grams: dietary fiber;

| 199. | Pickled Peppers |

Serving: 5 pint jars | Prep: | Cook: | Ready in: 1hours

Ingredients

- 4 red bell peppers, stemmed, seeded and cut into 1/2-inch-wide strips
- 4 yellow bell peppers, stemmed, seeded and cut into 1/2-inch-wide strips
- 4 green bell peppers, stemmed, seeded and cut into 1/2-inch-wide strips
- 3 cups white vinegar
- 3 cups sugar
- 2 tablespoons kosher salt
- 5 cloves garlic
- 5 teaspoons olive oil

Direction

- Sterilize jars: wash 5 pint (2-cup) canning jars with new 1- or 2-piece lids in hot, soapy water and rinse well. Place jars on a rack in a large kettle. (Jars should not touch the bottom of the kettle.) Fill kettle with water until jars are completely covered. Bring to a boil and boil 15 minutes. Leave jars in the hot water, removing them with tongs as you fill them. Place lids in a large saucepan and cover with water. Bring to a boil and boil 5 minutes. Leave lids in hot water, taking them out as you need them.
- Bring a large kettle 1/4 full of lightly salted water to a boil and add the peppers. Simmer until tender, about 10 minutes. Drain and set aside.
- Return kettle to the heat and add the vinegar, sugar and salt. Bring to a boil, stirring, and add the peppers. Return to a boil. Place 1 clove

of garlic and 1 teaspoon of olive oil in each jar and pack the peppers gently into the jars, leaving about 1/4inch of space below the lip. Pour enough liquid into the jars to cover the peppers. Wipe rims with a clean, damp towel and screw lids on securely but not too tightly.

- Fill a large kettle fitted with a rack halfway with water and bring to a boil. Meanwhile, bring a teapot full of water to a boil. Place the filled jars on the rack (they must not touch -- work in batches if necessary) and pour in boiling water from the teapot until jar tops are covered by 2 inches. Bring to a boil and boil 10 minutes.
- Using tongs, remove jars from the kettle. Using potholders, tighten lids. Allow to cool. Store in a cool, dark place.

Nutrition Information

- 623: calories;
- 5 grams: dietary fiber;
- 1 gram: polyunsaturated fat;
- 3 grams: protein;
- 140 grams: carbohydrates;
- 126 grams: sugars;
- 1412 milligrams: sodium;

---

200.   Pierogi Ruskie (Potato And Cheese Pierogi)

Serving: 24 to 30 pierogi | Prep: | Cook: | Ready in: 1hours30mins

Ingredients

- For the Dough:
- 2 cups/255 grams all-purpose flour (preferably unbleached), plus more as needed
- 1 teaspoon kosher salt
- 3 tablespoons unsalted butter
- 1 large egg, beaten
- For the Filling:
- ½ pound waxy or all-purpose potatoes

- Salt and pepper
- 3 tablespoons unsalted butter
- 3 medium yellow onions (about 8 ounces each), finely chopped
- ½ cup quark cheese, cottage cheese or sour cream (about 4 ounces)
- For Serving:
- Butter, for pan-frying (optional)
- Sour cream, for garnish
- Chopped fresh parsley or dill, for garnish

Direction

- Prepare the dough: Add the flour and salt to a large bowl; whisk to combine. In a small saucepan, heat 1/2 cup water and the butter over medium-high until butter is melted, about 3 minutes. Pour the buttery liquid into the flour gradually, stirring it in as you add it. (The dough will be quite crumbly and flaky at this point, like a biscuit dough.) Stir in the egg until combined then move the dough to a lightly floured surface and knead until smooth, 5 to 7 minutes. Cover the dough with a dampened towel or plastic wrap and let rest at room temperature for 30 minutes.
- Prepare the filling: Peel the potatoes and cut into 1-inch cubes. Add them to a large pot, sprinkle with 1 tablespoon salt and cover with cold water by about 2 inches. Bring to a boil over high and continue to cook at a simmer until potatoes are tender, about 25 minutes.
- While the potatoes cook, prepare the onions: In a large skillet, melt the butter over medium-high. Add the onions, season generously with salt and pepper, and cook, stirring occasionally, until golden-brown and softened, about 12 minutes. Set aside about 1 cup of onions for garnish and add the rest to a medium bowl.
- Transfer the cooked potatoes to a colander to drain, then transfer to the medium bowl with the onions. Add the cheese, stir to combine, season generously with salt and pepper, then let cool.
- Bring a large pot of heavily salted water to a boil over high.

- Prepare the wrappers: Cut the dough into two even pieces. (You'll want to leave one piece under the towel to stay moist while you work with the other piece.) You'll also want a small bowl of flour, a small bowl of water and a towel handy for keeping your hands clean. Dust some flour onto a baking sheet (for holding the pierogi) and your work surface, then roll out one portion of dough until 1/8-inch thick. Using a 3-inch cookie cutter or inverted glass, punch 12 to 15 disks of dough. (Save and refrigerate the scraps to boil as a rustic pasta, in soup or another use.)
- Assemble the pierogi: Working with one disk at time, spoon a scant tablespoon of filling onto the middle of it. Fold the dough in half to enclose the filling, bringing the edges together to form a crescent shape. Pinch the two sides together at the top, then work your way down on both sides, pinching the dough over the filling and pushing in the filling as needed, making sure the potato mixture does not break the seal. If needed, you can dip your fingertip into water and moisten the dough in spots as needed to help the two sides adhere together.
- To form a rustic pattern on the curved seal, pinch the rounded rim underneath using your pointer finger and middle finger and press an indentation on top with your thumb, working your way along the rounded rim. Transfer to the prepared baking sheet. (If you've gotten some filling on your fingers, dip your fingertips into the bowl of water then dry them off on the towel.)
- Repeat with remaining disks, then repeat the entire process with the remaining portion of dough. You'll want to work fairly quickly, as the pierogi can be harder to seal if they start to dry out. (If cooking the pierogi at a later point, transfer them on the baking sheet to the freezer until frozen solid, then transfer the pierogi to a resealable bag and freeze.)
- To cook the pierogi, add a single layer of pierogi to the pot of boiling water. Let them cook until they rise to the surface, about 2 minutes, then cook another 2 to 3 minutes until puffy. (With frozen dumplings, you will need to increase the cooking time by a couple of minutes.) Use a slotted spoon to transfer cooked dumplings to a colander to drain, then boil remaining dumplings.
- If you want to pan-fry your pierogi, working in batches, melt 1 to 2 tablespoons of butter in a large skillet over medium-high until crackling. Add a few boiled pierogi in a single layer to avoid overcrowding, and cook until crisp and golden, 1 to 2 minutes per side. Repeat with remaining pierogi, adding butter as needed.
- Serve hot. Top with any browned butter from the pan, warmed reserved onions, sour cream and herbs.

---

201. Pierre Franey Potato Gnocchi

Serving: 6 servings | Prep: | Cook: | Ready in: 35mins

Ingredients

- 3 large potatoes, preferably Idaho variety, about 1 3/4 pounds
- 2 egg yolks
- 1 ¾ cup flour, plus 1/4 cup for rolling the dough
- Salt to taste

Direction

- Boil potatoes in lightly salted water until soft. Drain and run them through sieve, or mash well, and let dry on top of stove in warm oven.
- To the potatoes add egg yolks and blend well. Add only enough flour to make a firm, yet delicate dough. If too much flour is added the dumplings become tough when cooked.
- On lightly floured surface roll dough into strips measuring 1 by 8 inches. Dust them with flour. Lower strips, one at a time, into the top chute of gnocchi machine while cranking handle slowly. Gnocchi will roll out the

bottom chute. Cover them with a towel until ready to cook.

- Cook gnocchi in large pot of boiling salted water. When they rise to the surface they are done. Serve with sauce of choice.

Nutrition Information

- 308: calories;
- 0 grams: polyunsaturated fat;
- 64 grams: carbohydrates;
- 5 grams: dietary fiber;
- 9 grams: protein;
- 536 milligrams: sodium;
- 2 grams: sugars;
- 1 gram: monounsaturated fat;

202.   Pizza With Spring Onions And Fennel

Serving: One 12- to 14-inch pizza | Prep: | Cook: | Ready in: 45mins

Ingredients

- 2 tablespoons extra virgin olive oil
- 1 medium size sweet spring onion, chopped, about 1 cup
- Salt, preferably kosher salt
- freshly ground pepper
- 1 ¼ pounds trimmed fennel bulbs, tough outer layers removed, cored and chopped
- 2 large garlic cloves, minced
- 2 tablespoons minced fennel fronds
- ½ recipe whole wheat pizza dough (see recipe)
- Parmesan

Direction

- Preheat the oven to 450 degrees, preferably with a baking stone in it. Heat 1 tablespoon of the olive oil over medium heat in a large, heavy skillet, and add the onion and about 1/2 teaspoon salt. Cook, stirring often, until the

onion is tender, about five minutes. Add the fennel and garlic, and stir together. Cook, stirring often, until the fennel begins to soften, about five minutes. Turn the heat to low, cover and cook gently, stirring often, until the fennel is very tender and sweet and just beginning to color, about 15 minutes. Season to taste with salt and pepper. Stir in the chopped fennel fronds, and remove from the heat.

- Roll or press out the pizza dough and line a 12- to 14-inch pan. Brush the pizza crust with the remaining tablespoon of olive oil and sprinkle on the Parmesan. Spread the fennel mixture over the crust in an even layer. Place on top of the pizza stone, and bake 15 to 20 minutes, until the edges of the crust are brown and the topping is beginning to brown. Remove from the heat. Serve hot, warm or room temperature.

203.   Plum Sorbet Or Granita

Serving: 6 servings | Prep: | Cook: | Ready in: 3hours30mins

Ingredients

- 125 grams (1/2 cup) red wine
- 1 clove
- 2 black peppercorns
- 1 teaspoon vanilla
- 83 to 100 grams (about 1/3 cup plus 1 teaspoon to 1/2 cup) sugar, to taste
- 900 grams (2 pounds) ripe red plums, pitted
- 20 grams (1 tablespoon) clover honey
- 33 grams (1 tablespoon plus 2 teaspoons) corn syrup

Direction

- Combine the red wine, clove, peppercorns, vanilla and sugar in a saucepan. Bring to a boil, reduce the heat and simmer 5 minutes. Remove from the heat and strain into a bowl. Allow to cool. Blend the plums with the honey, corn syrup and wine syrup in a blender until smooth. Chill for 2 hours or overnight.

- If you are making granita, place a 9-by-11-inch baking dish in the freezer. You may omit the corn syrup and reduce the sugar if desired.
- Using an immersion blender, blend the plum mixture for 30 seconds. If making sorbet, freeze in an ice cream maker following the manufacturer's directions. If making granita, scrape into the chilled baking dish and place back in the freezer. Set the timer for 30 minutes. Using a fork, scrape the ice crystals from the outside of the baking dish toward the center. Return to the freezer and set the timer for another 30 minutes. Continue to scrape the mixture with a fork every 30 minutes until you have a uniform frozen mixture. It should not be frozen solid. If you forget to scrape and the mixture does freeze like an ice cube, cut into chunks and use a food processor fitted with the steel blade to break it up. Transfer to a container and freeze. Allow to soften for 15 minutes in the refrigerator before serving.

---

204. Plum And Grapefruit Salsa

Serving: 2 cups | Prep: | Cook: | Ready in: 40mins

Ingredients

- 2 grapefruits
- 8 plums, halved, pitted and thinly sliced
- 1 jalapeno, finely chopped
- 1 tablespoon finely chopped ginger
- 3 tablespoons coarsely chopped cilantro
- 1 tablespoon coarsely chopped mint
- Kosher salt and freshly ground pepper to taste

Direction

- Using a knife, remove the peel and pith from the grapefruit and discard. Cut the sections out from between the membranes and cut each section in half lengthwise.

- Transfer to a medium bowl and add the plums, jalapeno, ginger, cilantro and mint. Toss and season with salt and pepper.
- Let sit at room temperature for at least half an hour and up to 1 hour. Serve with grilled chicken, seafood or tortilla chips. (Can be covered and refrigerated for one day.)

Nutrition Information

- 105: calories;
- 603 milligrams: sodium;
- 1 gram: fat;
- 0 grams: polyunsaturated fat;
- 26 grams: carbohydrates;
- 4 grams: dietary fiber;
- 22 grams: sugars;
- 2 grams: protein;

---

205. Poached Chicken With Rice

Serving: 4 servings | Prep: | Cook: | Ready in: 1hours15mins

Ingredients

- 1 chicken (about 3 pounds), cut into 4 pieces
- 2 leeks, trimmed and washed well
- 3 ribs celery
- 4 parsley sprigs
- 2 sprigs fresh thyme or 1 teaspoon dried
- 1 bay leaf
- 3 medium carrots, scraped
- 1 medium onion, peeled, stuck with 2 cloves
- 6 peppercorns
- Salt to taste
- 2 tablespoons butter
- 4 tablespoons flour
- ½ cup cream
- ½ cup half and half
- ¼ teaspoon freshly grated nutmeg
- 1 pinch cayenne pepper

- 2 tablespoons fresh lemon juice

Direction

- Rinse the chicken well in cold water. Place the chicken in a Dutch oven and barely cover with water.
- Tie the leeks, celery, parsley and thyme sprigs with a string to form a bouquet garni. Add it to the Dutch oven, then add the bay leaf, carrots, onion with cloves, peppercorns and salt. Bring to a boil, reduce heat to simmer and cook until chicken is tender, about 45 minutes. Skim the surface often to remove fat.
- Remove the chicken from the broth and keep warm while preparing the sauce. Reserve the broth.
- Melt the butter in a saucepan, add the flour, and mix well with a wire whisk over low heat. When blended, add 2 cups of the chicken broth, stir vigorously with the whisk. Bring to a boil and simmer for 10 minutes.
- Strain through a sieve and add cream, half and half, nutmeg, cayenne and lemon juice. Bring to a boil. Check for seasoning and simmer for 5 minutes.
- Serve one chicken quarter per person. Remove skin if desired, spoon a little of the sauce over the chicken and serve the remainder in a sauce boat. Serve with rice and the poached vegetables.

Nutrition Information

- 776: calories;
- 7 grams: sugars;
- 23 grams: saturated fat;
- 0 grams: trans fat;
- 8 grams: polyunsaturated fat;
- 3 grams: dietary fiber;
- 56 grams: fat;
- 20 grams: monounsaturated fat;
- 21 grams: carbohydrates;
- 47 grams: protein;
- 1269 milligrams: sodium;

| 206. | Pocket Sandwiches |

Serving: 4 servings | Prep: | Cook: | Ready in: 20mins

Ingredients

- 1 ½ pounds ground turkey
- 1 large onion, chopped
- 1 large clove garlic, minced, or 1 teaspoon minced garlic in oil
- 2 large red or yellow peppers or one of each, chopped
- 1 tablespoon fresh oregano leaves or 1 teaspoon crushed, dried oregano
- 1 tablespoon fresh thyme leaves or 1 teaspoon crushed, dried thyme
- Freshly ground black pepper to taste
- 4 tablespoons red-wine vinegar
- 4 large whole-wheat pitas
- 2 large ripe tomatoes, sliced
- 8 scallions, sliced thin

Direction

- Heat nonstick skillet and saute turkey, breaking it up as you stir, until meat begins to brown.
- Add onion, garlic, peppers, oregano, thyme and pepper. Cook over medium heat until onion softens.
- Add vinegar and cook quickly to reduce liquid. Adjust seasonings.
- Toast the pitas and cut in half.
- Either serve the meat topped with cucumbers and yogurt salad (see recipe), with tomatoes and scallions on the side, or spoon some of the meat mixture into a pita half, add a tomato slice and scallions and serve the cucumber salad on the side.

Nutrition Information

- 495: calories;
- 0 grams: trans fat;
- 5 grams: sugars;

- 52 grams: carbohydrates;
- 42 grams: protein;
- 15 grams: fat;
- 4 grams: saturated fat;
- 395 milligrams: sodium;
- 9 grams: dietary fiber;

207.   Polenta With Zucchini And Tomatoes

Serving: Serves four to six | Prep: | Cook: | Ready in: 1hours

Ingredients

- 1 recipe Easy Oven-Baked Polenta, with Parmesan if desired
- 1 tablespoon extra virgin olive oil
- 1 small onion, chopped
- 2 large garlic cloves, minced
- 1 ¼ to 1 ½ pounds zucchini, cut in half lengthwise if thick, and sliced about 1/4 inch thick
- Salt, preferably kosher salt, to taste
- 1 pound tomatoes, peeled, seeded and chopped, or 1 (14-ounce) can, chopped (see note)
- Pinch of sugar
- 1 tablespoon chopped fresh parsley
- 1 tablespoon chopped fresh mint
- Freshly ground black pepper
- Freshly grated Parmesan

Direction

- Begin making the polenta. While it's in the oven, cook the squash. Heat the oil over medium heat in a large, heavy nonstick skillet, and add the onion. Cook, stirring often, until just about tender, about five minutes. Add the garlic and cook, stirring, for a minute or two, until fragrant. Stir in the squash and 1/2 teaspoon salt, and toss together for five to eight minutes, until it is coated with oil and beginning to soften. Add the tomatoes and their juice, the sugar and salt to taste. Turn the heat to medium-high. Cook, stirring often, for five to 10 minutes, until the tomatoes have cooked down slightly. Turn the heat back down to medium and cook, uncovered, for 20 minutes, until the vegetables are soft and aromatic. If they begin to dry and stick to the pan before the end of the cooking time (if you're using fresh tomatoes, this may happen because there isn't as much juice as with canned tomatoes), add up to 1/4 cup water. Stir in the parsley and mint, and simmer for a few more minutes. Remove from the heat, taste, adjust the salt and add pepper.
- When the polenta is ready, remove from the oven. If adding Parmesan, stir it in. Spoon onto plates, and make a depression in the center. Top with the zucchini. Garnish with additional Parmesan, and serve.

Nutrition Information

- 77: calories;
- 448 milligrams: sodium;
- 4 grams: protein;
- 1 gram: saturated fat;
- 2 grams: dietary fiber;
- 0 grams: polyunsaturated fat;
- 8 grams: carbohydrates;
- 5 grams: sugars;

208.   Pork Cutlets With Paprika Sauce

Serving: 4 servings | Prep: | Cook: | Ready in: 30mins

Ingredients

- 8 boneless pork loin cutlets, about 3 ounces each, trimmed of excess fat
- Salt and freshly ground pepper to taste
- 1 tablespoon vegetable oil
- ½ cup finely chopped onion

- 2 teaspoons chopped fresh marjoram or 1 teaspoon dried
- 1 teaspoon finely chopped garlic
- 1 teaspoon paprika
- 2 tablespoons vodka or gin
- ½ cup fresh or canned chicken broth
- ¼ cup sour cream

Direction

- Sprinkle the cutlets with salt and pepper.
- Heat the oil in a skillet large enough to hold the cutlets in one layer. When the oil is very hot, add the meat and cook over medium high heat for about 5 minutes or until browned. Turn the slices and cook 5 minutes more.
- Remove the fat from the skillet and scatter the onion, marjoram, garlic and paprika around the pork. Cook and stir until lightly browned. Add the vodka and chicken broth and bring to a boil. Simmer for 15 minutes. If there is too much liquid, reduce it. Stir in the sour cream; reheat but do not boil.

Nutrition Information

- 327: calories;
- 0 grams: trans fat;
- 1 gram: sugars;
- 31 grams: protein;
- 18 grams: fat;
- 4 grams: carbohydrates;
- 6 grams: monounsaturated fat;
- 2 grams: polyunsaturated fat;
- 578 milligrams: sodium;

209. Pork And Potato Hash

Serving: 6 servings | Prep: | Cook: | Ready in: 50mins

Ingredients

- 1 ¾ pounds all-purpose potatoes, peeled, cut into 1/4-inch slices and washed in cold water

- 1 ½ cups water
- ¾ pound onions (about 2 medium-size onions), peeled and cut into 1/2-inch dice
- A few tablespoons of juice left over from the pork roast, if any remains (see recipe)
- 3 to 4 cloves garlic, peeled, crushed and chopped (about 1 tablespoon)
- ⅓ cup minced scallion (3 to 4 scallions)
- 3 tablespoons olive oil
- ¼ teaspoon Tabasco sauce
- ¾ teaspoon salt
- 2 teaspoons Worcestershire sauce
- 10 to 12 ounces leftover pork roast (see recipe), cut into 1/2-inch dice (about 2 1/2 cups)
- 1 fried egg, for garnish (optional)

Direction

- In a 12-inch nonstick skillet (or 2 smaller nonstick skillets), place the sliced potatoes with the water, onion and juice from the pork roast. Bring to a boil, cover and boil over medium heat for 10 minutes. Then add the garlic, scallion, olive oil, Tabasco, salt, Worcestershire sauce and the leftover pork roast. Mix well and cook, uncovered, stirring over high heat for about 5 minutes.
- Most of the moisture will have evaporated by now and the mixture should start to sizzle. Since the hash will begin to stick at this point, use a flat wooden spatula to scrape up the crusty bits sticking in the bottom of the pan and stir them into the uncooked mixture. Continue to cook over medium heat for about 20 minutes, stirring every 3 or 4 minutes. The mixture will brown faster in the last 10 minutes of cooking and should then be stirred every 2 or 3 minutes.
- At the end of the cooking time, the mixture will stop sticking to the pan. Press on the mixture to make it hold together and fold the solid mass into an oval omelet shape. Invert onto a large platter. Serve immediately as is or with one fried egg on top.

Nutrition Information

- 298: calories;
- 28 grams: carbohydrates;
- 15 grams: protein;
- 2 grams: polyunsaturated fat;
- 3 grams: sugars;
- 353 milligrams: sodium;
- 14 grams: fat;
- 4 grams: dietary fiber;
- 8 grams: monounsaturated fat;

---

210. Portobello Mushroom Cheeseburgers

Serving: Serves 4 | Prep: | Cook: |Ready in: 1hours

Ingredients

- 1 tablespoon red wine vinegar or sherry vinegar
- Salt
- freshly ground pepper to taste
- 1 garlic clove, green shoot removed, minced or pureed
- 3 tablespoons extra virgin olive oil
- 4 large portobello mushrooms, stems removed
- 1 6-ounce bag baby spinach
- 4 1/2-ounce slices cheddar or Gruyère cheese
- Whole grain hamburger buns and the condiments of your choice
- condiments of your choice

Direction

- Whisk together the vinegar, salt, pepper, garlic and olive oil. Toss with the mushroom caps in a wide bowl. Rub the marinade over the tops of the mushroom caps and place them on a baking sheet, rounded side up. Let sit for 15 minutes. Don't rinse the bowl, because you'll use any oil and vinegar residue to dress the spinach.
- Bring a large pot of water to a boil, salt generously and blanch the spinach for 20 seconds. Transfer to a bowl of ice water, drain and squeeze dry. Chop coarsely and toss in the bowl with the residue of the marinade. Set aside.
- Prepare a medium-hot grill, heat a heavy skillet over medium-high heat, or preheat an electric grill or panini pan on medium-high. Season the mushrooms as desired with salt and pepper. Place the mushrooms on the hot grill or pan, rounded side down. Cook them for about 6 to 8 minutes, depending on the thickness, until lightly browned, and moist. Turn over and cook for another 6 minutes. Turn over for a minute to reheat the top, then flip back over and place the cheese on top. Continue to cook until the cheese melts. If using a panini grill, cook 6 to 8 minutes. Open the grill and place the cheese on top. Wait for it to melt. Place a mound of spinach on the bottom half of each hamburger bun and place the mushrooms, rounded side up, on top of the spinach. Top with your choice of condiments and serve.

---

211. Potato Focaccia With Oyster Mushrooms

Serving: 1 large focaccia, serving 12 | Prep: | Cook: |Ready in: 3hours50mins

Ingredients

- For the sponge
- 1 teaspoon / 4 grams active dry yeast
- ½ cup / 120 ml lukewarm water
- ¾ cup / 90 grams unbleached all-purpose flour
- For the dough
- 8 ounces / 225 g potatoes, such as Yukon gold, peeled and diced
- 1 teaspoon / 4 grams active dry yeast
- 1 cup / 240 ml lukewarm water
- 3 tablespoons extra-virgin olive oil
- ¾ to 1 cup / 100 to 125 grams unbleached all-purpose flour, as needed

- 2 cups / 250 grams whole wheat flour or durum flour
- 1 ¾ teaspoons/ 12 grams fine sea salt
- For the topping
- 2 tablespoons extra-virgin olive oil
- 2 teaspoons finely chopped fresh sage
- 1 to 2 garlic cloves, to taste (optional)
- ½ pound oyster mushrooms
- Salt and freshly ground pepper to taste
- 12 to 24 small sage leaves

Direction

- Make sponge. Combine yeast and water in the bowl of a stand mixer and stir to dissolve. Whisk in flour. Cover with plastic wrap and let rise in a warm place until bubbly and doubled in volume, about 45 minutes.
- While starter is proofing, steam potatoes above 1 inch of boiling water until tender, 15 to 20 minutes. Mash with a potato masher or put through a potato ricer or sieve. Set aside to cool.
- Make dough. Whisk together yeast and water in a small bowl and let stand until creamy, a few minutes. Add to sponge in mixer bowl, along with the olive oil. Add mashed potatoes, flours (using smaller amount of unbleached flour) and salt and mix in with paddle attachment for 1 to 2 minutes, until ingredients are amalgamated. Change to dough hook and knead on medium speed for 8 to 10 minutes, adding more white flour if dough seems impossibly sticky (it will be sticky no matter what). The dough should come together and slap against the sides of the bowl. It will be tacky.
- Cover bowl tightly with plastic wrap and let dough rise in a warm spot until doubled, about 1 1/2 hours.
- Shape the focaccia. Coat a 12-x 17-inch sheet pan (sides and bottom) with olive oil. Line with parchment and flip the parchment over so exposed side is oiled. Turn dough onto the baking sheet. Oil or moisten your hands, as dough is sticky, and press out dough until it just about covers the bottom of the pan. Cover with a towel and allow it to relax for 10 minutes, then continue to press it out until it reaches the edges of the pan. Cover with a damp towel and let rise in a warm spot for 45 minutes to an hour, or until dough is full of air bubbles.
- Preheat oven to 425 degrees after 30 minutes of rising (30 minutes before you wish to bake), preferably with a baking stone in it. Place olive oil, sage and garlic in a small saucepan and heat over medium heat until the ingredients begin to sizzle in the oil. Allow to sizzle for 30 seconds, then remove from heat, swirl the oil in pan and transfer to a measuring cup or small bowl or ramekin. Allow to cool.
- Cut away the tough stems bottoms from the mushrooms and tear large mushrooms into smaller pieces. In a large bowl, toss with salt and pepper and the cooled olive oil mix. With lightly oiled fingertips or with your knuckles, dimple the dough, pressing down hard so you leave indentations. Arrange the mushrooms over the dough. Drizzle on any oil left in the bowl.
- Place pan in oven on baking stone. Spray oven with water 3 times during the first 10 minutes of baking, and bake 20 to 25 minutes, until edges are crisp and the top is golden. If you wish, remove the focaccia from the pan and bake directly on the stone during the last 10 minutes. Remove from oven, remove from pan at once and cool on a rack. Arrange the whole sage leaves over the top. If you want a softer focaccia, cover with a towel when you remove it from the oven. Serve warm or at room temperature.

Nutrition Information

- 216: calories;
- 35 grams: carbohydrates;
- 3 grams: dietary fiber;
- 0 grams: sugars;
- 264 milligrams: sodium;
- 6 grams: fat;
- 1 gram: polyunsaturated fat;

- 4 grams: monounsaturated fat;
- 5 grams: protein;

212. Potato Salad With White Wine

Serving: 4 servings | Prep: | Cook: | Ready in: 30mins

Ingredients

- 1 ½ pounds small Idaho, Washington or Yellow Gold potatoes
- Salt and freshly ground pepper
- ¼ cup dry white wine
- 4 tablespoons vegetable or olive oil

Direction

- Preheat oven to 200 degrees.
- Rinse potatoes and place them in a large saucepan with cold water to cover. Bring to a boil and simmer for 20 minutes or longer, depending on the size. Do not overcook.
- Drain potatoes, and when they are cool enough to handle, peel them and cut them into 1/4-inch slices. Place them in a heat-proof mixing bowl. Sprinkle with salt and pepper, wine and oil. Toss while warm. Cover bowl with foil. Place it in oven briefly to warm through. Turn into a serving dish and serve while warm.

Nutrition Information

- 263: calories;
- 14 grams: fat;
- 2 grams: saturated fat;
- 10 grams: monounsaturated fat;
- 1 gram: sugars;
- 30 grams: carbohydrates;
- 4 grams: protein;
- 461 milligrams: sodium;

213. Potato And Goat Cheese Pizza With Rosemary

Serving: 4 main-course servings | Prep: | Cook: | Ready in: 2hours25mins

Ingredients

- Basic dough (see recipe)
- 2 large baking potatoes, preferably long and thin
- 2 tablespoons plus 1/2 teaspoon olive oil
- 1 teaspoon salt
- Freshly ground pepper to taste
- 4 ounces goat cheese, crumbled
- 2 teaspoons minced fresh rosemary

Direction

- Prepare the dough and roll it out according to directions in basic dough recipe. While dough is rising, preheat oven to 375 degrees. Peel the potatoes, and cut them crosswise into slices 1/8-inch thick. Toss the slices with 1/2 teaspoon of the olive oil and place them in a single layer on a large baking sheet. Bake until the slices are tender, about 15 minutes.
- Increase oven temperature to 425 degrees. When the dough is rolled out, arrange the potato slices over the dough in concentric circles. Season with the salt and pepper. Sprinkle with the crumbled goat cheese and rosemary. Drizzle the remaining 2 tablespoons olive oil over the top, and bake until the crust is golden brown, about 20 minutes. Cut into wedges, and serve immediately.

214. Potato And Sorrel Gratin

Serving: Serves 6 to 8 | Prep: | Cook: | Ready in: 1hours30mins

Ingredients

- 2 pounds small or medium-size Yukon gold potatoes, scrubbed
- Salt to taste
- 8 ounces sorrel, stemmed and washed in 2 changes of water
- 1 garlic clove, peeled and cut in half
- Olive oil or butter for the baking dish
- 4 eggs
- 1 ½ cups milk (2 percent)
- 3 ounces Gruyère, grated (3/4 cup)
- 1 ounce Parmesan, grated (1/4 cup)
- Freshly ground pepper

Direction

- Place potatoes in a wide saucepan and cover with water. Add salt to taste and bring water to a boil over medium-high heat. Reduce heat to medium, cover partially and gently boil potatoes for 20 minutes, or until tender all the way through but firm enough to slice. Drain, return the potatoes to the pan, cover and let sit for 15 minutes. Remove from the pot and using a towel to grip the potatoes if they are too hot to handle, slice about 1/2 inch thick, or if you prefer, cut in dice. Transfer to a large bowl.
- Meanwhile stem and wash sorrel leaves. Heat a wide skillet over high heat and add the sorrel, in batches if necessary. Stir until sorrel has wilted in the liquid left on the leaves after washing. The color will go from bright green to drab olive and the sorrel will melt down to what looks like a purée. Don't worry, it will be chopped and mixed with the other ingredients and you won't mind the color. When all of the sorrel has wilted, remove from heat and transfer to a strainer or a colander. Rinse briefly with cold water, then press or squeeze out excess liquid. Chop medium-fine. Transfer to bowl with the potatoes, toss together and season with salt and pepper.
- Preheat oven to 375 degrees. Rub sides and bottom of a 2- to 2 1/2-quart baking dish or gratin with the cut side of the garlic clove. Oil dish with olive oil. Mince remaining garlic and add to potatoes and sorrel.

- Beat eggs in a medium bowl. Add salt to taste (I use about 1/2 teaspoon). Whisk in milk. Add to potatoes and sorrel and stir well to distribute sorrel evenly throughout the mixture. Stir in cheeses and freshly ground pepper, and scrape into the baking dish.
- Bake 45 minutes, or until set and the top and sides are nicely browned. Remove from the heat and allow to sit for 10 minutes or longer before serving.

Nutrition Information

- 253: calories;
- 4 grams: sugars;
- 533 milligrams: sodium;
- 12 grams: protein;
- 5 grams: monounsaturated fat;
- 0 grams: trans fat;
- 1 gram: polyunsaturated fat;
- 25 grams: carbohydrates;

---

215. Potato 'Salad' And Tomatillo Tacos

Serving: Makes 12 tacos | Prep: | Cook: | Ready in: 45mins

Ingredients

- 1 ½ pounds waxy potatoes like red bliss or white creamers, scrubbed and cut in 1/2-inch dice
- 2 tablespoons extra virgin olive oil, sunflower oil, grapeseed oil or canola oil
- 1 small red or white onion, quartered lengthwise, then cut across the grain in thin slices
- 1 teaspoon Mexican oregano or fresh thyme
- 1 garlic clove, minced
- 3 eggs, hard-boiled and chopped
- 1 cup quick fresh tomatillo salsa
- 12 corn tortillas

- About 1/4 cup chopped cilantro, plus more for garnish
- 3 ounces goat cheese or queso fresco, crumbled

Direction

- Steam the potatoes above 1 inch of water for 10 minutes, or until tender. Remove the potatoes from the heat but don't discard the steaming water.
- Heat the oil in a wide, heavy skillet over medium heat. Add the onion and cook, stirring, until tender, about 5 minutes. Add a generous pinch of salt and the potatoes and oregano or thyme, and continue to cook, stirring, for a few more minutes, until the onions are beginning to color on the edges. Add the garlic and stir until it begins to smell fragrant, about 30 seconds to a minute. Season to taste with salt and pepper. Remove from the heat and allow to cool for 5 minutes. Add 1/2 cup of the salsa and the cilantro and stir together.
- Heat the tortillas. Wrap them in a kitchen towel and place in the steamer. Bring the water back to a boil, cover and steam 1 minute. Turn off the heat and allow the tortillas to sit undisturbed for 10 to 15 minutes.
- Top the tortillas with the potato mixture and top the potatoes with another spoonful of salsa and some crumbled cheese. Garnish with more cilantro, fold the tortillas over and serve.

Nutrition Information

- 161: calories;
- 1 gram: polyunsaturated fat;
- 23 grams: carbohydrates;
- 215 milligrams: sodium;
- 6 grams: protein;
- 2 grams: sugars;
- 0 grams: trans fat;
- 3 grams: dietary fiber;

216.   Poussins Or Cornish Hens With Rosemary, Orange And Shallots

Serving: 8 servings | Prep: | Cook: | Ready in: P1DT4hours45mins

Ingredients

- For the stock:
- 4 pounds veal bones
- 2 pounds chicken necks and wings
- 1 large onion
- 3 cloves garlic
- 3 carrots, sliced
- 2 leeks, sliced, including green part
- ¾ bottle dry white wine
- 2 cups chopped plum tomatoes, with their juice
- 1 tablespoon tomato paste
- 1 teaspoon whole black peppercorns
- 6 sprigs fresh thyme
- 8 sprigs parsley
- 8 quarts water
- For the poussins or Cornish hens:
- 1 orange
- 8 poussins or Cornish hens, air-dried overnight in refrigerator
- 2 bunches fresh rosemary
- 4 tablespoons olive oil
- Coarse salt and freshly ground pepper to taste
- 16 large shallots
- 2 tablespoons unsalted butter

Direction

- The day before, start the stock. Roast the veal bones, chicken necks and bones, onion, garlic and carrots in the oven until well browned. Place in a stock pot with leeks, wine, tomatoes, tomato paste, peppercorns, thyme, parsley and water. Simmer uncovered, for four hours, adding water if necessary (cook for a half-hour after adding extra water). Strain the stock and refrigerate.
- Preheat oven to 375 degrees. Cut the orange in half and cut one half in four slices. Place half a

slice inside each poussin; squeeze the juice from the remaining orange half over each poussin. Place some rosemary leaves inside, leaving plenty for the garnish. Sprinkle with oil, season with salt and pepper and truss.

- Place the poussins on their side in a roasting pan with the shallots. Roast for 15 minutes, turn on the other side and roast a further 15 minutes. Finish breast-up, place in a serving dish and keep warm.
- Meanwhile, remove stock from refrigerator and take off the fat, which will be solid. Put the stock in a saucepan and reduce to one-and-a-half cups. Remove the shallots from the roasting pan and keep warm. Degrease the cooking juices from the poussins and add to the stock. Reduce to one-and-a-half cups and correct seasoning. Just before serving, swirl in the butter. Place in a heated sauce boat and keep warm.
- Place the poussins on a serving dish and then arrange shallots around them and garnish liberally with sprigs of rosemary. Pass the sauce separately.

---

217. Provençal Artichoke Ragout

Serving: Serves 6 to 8 | Prep: | Cook: | Ready in: 1hours15mins

Ingredients

- 2 pounds baby artichokes or globe artichokes if baby artichokes aren't available, trimmed (see below)
- 1 lemon, cut in half
- 2 tablespoons olive oil
- 1 large sweet onion, such as Vidalia or Maui, chopped, or 1 bunch of spring onions, chopped
- 2 celery stalks, from the inner hart, sliced
- 1 large or 2 small red bell peppers, diced
- 4 large garlic cloves, minced or pressed

- Salt
- 1 28-ounce can chopped tomatoes with juice, peeled, seeded and chopped
- ¾ to 1 cup water, as needed
- Freshly ground pepper
- 1 teaspoon fresh thyme leaves, or 1/2 teaspoon dried thyme
- 1 bay leaf
- 2 to 4 tablespoons chopped fresh basil or parsley
- 2 to 3 teaspoons fresh lemon juice

Direction

- How to trim artichokes: Fill a bowl with water, and add the juice of 1/2 lemon. Cut the stems off the artichokes, and with a sharp knife, cut away the tops — about 1/2 inch from the top for baby artichokes, 1 inch for larger artichokes. Rub the cut parts with the other half of the lemon. Break off the tough outer leaves until you reach the lighter green leaves near the middle. With a paring knife, trim the bottom of the bulb right above the stem by holding the knife at an angle and cutting around the artichoke, until you reach the light flesh beneath the tough bottoms of the leaves. Cut small baby artichokes in half, or large artichokes into quarters, and cut away the chokes if the artichokes are mature. Immediately place in the bowl of acidulated water.
- Heat the oil in a large, heavy nonstick skillet or casserole over medium heat, and add the onion and celery. Cook, stirring, until tender, about three to five minutes. Add the red pepper and about 1/4 teaspoon salt, and stir together for three to five minutes until the pepper begins to soften. Add the garlic, and stir together for another minute, until the garlic is fragrant. Add the tomatoes and a little more salt, and cook, stirring from time to time, for 10 minutes, until the tomatoes have cooked down and smell fragrant. Add the artichokes, thyme, bay leaf and enough water to cover the artichokes halfway, and bring to a simmer. Add salt and pepper, then cover and simmer

30 to 40 minutes, until the artichokes are tender and the sauce fragrant. Check from time to time and add water if necessary. Add the lemon juice, taste and adjust salt and pepper.

Nutrition Information

- 113: calories;
- 4 grams: sugars;
- 1 gram: polyunsaturated fat;
- 3 grams: monounsaturated fat;
- 19 grams: carbohydrates;
- 9 grams: dietary fiber;
- 5 grams: protein;
- 643 milligrams: sodium;

---

218.   Provençal Onion Pizza

Serving: One 12- to 14 inch pizza | Prep: | Cook: | Ready in: 1hours15mins

Ingredients

- 3 tablespoons olive oil
- 2 pounds sweet onions, finely chopped
- Salt
- freshly ground pepper
- 3 garlic cloves, minced
- ½ bay leaf
- 2 teaspoons fresh thyme leaves, or 1 teaspoon dried thyme
- 1 tablespoon capers, drained, rinsed and mashed in a mortar and pestle or finely chopped
- ½ recipe whole wheat pizza dough (see recipe)
- 12 anchovy fillets, soaked in water for five minutes, drained, rinsed and dried on paper towels
- 12 Niçoise olives

Direction

- Preheat the oven to 450 degrees, preferably with a pizza stone inside. Heat 2 tablespoons of the olive oil in a large, heavy nonstick skillet over medium-low heat. Add the onions and cook, stirring, until they begin to sizzle and soften, about three minutes. Add a generous pinch of salt and the garlic, bay leaf, thyme and pepper. Stir everything together, turn the heat to low, cover and cook slowly for 45 minutes, stirring often. The onions should melt down to a golden brown puree. If they begin to stick, add a few tablespoons of water. Stir in the capers, then taste and adjust seasonings. If there is liquid in the pan, cook over medium heat, uncovered, until it evaporates.
- Roll out the pizza dough and line a 12- to 14-inch pan. Brush the remaining tablespoon of oil over the bottom but not the rim of the crust. Spread the onions over the crust in an even layer. Cut the anchovies in half, and decorate the top of the crust with them, making twelve small X's and placing an olive in the middle of each X. Place on top of the pizza stone, and bake 15 to 20 minutes, until the edges of the crust are brown and the onions are beginning to brown. Remove from the heat. Serve hot, warm or room temperature.

Nutrition Information

- 189: calories;
- 9 grams: fat;
- 1 gram: polyunsaturated fat;
- 6 grams: monounsaturated fat;
- 23 grams: carbohydrates;
- 5 grams: protein;
- 2 grams: dietary fiber;
- 8 grams: sugars;
- 503 milligrams: sodium;

219. Prune Plum And Peach Compote

Serving: Forty servings | Prep: | Cook: |Ready in: 20mins

Ingredients

- 4 pounds prune plums
- 12 to 15 sprigs fresh mint, washed and tied with kitchen string
- 3 cups fruit preserves (a mixture of plum, raspberry and blueberry jam and currant jelly)
- 3 cups (1 bottle) dry red wine (a cabernet or merlot)
- 3 pounds ripe but firm peaches

Direction

- Halve the prune plums and discard the pits. Place the plums in a large stainless-steel saucepan with the mint, jam and wine.
- Peel the peaches with a sharp paring knife or vegetable peeler and cut each of them into six wedges, discarding the pits.
- Bring the plum mixture to a boil, stirring occasionally, and boil gently, covered, for 2 minutes. Add the peach wedges and bring the mixture back to a boil. Immediately remove the saucepan from the heat and let the mixture cool in the pan. When at room temperature, transfer to a bowl, cover with plastic wrap and refrigerate for at least 4 to 5 hours but for up to 5 to 6 days.
- At serving time, remove and discard the mint.

Nutrition Information

- 204: calories;
- 4 grams: dietary fiber;
- 32 grams: sugars;
- 1 gram: protein;
- 9 milligrams: sodium;
- 0 grams: polyunsaturated fat;
- 49 grams: carbohydrates;

220. Pumpkin Soup

Serving: 8 to 10 servings | Prep: | Cook: |Ready in: 45mins

Ingredients

- 1 large orange pumpkin
- 2 pounds pumpkin, peeled and de-seeded, cut into chunks
- 1 medium onion, finely chopped
- 1 clove garlic, minced
- 4 tablespoons unsalted butter
- Coarse salt and freshly ground pepper to taste
- 6 cups strong chicken stock
- 1 cup heavy cream
- 1 ½ tablespoons chopped parsley
- 3 cups croutons fried in butter

Direction

- Slice the top off the pumpkin to make a lid. Scrape out the seeds and scoop out the flesh required for the soup.
- Saute the onion and garlic in three tablespoons of the butter until tender but not brown.
- Add the pumpkin pieces, salt and pepper and cook gently for 10 minutes. Add the stock and simmer, stirring until the pumpkin is tender, about 15 to 20 minutes.
- Remove from the heat and puree in a food processor until smooth and satiny. Return to the pan, stir in the cream and remaining butter and heat through. Correct seasoning.
- Serve the soup in a warmed pumpkin shell or heated bowl or individual heated pumpkin shells. Pour in the soup, sprinkle with parsley and croutons and serve.

Nutrition Information

- 322: calories;
- 40 grams: carbohydrates;
- 16 grams: fat;
- 0 grams: trans fat;

- 5 grams: monounsaturated fat;
- 1 gram: polyunsaturated fat;
- 1365 milligrams: sodium;
- 9 grams: protein;
- 3 grams: dietary fiber;
- 14 grams: sugars;

221. Puréed Mushroom Soup

Serving: 16 shots or 6 to 8 bowls | Prep: | Cook: | Ready in: 1hours45mins

Ingredients

- ½ ounce dried porcinis
- 1 tablespoon extra virgin olive oil
- 1 medium onion, chopped
- 1 leek, white and light green part only, cut in half lengthwise, cleaned thoroughly and sliced or chopped
- Salt to taste
- 2 garlic cloves, minced (to taste, optional)
- 1 ½ pounds mushrooms (white or cremini) sliced or coarsely chopped
- ⅓ cup medium grain rice
- About 4 1/2 cups water, chicken stock or vegetable stock, or as needed
- A bouquet garni made with a bay leaf and a couple of sprigs each thyme and parsley and an optional Parmesan rind
- Freshly ground pepper to taste
- 1 tablespoon soy sauce (more to taste)
- 1 to 2 tablespoons dry sherry, to taste (optional)
- ½ cup milk or additional stock
- Garnish
- Chopped fresh parsley or torn leaves for garnish

Direction

- Place the dried porcinis in a bowl or pyrex measuring cup and cover with 2 cups boiling water. Let sit for 30 minutes. Line a strainer with cheesecloth and set over a bowl. Drain the porcinis through a cheesecloth-lined strainer. Squeeze the mushrooms over the strainer to extract as much flavorful liquid as possible. Rinse in several changes of water and set aside. Measure the mushroom soaking water and add water or stock to make 6 cups.
- Heat the olive oil over medium heat in a large, heavy soup pot or Dutch oven and add the onion and leek and a pinch of salt. Cook, stirring, until tender and, about 5 to 8 minutes. Do not brown. Add a generous pinch of salt and the garlic and cook, stirring, until the garlic smells fragrant, about 30 seconds. Add the fresh and reconstituted mushrooms and cook, stirring, until they begin to sweat and smell fragrant, 3 to 5 minutes.
- Add the rice, stock, bouquet garni, soy sauce and salt to taste, and bring to a boil. Reduce the heat, cover and simmer 45 minutes. Remove the bouquet garni and the parmesan rind if using.
- In batches, blend the soup until smooth. Fill the blender less than half way and cover the top with a towel pulled down tight, rather than airtight with the lid, because hot soup will jump and push the top off if the blender is closed airtight. Return to the pot, taste and adjust salt, and add pepper and the sherry, if using. Add the milk or another half cup of stock and heat through, stirring. If the soup still seems too thick, thin out a little more but remember to taste and adjust seasoning. Serve in espresso cups or in bowls, garnishing each serving with chopped or torn flat-leaf parsley.

Nutrition Information

- 44: calories;
- 2 grams: protein;
- 317 milligrams: sodium;
- 1 gram: sugars;
- 0 grams: polyunsaturated fat;
- 7 grams: carbohydrates;

222. Puréed Zucchini Soup With Curry

Serving: 4 to 6 servings | Prep: | Cook: | Ready in: 50mins

Ingredients

- 1 tablespoon extra virgin olive oil
- 1 small onion, chopped
- 2 garlic cloves, minced
- 2 pounds zucchini, diced (about 7 cups diced)
- 2 teaspoons curry powder
- 6 cups chicken stock, vegetable stock or water
- ¼ cup basmati rice
- Salt to taste
- Freshly ground pepper (I like a lot of it in this soup)
- Pinch of cayenne
- 2 tablespoons fresh lemon juice
- For garnish
- 2 tablespoons chopped chives
- 1 small zucchini, sliced paper-thin, tossed with salt and, if desired, lemon juice, and marinated for 15 minutes or longer
- Garlic croutons (optional)

Direction

- Heat the olive oil over medium heat in a large, heavy soup pot and add the onion. Cook, stirring, until it is tender, about 5 minutes. Add a generous pinch of salt, the garlic and the zucchini and stir for about a minute, until the garlic smells fragrant. Add the curry powder, stir together, and add the stock or water, the rice and salt to taste. Bring to a boil, reduce the heat, cover and simmer 30 minutes. Taste and adjust salt.
- Purée the soup with an immersion blender or a food mill or in batches in a blender, taking care to remove the lid or take out the center insert and to cover with a towel to avoid hot splashes. Return to the pot, heat through, add pepper and cayenne to taste and stir in the lemon juice. Serve, garnishing each bowl with paper-thin slices of zucchini, chopped chives and croutons if desired.

Nutrition Information

- 175: calories;
- 1 gram: polyunsaturated fat;
- 3 grams: dietary fiber;
- 23 grams: carbohydrates;
- 8 grams: sugars;
- 9 grams: protein;
- 999 milligrams: sodium;
- 6 grams: fat;

223. Quail In Escabeche (From Pedro Larumbe's Recipe)

Serving: 4 servings | Prep: | Cook: | Ready in: 1hours

Ingredients

- ½ cup olive oil
- 1 medium-size onion, coarsely chopped
- 2 cloves garlic, crushed
- Some sprigs of fresh thyme or 1/2 teaspoon dried
- 1 small stalk of fresh celery
- 6 black peppercorns, crushed
- 8 quails
- ½ cup red wine vinegar
- 2 cups meat broth (any meat, dark or white)
- 3 or 4 bay leaves
- Salt to taste

Direction

- Heat oil in deep saucepan and saute onion, garlic cloves, thyme, celery stalk and peppercorns over low heat, approximately 5 minutes.
- When onion is soft and transparent but not golden, add whole quails and saute until lightly browned on one side, about 5 minutes.

Turn and brown about another 5 minutes on the other side.

- Add vinegar, broth and bay leaves. Cover pan and simmer about 45 minutes or until quails are soft. Let cool. Dish can be eaten lukewarm or cold. It can be stored in the refrigerator for 2 weeks.

---

224. Quick Chile Sauce

Serving: 1 1/2 cups | Prep: | Cook: | Ready in: 5mins

Ingredients

- 9 Fresno chiles (about 5 ounces/140 grams) or other medium-heat chiles, preferably red, such as jalapeño or serrano, destemmed and roughly chopped
- 1 ¼ teaspoons kosher salt
- 3 ounces/85 grams cherry tomatoes (about 12) or 1 small vine tomato, roughly chopped
- 3 tablespoons white wine vinegar, apple cider vinegar or other light vinegar
- ¼ cup/60 milliliters extra-virgin olive oil

Direction

- Place the chiles and salt in the bowl of a food processor, and pulse a few times until chiles are chopped. (You don't want to go too far and turn them into paste.)
- Add the tomatoes and vinegar, and pulse again in two or three short bursts, just enough to break down the tomatoes.
- Transfer to a lidded container and top with the oil. Cover and keep in the fridge up to 1 week.

---

225. Quick Fresh Tomatillo Salsa

Serving: 2 cups, serving 8 | Prep: | Cook: | Ready in: 45mins

Ingredients

- 1 pound tomatillos, husked and rinsed
- 2 to 4 jalapeño or serrano chiles, seeded for a milder salsa, coarsely chopped
- ¼ cup chopped onion, soaked for 5 minutes in cold water, drained and rinsed
- ¼ to ½ cup coarsely chopped cilantro (to taste)
- Salt to taste (about 1/2 teaspoon)
- ¼ to ½ cup water, as needed

Direction

- Place the tomatillos in a saucepan, cover with water and bring to a boil. Reduce the heat and simmer for 8 to 10 minutes, flipping them over halfway through, until softened and olive green. Remove from the heat. Transfer to a blender. Add the chiles, onion, cilantro, and 1/4 cup water to the blender and blend to a coarse puree. Transfer to a bowl, add salt, and thin out as desired with water. Taste and adjust salt, and set aside for at least 30 minutes before serving, to allow the flavors to develop.

Nutrition Information

- 21: calories;
- 4 grams: carbohydrates;
- 3 grams: sugars;
- 170 milligrams: sodium;
- 1 gram: protein;
- 0 grams: polyunsaturated fat;

---

226. Quick Quesadilla With Dukkah

Serving: 1 serving | Prep: | Cook: | Ready in: 10mins

Ingredients

- 2 corn tortillas
- 1 ounce melting cheese, like Monterey Jack, mozzarella or Mexican string cheese, shredded

- ½ to 1 teaspoon pumpkin seed dukkah (to taste) (see recipe)

Direction

- Top one of the tortillas with the cheese and the dukkah. Place the other tortilla on top. Zap for 1 minute in the microwave, or heat in a dry skillet, flipping the quesadilla from time to time, until the cheese melts. The tortilla will be crispier using the pan method. Cut into quarters and serve.

Nutrition Information

- 225: calories;
- 1 gram: sugars;
- 23 grams: carbohydrates;
- 10 grams: fat;
- 5 grams: saturated fat;
- 3 grams: dietary fiber;
- 11 grams: protein;
- 41 milligrams: sodium;
- 0 grams: trans fat;

---

227.   Quinoa Salad With Avocado And Kalamata Olives

Serving: Serves 4 to 6 | Prep: | Cook: | Ready in: 45mins

Ingredients

- ¾ cup quinoa
- 1 ¼ cups water
- Salt to taste
- 1 small cucumber, cut in half lengthwise, seeded and sliced, or 1 Persian cucumber, sliced; or 1/2 cup sliced or diced celery (from the inner heart)
- ¼ cup kalamata olives, pitted and halved (about 12 olives)
- 1 ripe avocado, diced
- 1 tablespoon slivered fresh mint leaves
- 2 tablespoons chopped fresh parsley

- 1 ½ ounces feta cheese, crumbled (1/3 cup, optional)
- 1 6-ounce bag mixed spring salad greens, baby spinach, arugula, or a combination
- For the dressing
- 1 tablespoon freshly squeezed lemon juice
- 1 tablespoon sherry vinegar
- 1 teaspoon Dijon mustard
- 1 small garlic clove, pureed
- Salt to taste
- 2 tablespoons extra virgin olive oil
- ⅓ cup buttermilk or plain low-fat yogurt
- Freshly ground pepper

Direction

- Place the quinoa in a strainer and rinse several times with cold water. Place in a medium saucepan with 1 1/4 cups water and salt to taste. Bring to a boil, cover and simmer 15 minutes, until the grains display a thread-like spiral and the water is absorbed. Remove from the heat, remove the lid and place a dish towel over the pan, then return the lid to the pan and let sit for 10 minutes or longer undisturbed. Transfer to a salad bowl and fluff with forks. Allow to cool.
- Add the remaining salad ingredients except the salad greens to the bowl. Whisk together the dressing ingredients. If using yogurt, thin out if desired with a tablespoon of water.
- Just before serving toss the lettuces with 3 tablespoons of the dressing. Toss the quinoa mixture with the rest of the dressing. Line a salad bowl or platter with the greens, top with the quinoa, and serve. Or if preferred, toss together the greens and quinoa mixture before serving.

Nutrition Information

- 208: calories;
- 21 grams: carbohydrates;
- 6 grams: protein;
- 12 grams: fat;
- 2 grams: polyunsaturated fat;
- 8 grams: monounsaturated fat;

- 3 grams: sugars;
- 486 milligrams: sodium;
- 0 grams: trans fat;
- 5 grams: dietary fiber;

228. Rainbow Quinoa Salad

Serving: Serves 6 to 8 | Prep: | Cook: | Ready in: 35mins

Ingredients

- For the salad:
- 4 cups water
- ⅔ cup chopped dried fruit (such as apricots, raisins, cranberries, figs, currants)
- ¼ cup chopped cilantro
- ¼ cup chopped fresh mint
- ½ cup chopped fresh parsley
- Salt to taste
- 1 cup red quinoa or rainbow quinoa, rinsed
- ¼ cup lightly toasted pistachios
- ¼ cup lightly toasted almonds, chopped
- ¼ cup chopped walnuts
- 2 teaspoons lemon zest
- For the dressing:
- ¼ cup fresh lemon juice
- Salt to taste
- 1 small garlic clove, puréeed (optional)
- ¼ teaspoon ground cinnamon
- 1 teaspoon pomegranate molasses
- ⅓ cup extra- virgin olive oil

Direction

- Bring water to a boil in a 3-quart saucepan and add quinoa and salt to taste. Bring back to a rolling boil, then reduce heat slightly and boil gently for 20 minutes, or until you see a thread emerge from the blond and red quinoa. Drain and shake well in the strainer, then return to pot. Cover pot with a dishtowel and then , then place a lid over the dishtowel and let sit for 10 to 15 minutes undisturbed. Transfer to a large bowl.

- Meanwhile, whisk together lemon juice, salt, garlic, cinnamon, and pomegranate molasses. Whisk in olive oil.
- Toss together quinoa and dressing. Add remaining ingredients and toss together. Transfer to a platter, a wide bowl or individual plates and serve.

Nutrition Information

- 266: calories;
- 4 grams: dietary fiber;
- 6 grams: protein;
- 441 milligrams: sodium;
- 17 grams: fat;
- 2 grams: saturated fat;
- 26 grams: carbohydrates;
- 7 grams: sugars;
- 9 grams: monounsaturated fat;
- 5 grams: polyunsaturated fat;

229. Red Pepper With Tarragon Vinaigrette

Serving: 1 cup | Prep: | Cook: | Ready in: 25mins

Ingredients

- 2 shallots
- 1 clove garlic
- 1 red pepper
- ¼ cup fresh tarragon leaves
- ¾ cup extra-virgin olive oil
- Approximately 1/4 cup red wine vinegar (to taste)
- Course salt and freshly ground pepper to taste

Direction

- Mince the shallots and the garlic and place in a bowl.
- Preheat broiler. Cut the pepper into quarters or sixths and place skin side up on foil paper on a broiling pan. Broil until the skin blisters.

Place the pepper in a paper bag and let cool. Peel away the skin and chop the pepper. Add to the bowl containing the shallots and garlic.

- Add the tarragon leaves and olive oil. Mix thoroughly. Add the vinegar, salt, and pepper and taste to correct seasoning. Place in a serving bowl and serve spooned over the fish at the table.

Nutrition Information

- 801: calories;
- 82 grams: fat;
- 17 grams: carbohydrates;
- 7 grams: sugars;
- 550 milligrams: sodium;
- 59 grams: monounsaturated fat;
- 9 grams: polyunsaturated fat;
- 4 grams: dietary fiber;
- 3 grams: protein;
- 11 grams: saturated fat;

---

230. Red Quinoa, Cauliflower And Fava Bean Salad

Serving: 4 to 6 servings | Prep: | Cook: | Ready in: 1hours15mins

Ingredients

- 1 cup red quinoa
- 1 ½ cups water
- Salt to taste
- 1 ½ pounds fava beans
- ½ head cauliflower, broken into small florets
- 2 tablespoons chopped chives
- For the dressing
- 1 tablespoon freshly squeezed lemon juice
- 1 tablespoon sherry vinegar
- ½ teaspoon curry powder
- 1 teaspoon Dijon mustard
- 1 small garlic clove, puréed
- Salt to taste
- 2 tablespoons grapeseed oil

- 5 tablespoons buttermilk
- Freshly ground pepper

Direction

- Rinse the quinoa in several changes of water. Heat a heavy medium-size saucepan over medium-high heat and add the quinoa. Stir until the water on the grains has evaporated and the quinoa begins to crackle and smell toasty. Add the water and salt to taste. Bring to a boil, cover and reduce the heat to low. Simmer 20 minutes, until some of the quinoa grains display a little white spiral and the water has been absorbed. Remove from the heat, place a dish towel over the top of the pot and return the lid. Let sit for 15 minutes. Fluff the quinoa with a fork.
- Meanwhile, shell and skin the fava beans. Bring a medium pot of salted water to a boil. Fill a bowl with ice water. Drop the shelled fava beans into the boiling water and boil 5 minutes. Remove from the pot with a slotted spoon and transfer immediately to the cold water. Allow the beans to cool for several minutes, then slip off their skins by pinching off the eye of the skin and squeezing gently. Hold several beans in one hand and use your other thumb and forefinger to pinch off the eyes; have a bowl for the shelled favas close at hand, and this will not take a very long time.
- Bring the water in the pot back to a boil and drop in the cauliflower. Boil 3 to 5 minutes, until just tender. Transfer to a bowl of ice water, drain and dry on paper towels. Alternatively, steam the cauliflower for 4 to 5 minutes, or see the roasting variation below.
- Whisk together the dressing ingredients. Toss the quinoa, fava beans, cauliflower and chives in a bowl. Toss with the dressing and serve.

Nutrition Information

- 265: calories;
- 630 milligrams: sodium;
- 1 gram: monounsaturated fat;
- 0 grams: trans fat;

- 12 grams: sugars;
- 42 grams: carbohydrates;
- 14 grams: protein;
- 7 grams: fat;
- 5 grams: polyunsaturated fat;

231. Refried Bean, Zucchini And Corn Gratin

Serving: 6 to 8 servings | Prep: | Cook: | Ready in: 1hours15mins

Ingredients

- For the beans
- 3 cups simmered black beans or pinto beans, with liquid (see recipe)
- 2 tablespoons grapeseed or sunflower oil
- 2 teaspoons cumin seeds, ground
- 1 chipotle in adobo, seeded and minced (optional)
- Salt to taste
- 1 teaspoon mild or hot chili powder (more to taste)
- For the squash:
- 2 tablespoons extra virgin olive oil
- ½ cup minced onion
- Salt to taste
- 2 garlic cloves, minced
- 1 ½ pounds zucchini or mixed zucchini and yellow squash, sliced about 1/4 inch thick
- ½ to 1 teaspoon oregano, preferably Mexican oregano, to taste
- For the corn
- 2 cups corn kernels (fresh or frozen)
- 1 ¼ cups milk
- 1 serrano chile, minced
- ¼ cup cornmeal or polenta
- Salt to taste
- ½ cup grated asadero, Monterey Jack or pecorino
- ¼ cup crumbled queso cotijo, queso fresco, or feta
- 1 tablespoon butter or extra virgin olive oil

Direction

- Heat oven to 375 degrees. Oil or butter a 2-quart baking dish or gratin dish.
- Refry beans: Drain off about 1/2 cup of liquid from beans, retaining it in a separate bowl to use later for moistening beans, should they dry out. Heat oil over medium-high heat in a large, heavy nonstick frying pan and add ground cumin and chili. Cook, stirring over medium heat, for about a minute, until the spices begin to sizzle and cook. Add beans and optional chipotle. Fry beans, stirring and mashing with the back of a spoon, until they thicken and form a thin crust on the bottom of the pan. Stir up crust and mix into the beans. Cook until beans are thick but not dry, about 10 minutes. Add liquid you saved from the beans if they seem too dry. Taste refried beans and adjust salt (they probably won't need any as the broth reduces when you refry them). Spread in an even layer in the baking dish. (Note: If you use canned beans, do not drain. The frying process will go more quickly.)
- Clean and dry skillet. Heat over medium heat and add olive oil. Add onion and cook, stirring, until tender, about 5 minutes. Add a pinch of salt and garlic and cook, stirring, until garlic is fragrant, about 30 seconds. Add squash, oregano, salt and pepper, and turn up heat slightly. Cook, stirring often or tossing in pan, until squash is translucent and tender, 5 to 10 minutes. Taste and adjust seasoning. Spread in an even layer over the beans.
- Combine corn and milk in a saucepan and bring to a simmer. Simmer 5 minutes, until corn is just tender. Stir in cornmeal and minced serrano, add salt to taste, and continue to simmer until mixture is thick, 3 to 5 minutes. Stir in grated cheese. Remove from heat and spread in an even layer over squash. Sprinkle crumbled cheese over top. Dot with butter or drizzle on oil.
- Place in oven and bake 25 minutes, until bubbly and crumbled cheese is lightly browned. Serve hot or warm.

Nutrition Information

- 524: calories;
- 76 grams: carbohydrates;
- 10 grams: sugars;
- 24 grams: protein;
- 16 grams: dietary fiber;
- 4 grams: saturated fat;
- 3 grams: polyunsaturated fat;
- 1021 milligrams: sodium;
- 0 grams: trans fat;
- 7 grams: monounsaturated fat;

232.   Rice Salad With Cucumber, Lemon And Scallion

Serving: Four servings | Prep: | Cook: | Ready in: 1hours30mins

Ingredients

- 1 tablespoon grated lemon rind
- ¼ cup fresh lemon juice
- ¼ cup olive oil
- ½ teaspoon salt
- 1 teaspoon fresh ground pepper
- 2 medium-size cucumbers, peeled, halved lengthwise and seeded
- 4 scallions, rinsed and minced
- 1 ½ cups long-grain rice

Direction

- Combine the lemon rind and lemon juice in a large salad bowl. Slowly whisk in the olive oil and add the salt and pepper. Set aside. Cut the cucumbers into half-moon slices, 1/2 inch thick. Add the cucumber slices and scallions to the lemon vinaigrette. Toss.
- Cook the rice in water according to the directions on the package. When tender but still firm, remove from heat. Place in a colander and chill briefly under cold running water until the rice is at room temperature. Drain well. Add the rice to the salad bowl.

Toss. Cover and refrigerate for at least 1 hour before serving. This can be made up to 24 hours ahead of time.

Nutrition Information

- 401: calories;
- 6 grams: protein;
- 300 milligrams: sodium;
- 14 grams: fat;
- 2 grams: dietary fiber;
- 10 grams: monounsaturated fat;
- 63 grams: carbohydrates;
- 3 grams: sugars;

233.   Risotto Alla Milanese

Serving: 6 servings | Prep: | Cook: | Ready in: 35mins

Ingredients

- 2 tablespoons butter
- ½ cup finely minced shallots
- 1 ½ cups imported Italian rice
- 5 cups well-flavored chicken stock (approximately)
- Large pinch of powdered saffron
- Salt and freshly ground black pepper
- Freshly grated imported Italian Parmesan cheese

Direction

- Heat butter in a large, heavy saucepan. Add shallots and saute over medium heat until soft but not brown. Stir in rice and cook for several minutes, until the rice is well coated with butter.
- Place the stock in another saucepan and keep it simmering.
- Dissolve the saffron in a little of the stock in a small dish and stir into the rice.
- Then, stirring the rice constantly, add the simmering stock, about one-half cup at a time,

adding additional stock every few minutes as the rice absorbs it. After about 25 minutes, the rice should have absorbed most of the stock and be "al dente" and cohere in a creamy mass. Do not overcook the rice. Season to taste.

- Serve at once with freshly grated Parmesan cheese.

---

234. Risotto With Kale And Red Beans

Serving: 6 servings | Prep: | Cook: |Ready in: 45mins

Ingredients

- 2 quarts chicken or vegetable stock, as needed
- 1 tablespoon extra virgin olive oil
- ½ cup minced onion
- 1 ½ cups arborio or carnaroli rice
- 1 to 2 garlic cloves (to taste), green shoots removed, minced (optional)
- 1 teaspoon fresh thyme leaves, roughly chopped
- Freshly ground pepper to taste
- ½ cup dry white wine, like pinot grigio or sauvignon blanc, or rosé
- 1 bunch red kale, stemmed and washed thoroughly in 2 changes of water
- 1 15-ounce can red beans, drained and rinsed
- ⅓ cup freshly grated Parmesan cheese (1 1/2 ounces)

Direction

- Put the stock or broth into a saucepan and bring it to a simmer over low heat, with a ladle nearby or in the pot. Stack the kale leaves and cut crosswise into thin ribbons. Set aside.
- Heat the olive oil over medium heat in a wide, heavy skillet or in a large, wide saucepan. Add the onion and a generous pinch of salt, and cook gently until it is just tender, about 3 minutes. Do not brown.
- Stir in the rice, thyme and the garlic (if using) and stir until the grains separate and begin to

crackle. Add the wine and stir until it is no longer visible in the pan. Begin adding the simmering stock, a couple of ladlefuls (about 1/2 cup) at a time. The stock should just cover the rice, and should be bubbling, not too slowly but not too quickly. Cook, stirring often, until it is just about absorbed. Add another ladleful or two of the stock and continue to cook in this fashion, stirring in more stock when the rice is almost dry. You do not have to stir constantly, but stir often.

- After the first two additions of stock, stir in the kale, and continue to cook in the same fashion until the rice is tender all the way through but still chewy, about 15 minutes. Taste and adjust seasoning, adding salt and pepper to taste. Add the beans and another ladleful of stock to the rice, along with the Parmesan, and remove from the heat. The mixture should be creamy (add more stock if it isn't). Stir for about half a minute, then serve.

Nutrition Information

- 472: calories;
- 9 grams: sugars;
- 3 grams: saturated fat;
- 7 grams: dietary fiber;
- 733 milligrams: sodium;
- 4 grams: monounsaturated fat;
- 1 gram: polyunsaturated fat;
- 72 grams: carbohydrates;
- 21 grams: protein;

---

235. Risotto With Tomato Consomme And Fresh Cheese

Serving: Four servings | Prep: | Cook: |Ready in: 40mins

Ingredients

- 6 tomatoes, chopped
- 1 medium carrot, peeled and diced
- 1 red bell pepper, seeded and diced

- 7 cups basic vegetable broth (see recipe)
- 1 teaspoon olive oil
- 1 leek, white part only, rinsed well and minced
- 1 clove garlic, peeled and finely minced
- 1 ½ cups Arborio rice
- ½ teaspoon salt, plus more to taste
- 1 ½ teaspoons freshly ground pepper, plus more to taste
- 1 pound fresh mozzarella, diced
- 1 cup roughly chopped basil leaves
- 1 tablespoon cracked black peppercorns

Direction

- Put the chopped tomatoes, carrot and bell pepper into a blender, add the vegetable broth and puree until smooth. Strain the broth into a large, heavy-bottomed skillet or pot and simmer.
- Heat the olive oil in a large saucepan at medium heat. Add the leek and the garlic and saute until soft, about 5 minutes. Add the rice and stir. Ladle in 1/2 cup of the vegetable broth and stir. Increase the heat to medium-high and, for the next 25 minutes, continue adding the broth, 1/2 cup at a time, stirring constantly. Season to taste with salt and pepper. The rice should be tender but firm. If not, add more vegetable broth until the rice is tender. Remove the rice from the heat immediately. Quickly stir in the mozzarella and the basil leaves. Divide among 4 bowls and garnish with the cracked black pepper.

Nutrition Information

- 694: calories;
- 33 grams: protein;
- 1092 milligrams: sodium;
- 78 grams: carbohydrates;
- 7 grams: dietary fiber;
- 28 grams: fat;
- 15 grams: saturated fat;
- 9 grams: sugars;
- 1 gram: polyunsaturated fat;

---

236. Risotto With Winter Squash And Collard Greens

Serving: Serves six | Prep: | Cook: | Ready in: 2 hours

Ingredients

- 1 ½ pounds winter squash, such as butternut, banana or hubbard, peeled, seeded and cut in 1/2 inch dice (about 2 cups diced squash)
- 2 tablespoons extra virgin olive oil
- Salt
- freshly ground pepper to taste
- 1 bunch collard greens, about 1 pound, stemmed and washed
- 2 quarts chicken or vegetable stock, or 1 quart chicken or vegetable broth and 1 quart water
- 1 small or 1/2 medium onion
- 2 large garlic cloves, green shoots removed, minced
- 1 ½ cups arborio or carnaroli rice
- ½ cup dry white wine, such as pinot grigio or sauvignon blanc
- Pinch of saffron (optional)
- ½ cup freshly grated Parmesan cheese (2 ounces)
- 3 to 4 tablespoons chopped flat-leaf parsley

Direction

- Preheat the oven to 425 degrees. Cover a baking sheet with foil. Toss the squash with 1 tablespoon of the olive oil, season with salt and pepper, and spread on the baking sheet in an even layer. Place in the oven, and roast for 30 to 40 minutes, stirring every 10 minutes until tender and caramelized. Remove from the heat.
- While the squash is roasting, blanch the collard greens. Bring a large pot of water to a boil. Fill a bowl with ice water. When the water comes to a boil, salt generously and add the collard greens. Blanch for four minutes and transfer to the ice water with a slotted spoon or skimmer. Drain and squeeze out extra water. Chop coarsely, or cut in ribbons.

- Bring the stock to a simmer in a saucepan. Heat the remaining oil over medium heat in a large, heavy nonstick frying pan or a wide saucepan, and add the onion. Cook, stirring, until the onion begins to soften, about three minutes, and add the garlic and about 1/2 teaspoon salt. Cook, stirring, until the onion is tender and the garlic fragrant, about one minute, and add the rice. Cook, stirring, until the grains of rice are separate.
- Stir in the wine, and cook over medium heat, stirring constantly. The wine should bubble but not too quickly. When the wine has just about evaporated, add the collard greens, a third of the squash and the saffron. Stir in a ladleful or two of the simmering stock, enough to just cover the rice. The stock should bubble slowly. Cook, stirring often, until it is just about absorbed. Add another ladleful of the stock, and continue to cook in this fashion -- not too fast and not too slowly, adding more stock when the rice is almost dry -- until the rice is tender all the way through but still chewy, 20 to 25 minutes. Taste and adjust seasonings.
- Add the remaining roasted squash and another 1/2 cup of stock to the rice. Stir in the Parmesan and parsley, and remove from the heat. Add freshly ground pepper, taste one last time and adjust salt. The mixture should be creamy (add more stock if it is not). Serve right away in wide soup bowls or on plates, spreading the risotto in a thin layer rather than a mound.

Nutrition Information

- 506: calories;
- 6 grams: dietary fiber;
- 82 grams: carbohydrates;
- 20 grams: sugars;
- 12 grams: fat;
- 3 grams: saturated fat;
- 1 gram: polyunsaturated fat;
- 17 grams: protein;
- 1639 milligrams: sodium;

237. Roast Cornish Hens With Herbs And Pancetta

Serving: 4 servings | Prep: | Cook: | Ready in: 45mins

Ingredients

- 4 fresh sage leaves
- 2 teaspoons fresh rosemary leaves
- 2 teaspoons fresh thyme
- 2 tablespoons unsalted butter, softened
- 4 poussins or Cornish hens, air-dried overnight in the refrigerator
- Coarse salt and freshly ground pepper to taste
- 8 slices smoked pancetta
- 2 tablespoons olive oil

Direction

- Preheat the oven to 375 degrees. Chop the sage, rosemary and thyme and mix with the butter. Push the herb butter under the loosened skin of the breasts of the poussins or hens. Truss the poussins, season with salt and pepper and cover the breasts with pancetta. Sprinkle with olive oil.
- Place the poussins in a roasting pan and roast for 45 minutes to 1 hour. Degrease the pan juices and season to taste. Place each poussin on a heated plate and pour a serving of sauce around each one.

Nutrition Information

- 1032: calories;
- 25 grams: saturated fat;
- 14 grams: polyunsaturated fat;
- 83 grams: fat;
- 0 grams: trans fat;
- 37 grams: monounsaturated fat;
- 2 grams: carbohydrates;
- 1 gram: sugars;
- 65 grams: protein;

- 955 milligrams: sodium;

238.   Roast Rabbit With Rosemary

Serving: Four servings | Prep: | Cook: | Ready in: 1hours10mins

Ingredients

- 1 young rabbit, about 2 1/2 pounds, cleaned weight, cut into serving pieces
- Salt to taste, if desired
- Freshly ground pepper to taste
- 2 tablespoons olive oil
- 2 tablespoons butter
- 1 teaspoon finely ground rosemary
- 2 tablespoons finely chopped shallots
- 1 teaspoon finely minced garlic
- ½ cup dry white wine
- ½ cup fresh or canned chicken broth
- ¼ cup finely chopped parsley

Direction

- Preheat oven to 450 degrees.
- Sprinkle the rabbit with salt and pepper.
- Heat the oil and half of the butter in a baking dish. Add the rabbit pieces in one layer. Sprinkle with rosemary.
- Place the dish in the oven and bake 30 minutes. Turn the rabbit pieces and continue baking five minutes. Sprinkle with shallots and garlic. Bake five minutes and add the wine and broth. Bake, turning the pieces occasionally, about 20 minutes. Stir in the remaining one tablespoon of butter. Sprinkle with parsley and serve.

Nutrition Information

- 684: calories;
- 1117 milligrams: sodium;
- 35 grams: fat;

- 0 grams: trans fat;
- 3 grams: carbohydrates;
- 1 gram: sugars;
- 80 grams: protein;
- 11 grams: saturated fat;
- 12 grams: monounsaturated fat;
- 5 grams: polyunsaturated fat;

239.   Roast Rack Of Venison With Cranberry Chutney

Serving: 6 servings | Prep: | Cook: | Ready in: 1hours

Ingredients

- 2 cups dry red wine
- 2 cloves garlic, crushed
- 1 teaspoon whole black peppercorns, crushed
- 2 bay leaves
- Juice of 1 lemon
- 2 tablespoons extra-virgin olive oil
- Salt and freshly ground pepper to taste
- 1 loin rack of venison, 4 to 5 pounds, with the bones cracked to permit easy carving
- 1 cup dried cranberries
- ½ cup red wine vinegar
- ½ cup sugar
- 1 tablespoon chopped fresh ginger
- ½ teaspoon Chinese 5-spice powder
- ½ cup beef broth

Direction

- Place the wine, garlic, half the peppercorns, the bay leaves, lemon juice, olive oil and salt and pepper to taste in a deep dish that will hold the venison. Place the venison in the bowl, turn it to coat all sides, cover it and refrigerate overnight. Turn the meat a few times while it is marinating.
- Place the cranberries in a non-reactive saucepan. Stir in the vinegar, sugar, ginger, five-spice powder and remaining peppercorns. Bring to a simmer and cook slowly, stirring from time to time, about 20 minutes. The

cranberries should be soft and there should be enough liquid in the pan just to moisten them. Remove from the heat and set aside until serving time.

- About two hours before serving remove the venison from the marinade and place it in a roasting pan so it comes to room temperature. Strain the marinade, place it in a saucepan and cook over high heat until the marinade is reduced to about three-fourths cup. Add the beef broth, cook the mixture down until there is about three-fourths cup, then season with salt and pepper. Remove from the heat.
- Preheat oven to 425 degrees. Place the venison in the oven and roast it about 12 minutes per pound for medium rare. It should register 120 degrees when an instant-read thermometer is inserted in the thick part of the meat, not touching any bone.
- Remove the meat from the oven and allow it to stand at room temperature 20 minutes before carving. Warm the dried-cranberry mixture and transfer it to a serving dish. Reheat the sauce made from the marinade. Check the seasonings again.
- Cut the venison into individual chops. If the butcher has cracked the large bone between the chops, cutting the chops should be extremely easy.
- Serve the venison moistened with some of the reheated sauce and with the cranberry mixture on the side.

Nutrition Information

- 259: calories;
- 2 grams: dietary fiber;
- 31 grams: sugars;
- 415 milligrams: sodium;
- 5 grams: fat;
- 1 gram: polyunsaturated fat;
- 3 grams: protein;
- 38 grams: carbohydrates;

---

240. Roasted Cauliflower Gratin With Tomatoes And Goat Cheese

Serving: Serves 4 to 6 | Prep: | Cook: | Ready in: 1hours20mins

Ingredients

- 1 medium-size head of cauliflower
- Salt and freshly ground pepper to taste
- 3 tablespoons extra virgin olive oil
- 1 small or 1/2 large red onion, cut in half or quarters (if using a whole onion) lengthwise, then sliced thin across the grain
- 2 garlic cloves, minced
- 1 teaspoon fresh thyme leaves
- 1 (14 8/10-ounce) can chopped tomatoes in juice
- ⅛ teaspoon cinnamon
- ½ teaspoon coriander seeds, lightly toasted and coarsely ground
- 2 eggs
- 2 ½ ounces soft goat cheese (about 1/2 cup plus 2 tablespoons)
- 2 to 3 teaspoon chopped chives

Direction

- Preheat oven to 450 degrees. Line a baking sheet with parchment or foil. Cut away the bottom of the cauliflower stem and trim off leaves. Cut cauliflower into 1/3 inch thick slices, letting the florets on the edges fall off. Toss all of it, including the bits that have fallen away, with 2 tablespoons of the olive oil, salt, and pepper. Place on baking sheet in an even layer.
- Roast for 15 to 20 minutes, stirring and flipping over the big slices after 8 minutes, until the slices are tender when pierced with a paring knife and the small florets are nicely browned. Remove from oven and cut large slices into smaller pieces. You should have about 2 cups. Transfer to a large bowl. Turn oven down to 375 degrees.

- Oil a 1-1/2 to 2-quart baking dish or gratin. Heat remaining oil over medium heat in a medium-size skillet or a wide saucepan and add onion. Cook, stirring, until tender, about 5 minutes. Add a generous pinch of salt and the garlic and thyme and continue to cook, stirring, until garlic is fragrant, 30 seconds to a minute. Add tomatoes, cinnamon, ground coriander seeds, and salt and pepper to taste and bring to a simmer. Cook, stirring often, over medium-low heat, for 10 to 15 minutes, until the tomatoes have cooked down and the sauce is fragrant. Taste and adjust seasoning. Add to bowl with the cauliflower and stir everything together. Scrape into prepared baking dish.
- Set aside 2 tablespoons of the goat cheese. Beat eggs, then add the remaining cheese and beat together until smooth. Pour over cauliflower mixture, making sure to scrape out every last bit with a rubber spatula. Dot top with small pieces of the remaining goat cheese and sprinkle on chives.
- Bake 30 minutes, until top is beginning to brown in spots. Remove from oven and allow to sit for 5 to 10 minutes before serving.

Nutrition Information

- 179: calories;
- 6 grams: monounsaturated fat;
- 11 grams: carbohydrates;
- 547 milligrams: sodium;
- 13 grams: fat;
- 4 grams: dietary fiber;
- 0 grams: trans fat;
- 1 gram: polyunsaturated fat;
- 5 grams: sugars;
- 8 grams: protein;

241. Roasted Cauliflower With Tahini Parsley Sauce

Serving: Serves four to six, with some sauce left over | Prep: | Cook: | Ready in: 1hours

Ingredients

- 1 large cauliflower, broken into florets
- Salt to taste
- Freshly ground pepper to taste
- 2 tablespoons extra virgin olive oil
- 2 to 3 garlic cloves, to taste, cut in half, green shoots removed
- 1 cup sesame tahini
- ¼ to ¾ cup fresh lemon juice, to taste
- 1 cup finely chopped flat-leaf parsley (2 bunches)

Direction

- Preheat the oven to 400 degrees. Meanwhile, bring a large pot of water to a boil, and fill a bowl with ice water. When the water comes to a boil, salt generously and add the cauliflower. Blanch for two minutes, and transfer to the ice water. Drain and blot dry. Transfer to a baking dish.
- Season the cauliflower with salt and pepper, and toss with the olive oil. Place in the oven, and roast for 30 to 40 minutes, stirring from time to time, until tender and lightly browned.
- Puree the garlic cloves with 1/4 teaspoon salt in a mortar and pestle. Transfer to a bowl, and whisk in the sesame tahini. Whisk in the lemon juice, beginning with the smaller amount. The mixture will stiffen up. Gradually whisk in up to 1/2 cup water, until the sauce has the consistency of thick cream (or runny yogurt). Stir in the parsley. Taste, and adjust salt and lemon juice. Serve with the cauliflower. You will have some sauce left over.

Nutrition Information

- 328: calories;

- 27 grams: fat;
- 4 grams: sugars;
- 12 grams: monounsaturated fat;
- 10 grams: protein;
- 19 grams: carbohydrates;
- 7 grams: dietary fiber;
- 527 milligrams: sodium;

242. Roasted Eggplant Dip

Serving: Four servings | Prep: | Cook: |Ready in: 1hours20mins

Ingredients

- Vegetable oil spray
- 1 large eggplant, about 1 1/2 pounds, halved crosswise
- 1 jalapeno pepper, seeded, deveined and minced
- 1 shallot, peeled and minced
- 1 teaspoon fresh lemon juice
- 1 teaspoon fresh lime juice
- 1 ¼ teaspoons ground cumin seed
- ⅛ teaspoon ground cinnamon
- ½ teaspoon coarse salt, plus more to taste
- 1 teaspoon freshly ground pepper, plus more to taste
- 1 cup minced coriander leaves, for garnish

Direction

- Preheat oven to 350 degrees. Spray a small baking sheet with vegetable oil. Place the eggplant cut side down, and bake until soft, about 35 to 45 minutes. Set aside until cool and chop coarsely.
- Combine remaining ingredients except coriander in a glass or ceramic bowl. Marinate for 30 minutes. Combine the mixture in a blender or food processor. Puree until smooth. Season with salt and pepper to taste. Garnish with coriander. Serve with sesame pita chips (recipe below).

Nutrition Information

- 74: calories;
- 241 milligrams: sodium;
- 0 grams: trans fat;
- 2 grams: protein;
- 1 gram: polyunsaturated fat;
- 5 grams: dietary fiber;
- 6 grams: sugars;
- 3 grams: fat;
- 12 grams: carbohydrates;

243. Roasted Garlic And Shallot Soup

Serving: 6 to 8 servings | Prep: | Cook: |Ready in: 2hours30mins

Ingredients

- 5 whole heads garlic, cloves from 2 1/2 heads peeled
- ¾ pound shallots, half of them peeled and coarsely chopped
- 4 tablespoons olive oil
- Kosher salt and freshly ground pepper
- 4 tablespoons unsalted butter
- 2 large yellow onions, peeled and coarsely chopped
- ¾ pound russet potatoes, peeled and quartered
- 4 cups well-seasoned chicken stock, approximately
- 1 cup heavy cream, half-and-half or milk, approximately
- 1 tablespoon fresh thyme leaves

Direction

- Preheat oven to 350 degrees.
- Combine unpeeled garlic heads and unpeeled shallots in large bowl, pour the olive oil over them and toss to coat. Season generously with salt and pepper and place them in a single layer in a baking dish along with any oil

remaining in bowl. Cover with foil and bake 35 minutes. If shallots are soft by then, remove them. Bake them a little longer if necessary. Continue baking the garlic another 30 minutes or so until it is soft. Allow garlic and shallots to cool.

- Meanwhile, melt the butter in a heavy three- to four-quart saucepan. Add onions and cook gently for 15 minutes. Do not allow to brown. Add peeled, unroasted shallots and peeled garlic cloves. Cook over low heat 10 minutes longer. Add potatoes, about 1/2 teaspoon salt or to taste, the chicken stock, cream and thyme. Cover and cook about 40 minutes, until potatoes are very soft.
- Peel roasted shallots. Cut roasted garlic heads in half horizontally and squeeze in a potato ricer or by hand to extract the soft pulp. Add garlic pulp and shallots to saucepan and cook 10 minutes longer.
- Puree the soup in a blender or food processor. Season to taste with salt and pepper and, if desired, adjust the consistency of the soup with some additional stock, cream or milk or water. Reheat before serving.

Nutrition Information

- 386: calories;
- 0 grams: trans fat;
- 2 grams: polyunsaturated fat;
- 35 grams: carbohydrates;
- 4 grams: dietary fiber;
- 12 grams: saturated fat;
- 8 grams: protein;
- 743 milligrams: sodium;
- 25 grams: fat;
- 10 grams: monounsaturated fat;

244.   Roasted Sweet Potatoes And Fresh Figs

Serving: 4 servings | Prep: | Cook: | Ready in: 45mins

Ingredients

- 4 small sweet potatoes (2 1/4 pounds total)
- 5 tablespoons olive oil
- Scant 3 tablespoons balsamic vinegar (you can use a commercial rather than a premium aged grade)
- 1 ½ tablespoons superfine sugar
- 12 green onions, halved lengthwise and cut into 1 1/2-inch segments
- 1 red chili, thinly sliced
- 6 ripe figs (8 1/2 ounces total), quartered
- 5 ounces soft goat's milk cheese (optional)
- Maldon sea salt and freshly ground black pepper

Direction

- Preheat oven to 475 degrees. Wash the sweet potatoes, halve them lengthwise, and then cut each half into 3 long wedges. Mix with 3 tablespoons of the olive oil, 2 teaspoons salt and some black pepper.
- Spread the wedges out, skin side down, on a baking sheet and cook for about 25 minutes, until they are soft but not mushy. Remove from the oven and leave to cool.
- To make the balsamic reduction, place the balsamic vinegar and sugar in a small saucepan. Bring to a boil, then decrease the heat and simmer for 2 to 4 minutes, until it thickens. Be sure to remove the pan from the heat when the vinegar is still runnier than honey; it will continue to thicken as it cools. Stir in a drop of water before serving if it does become too thick to drizzle
- Arrange the sweet potatoes on a serving platter. Heat the remaining oil in a medium saucepan over medium heat and add the green onions and chili. Fry for 4 to 5 minutes, stirring often to make sure not to burn the chili. Spoon the oil, onions and chili over the sweet potatoes. Dot the figs among the wedges, and then drizzle over the balsamic reduction. Serve at room temperature. Crumble the cheese over the top, if using.

Nutrition Information

- 343: calories;
- 47 grams: carbohydrates;
- 7 grams: dietary fiber;
- 619 milligrams: sodium;
- 17 grams: fat;
- 2 grams: polyunsaturated fat;
- 12 grams: monounsaturated fat;
- 26 grams: sugars;
- 3 grams: protein;

---

245. Roasted Pear Poundcake With Chocolate Sauce

Serving: Eight to ten servings | Prep: | Cook: | Ready in: 1hours25mins

Ingredients

- The cake:
- 4 large, firm pears, peeled, halved, cored and cut across into 1/4-inch-thick slices
- 1 cup unsalted butter, softened
- 2 ½ cups sugar
- 4 eggs
- 1 ½ teaspoons vanilla extract
- 4 cups all-purpose flour
- 1 teaspoon salt
- 3 teaspoons baking powder
- The sauce:
- 6 ounces bittersweet chocolate, coarsely chopped
- 1 cup heavy cream
- 2 tablespoons brandy

Direction

- For the cake, preheat oven to 400 degrees. Place the pear slices on a baking sheet and roast until tender, about 10 minutes. Meanwhile, butter and flour a 10-inch tube pan. Place the pears in a food processor and puree until smooth. Set aside. Reduce the oven temperature to 350 degrees. Cream the butter

and sugar with an electric mixer until light and fluffy. Add the eggs one at a time, mixing until very light; batter will appear curdled at this point. Mix in the vanilla and the pear puree.
- Sift together the flour, salt and baking powder. Mix the dry ingredients into the batter just until combined. Scrape the batter into the prepared pan and bake until the top springs back when touched in the center, about 1 hour. Place on a rack to cool. Turn the cake out of the pan and reinvert onto a cake plate.
- To make the sauce, place the chocolate in a double boiler over barely simmering water, stirring occasionally until melted. Whisk in the cream and brandy. If making the sauce in advance, rewarm before serving. To serve, place a slice of cake on a plate and spoon the chocolate sauce beside it.

Nutrition Information

- 777: calories;
- 2 grams: polyunsaturated fat;
- 5 grams: dietary fiber;
- 9 grams: protein;
- 382 milligrams: sodium;
- 35 grams: fat;
- 21 grams: saturated fat;
- 1 gram: trans fat;
- 10 grams: monounsaturated fat;
- 112 grams: carbohydrates;
- 67 grams: sugars;

---

246. Romaine And Radish Salad With Buttermilk Lemon Dressing

Serving: 4 to 6 servings | Prep: | Cook: | Ready in: 10mins

Ingredients

- 2 hearts of romaine (the lighter, more delicate inner part of a head of romaine lettuce)
- 1 cup thinly sliced radishes (about 1 bunch)
- 1 to 2 tablespoons chopped chives, or a mixture of chives and tarragon
- For the buttermilk dressing
- 2 tablespoons freshly squeezed lemon juice
- 1 small garlic clove, puréed
- Salt to taste
- 1 tablespoon extra virgin olive oil
- 5 tablespoons buttermilk
- Freshly ground pepper

Direction

- Combine the romaine, radishes and herbs in a large salad bowl.
- Whisk together the lemon juice, garlic, salt, olive oil and buttermilk. Just before serving, toss with the salad mix. Add salt and freshly ground pepper to taste, toss again, and serve.

Nutrition Information

- 45: calories;
- 3 grams: fat;
- 0 grams: polyunsaturated fat;
- 2 grams: protein;
- 5 grams: carbohydrates;
- 290 milligrams: sodium;

247.   Rosemary Lime Sorbet

Serving: about 1 quart | Prep: | Cook: | Ready in: 20mins

Ingredients

- ¾ cup sugar
- 3 cups half-and-half
- 2 tablespoons chopped rosemary
- ¼ cup light corn syrup
- Juice of 3 limes

Direction

- In a large saucepan, combine sugar, half-and-half, rosemary and corn syrup. Whisk lightly and bring to a boil, making sure mixture does not boil over, then strain into a bowl. Let cool, then chill in refrigerator. Remove from refrigerator and slowly whisk in lime juice. If mixture shows signs of curdling, whisk harder or transfer to a blender.
- Pour mixture into an ice cream maker and follow manufacturer's instructions.

Nutrition Information

- 153: calories;
- 7 grams: fat;
- 4 grams: saturated fat;
- 2 grams: protein;
- 22 grams: carbohydrates;
- 21 grams: sugars;
- 30 milligrams: sodium;
- 0 grams: polyunsaturated fat;
- 1 gram: dietary fiber;

248.   Saks' Signature Cheesecake

Serving: Ten servings | Prep: | Cook: | Ready in: 1hours30mins

Ingredients

- For the crust:
- ⅔ cup graham crackers (one package)
- ⅓ cup brown sugar
- ⅓ cup melted butter
- Spray shortening for greasing pan
- For the filling:
- 2 pounds cream cheese
- ½ cup unsalted butter
- 1 cups sugar
- 1 pound sour cream
- 2 tablespoons cornstarch
- 1 teaspoon lemon extract
- 1 teaspoon vanilla extract

- 5 eggs

Direction

- Preheat the oven to 325 degrees. Coarsely chop the graham crackers, place in a food processor and grind completely. Add the brown sugar and melted butter. Spray a springform pan 10 inches in diameter with shortening. Press the crumb crust into the pan, distributing it evenly. Chill crust while making the filling.
- For the filling, coarsely chop the cream cheese and butter in a large bowl. Using a mixer, soften the two. Continue beating while adding the sugar. In a separate bowl, combine the sour cream, cornstarch, lemon and vanilla extracts and eggs. Add this mixture to the cream-cheese mixture and combine until completely smooth.
- Place the springform pan in a larger baking dish and fill the dish with hot water to reach halfway up the sides of the pan. Pour the mixture into the pan and bake for 35 minutes. Reduce the temperature to 300 degrees and continue baking for 35 more minutes, until a toothpick inserted in the center of the cheesecake is clean. Refrigerate overnight. Remove from the pan and serve.

Nutrition Information

- 843: calories;
- 34 grams: saturated fat;
- 16 grams: monounsaturated fat;
- 574 milligrams: sodium;
- 62 grams: fat;
- 1 gram: dietary fiber;
- 5 grams: polyunsaturated fat;
- 63 grams: carbohydrates;
- 39 grams: sugars;
- 12 grams: protein;

249.   Salad Of Bulgur, Corn And Avocado

Serving: 6 to 8 servings | Prep: | Cook: | Ready in: 2hours30mins

Ingredients

- 1 cup bulgur
- 4 cups boiling water
- 1 ripe avocado
- 2 cups cooked corn kernels
- ¼ cup lemon juice
- ½ cup chopped scallions
- ½ cup minced sweet red pepper
- ⅓ cup chopped fresh parsley
- ⅓ cup extra virgin olive oil
- Salt and freshly-ground black pepper to taste

Direction

- Place bulgur in bowl, pour the boiling water over it and let soften for two hours. Drain it well, squeezing out as much water as possible. Transfer the bulgur to a serving bowl.
- Peel, pit and dice the avocado. Toss it gently with the lemon juice in a small bowl.
- Mix the corn kernels, scallions, red pepper, parsley and olive oil with the bulgur. Gently fold in the avocado and lemon juice. Season to taste with salt and pepper and serve.

Nutrition Information

- 233: calories;
- 13 grams: fat;
- 2 grams: sugars;
- 9 grams: monounsaturated fat;
- 26 grams: carbohydrates;
- 5 grams: dietary fiber;
- 4 grams: protein;
- 537 milligrams: sodium;

250. Salade Niçoise With Yogurt Vinaigrette

Serving: 6 servings | Prep: | Cook: | Ready in: 45mins

Ingredients

- For the vinaigrette:
- 2 tablespoons good-quality red or white wine vinegar or sherry vinegar
- 1 tablespoon fresh lemon juice
- 1 garlic clove, small or large to taste, green shoot removed, puréed with a garlic press or in a mortar and pestle
- Salt and freshly ground pepper to taste
- 1 teaspoon Dijon mustard
- ¼ cup extra virgin olive oil
- 5 tablespoons plain low-fat yogurt (you can omit this and use a total of 1/2 cup extra virgin olive oil)
- For the salad:
- ¾ pound medium Yukon gold or fingerling potatoes, cut in 3/4-inch dice
- 1 5 1/2-ounce can light (not albacore) tuna packed in water, drained
- 6 ounces green beans, trimmed, and cut in half if long
- 1 small red or green pepper, thinly sliced or diced
- 1 small cucumber (preferably Persian), cut in half lengthwise and then sliced in half-moons
- 2 hard-cooked eggs, preferably free range, peeled and cut in wedges
- 1 small head of Boston lettuce, 1 romaine heart, or 4 to 5 cups mixed baby salad greens, washed and dried
- 2 to 4 tablespoons chopped fresh herbs, like parsley, basil, tarragon, chives and marjoram
- 3 or 4 tomatoes, cut in wedges, or 1/2 pint cherry tomatoes, cut in half
- Optional:
- 6 to 12 anchovy fillets, rinsed and drained on paper towels
- 12 imported black olives

Direction

- Using a fork or a small whisk, mix together the vinegar and lemon juice with the garlic, salt, pepper and Dijon mustard. Whisk in the olive oil and yogurt.
- Steam the potatoes above 1 inch simmering water for 10 to 15 minutes, until tender. Transfer to a large salad bowl and season with salt and pepper. Add the tuna and toss with 1/4 cup of the dressing while the potatoes are hot.
- Bring a pot of water to a boil, and fill a bowl with ice water. When the water comes to a boil, add a generous amount of salt and add the green beans. Cook 4 to 5 minutes, until just tender. Transfer to the ice water, then drain. Dry on paper towels. Add to the salad bowl, along with the red or green pepper, cucumber, hard-boiled eggs, lettuce and herbs. Garnish with the tomatoes, anchovies and olives, and serve.

Nutrition Information

- 218: calories;
- 2 grams: polyunsaturated fat;
- 0 grams: trans fat;
- 3 grams: dietary fiber;
- 12 grams: protein;
- 8 grams: monounsaturated fat;
- 17 grams: carbohydrates;
- 4 grams: sugars;
- 536 milligrams: sodium;

251. Salmon Or Tuna Carpaccio With Wasabi Sauce

Serving: Serves 4 | Prep: | Cook: | Ready in: 30mins

Ingredients

- 12 ounces sushi-grade salmon or ahi tuna, cut into four 3-ounce pieces
- ½ teaspoon wasabi paste
- 1 tablespoon seasoned rice vinegar

- ½ teaspoon soy sauce
- 1 tablespoon Greek yogurt
- 1 tablespoon heavy cream
- Shiso for garnish
- cilantro sprigs or chervil sprigs for garnish
- For the cucumber accompaniment
- 1 cup finely diced cucumber
- 2 tablespoons seasoned rice vinegar
- 1 tablespoon sesame oil

Direction

- Lightly brush a sheet of plastic with olive oil and lay a piece of fish on it. Lightly brush surface of fish with olive oil and lay another sheet of plastic on top. Using the flat side of a meat tenderizer or a rolling pin, gently pound fish until it is very thin, 1/4 to 1/8 inch thick. Take care not to tear the fish; if it seems that it will break apart, stop when it's a little thicker than 1/4 inch. Repeat with remaining pieces. Gently unpeel top layer of plastic and then set it back over the fish. Place in the refrigerator for at least 30 minutes.
- Whisk together wasabi, vinegar, soy sauce, yogurt, and cream in a small bowl or measuring cup.
- Toss cucumber with rice vinegar and sesame oil.
- Cut each piece of flattened fish into smaller pieces and fan out on plates or on a platter. Using a pastry brush, brush each piece of fish with the wasabi sauce. Place a spoonful of the cucumber salad on each plate, garnish with shiso, cilantro or chervil and serve.

Nutrition Information

- 147: calories;
- 21 grams: protein;
- 79 milligrams: sodium;
- 5 grams: fat;
- 2 grams: polyunsaturated fat;
- 0 grams: dietary fiber;
- 1 gram: sugars;

252.   Salt Baked Chicken

Serving: Four servings | Prep: | Cook: | Ready in: 2hours20mins

Ingredients

- About 4 pounds kosher salt
- 1 4-pound chicken

Direction

- Preheat the oven to 350 degrees. Put the salt in a heavy pot with a lid, slightly larger than the chicken. Place the pot, uncovered, over medium heat until the salt is very hot, stirring from time to time, about 30 minutes.
- Scoop most of the salt into a large bowl, leaving a 1 1/2-to-2-inch layer of salt in the bottom of the pot. Place the chicken over the salt layer, breast side up. Spoon the remaining salt over and around the chicken, so that it is completely buried in salt.
- Cover the pot with the lid. Bake until the chicken is cooked through, about 1 1/2 hours. Scrape the salt from the chicken and remove from the pot. Wipe off as much of the salt as possible and let stand for 10 minutes. Carve the chicken and serve.

Nutrition Information

- 663: calories;
- 0 grams: trans fat;
- 19 grams: monounsaturated fat;
- 10 grams: polyunsaturated fat;
- 57 grams: protein;
- 1055 milligrams: sodium;
- 46 grams: fat;
- 13 grams: saturated fat;

253. Samuel's Roasted Mushroom Base

Serving: 1 1/4 pounds (about 3 cups) | Prep: | Cook: | Ready in: 30mins

Ingredients

- ¼ cup extra virgin olive oil
- 2 pounds cremini mushrooms, cut in small dice if large, quartered if small
- Kosher salt to taste
- ¼ teaspoon ground black pepper
- 1 teaspoon mushroom powder, made by pulverizing dried mushrooms in a spice mill (optional)

Direction

- Preheat the oven to 400 degrees. Line 2 baking sheets with parchment.
- In a large bowl mix together the olive oil, mushrooms, salt and pepper. Spread in an even layer on the baking sheets.
- Bake 1 sheet at a time on the middle rack of the preheated oven for 15 to 20 minutes, stirring every 5 minutes, until the mushrooms are tender. They will reduce considerably in volume. Remove from the heat and allow to cool. Process in a food processor fitted with the steel blade until chopped fine but still retaining some texture. Taste and adjust seasonings. Mix in mushroom powder if desired.

Nutrition Information

- 170: calories;
- 14 grams: fat;
- 2 grams: polyunsaturated fat;
- 10 grams: carbohydrates;
- 1 gram: dietary fiber;
- 4 grams: sugars;
- 6 grams: protein;
- 559 milligrams: sodium;

254. Sardines In Vinegar (Escabeche)

Serving: Serves 4 | Prep: | Cook: | Ready in: 25mins

Ingredients

- 1 pound sardines, (or 4 to 6 per person depending on the size), cleaned, heads removed
- Salt and freshly ground pepper
- 3 tablespoons extra-virgin olive oil
- ¼ cup red wine vinegar or sherry vinegar
- 2 garlic cloves, peeled, halved, and green shoots removed
- Pinch of saffron threads
- Pinch of ground ginger
- 2 onions, sliced or chopped
- ½ teaspoon coriander seeds, crushed
- 2 small bay leaves
- 1 lemon, sliced in rounds
- Chopped fresh parsley for garnish

Direction

- Pat sardines dry and season on both sides with salt and pepper. Heat 2 tablespoons of the oil over medium-high heat in a large, heavy skillet and add sardines. Cook on one side for about 2 1/2 minutes, flip over and cook on the other side for another 2 1/2 minutes, or until flesh is opaque and flakes when poked with a fork. Add 2 tablespoons of the vinegar, toss together and scrape bottom of pan with a spoon to deglaze. Remove from heat and transfer to a ceramic baking dish.
- In a mortar and pestle, mash together garlic, a generous pinch of salt, saffron and ginger.
- Heat remaining olive oil over medium heat in the skillet in which you cooked the sardines and add onions and pinch of salt. Cook, stirring, until onions are tender, about 5 minutes. Add garlic mix, coriander seeds and bay leaves and continue to cook, stirring often, until onions are very soft but not browned (add a little salt if they begin to stick), another

166

3 to 5 minutes. Stir in remaining vinegar and turn heat to medium low. Simmer for another 5 minutes. Season to taste with salt and pepper and add to dish with sardines. Toss together gently.

- Top sardines with lemon slices. Cover dish and refrigerate for at least 1 hour (as long as overnight). Before serving, sprinkle with parsley.

Nutrition Information

- 275: calories;
- 16 grams: fat;
- 3 grams: sugars;
- 9 grams: monounsaturated fat;
- 8 grams: carbohydrates;
- 2 grams: dietary fiber;
- 24 grams: protein;
- 507 milligrams: sodium;

255.	Sauce

Serving: Six cups | Prep: | Cook: | Ready in: 40mins

Ingredients

- 2 tablespoons olive oil
- ½ cup finely diced celery
- ½ cup finely diced green pepper
- 1 bay leaf
- 1 large clove garlic, minced
- 1 ½ teaspoons dried basil
- 1 teaspoon dried thyme
- ½ teaspoon dried oregano
- 1 teaspoon salt
- 1 teaspoon black pepper
- 2 tablespoons Worcestershire sauce
- 2 dashes Tabasco sauce
- 4 cups canned tomatoes, with their juice
- 1 tablespoon tomato paste
- 3 tablespoons chopped parsley

Direction

- Heat the olive oil in a large skillet and saute the vegetables for 5 minutes or until soft. Add the bay leaf, garlic, herbs, salt and pepper, Worcestershire and Tabasco. Cook over low heat for 3 minutes, or until all ingredients are combined.
- Chop the tomatoes and add to the skillet with their juice. Cook gently until the sauce begins to thicken, about 20 minutes.
- Stir in the tomato paste. Cook 5 minutes. Add the parsley and stir well. Serve over Basic Texas Meat Loaf.

Nutrition Information

- 40: calories;
- 1 gram: protein;
- 230 milligrams: sodium;
- 3 grams: sugars;
- 0 grams: polyunsaturated fat;
- 2 grams: dietary fiber;
- 5 grams: carbohydrates;

256.	Sauteed Striped Bass With Wild Mushrooms

Serving: 4 servings | Prep: | Cook: | Ready in: 45mins

Ingredients

- 3 large Idaho or Washington potatoes, peeled and cut into ovals 1/8-inch thick
- 6 tablespoons vegetable oil, plus more if needed
- Salt
- 3 cups coarsely sliced cepes or porcini (about 1 pound)
- 1 cup coarsely sliced chanterelles (about 1/3 pound)
- Freshly ground pepper to taste
- 4 tablespoons finely chopped shallots
- 1 teaspoon finely chopped garlic
- 4 tablespoons finely chopped parsley

- 4 striped bass fillets, about 6 ounces each, with skin removed
- ¼ cup flour for dredging
- 4 tablespoons butter
- 1 tablespoon lemon juice
- 4 tablespoons chopped chives

Direction

- Rinse potato slices under cold running water, drain well and pat dry.
- Heat 2 tablespoons of oil in a large, nonstick skillet over high heat. Add potatoes, salt to taste, and cook until lightly browned on both sides. Remove from skillet; keep warm.
- Add a little more oil to the pan if necessary, and add the cepes and chanterelles. Salt and pepper to taste. Cook over high heat until the mushrooms wilt. Add the shallots, garlic and parsley. Cook for about a minute, stirring gently; then, set aside. Keep warm.
- Dredge the fish in flour, and shake off the excess. Set aside.
- In another large, nonstick skillet, add 4 remaining tablespoons of vegetable oil over medium heat. Add the fillets, and season well. Cook until lightly browned, about 3 or 4 minutes. Reduce the heat to medium, gently flip the fish and cook 3 to 4 minutes more, or until done. Do not overcook. Remove and keep warm.
- Divide the potatoes evenly over four plates in a ring pattern. Place the fish over the center, and put the mushroom mixture over the fish.
- In a saucepan over medium-high heat, melt the butter, and cook, swirling occasionally, until lightly browned. Add lemon juice, then pour lemon butter equally over each serving. Sprinkle with chives and serve.

Nutrition Information

- 659: calories;
- 37 grams: fat;
- 10 grams: saturated fat;
- 7 grams: dietary fiber;
- 38 grams: protein;

- 1271 milligrams: sodium;
- 5 grams: sugars;
- 1 gram: trans fat;
- 19 grams: monounsaturated fat;
- 6 grams: polyunsaturated fat;
- 45 grams: carbohydrates;

257.   Sauteed Wild Mushrooms With Shallots And Garlic

Serving: 4 servings | Prep: | Cook: | Ready in: 15mins

Ingredients

- 1 pound fresh wild mushrooms, like chanterelles, morels, porcini or any cultivated mushrooms of your choice
- 2 tablespoons olive oil
- Salt and freshly ground pepper to taste
- 1 tablespoon butter
- 2 tablespoons fine bread crumbs
- 1 tablespoon finely chopped shallots
- 1 teaspoon finely chopped garlic
- 2 tablespoons finely chopped parsley

Direction

- Trim the mushrooms, wash them in cold water and drain well.
- If the mushrooms are large, slice them or cut them in halves or quarters.
- Heat a large, heavy skillet and add the olive oil. When it is very hot and almost smoking, add the mushrooms, salt and pepper. Cook over high heat, shaking and tossing the skillet so that the mushrooms cook evenly until they are browned and crisp. They should be almost mahogany in color.
- Add the butter, and quickly sprinkle in the bread crumbs, shallots and garlic, and toss well for 10 seconds. Add the parsley and serve immediately.

Nutrition Information

- 128: calories;
- 4 grams: protein;
- 308 milligrams: sodium;
- 3 grams: sugars;
- 0 grams: trans fat;
- 6 grams: monounsaturated fat;
- 2 grams: dietary fiber;
- 10 grams: fat;
- 1 gram: polyunsaturated fat;
- 7 grams: carbohydrates;

258.   Sautéed Chanterelles

Serving: 4 servings | Prep: | Cook: | Ready in: 20mins

Ingredients

- 1 pound chanterelles
- 2 to 3 tablespoons unsalted butter
- ¼ cup dry white wine
- About 3/4 cup chicken stock, preferably homemade
- Coarse salt and freshly ground pepper to taste
- 1 tablespoon chopped parsley, fresh thyme leaves or chives

Direction

- Cut the base of the stems of the chanterelles. If the mushrooms are very gritty, rinse them quickly under cold running water and pat them dry. Otherwise, clean them carefully with a soft paint or pastry brush. Cut the large mushrooms into bite-size pieces; leave the smaller ones whole.
- Heat the butter in a frying pan. Add the chanterelles and saute for two to three minutes or until they start to become soft. Add the wine and when it has evaporated, add the chicken stock. Cook over high heat until it has almost evaporated. Season to taste with salt and pepper and sprinkle with parsley, thyme or chives.

Nutrition Information

- 136: calories;
- 10 grams: carbohydrates;
- 425 milligrams: sodium;
- 0 grams: polyunsaturated fat;
- 2 grams: sugars;
- 4 grams: dietary fiber;
- 3 grams: protein;
- 8 grams: fat;
- 5 grams: saturated fat;

259.   Sautéed Red Snapper With Rhubarb Sauce

Serving: 4 servings | Prep: | Cook: | Ready in: 30mins

Ingredients

- 1 pound rhubarb, washed and trimmed
- ⅓ cup sugar
- Pinch saffron
- Salt and pepper to taste
- 2 tablespoons olive oil
- 2 tablespoons butter (or a little more oil)
- 4 6-ounce red snapper fillets
- Chopped mint or parsley for garnish (optional)

Direction

- Combine the rhubarb, sugar and saffron in a small saucepan, cover and turn the heat to low. Cook, stirring only occasionally, for about 20 minutes, or until the rhubarb becomes saucy. Add salt to taste and a little more sugar if necessary. If the mixture is very soupy, continue to cook a little longer to make it thicker.
- When you judge the rhubarb to be nearly done, put a large skillet, preferably nonstick, over medium-high heat. A minute later, add the oil and butter. When the butter foam subsides, add the fillets, skin side down. Cook for 4 or 5 minutes, or until the fish is nearly

done; turn carefully; and lightly brown the flesh side, seasoning it with salt and pepper as it cooks. Transfer the fish to a plate lined with paper towels to absorb excess oil.

- Serve the fish napped with a bit of the sauce and garnished, if you like, with the herb.

Nutrition Information

- 371: calories;
- 0 grams: trans fat;
- 7 grams: monounsaturated fat;
- 22 grams: carbohydrates;
- 36 grams: protein;
- 732 milligrams: sodium;
- 15 grams: fat;
- 5 grams: saturated fat;
- 2 grams: dietary fiber;
- 18 grams: sugars;

260. Sautéed Shredded Cabbage And Squash

Serving: The sautéed vegetables alone serve 4; the gratin serves 6. | Prep: | Cook: |Ready in: 1hours30mins

Ingredients

- For the shredded vegetable sauté:
- 2 tablespoons extra virgin olive oil
- 1 pound winter squash, peeled and shredded
- ½ cup chopped onion
- ¾ pound green cabbage, shredded
- 2 garlic cloves, minced
- 2 teaspoons finely chopped fresh sage
- 2 teaspoons chopped fresh thyme leaves
- For the gratin:
- 3 eggs
- ½ cup low-fat milk
- Salt and freshly ground pepper
- 1 cup cooked barley, rice (preferably brown) or quinoa
- 2 ounces Gruyère, grated (1/2 cup)
- 1 ounce Parmesan, grated (1/4 cup)

Direction

- If serving the vegetables with grains, begin cooking the grains of your choice first.
- Heat 1 tablespoon of the olive oil over medium heat in a large, heavy skillet or a wok and add the onion. Cook, stirring, until it begins to soften, about 3 minutes. Add the shredded winter squash and the garlic and a generous pinch of salt. Cook, stirring often, until not quite tender, about 10 minutes, and add the remaining oil, the cabbage, sage, thyme, and salt and pepper to taste. Continue to cook, stirring often, until the vegetables are tender and fragrant, 8 to 10 minutes. Serve with grains or use the vegetables for the gratin below.
- If making a gratin, preheat the oven to 375 degrees and oil a 2-quart baking dish or gratin dish. In a large bowl, whisk together the eggs and milk. Add salt to taste (about 1/2 teaspoon) and freshly ground pepper, and stir in the cooked grains (I used cooked purple barley, and it was a beautiful and tasty combination with lots of texture) and the cooked vegetables. Add the cheeses and stir everything together, then scrape into the prepared baking dish.
- Bake 40 to 45 minutes, or until the top is lightly browned and the gratin is set. Allow to cool for 15 minutes or longer before cutting into wedges and serving. The gratin is good hot, warm or at room temperature, and you can cut it into smaller pieces to serve as an hors d'oeuvre.

Nutrition Information

- 448: calories;
- 21 grams: protein;
- 833 milligrams: sodium;
- 7 grams: saturated fat;
- 0 grams: trans fat;
- 9 grams: monounsaturated fat;
- 48 grams: carbohydrates;
- 8 grams: sugars;
- 20 grams: fat;

- 3 grams: polyunsaturated fat;

261. Savory Whole Wheat Buttermilk Scones With Rosemary And Thyme

Serving: 12 small scones | Prep: | Cook: |Ready in: 30mins

Ingredients

- 150 grams (approximately 1 1/4 cups) whole-wheat flour
- 100 grams (approximately 3/4 cup) unbleached all-purpose flour
- 10 grams (2 teaspoons) baking powder
- 5 grams (1/2 teaspoon) baking soda
- 4 grams (approximately 1 teaspoon) brown sugar
- 5 grams (approximately 3/4 teaspoon) salt
- 70 grams (2 1/2 ounces / 5 tablespoons) unsalted butter
- 1 tablespoon finely chopped mixed fresh rosemary and thyme
- 125 grams (approximately 1/2 cup) buttermilk

Direction

- Preheat oven to 400 degrees. Line a baking sheet with parchment.
- Sift together flours, baking powder, baking soda, sugar and salt. Rub in butter, or place in a stand mixer fitted with the paddle and beat at low speed until incorporated. Add chopped rosemary and thyme and buttermilk and mix just until the dough comes together.
- Transfer to a lightly floured work surface and gently shape into a 1/2-inch thick rectangle. Either cut 2-inch circles with a biscuit cutter or cut into 6 squares, then cut each square in half on the diagonal. Transfer to baking sheet. Bake 15 minutes, until browned on the bottom. Flip over, bake 2 more minutes, and remove from the heat. Serve warm or allow to cool.

Nutrition Information

- 121: calories;
- 0 grams: polyunsaturated fat;
- 1 gram: sugars;
- 17 grams: carbohydrates;
- 2 grams: dietary fiber;
- 201 milligrams: sodium;
- 5 grams: fat;
- 3 grams: protein;

262. Scallop Cakes With Artichoke Hearts

Serving: Four servings | Prep: | Cook: |Ready in: 20mins

Ingredients

- ½ pound sea scallops, coarsely chopped
- 3 artichoke hearts, cooked until tender, cooled and coarsely chopped
- 1 tablespoon minced fresh parsley
- 1 teaspoon minced fresh mint
- 1 egg, beaten
- ½ teaspoon salt
- Freshly ground black pepper to taste
- ¼ cup cracker crumbs

Direction

- Combine all ingredients in a medium bowl. With slightly moistened hands, form the mixture into 8 cakes, each about 1/2 inch thick.
- Coat a large nonstick skillet lightly with oil. Heat over medium-low heat until hot. Add as many fish cakes as will comfortably fit in pan. Cook until nicely browned on both sides and scallops are cooked through, about 4 minutes per side.

Nutrition Information

- 88: calories;

- 292 milligrams: sodium;
- 2 grams: dietary fiber;
- 1 gram: sugars;
- 0 grams: trans fat;
- 8 grams: carbohydrates;
- 10 grams: protein;

263. Sea Scallops With Red Peppers And Tomatoes

Serving: 4 servings | Prep: | Cook: | Ready in: 20mins

Ingredients

- 1 ½ pounds sea scallops
- ¼ cup milk
- Salt and freshly ground pepper to taste
- Flour for dredging
- 4 tablespoons olive oil
- 1 sweet red pepper, cored, seeded and cut into 1/4-inch pieces
- 1 cup ripe plum tomatoes, seeded, peeled and cut into 1/2-inch cubes
- 2 tablespoons finely chopped shallots
- 1 teaspoon finely chopped garlic
- 1 tablespoon fresh lemon juice
- 4 tablespoons coarsely chopped parsley

Direction

- Cut the scallops crosswise if they are more than 1 1/4 inches across.
- Place the scallops in a mixing bowl and add the milk, salt and pepper. Set aside. Place the flour in a flat dish and set it aside.
- Heat 2 tablespoons of the oil in a nonstick skillet over medium-high heat. Add the red pepper, tomatoes, salt and pepper. Cook and stir until wilted. This should take a few minutes.
- Drain the scallops and dredge them in the flour. Shake off the excess.
- Meanwhile, heat the remaining oil over high heat in a nonstick skillet large enough to hold the scallops in one layer. If the skillet cannot

accommodate all the scallops, cook them in two batches. Add the scallops and cook, stirring, until golden brown. Do not overcook.
- Add the shallots, garlic and lemon juice, shaking the pan. Cook about 30 seconds. Add the pepper and tomato mixture and stir and toss well for about 2 minutes. Add the parsley and serve immediately with rice Creole (see recipe).

Nutrition Information

- 280: calories;
- 10 grams: monounsaturated fat;
- 22 grams: protein;
- 15 grams: fat;
- 0 grams: trans fat;
- 13 grams: carbohydrates;
- 4 grams: sugars;
- 680 milligrams: sodium;
- 2 grams: dietary fiber;

264. Seared Fish With Beet Salsa

Serving: Serves 4 | Prep: | Cook: | Ready in: 1hours

Ingredients

- For the salsa
- 3 medium or 4 small beets, preferably a mix of golden, Chioggia and red, roasted, peeled and cut in very small dice (smaller than 1/4 inch) (about 1 cup very small dice)
- 2 to 3 serrano or jalapeño chiles, minced
- ¼ cup chopped cilantro (more to taste)
- Salt to taste
- 2 tablespoons fresh lime juice (more to taste)
- 2 tablespoons minced shallot or chives (optional)
- ½ small tart apple, cored and cut in very small dice (smaller than 1/4 inch)
- 2 tablespoons extra virgin olive oil
- For the fish

- 1 ½ pounds cod fillets (or other light-fleshed fish of your choice, like halibut or tilapia
- Salt and freshly ground pepper
- 1 tablespoon sunflower oil, grapeseed oil or extra virgin olive oil
- Juice of 1 lime

Direction

- Combine all of the ingredients for the salsa in a medium bowl. Stir together, taste and adjust salt. Set aside for 30 minutes or longer.
- Preheat the oven to 400 degrees. Season the fish with salt and pepper. Heat a heavy ovenproof skillet over high heat and add the oil. Tilt the pan to film the bottom. Add the fish fillets and cook for 1 minute, or until you can easily slide a spatula underneath and turn the fish over (you may have to do this in two batches so that you don't crowd the fish).
- Turn the fish over and place in the oven for 5 to 10 minutes, depending on the thickness of the fillet (5 minutes per 1/2 inch thickness), until the fish is opaque and can be pulled apart with the tines of a fork. Remove from the heat and transfer to plates or a platter. Squeeze lime juice over each piece of fish and serve, garnishing each serving with a generous spoonful of salsa.

Nutrition Information

- 287: calories;
- 10 grams: carbohydrates;
- 3 grams: dietary fiber;
- 6 grams: sugars;
- 2 grams: polyunsaturated fat;
- 7 grams: monounsaturated fat;
- 33 grams: protein;
- 650 milligrams: sodium;
- 13 grams: fat;

265.   Seared Salmon With Mashed Vegetables And Seaweed

Serving: six servings | Prep: | Cook: | Ready in: 30mins

Ingredients

- For the seaweed:
- 2 to 3 tablespoons canola oil
- 12 1-by-3-inch strips dulse seaweed
- For the vegetables:
- 2 medium Idaho potatoes, peeled and cubed
- 2 medium parsnips, peeled and cubed
- 2 small white turnips, peeled and cubed
- 1 clove garlic, minced
- ½ cup chopped onion
- 1 leek, chopped
- Coarse salt and freshly ground pepper to taste
- ¼ cup olive oil
- ¼ cup heavy cream
- For the shallot sauce:
- 8 ounces shallots, peeled and sliced
- 2 tablespoons olive oil
- ⅓ cup flour
- 1 pint fish stock or clam juice
- ½ tablespoon crushed black peppercorns
- 2 tablespoons balsamic vinegar
- For the salmon:
- 6 6-ounce salmon fillets
- Coarse sea salt and freshly ground pepper to taste
- 2 tablespoons canola or grapeseed oil

Direction

- Heat the oil in a heavy skillet and fry the seaweed for one minute. Remove and drain on paper towels.
- Prepare the vegetables. Simmer the first six ingredients together in boiling, salted water for 12 to 15 minutes. Drain and mash. Season to taste and add the olive oil and heavy cream. Mix well and keep warm.
- Saute the shallots over medium heat in the oil until caramelized (about 10 to 15 minutes). Sprinkle with flour and stir well. Add the fish

stock and cook slowly over moderate heat, stirring until any lumps have disappeared. Season to taste with salt, add the crushed peppercorns and vinegar and simmer five more minutes. Set aside and keep warm.

- Season the salmon with salt and pepper to taste. Heat the oil in a saute pan and sear the salmon for two-and-a-half to three minutes on each side for rare, more for well done.
- While the fish is cooking, place a mound of potato mixture in the center of six individually heated plates. Spoon sauce around the potato and top it with the salmon fillet. Sprinkle the seaweed on top.

Nutrition Information

- 788: calories;
- 22 grams: monounsaturated fat;
- 13 grams: polyunsaturated fat;
- 41 grams: carbohydrates;
- 9 grams: sugars;
- 52 grams: fat;
- 10 grams: saturated fat;
- 0 grams: trans fat;
- 7 grams: dietary fiber;
- 42 grams: protein;
- 1174 milligrams: sodium;

- ½ teaspoon freshly ground pepper
- 1 tablespoon unbleached all-purpose flour
- ¾ cup white wine
- ¼ cup capers, drained
- 2 cups vegetable stock or water
- 1 bay leaf
- 1 tablespoon minced fresh flat-leaf parsley, plus 1/4 cup chopped fresh flat-leaf parsley for garnish (optional)
- 1 teaspoon minced fresh thyme leaves
- ⅛ teaspoon ground turmeric
- ¼ cup freshly squeezed lemon juice
- Garnish
- Caper berries, for garnish
- 1 lemon, thinly sliced, for garnish (optional)
- Seitan Cutlets
- 7 cups unbleached bread flour
- 3 cups whole-wheat bread flour
- 4 ½ cups water
- 1 ½ teaspoons sea salt
- 8 cups vegetable stock or water
- ¼ cup tamari
- 1 piece of kombu
- 1 piece of wakame

Direction

-
-

---

266.   Seitan Piccata

Serving: 6 to 8 cutlets, about 1 1/2 pounds. | Prep: | Cook: | Ready in: 4hours

Ingredients

- 6 seitan cutlets (about 1 1/2 pounds; see recipe below)
- Whole-wheat flour, for dredging
- 6 tablespoons extra-virgin olive oil
- ¼ cup minced shallots
- ¼ cup finely sliced leek, white and pale green parts
- 1 teaspoon sea salt

---

267.   Shell Bean Succotash

Serving: Serves 6 | Prep: | Cook: | Ready in: 1hours15mins

Ingredients

- 1 pound shell beans (about 1 3/4 cups)
- 1 onion, halved
- 7 cups water
- 3 large garlic cloves, crushed
- A bouquet garni made with a few sprigs each of parsley and thyme, a sprig of sage and a bay leaf
- Salt to taste

- 2 tablespoons extra virgin olive oil
- 1 small red onion, finely chopped
- ½ pound summer squash, cut in small dice
- 2 garlic cloves, minced (optional)
- Kernels from 4 ears of corn
- 2 or 3 sage leaves, minced
- Freshly ground pepper

Direction

- Combine the beans, onion, water, garlic, bouquet garni and salt in a heavy saucepan or soup pot, and bring to a simmer. Cover and simmer 45 minutes, or until the beans are tender. Taste and adjust salt. Remove and discard the onion, the bouquet garni and the garlic cloves. Drain though a strainer or colander set over a bowl.
- Heat the olive oil in a large, heavy skillet over medium heat, and add the red onion. Cook, stirring, until it begins to soften, for about three minutes. Add the squash, and salt to taste. Cook, stirring, until the squash begins to soften and look translucent, three to four minutes. Add the garlic and corn. Cook for about four minutes, stirring often. Season with salt and pepper. Add the beans and sage, and continue to cook, stirring, for another minute or two. Taste and adjust seasonings. If you want this to be more moist, stir in some of the bean broth.

Nutrition Information

- 90: calories;
- 2 grams: sugars;
- 900 milligrams: sodium;
- 5 grams: fat;
- 1 gram: polyunsaturated fat;
- 3 grams: protein;
- 10 grams: carbohydrates;

---

268. Shrimp Broth

Serving: About four cups | Prep: | Cook: | Ready in: 30mins

Ingredients

- Shells from raw shrimp
- 5 cups water
- 6 black peppercorns
- ¼ cup coarsely chopped onions
- 2 ribs celery coarsely chopped
- 1 bay leaf

Direction

- Put all the ingredients in a saucepan and bring to a boil. Simmer for 20 minutes and strain.

---

269. Shrimp And Corn Curry

Serving: 4 servings (5 cups) | Prep: | Cook: | Ready in: 40mins

Ingredients

- 2 tablespoons vegetable oil, preferably canola
- 3 tablespoons curry powder
- 1 medium onion, chopped
- 1 tablespoon black mustard seeds
- 1 ½ pounds shrimp, peeled and de-veined
- 2 medium tomatoes, cored and chopped
- 2 cups cooked corn kernels (see Micro-Tips)
- 1 tablespoon peeled and grated fresh ginger
- 1 to 2 tablespoons fresh lemon juice
- ¼ cup chopped cilantro
- 1 ½ teaspoons kosher salt
- Freshly ground black pepper to taste

Direction

- Place oil, curry, onion and mustard seeds in a 2 1/2-quart souffle dish with a tightly fitting lid. Cook, uncovered, at 100 percent power in a high-power oven for 4 minutes.
- Stir in shrimp. Cook, covered, for 3 minutes.

- Remove from oven. Stir in tomatoes, corn and ginger. Cook, covered, for 5 minutes.
- Remove from oven. Stir in remaining ingredients.

Nutrition Information

- 326: calories;
- 0 grams: trans fat;
- 3 grams: polyunsaturated fat;
- 29 grams: carbohydrates;
- 28 grams: protein;
- 11 grams: fat;
- 1 gram: saturated fat;
- 973 milligrams: sodium;
- 6 grams: sugars;

---

270. Silvano Marchetto's Penne All'Arrabiata

Serving: 4 to 6 servings | Prep: | Cook: | Ready in: 30mins

Ingredients

- ¼ cup Tuscan extravirgin olive oil
- 2 whole cloves garlic
- 1 chopped clove garlic
- 1 16-ounce can imported Italian plum tomatoes
- 10 leaves fresh basil
- 1 whole dried hot red chili pepper
- Salt and freshly ground black pepper to taste
- 1 pound penne (short tubular pasta)
- 1 tablespoon salt

Direction

- Over medium heat, brown the 2 garlic cloves in the olive oil. When thoroughly brown, remove and discard.
- Add the chopped garlic clove and let sizzle for a moment, watching carefully that it doesn't burn.

- Add tomatoes and their juice to the garlic in the pan, breaking up the tomatoes with a fork. Leave to cook for 10 minutes to reduce the sauce slightly.
- While tomatoes are cooking, wash and dry the basil leaves and cut into ribbons. Cut the whole chili pepper in half and discard the seeds. Chop the pepper roughly. Add chili pepper and basil to the sauce in the pan, stir well and taste for seasoning, adding salt and pepper if desired. Leave to simmer over low heat while preparing pasta.
- Bring 4 quarts of water to a rolling boil. Add 1 tablespoon of salt and when water reboils, add pasta all at once. Stir vigorously with a long-handled wooden spoon or fork to bring quickly back to a boil. Cook until done.
- Drain and turn into a warmed serving bowl. Dress with the sauce and serve immediately.

Nutrition Information

- 378: calories;
- 7 grams: monounsaturated fat;
- 60 grams: carbohydrates;
- 4 grams: sugars;
- 11 grams: protein;
- 379 milligrams: sodium;
- 10 grams: fat;
- 1 gram: polyunsaturated fat;

---

271. Smoked Chicken Breasts

Serving: Four servings | Prep: | Cook: | Ready in: 45mins

Ingredients

- 1 tablespoon wood chips
- 2 chicken breasts, split, skinned but not boned

Direction

- Place the wood chips in the bottom of a stove-top smoker and place the chicken on the rack over the chips. Place over medium heat until the wood begins to smolder. Cover and cook until the chicken is cooked through, about 45 minutes.

272.   Smoked Mozzarella And Sun Dried Tomato Pizza

Serving: 4 main-course servings | Prep: | Cook: | Ready in: 2hours25mins

Ingredients

- Basic dough (see recipe)
- ½ pound sun-dried tomatoes, packed in oil, drained, oil reserved
- ½ pound smoked mozzarella, halved lengthwise and sliced thin

Direction

- Prepare the dough.
- Preheat oven to 425 degrees. Brush the top of dough with 1 1/2 tablespoons of the oil reserved from the sun-dried tomatoes. Bake for 15 minutes. Remove the dough from the oven and arrange the tomatoes over the top in a pinwheel fashion. Arrange the cheese slices in between the tomatoes. Bake until the cheese is melted and the dough is golden brown, about 5 minutes longer.

273.   Smoked Sturgeon Salad With Leeks, Haricots Verts And Frisee

Serving: 4 servings | Prep: | Cook: | Ready in: 1hours

Ingredients

- Zest and juice from 2 lemons
- 1 tablespoon chopped parsley
- 1 tablespoon chopped shallots
- 2 teaspoons green peppercorns packed in water or vinegar, drained, mashed
- ¼ cup extra virgin olive oil
- Kosher salt
- 2 teaspoons sugar
- 1 teaspoon turmeric
- ¼ cup champagne vinegar
- ⅔ cup grape-seed oil
- Freshly ground black pepper
- ¼ pound smoked sturgeon, flaked into bite-sized pieces
- 2 Idaho potatoes, peeled and cut into 1/2-inch dice
- ¼ pound haricots verts
- 2 leeks, white part only, cleaned and cut into 1/2-inch slices
- 3 slices country bread, cut into 4-inch-long sticks
- 2 tablespoons butter, melted
- 1 head frisee lettuce, green leaves only, cut into bite-size pieces

Direction

- Make green peppercorn dressing: in a small bowl, combine lemon zest, parsley, shallots and peppercorns. Add lemon juice and gradually whisk in olive oil. Season to taste with salt.
- In a small saucepan over medium heat, combine sugar with 2 tablespoons water. Stir until sugar is dissolved. In a medium bowl combine sugar water and turmeric. Whisk in the vinegar, then the grape-seed oil. Season to taste with salt and pepper. Add sturgeon to mixture, stirring to coat. Season to taste with salt and pepper, and set aside.
- In a small pan over high heat, combine 2 quarts of water with 1/2 teaspoon salt. Bring to a boil, add diced potatoes and cook until tender. Drain, rinse with cold water, and drain again. In the same pan, again combine 2 quarts of water with 1/2 teaspoon salt, and bring to a boil. Add haricots verts, and cook until tender, but still slightly crisp. Drain, transfer to a bowl of ice water, and drain again. In a large bowl,

combine potatoes and haricots verts, and set aside.

- In a medium saucepan, combine leeks with enough water to cover. Season with salt and pepper to taste. Bring to a boil, cover, and cook until tender, about 3 minutes. Drain, cool and add to the bowl of potatoes and haricots verts.
- Preheat oven to 350 degrees. Brush bread sticks with melted butter, and bake until golden brown, about 10 minutes. Remove, and season to taste with salt and pepper.
- Add frisee to vegetables. Add vinaigrette a little at a time, tossing to mix well and reserving about 2 tablespoons for drizzling over the finished salad. On each of 4 plates, place 1/4 of the sturgeon. Top with a mound of vegetables, and drizzle with vinaigrette. Garnish with bread sticks.

Nutrition Information

- 729: calories;
- 7 grams: dietary fiber;
- 8 grams: sugars;
- 58 grams: fat;
- 0 grams: trans fat;
- 18 grams: monounsaturated fat;
- 28 grams: polyunsaturated fat;
- 45 grams: carbohydrates;
- 884 milligrams: sodium;
- 10 grams: saturated fat;
- 11 grams: protein;

---

274. Smoked Tomato And Chicken Pasta

Serving: Four servings | Prep: | Cook: | Ready in: 45mins

Ingredients

- 1 ½ tablespoons wood chips
- 2 chicken breasts, split, skinned but not boned
- 12 plum tomatoes, cored and halved lengthwise

- 1 teaspoon salt, plus more to taste
- Freshly ground pepper to taste
- 1 pound farfalle
- ¼ cup fresh basil, cut across into thin strips

Direction

- Smoke the chicken breasts as in the recipe above, using 1 1/2 tablespoons of wood chips. Sprinkle the tomatoes with 1/4 teaspoon of salt and pepper to taste. Remove the chicken from the rack and add the tomatoes, cut side up. Cover and smoke until the tomatoes are soft, about 25 minutes.
- Meanwhile, take the chicken off the bone and shred. Bring a large pot of salted water to a boil. Add the pasta and cook until al dente, about 10 minutes. Drain. Cut the tomato pieces in half crosswise.
- Place the pasta in a large bowl and toss with the chicken, tomatoes, remaining salt, pepper and basil. Divide among 4 plates and serve.

---

275. Sorghum Sweet Potatoes

Serving: 8 servings | Prep: | Cook: | Ready in: 20mins

Ingredients

- 3 pounds sweet potatoes, peeled and cut into 1-inch cubes
- 1 teaspoon kosher salt
- 3 tablespoons unsalted butter
- 1 red jalapeno chile, minced
- ¼ teaspoon grated orange zest
- ½ cup heavy cream
- ¼ cup vegetable stock
- 2 tablespoons sorghum or maple syrup
- ¼ teaspoon freshly grated nutmeg

Direction

- Place the sweet potatoes in a large pot and cover with water. Bring to a boil, season with 1/2 teaspoon of the salt and cook until tender.

- While the sweet potatoes are cooking, melt the butter in a small saucepan, and when the butter bubbles and froths, add the jalapeno and the orange zest. Cook for 1 minute, turn off the heat and then add the cream. Set aside.
- When the sweet potatoes are fork tender, drain them in a colander set up in your sink. Let them drain completely, and then pass them through a ricer or mash them well with a potato masher.
- Add the flavored cream, stock, sorghum, nutmeg and the remaining 1/2 teaspoon of salt. Mix well and transfer to a serving bowl.

Nutrition Information

- 250: calories;
- 11 grams: sugars;
- 337 milligrams: sodium;
- 38 grams: carbohydrates;
- 5 grams: dietary fiber;
- 10 grams: fat;
- 6 grams: saturated fat;
- 0 grams: polyunsaturated fat;
- 3 grams: protein;

---

276. Southeast Asian Shrimp And Grapefruit Salad

Serving: 4 servings | Prep: | Cook: | Ready in: 30mins

Ingredients

- 1 to 1 ½ pounds shrimp
- Salt
- 3 tablespoons nam pla (fish sauce) or soy sauce
- 1 tablespoon sugar
- Juice of 2 limes
- 6 cups lettuce or mesclun, washed and dried
- 2 grapefruit, peeled and sectioned, tough white pith removed, each section cut in half
- ¼ cup chopped mint
- ¼ cup chopped cilantro
- Minced chilies or dried red pepper flakes, optional
- ½ cup chopped dry-roasted peanuts, optional

Direction

- Put shrimp in a saucepan with salted water to cover; bring to a boil, then turn off heat and let sit for 5 minutes, or until shrimp are opaque in center. (Alternatively, grill or saute, sprinkling shrimp with salt as they cook.) Cool in refrigerator or under cold running water, then peel (and devein if you like). Cut shrimp in half if they're large.
- Combine nam pla or soy sauce with 2 tablespoons water, sugar and lime juice, and blend or whisk until smooth.
- Arrange the lettuce on 4 plates; top each portion with a few grapefruit pieces, some shrimp, and the mint and cilantro; drizzle with the dressing, then sprinkle with a little of the minced chilies and chopped peanuts if you like, or pass them at the table.

Nutrition Information

- 182: calories;
- 2 grams: fat;
- 13 grams: sugars;
- 1468 milligrams: sodium;
- 0 grams: monounsaturated fat;
- 1 gram: polyunsaturated fat;
- 21 grams: carbohydrates;
- 4 grams: dietary fiber;
- 23 grams: protein;

---

277. Southern Black Eyed Peas And Cauliflower

Serving: | Prep: | Cook: | Ready in: 30mins

Ingredients

- 2 tablespoons olive oil

- 1 large onion, finely chopped
- 1 green bell pepper, seeded and diced
- 2 cups cauliflower florets, roughly chopped into 1/2-inch pieces
- 2 cloves garlic, minced
- 1 tablespoon ground cumin
- 1 teaspoon chili powder
- ½ teaspoon ground cinnamon
- ¼ teaspoon cayenne pepper
- ½ teaspoon sea salt
- 2 (15-ounce) cans black-eyed peas, rinsed and drained
- 1 (14-ounce) can tomato sauce
- 1 cup water
- ¼ cup soy sauce
- ⅓ cup packed brown sugar or maple syrup
- 2 tablespoons white or apple cider vinegar

Direction

- In a large pot, heat oil over medium-high heat and sauté onions and green peppers until soft. Add cauliflower and cook, stirring frequently, until it is lightly browned, about 5 to 8 minutes. Add garlic, cumin, chili powder, cinnamon, cayenne and salt, and cook a few more minutes.
- Stir in black-eyed peas, tomato sauce, water, soy sauce, brown sugar and vinegar. Reduce heat to medium. Simmer, uncovered, for 10 to 15 minutes. Adjust seasoning to taste. Serve in soup bowls with biscuits and whipped maple "butter" on the side.

Nutrition Information

- 186: calories;
- 1 gram: polyunsaturated fat;
- 12 grams: sugars;
- 1009 milligrams: sodium;
- 5 grams: fat;
- 3 grams: monounsaturated fat;
- 31 grams: carbohydrates;
- 6 grams: dietary fiber;
- 7 grams: protein;

278. Southwestern Chicken Salad With Chipotle Chiles

Serving: Serves four to six | Prep: | Cook: | Ready in: 40mins

Ingredients

- For the poached and shredded chicken breasts
- 1 whole chicken breast on the bone, skinned and split, or 2 boneless, skinless chicken breasts, 1 1/3 to 1 1/2 pounds
- 2 ½ quarts water
- 1 onion, quartered
- 2 garlic cloves, peeled and crushed
- ½ teaspoon dried thyme or oregano, or a combination
- Salt to taste 1 to 1 1/2 teaspoons
- For the dressing
- 2 tablespoons fresh lime juice
- 2 tablespoons white wine vinegar or cider vinegar
- Salt
- freshly ground pepper to taste
- 1 small or medium garlic clove, minced
- 1 scant teaspoon cumin seeds, toasted and coarsely ground
- ¼ cup extra virgin olive oil
- ¼ cup buttermilk
- 2 to 4 tablespoons chicken stock from poaching the chicken breasts, as needed
- For the salad
- 1 whole chicken breast or 2 large boneless skinless breasts, poached and shredded about 4 cups shredded chicken
- Salt
- freshly ground pepper
- 4 large radishes, diced, plus 2 radishes, sliced
- ¼ cup chopped fresh cilantro
- 2 to 3 chipotle chiles en adobo, rinsed, seeded and cut into thin strips
- 8 romaine lettuce leaves, cut crosswise into wide strips
- 1 small avocado, sliced

Direction

- Combine the water, the quartered onion and the whole crushed garlic cloves in a 2-quart saucepan, and bring to a simmer over medium heat. Add the chicken breasts, and bring back to a simmer. Skim off any foam that rises, and then add the dried herbs. Cover partially, reduce the heat to low and simmer 15 to 20 minutes, until the chicken is cooked through. (Cut one in half; the meat should not be pink.) Add salt to taste. Allow the chicken to cool in the broth if there is time. Remove the chicken from the broth when cool enough to handle. Remove from the bone and shred, pulling strips of chicken off the top of the breast. Pull with the grain, and the meat comes apart naturally. You should have about 4 cups of shredded chicken. Strain the chicken broth, and refrigerate overnight. The next morning, skim off and discard the fat, and freeze the broth in smaller containers.
- Mix together the ingredients for the dressing.
- Place the shredded chicken in a large bowl and season to taste with salt and pepper. Toss with the diced radishes, cilantro, chipotles and all but 2 tablespoons of the dressing.
- Toss the romaine lettuce with the remaining dressing, and arrange on a platter. Top with the salad. Garnish the top of the salad with the sliced radishes and the sliced avocado, and serve.

---

279. Soy, Ginger And Mustard Coated Bluefish With Grilled Scallions

Serving: Four servings | Prep: | Cook: | Ready in: 45mins

Ingredients

- 1 teaspoon Dijon mustard
- 2 teaspoons soy sauce
- 2 teaspoons minced fresh ginger
- 1 bluefish fillet (about 1 1/2 pounds)
- 12 scallions, trimmed

Direction

- Preheat a charcoal grill. Combine the mustard, soy sauce and ginger and rub the mixture over the flesh side of the bluefish. Let stand for 10 minutes. Place the fish on the grill, flesh side down. Grill for 7 minutes. Carefully turn the fish over and grill until just cooked through, about 5 minutes more.
- Meanwhile, place the scallions on the grill and grill until tender, about 10 minutes, turning once. Cut the fish in half lengthwise; cut again crosswise, making roughly equal pieces. Place 1 piece of fish and 3 scallions on each of 4 plates and serve immediately.

Nutrition Information

- 228: calories;
- 2 grams: polyunsaturated fat;
- 0 grams: trans fat;
- 3 grams: monounsaturated fat;
- 1 gram: sugars;
- 7 grams: fat;
- 4 grams: carbohydrates;
- 35 grams: protein;
- 269 milligrams: sodium;

---

280. Spaghetti With Clams And Green Beans

Serving: 4 servings | Prep: | Cook: | Ready in: 40mins

Ingredients

- 18 cherrystone clams, shucked, with clam juice reserved, about 2 cups
- 1 pound green beans
- 12 cups water
- Salt to taste
- 1 pound imported spaghetti
- 2 tablespoons olive oil

- 1 tablespoon finely chopped garlic
- 5 ripe plum tomatoes, about 1 pound, cut into 1/2-inch cubes
- ⅛ teaspoon red hot-pepper flakes
- ⅓ cup Absolut lemon vodka or regular vodka flavored with the juice of 1/2 lemon, optional
- ⅓ cup heavy cream
- Freshly ground pepper to taste
- ½ cup coarsely chopped fresh basil leaves or 1/2 cup chopped Italian parsley
- Freshly grated peccorino or Parmesan cheese, optional

Direction

- Chop the clams coarsely; there should be about 1 cup.
- Trim or break off the ends of the beans and remove the strings. Cut the beans into 2-inch lengths.
- Bring the water, salted to taste, to a boil in a kettle and add the green beans. Bring to a simmer and cook for 6 to 7 minutes. Do not overcook; the beans should remain crisp. Drain and reserve the cooking liquid.
- Bring the reserved cooking liquid to a boil. Add the spaghetti, stir and cook for about 6 minutes. Drain.
- Meanwhile, heat the oil in a large skillet. Add the garlic and cook briefly, stirring, without browning. Add the tomatoes, pepper flakes and the reserved clam juice. Cook, stirring, over medium heat until the liquid has been reduced to about 2 cups.
- Add the drained spaghetti, beans, vodka, if desired, cream and freshly ground pepper. Bring to a simmer. Cook until the spaghetti is al dente, stirring, and add the clams and basil. Toss and cook 1 minute. Serve immediately with peccorino or Parmesan cheese, if desired.

281. Spaghetti With Feta, Olives And Garlic Beans

Serving: Serves 6 | Prep: | Cook: | Ready in: 1hours

Ingredients

- ¼ cup olive oil
- 1 medium-sized onion, diced
- 3 large cloves garlic, peeled and minced
- 1 pound mixture of green and yellow beans, ends trimmed, and sliced at an angle into 1/2-inch pieces
- Salt and freshly ground pepper to taste
- 1 ¼ pounds spaghetti, fresh or dried
- 30 Calamata olives, pitted and chopped
- 2 cloves garlic, finely chopped
- 2 large tomatoes, peeled, seeded and diced
- 2 teaspoons fresh lemon juice
- 6 tablespoons butter
- ½ pound feta cheese, cubed

Direction

- In a small saute pan, heat the olive oil over medium-low heat, add the onion and cook slowly until it is translucent. Add the three cloves of minced garlic and continue cooking for one minute. Add the beans and cover the pan. Cook slowly for about 30 minutes, until the beans are soft. If the mixture dries, add a few tablespoons of water. Season with salt and pepper.
- Meanwhile, bring a large pot of water to a rolling boil. Add the spaghetti and boil for about two to three minutes if using fresh pasta or 10 to 12 minutes if using dried, until the spaghetti is al dente. (Depending on the brand of spaghetti, cooking times may vary.) Drain well.
- In a small bowl, combine the chopped olives with the finely chopped garlic. Set aside.
- In another small bowl, toss the diced tomatoes with the fresh lemon juice. Set aside.
- In a large saute pan, heat the butter until it is nut-colored. Add the cooked pasta and toss.

Add the feta cheese and stir until slightly softened, about five to seven minutes.

- Transfer a portion of the pasta onto each plate. In a straight line down the center of the plate, top the spaghetti with one mound of the bean mixture, one of the tomato-lemon mixture and a pile of the olive-garlic mixture. Serve immediately.

Nutrition Information

- 698: calories;
- 13 grams: monounsaturated fat;
- 84 grams: carbohydrates;
- 7 grams: dietary fiber;
- 6 grams: sugars;
- 20 grams: protein;
- 32 grams: fat;
- 15 grams: saturated fat;
- 0 grams: trans fat;
- 2 grams: polyunsaturated fat;
- 751 milligrams: sodium;

282. Spaghetti With Tomatoes And Garlic

Serving: 4 servings | Prep: | Cook: | Ready in: 15mins

Ingredients

- ¾ pound spaghetti
- ¾ pound ripe plum tomatoes with skin removed or 1 cup canned crushed tomatoes
- 2 tablespoons olive oil
- 1 tablespoon finely chopped garlic
- 1 teaspoon finely chopped jalapeno pepper (optional)
- Salt and pepper to taste
- 2 tablespoons fresh chopped basil or Italian parsley
- 4 tablespoons grated Parmesan or pecorino cheese

Direction

- Bring two quarts of salted water to boil in a kettle. Add the spaghetti, stir well and bring back to a boil, stirring while cooking. Cook to the desired degree of doneness. Reserve a quarter-cup of the cooking liquid.
- Meanwhile, cut the tomatoes into 1/4 inch cubes.
- In a skillet or kettle, add olive oil and the garlic. Cook briefly, stirring. Do not brown. Add the tomatoes, jalapeno pepper, salt and pepper to taste. Cook for 2 minutes, stirring. Add the spaghetti, basil or parsley, reserved cooking liquid and cheese, toss well and serve.

Nutrition Information

- 440: calories;
- 441 milligrams: sodium;
- 11 grams: fat;
- 3 grams: saturated fat;
- 1 gram: polyunsaturated fat;
- 71 grams: carbohydrates;
- 5 grams: dietary fiber;
- 6 grams: sugars;
- 15 grams: protein;

283. Sparkling Pineapple Soup

Serving: | Prep: | Cook: | Ready in: 10mins

Ingredients

- 2 cups sparkling wine
- 3 cupsgrated pineapple flesh
- 2 tablespoons lemon juice
- Toasted coconut

Direction

- In a bowl, whisk together 2 cups sparkling wine
- In another bowl,combine 3 cups grated pineapple flesh, 2 tablespoons lemon juice

- Combine everything in one bowl, stir gently and serve immediately; do not refrigerate.
- Garnish: Toasted coconut.

---

284.   Spiced Lamb Loaf

Serving: 6 or more servings | Prep: | Cook: |Ready in: 1hours15mins

Ingredients

- 2 pounds ground lean meat, preferably lamb
- 1 tablespoon corn, peanut or vegetable oil
- 1 cup finely chopped onion
- 1 cup finely diced celery
- 1 cup finely chopped green pepper
- 1 teaspoon finely minced garlic
- Salt to taste if desired
- Freshly ground pepper to taste
- ⅛ teaspoon freshly grated nutmeg
- 1 teaspoon ground cumin
- 2 teaspoons Worcestershire sauce
- ⅛ teaspoon Tabasco sauce
- 1 tablespoon Dijon-style mustard
- ½ cup fine, fresh bread crumbs
- 1 egg, lightly beaten

Direction

- Preheat oven to 400 degrees.
- Put meat in mixing bowl and set aside.
- Heat oil in saucepan and add onion, celery, green pepper and garlic. Cook, stirring, until vegetables are wilted. Set aside to cool briefly.
- Add cooked vegetables to meat. Add salt, pepper, nutmeg, cumin, Worcestershire sauce, Tabasco sauce, mustard, bread crumbs and egg. Blend well with the fingers.
- Pack mixture into 6-cup loaf pan. Smooth over the top.
- Place pan in oven and bake 50 minutes. Remove from oven and let stand 10 minutes. Slice and serve.

Nutrition Information

- 1072: calories;
- 0 grams: trans fat;
- 12 grams: protein;
- 2 grams: dietary fiber;
- 3 grams: sugars;
- 568 milligrams: sodium;
- 108 grams: fat;
- 54 grams: saturated fat;
- 5 grams: polyunsaturated fat;
- 44 grams: monounsaturated fat;

---

285.   Spiced Pepper Purée

Serving: About 1 cup | Prep: | Cook: |Ready in: 30mins

Ingredients

- 4 large bell peppers, yellow, orange or red, about 2 pounds
- 2 teaspoons cumin seeds, or 2 teaspoons ground cumin
- 1 inchlong piece of ginger, peeled
- Salt and pepper to taste

Direction

- adjust a rack about 4 inches from the heat source. Grill or broil the peppers, turning frequently as they blacken, until they collapse, about 15 minutes. Wrap in aluminum foil and let cool.
- Toast cumin seeds in a dry skillet over medium heat, shaking pan occasionally and removing from heat when fragrant. Grind to a powder in a coffee or spice grinder.
- When peppers are cool, remove core, skin and all seeds. Place peppers in a food processor with cumin and ginger; add a large pinch of salt and purée. Stop machine, adjust salt and pepper to taste. Store, well covered, in the refrigerator for several days, or the freezer for up to a month. Return to room temperature before serving.

Nutrition Information

- 104: calories;
- 1 gram: fat;
- 0 grams: polyunsaturated fat;
- 25 grams: carbohydrates;
- 5 grams: dietary fiber;
- 17 grams: sugars;
- 2 grams: protein;
- 467 milligrams: sodium;

---

286.   Spiced Pumpkin Pie

Serving: 8 servings | Prep: | Cook: | Ready in: 3hours

Ingredients

- For the crust:
- 1 ¼ cups/160 grams all-purpose flour
- ¼ teaspoon fine sea salt
- 10 tablespoons/140 grams unsalted butter, chilled and cubed
- 2 to 4 tablespoons ice water, as needed
- For the filling:
- 1 cup heavy cream
- 1 cinnamon stick
- 2 petals from a star-anise pod (not the whole pod)
- 1 whole clove
- 1 tablespoon grated fresh ginger
- 1 teaspoon cardamom pods
- ½ teaspoon whole black peppercorns
- 1 ¾ cups pumpkin or butternut squash purée (homemade or from a 15-ounce can)
- ¾ cup/165 grams dark brown sugar
- 2 large eggs
- 2 large egg yolks
- 2 tablespoons dark rum
- 2 teaspoons ground ginger
- ½ teaspoon kosher salt
- ¼ teaspoon freshly grated nutmeg

Direction

- Make the crust: In a large bowl, whisk together the flour and salt. Using your fingers, rub in the butter until it is the size of peas. Drizzle in water until the dough comes together when squeezed.
- Transfer dough to a lightly floured surface. Working a palm-size chunk at a time, use the heel of your hand to smear the dough across the work surface. Continue until all the dough has been smeared, then gather it all together, flatten into a disk, and wrap in plastic wrap. Chill for at least 1 hour and up to 2 days.
- On a lightly floured surface, roll dough into a 12-inch circle. Transfer to a 9-inch pie plate; fold the edges over and crimp. Prick crust all over with a fork and chill for at least 30 minutes.
- Heat oven to 425 degrees. Line chilled crust with foil and pie weights, then bake for 15 minutes. Remove foil and bake until pale golden, 5 to 10 minutes longer. Transfer to a rack to cool. Lower oven temperature to 325 degrees.
- Make the filling: In a medium pot, combine the cream, cinnamon stick, star anise petals, clove, fresh ginger, cardamom and peppercorns, and bring to a simmer. Remove from heat, cover, and let steep for 1 hour. Strain through a fine-mesh sieve into a large bowl.
- Whisk in pumpkin, brown sugar, eggs, yolks, rum, ground ginger, salt and nutmeg. Pour into par-baked shell, transfer to a baking sheet, and bake until crust is golden and center is slightly jiggly, 50 to 60 minutes. Cool completely before serving.

Nutrition Information

- 467: calories;
- 28 grams: fat;
- 17 grams: saturated fat;
- 2 grams: polyunsaturated fat;
- 3 grams: dietary fiber;
- 8 grams: monounsaturated fat;
- 49 grams: carbohydrates;

- 23 grams: sugars;
- 6 grams: protein;
- 234 milligrams: sodium;
- 1 gram: trans fat;

287. Spiced Sweet Potato Fries With Chili Cilantro Cream

Serving: 6 servings | Prep: | Cook: |Ready in: 1hours

Ingredients

- For the Potato Fries
- 2 large sweet potatoes, cut in matchsticks/batons, approximately 1/4 × 2 inches (no need to peel)
- 2 tablespoons olive oil
- 2 teaspoons salt
- 1 teaspoon ground cumin
- 1 teaspoon chili powder
- 1 teaspoon paprika
- 1 teaspoon freshly ground black pepper
- ½ teaspoon cayenne pepper, or to taste
- For the Chili-Cilantro Sour Cream
- 1 cup sour cream
- 1 tablespoon freshly squeezed lime juice
- 2 teaspoons sweet chili sauce
- 1 small garlic clove, minced
- ½ teaspoon salt
- ½ teaspoon freshly ground black pepper
- 1 heaping tablespoon chopped cilantro

Direction

- Heat oven to 425 degrees. Toss the sweet potatoes and olive oil in a large bowl.
- Combine the salt, cumin, chili powder, paprika, pepper and cayenne in a small bowl. Add to the potatoes and toss to coat.
- Arrange the potatoes in one layer on a large baking sheet. Bake on the lowest rack of the oven until the undersides are browned, 12 to 15 minutes. Turn the potatoes with a spatula and bake for 10 more minutes.

- While the potatoes are cooking, make the sour cream sauce. Combine all the ingredients except the cilantro in a medium bowl and whisk together. Stir in the cilantro.
- Remove the potatoes from the oven and cool for a few minutes. Serve with the sour cream.

Nutrition Information

- 169: calories;
- 12 grams: fat;
- 5 grams: monounsaturated fat;
- 1 gram: polyunsaturated fat;
- 14 grams: carbohydrates;
- 2 grams: protein;
- 4 grams: sugars;
- 242 milligrams: sodium;

288. Spicy Celery With Garlic

Serving: 6 servings | Prep: | Cook: |Ready in: 35mins

Ingredients

- 1 bunch celery (2 pounds)
- 4 cloves garlic, peeled and thinly sliced (2 tablespoons)
- ½ cup chicken stock, preferably unsalted homemade stock, or canned light chicken broth
- ¼ cup hot red salsa
- ¼ cup olive oil
- Salt to taste

Direction

- Using a vegetable peeler, remove the tough, fibrous strings from the celery ribs. Cut the celery into 2-inch pieces. You should have about 8 cups.
- Place the celery pieces in a large bowl, cover with cold water and wash them thoroughly.
- Place the celery, still wet, in a large saucepan with the remainder of the ingredients. Bring

the mixture to a boil, uncovered; then, reduce the heat, cover and cook gently for about 25 minutes until most of the liquid has evaporated and the celery is tender.

- Serve immediately, or if you want to serve the dish later, cool, cover, refrigerate and reheat briefly in a microwave oven or in a saucepan on top of the stove.

Nutrition Information

- 118: calories;
- 10 grams: fat;
- 1 gram: polyunsaturated fat;
- 7 grams: carbohydrates;
- 3 grams: sugars;
- 2 grams: protein;
- 451 milligrams: sodium;

289. Spicy Pumpkin Roti Filling

Serving: Filling for 4 rotis | Prep: | Cook: | Ready in: 45mins

Ingredients

- 1 tablespoon vegetable oil or ghee
- 1/2-inch knob of peeled, fresh ginger
- 1 cinnamon stick
- 2 ½ pounds peeled and seeded Jamaican pumpkin (see note), cut into 1-inch cubes (about 3 1/4 pounds unpeeled pumpkin)
- 1 teaspoon garam masala (preferably Turban or Chief brand)
- Salt to taste

Direction

- Heat the oil or ghee in a large pot over high heat. Add the ginger and cinnamon stick and sizzle for 1 minute.
- Add the pumpkin and sprinkle with the garam masala. Stir for 1 or 2 minutes over high

heat, until the pumpkin is coated with the spices. Watch carefully; do not burn the spices.

- Reduce the heat to medium, cover, and let simmer, stirring occasionally, for 20 to 30 minutes, or until the pumpkin is soft.
- Remove and discard the ginger and cinnamon. Mash the pumpkin with a potato masher into a course puree. Add salt to taste, stir and simmer for 3 to 4 minutes over low heat, or until the excess moisture evaporates. (The mixture should be the consistency of a thick puree). Let cool a few minutes before adding to roti.

Nutrition Information

- 111: calories;
- 2 grams: dietary fiber;
- 8 grams: sugars;
- 679 milligrams: sodium;
- 1 gram: polyunsaturated fat;
- 3 grams: protein;
- 20 grams: carbohydrates;
- 4 grams: fat;
- 0 grams: trans fat;

290. Spicy Thai Seafood Salad

Serving: 4 servings | Prep: | Cook: | Ready in: 25mins

Ingredients

- 3 cloves garlic, green part removed
- 2 green chilies
- 1 bunch coriander
- 1 teaspoon sugar
- 3 tablespoons Thai fish sauce
- ½ cup fresh lime juice
- 4 cups water
- ½ pound medium shrimps, peeled
- ½ pound white fish fillets, like sea bass or monkfish, cut in 1/2-inch pieces
- ½ pound bay scallops, or sea scallops halved
- Coarse salt and freshly ground pepper to taste

- 3 scallions, sliced
- 1 red chili
- Coriander leaves to garnish

Direction

- Combine garlic, green chilies, coriander, sugar, fish sauce and one-fourth cup lime juice in blender's bowl. Puree.
- Bring water to boil in a saucepan with one-fourth teaspoon salt and remaining lime juice. Poach seafood two to three minutes, or until cooked. Drain and toss in a bowl with the coriander dressing. Add pepper, scallions and red chili. Garnish with coriander leaves and serve warm or at room temperature.

Nutrition Information

- 196: calories;
- 1659 milligrams: sodium;
- 3 grams: fat;
- 1 gram: polyunsaturated fat;
- 0 grams: trans fat;
- 16 grams: carbohydrates;
- 4 grams: sugars;
- 28 grams: protein;

---

291.   Spicy Tunisian Carrot Frittata

Serving: Serves 6 | Prep: | Cook: | Ready in: 1hours

Ingredients

- 1 pound carrots, peeled and sliced
- 1 tablespoon caraway seeds, ground
- 1 to 2 tablespoon harissa, to taste (see note)
- 4 large garlic cloves, minced
- 1 teaspoon salt
- ½ teaspoon freshly ground black pepper
- ¼ cup finely chopped flat leaf parsley
- 8 large eggs
- 1 tablespoon extra virgin olive oil

Direction

- Either boil the carrots in salted water, or steam until thoroughly tender, about 15 minutes. Drain and mash with a fork, or puree in a food processor fitted with the steel blade. Add the caraway, harissa, and garlic, and blend together.
- Beat the eggs in a large bowl. Beat in the salt and pepper, and add the carrot mixture and the parsley. Mix together well. Heat the olive oil over medium-high heat in a heavy 10-inch nonstick skillet. Hold your hand above it; it should feel hot. Drop a bit of egg into the pan and if it sizzles and cooks at once, the pan is ready. Pour in the egg mixture. Swirl the pan to distribute the eggs and filling evenly over the surface. Shake the pan gently, tilting it slightly with one hand while lifting up the edges of the omelet with a spatula, to let the eggs run underneath during the first few minutes of cooking.
- Cover the pan, turn the heat down to low and cook 15 minutes, shaking the pan gently every once in a while, until the frittata is almost set. From time to time remove the lid and loosen the bottom of the omelet with a spatula, tilting the pan, so that the bottom doesn't burn. Meanwhile, preheat the broiler.
- Finish under the broiler for 1 to 3 minutes, watching very carefully to make sure the top doesn't burn (it should brown slightly, and it will puff under the broiler). Remove from the heat, shake the pan to make sure the frittata isn't sticking, and allow to cool for at least 5 minutes and up to 15. Loosen the edges with a wooden or plastic spatula. Carefully slide from the pan onto a large round platter. Serve warm or room temperature.

Nutrition Information

- 157: calories;
- 10 grams: protein;
- 3 grams: dietary fiber;
- 361 milligrams: sodium;
- 9 grams: fat;

- 2 grams: polyunsaturated fat;
- 0 grams: trans fat;
- 4 grams: sugars;

292. Spicy Wine Poached Pears With Hubbardston Blue

Serving: Five servings and a snack for the cook (the test pear) | Prep: | Cook: |Ready in: 1hours

Ingredients

- ½ bottle zinfandel, 1 2/3 cups
- ¼ bottle dry vermouth, 3/4 cup plus 2 tablespoons
- ½ cup sugar
- Zest of 1 medium orange, cut in long strips
- Zest of 1 lemon, cut in long strips
- 2 cinnamon sticks, 3 inches long
- 5 whole cloves
- 5 black peppercorns
- 2 quarter-sized slices fresh ginger
- 11 Seckel pears, just ripe
- 1 round, approximately 3 1/2 ounces, Hubbardston blue cheese
- 1 tablespoon sugar (optional)

Direction

- Bring the first nine ingredients to a boil in a large, noncorrodable saucepan. Turn off the heat and allow to cool.
- Peel and core the pears, opening a generous hollow for the stuffing, but leaving the stems on. Drop each into the liquid as it is completed.
- Wring out a detergent-free dish towel (or five layers of cheesecloth) in hot water and lay it on top of the pears. Bring the liquid to a fast simmer and cook for about 30 minutes, or until a sample pear is tender enough to cut with a spoon edge and still firm enough so it will hold up to being stuffed.
- Remove the pears with a slotted spoon, reserve and refrigerate, if desired. Return the

pan to the heat and boil until the liquid is reduced by about a third. You should have a thick syrup that will evenly coat the spoon. Strain and chill it, reserving the peels if desired (see note).

- At serving time, bring the pears to room temperature. Whip the cheese until it is light and fluffy, adding the tablespoon of sugar if a sweeter dessert is desired. Use a pastry bag to pipe each pear full of the cheese and place two on each plate. Spoon about one tablespoon of syrup over each. There should be just enough to streak and flavor the pears and form a bit of a puddle around them. Some syrup will probably be left over.

293. Spinach And Garlic Omelet

Serving: 1 serving. | Prep: | Cook: |Ready in: 15mins

Ingredients

- For each omelet:
- 2 ounces baby spinach or stemmed, washed bunch spinach (2 cups, tightly packed)
- 1 large or 2 small garlic cloves, minced or puréed
- Salt and freshly ground pepper
- 2 eggs
- 2 to 3 teaspoons low-fat milk
- 2 teaspoons extra virgin olive oil
- 2 teaspoons freshly grated Parmesan

Direction

- Wash the spinach and wilt in a frying pan over medium-high heat. The water remaining on the spinach leaves after washing will be sufficient. Drain, allow to cool and squeeze out excess water. Chop medium-fine and toss with half the garlic and salt and pepper to taste.
- Break the eggs into another bowl and beat with a fork or a whisk until they are frothy.

Whisk in the remaining garlic, salt and pepper to taste and 2 to 3 teaspoons milk.

- Heat an 8-inch nonstick omelet pan over medium-high heat. Add 2 teaspoons olive oil. Hold your hand an inch or two above the pan, and when it feels hot, pour the eggs into the middle of the pan, scraping every last bit into the pan with a rubber spatula. Swirl the pan to distribute the eggs evenly over the surface. Shake the pan gently, tilting it slightly with one hand while lifting up the edges of the omelet with the spatula in your other hand, to let the eggs run underneath during the first few minutes of cooking.

- As soon as the eggs are set on the bottom, sprinkle the spinach over the middle of the egg pancake and top with the Parmesan, then jerk the pan quickly away from you then back toward you so that the omelet folds over on itself. If you don't like your omelet runny in the middle (I do), jerk the pan again so that the omelet folds over once more. Cook for a minute or two longer. Tilt the pan and roll the omelet out onto a plate.

Nutrition Information

- 262: calories;
- 3 grams: polyunsaturated fat;
- 1 gram: sugars;
- 16 grams: protein;
- 411 milligrams: sodium;
- 0 grams: trans fat;
- 20 grams: fat;
- 6 grams: saturated fat;
- 10 grams: monounsaturated fat;
- 5 grams: carbohydrates;

294. Spinach And Millet Timbale With Tomato Sauce

Serving: 6 main dish servings | Prep: | Cook: | Ready in: 2hours30mins

Ingredients

- 6 eggs
- 2 cups, tightly packed, blanched spinach* (about 10 ounces blanched; 1 1/2 pounds baby spinach or 3 pounds bunch, on the stem), finely chopped
- 2 teaspoons chopped fresh thyme leaves
- 2 garlic cloves, finely minced (optional)
- 1 cup cooked millet
- 3 ounces Gruyère cheese, grated (3/4 cup)
- ⅔ cup 2 percent milk
- Salt and freshly ground pepper to taste
- 1 ½ cups marinara sauce

Direction

- Heat the oven to 350 degrees. Bring a kettle of water to a boil. Butter a 2-quart soufflé dish or 6 1-cup ramekins, making sure to butter the bottoms generously, and place them in a baking pan that is deep enough so that you can fill it with enough water to come halfway up the sides of the mold or ramekins.

- Beat the eggs in a large bowl and stir in the remaining ingredients (I usually season with 3/4 to 1 teaspoon of kosher salt). Scrape into the molds, filling them a little more than halfway full.

- Add boiling water to the baking pan, enough to come halfway up the sides of the molds. Place in the oven and bake for 5 minutes, then lower the heat to 325 degrees. Bake small molds for another 40 minutes, or until set and a skewer inserted in the center comes out almost clean. Large timbales will take between 1 to 1 1/2 hours. Make sure the water bath does not boil.

- Remove the timbales from the oven and allow to sit for 10 minutes while you heat the tomato sauce.

- Spoon about 3 to 4 tablespoons of tomato sauce onto each plate if you made individual timbales. Run a knife around the edges of the ramekins and unmold onto the plates. If serving 1 large timbale unmold onto a platter and cut into wedges.

Nutrition Information

- 212: calories;
- 5 grams: sugars;
- 0 grams: trans fat;
- 2 grams: dietary fiber;
- 14 grams: carbohydrates;
- 472 milligrams: sodium;
- 11 grams: fat;
- 4 grams: monounsaturated fat;
- 13 grams: protein;

---

295.   Spinach And Yogurt Dip

Serving: 2 cups | Prep: | Cook: |Ready in: 20mins

Ingredients

- 1 ½ pounds spinach, stemmed and washed thoroughly in 2 changes of water (or 12 ounces baby spinach)
- 1 to 2 large garlic cloves (to taste)
- Salt to taste
- 1 cup thick plain yogurt
- 2 tablespoons extra virgin olive oil
- 2 allspice berries, ground, or 1/8 teaspoon ground allspice (more to taste)
- 1 clove, ground, or 1/8 teaspoon ground clove
- ⅛ teaspoon freshly grated nutmeg
- ⅛ teaspoon ground cinnamon
- 1 scant teaspoon coriander seeds, or 1 teaspoon freshly ground coriander
- Chopped walnuts for garnish (optional)

Direction

- Blanch the spinach for 20 to 30 seconds or steam for 2 to 3 minutes. Rinse and squeeze out excess water and chop coarsely.
- Pound the garlic to a paste with salt in a mortar and pestle. Stir into the yogurt and set aside.

- Heat the olive oil over medium heat in a wide, heavy skillet and add the spices. Cook, stirring, until they begin to sizzle, and add the spinach. Cook, stirring, until heated through and coated with the oil and spices, 2 to 3 minutes. Transfer to a food processor and pulse to a puree. Add the yogurt and blend together. Transfer to a bowl or platter. Serve on croutons or with crudités such as red pepper squares, or with pita triangles. Garnish with chopped walnuts if desired. Serve with pita bread.

Nutrition Information

- 143: calories;
- 10 grams: fat;
- 562 milligrams: sodium;
- 11 grams: carbohydrates;
- 4 grams: sugars;
- 7 grams: protein;
- 2 grams: saturated fat;
- 0 grams: trans fat;
- 6 grams: monounsaturated fat;
- 1 gram: polyunsaturated fat;

---

296.   Spinach, Sardine And Rice Gratin

Serving: Serves 4 | Prep: | Cook: |Ready in: 45mins

Ingredients

- 2-3 3/4-ounce cans boneless, skinless and boneless sardines packed in olive oil
- 2 pounds spinach (2 generous bunches), stemmed and washed in two changes of water or 1 pound baby spinach
- 1 tablespoon extra virgin olive oil
- Salt and freshly ground pepper to taste
- 1 medium onion, finely chopped
- 2 to 4 garlic cloves, minced
- 1 teaspoon fresh thyme leaves, roughly chopped, or 1/2 teaspoon dried thyme

- 1 teaspoon all-purpose flour
- ½ cup low-fat milk
- 1 cup cooked rice (brown or white; I like to use Arborio)
- ¼ cup fresh or dry bread crumbs

Direction

- Preheat the oven to 425 degrees. Oil a 1 1/2 to 2-quart gratin or baking dish. Remove the sardines from the oil and separate them into fillets. Set the oil aside.
- Wilt the spinach either by steaming or blanching. To blanch bring a large pot of water to a boil, salt generously and add the spinach. Blanch for no more than 20 seconds (do this in batches). Transfer to a bowl of cold water, drain and squeeze out excess water. If you prefer, you can wilt the spinach by steaming for about 1 minute over an inch of boiling water. Chop medium-fine.
- Heat the olive oil (not the oil from the sardines) in the skillet over medium heat and add the onion and a pinch of salt. Cook, stirring, until tender, 5 to 8 minutes. Add a generous pinch of salt, stir in the garlic and thyme and cook, stirring, until fragrant, 30 seconds to a minute, then add the chopped wilted spinach, flour, and salt and pepper to taste. Stir together for 1 minute, until everything is blended. Add the milk and cooked rice and stir together for about 1 minute, until you no longer see liquid in the pan. Remove from the heat. Taste and adjust salt and pepper.
- Spread half the rice and spinach in the bottom of the baking dish. Top with the sardine fillets in one layer. Drizzle a tablespoon of the oil from the cans over the sardines, then top with the remaining rice and spinach in an even layer. Sprinkle on the breadcrumbs and drizzle on another tablespoon of the oil from the sardine cans. Place in the oven and bake 15 minutes, until sizzling. Serve hot or warm.

Nutrition Information

- 373: calories;
- 4 grams: sugars;
- 6 grams: dietary fiber;
- 25 grams: fat;
- 18 grams: monounsaturated fat;
- 3 grams: polyunsaturated fat;
- 30 grams: carbohydrates;
- 10 grams: protein;
- 835 milligrams: sodium;

---

297.   Spinach Basil Pesto

Serving: 4 cups | Prep: | Cook: | Ready in: 30mins

Ingredients

- ¼ cup roughly chopped walnuts
- 4 cups baby spinach leaves
- 2 cups fresh basil
- 1 teaspoon salt or to taste
- ½ cup olive oil
- ¼ cup grated rennet-free Parmesan cheese

Direction

- Preheat oven to 350 degrees. Spread out the walnuts on a small rimmed baking sheet and roast in oven for about 12 minutes, giving them a shake after 6 minutes. Continue roasting until golden brown and toasted. Set aside and allow to cool thoroughly.
- Fill a large stockpot three-quarters full with water, and bring to a boil over high heat. Meanwhile, fill a large bowl half way up with ice and water and set close to the sink.
- Dump the spinach and basil into the boiling water and stir. After 1 minute, strain the greens, and plunge them into the bowl with ice water. Drain the greens again and squeeze them tightly to get as much water out as possible. Chop the greens roughly.
- Combine the greens and walnuts with the salt, olive oil and Parmesan in a food processor and process until a smooth consistency is reached.

Taste and season with additional salt, if desired.

Nutrition Information

- 40: calories;
- 0 grams: sugars;
- 18 milligrams: sodium;
- 4 grams: fat;
- 1 gram: protein;
- 3 grams: monounsaturated fat;

298.   Spring Vegetable Stew

Serving: Serves 4 | Prep: | Cook: | Ready in: 40mins

Ingredients

- Juice of 1 lemon
- 6 baby artichokes
- 2 tablespoons olive oil
- ½ pound spring onions, white and light green parts only, chopped (about 1 1/2 cups)
- ½ cup chopped celery, preferably from the heart of the bunch
- 1 bulb green garlic, papery shells removed, chopped
- 1 large fennel bulb (1 to 1 1/4 pounds), trimmed, quartered, cored, and chopped (3 to 3 1/2 cups chopped)
- Salt and freshly ground black pepper to taste
- ½ cup water
- 2 tablespoons chopped fennel fronds or chopped fresh mint (or a combination)

Direction

- Fill a bowl with water and add lemon juice. Trim artichokes, quarter them and place in the water as you go along.
- Heat oil over medium heat in a large, heavy, lidded skillet or Dutch oven and add onions and celery. Cook, stirring, until tender, about 5 minutes. Add garlic, stir for about a minute

until you can smell the fragrance of the garlic, and add fennel and a generous pinch of salt. Cook, stirring often, for 5 to 8 minutes more, until the fennel has softened.

- Drain artichoke hearts and add to the pan. Cook, stirring often, for 5 minutes. Add water and salt to taste and bring to a simmer. Cover, reduce heat to low, and simmer for 10 to 15 minutes, or until all of the vegetables are very tender and fragrant. Stir in chopped fennel fronds and/or mint and simmer for a few more minutes. Taste and adjust salt and pepper. Serve hot or warm, on its own as a side, tossed with pasta or as a topping for grains.

Nutrition Information

- 246: calories;
- 43 grams: carbohydrates;
- 18 grams: dietary fiber;
- 11 grams: protein;
- 1093 milligrams: sodium;
- 8 grams: fat;
- 1 gram: polyunsaturated fat;
- 5 grams: monounsaturated fat;
- 9 grams: sugars;

299.   Squash Sauce

Serving: about a quart | Prep: | Cook: | Ready in: 45mins

Ingredients

- 2 tablespoons grapeseed or extra virgin olive oil
- 1 ½ cups peeled and cubed butternut squash
- ¼ cup diced onion
- 4 cups vegetable stock
- Salt and freshly ground black pepper
- Raw cane sugar to taste
- Raz al hanout to taste

Direction

- In a saucepan, warm oil over medium heat. Add squash and onion, and saute until onion is soft, 2 to 3 minutes. Add stock, bring to a simmer and cook until squash is soft, about 15 minutes. Season to taste with salt, pepper, sugar and raz al hanout.

300. Squid And Arugula Salad With Sesame Seeds

Serving: 4 servings | Prep: | Cook: | Ready in: 25mins

Ingredients

- 1 sprig thyme
- 1 bay leaf
- 10 coriander seeds
- Juice of 2 lemons
- ½ pound squid, cleaned, washed and drained
- 2 sweet red peppers, split and seeded
- 3 tablespoons olive oil
- 1 small clove garlic, peeled and chopped
- 2 sprigs fresh coriander, leaves only, chopped
- ½ tablespoon sesame oil
- 1 tablespoon shallots, peeled and finely chopped
- 1 sprig fresh mint, leaves only, half of them chopped
- 2 bunches arugula, leaves only
- 1 tablespoon chives, minced
- 1 tablespoon sesame seeds
- Coarse salt and freshly ground pepper to taste

Direction

- In a large pot over high heat, combine one quart water with one teaspoon salt, thyme, bay leaf, coriander seeds, the juice of half a lemon and freshly ground pepper. Bring to boil and cook for three minutes. Add the squid and boil again for another two to three minutes. Drain the squid and set aside to cool. Discard the cooking liquid with the herbs and condiments. Slice the squid into fourth-inch pieces and set aside.

- Preheat the broiler. Brush the skin of the sweet red peppers with a half tablespoon of the oil and place on a baking sheet. Cook under the broiler until the skin turns black, about five to seven minutes. Remove from heat, let cool and wash the burned skin off under running water. Pat dry and cut the roasted pepper into thin strips. Set aside.
- In a bowl, mix the squid, the red pepper strips, the juice of one lemon, one-and-a-half tablespoons of the olive oil, the garlic, half of the chopped coriander leaves, the sesame oil, the shallots, the chopped mint leaves and salt and pepper to taste.
- In a separate bowl, mix the arugula with half of the chives, half of the sesame seeds, juice from one-half lemon, the remaining tablespoon olive oil and salt and pepper to taste.
- Toast the remaining sesame seeds in a dry pan over medium heat or under the broiler, tossing often for one to two minutes or until golden, and set aside. Divide the arugula among four plates and spoon even amounts of squid on top of each bed of leaves. Sprinkle with the remaining minced chives, toasted sesame seeds, coriander leaves and mint leaves.

Nutrition Information

- 245: calories;
- 2 grams: saturated fat;
- 17 grams: carbohydrates;
- 14 grams: protein;
- 16 grams: fat;
- 7 grams: dietary fiber;
- 6 grams: sugars;
- 660 milligrams: sodium;
- 9 grams: monounsaturated fat;
- 3 grams: polyunsaturated fat;

301.   Steamed Broccoli With Garlic

Serving: 4 servings | Prep: | Cook: | Ready in: 10mins

Ingredients

- 1 bunch broccoli
- 2 tablespoons olive oil
- 2 teaspoons finely chopped garlic
- Salt and freshly ground pepper

Direction

- Using a paring knife, cut off and discard tough bottoms of broccoli stalks. Cut broccoli into florets.
- Place broccoli in a steamer for 3 to 4 minutes. Do not overcook.
- Heat oil in a skillet, add garlic, broccoli and salt and pepper to taste. Saute briefly, being careful not to burn garlic. Serve immediately.

Nutrition Information

- 115: calories;
- 7 grams: fat;
- 1 gram: polyunsaturated fat;
- 5 grams: monounsaturated fat;
- 11 grams: carbohydrates;
- 4 grams: protein;
- 3 grams: sugars;
- 374 milligrams: sodium;

302.   Stir Fried Balsamic Ginger Carrots

Serving: 8 servings | Prep: | Cook: | Ready in: 15mins

Ingredients

- 1 ¼ teaspoon salt
- 1 ½ pounds carrots, cut diagonally into 2-inch pieces (about 5 cups)
- 1 tablespoon plus 1 teaspoon balsamic vinegar
- 1 tablespoon dry sherry
- 2 teaspoons soy sauce (low-sodium if desired)
- ¾ teaspoon sugar
- ¼ teaspoon freshly ground pepper
- 2 tablespoons peanut or canola oil
- 2 tablespoons minced ginger
- 2 tablespoons finely chopped chives

Direction

- In a 3-quart saucepan, bring 1 1/2 quarts water to a boil over high heat. Add 1/2 teaspoon of the salt and the carrots and return to a full boil, about 5 minutes. Boil for 2 additional minutes. Drain the carrots in a colander, shaking well to remove excess water. Combine the vinegar, sherry and soy sauce in a cup. Combine the sugar, pepper and the remaining 3/4 teaspoon salt in a small dish.
- Heat a 14-inch flat-bottomed wok or a 12-inch skillet over high heat until a drop of water evaporates within a second or two when added to the pan. Swirl in the oil by adding it to the sides of the pan and swirling the pan, then add the ginger and stir-fry no more than 10 seconds, until the ginger is fragrant. Add the carrots and stir-fry for 1 minute, until the carrots are well coated in oil and ginger. Swirl the vinegar mixture into the wok, sprinkle with the sugar mixture, and stir-fry for 1 minute, until the carrots are crisp-tender. Immediately transfer to a serving bowl and sprinkle with chives.

Nutrition Information

- 75: calories;
- 226 milligrams: sodium;
- 4 grams: fat;
- 0 grams: trans fat;
- 2 grams: dietary fiber;
- 1 gram: protein;
- 10 grams: carbohydrates;
- 5 grams: sugars;

303.   Stracciatella With Spinach

Serving: 4 servings | Prep: | Cook: | Ready in: 1hours

Ingredients

- 1 ½ quarts chicken or turkey stock
- Salt
- freshly ground pepper to taste
- 2 large or extra large eggs
- 1 ½ tablespoons semolina
- ⅓ cup freshly grated Parmesan (1 1/2 ounces)
- 1 6-ounce bag baby spinach, or 1 bunch spinach, stemmed, washed, dried and coarsely chopped

Direction

- Place the stock in a large saucepan or soup pot. Remove 1/3 cup and set aside. Bring the rest to a simmer. Season to taste with salt and freshly ground pepper. If there is any visible fat, skim it away.
- Beat the eggs in a bowl, and stir in the 1/3 cup of stock, the semolina and the cheese.
- Stir the spinach into the simmering stock, then drizzle in the egg mixture, scraping all of it in with a rubber spatula. Stir very slowly with the spatula, paddling it back and forth until the little "rags" form. Taste, adjust seasoning and serve at once.

Nutrition Information

- 238: calories;
- 6 grams: sugars;
- 1038 milligrams: sodium;
- 10 grams: fat;
- 4 grams: monounsaturated fat;
- 0 grams: trans fat;
- 1 gram: dietary fiber;
- 18 grams: protein;

304.   Strawberry Charlotte

Serving: Serves 8 | Prep: | Cook: | Ready in: 1hours45mins

Ingredients

- 3 ½ teaspoons gelatin
- ½ cup boiling water
- ¾ cup sugar
- 1 tablespoon lemon juice
- 1 cup crushed or puréed strawberries, plus a handful of whole berries for garnish
- 3 egg whites, beaten to soft peaks
- 1 cup heavy cream, whipped to stiff peaks

Direction

- In a medium bowl, soften the gelatin in 1/4 cup cold water. Add the boiling water to the mixture and stir until the gelatin is fully dissolved.
- Add the sugar, the lemon juice and the crushed strawberries and stir gently to combine. Let cool, then chill in the refrigerator until it begins to set.
- Whip the gelatin mixture until somewhat fluffy. Fold in the egg whites, followed by the cream.
- Pour into a 1-quart mold, which, if desired, may be garnished by placing extra whole strawberries on the bottom. Chill in the refrigerator until firm. To serve, unmold the charlotte by dipping the base of the mold in hot water and then inverting it onto a serving plate. Decorate with a few whole berries with the stems intact. Serve plain or use sweetened, crushed strawberries as a sauce.

Nutrition Information

- 184: calories;
- 7 grams: saturated fat;
- 3 grams: protein;
- 0 grams: dietary fiber;
- 20 grams: sugars;
- 31 milligrams: sodium;

- 11 grams: fat;

305.   Strawberry Summer Pudding

Serving: 6 servings | Prep: | Cook: |Ready in: 15mins

Ingredients

- 1 ¼ pounds (about 1 1/2 pints) ripe strawberries
- ½ cup sugar
- 6 ounces white bread
- 1 cup sour cream (optional)

Direction

- Clean and hull the strawberries. Cut 12 of them into thin slices (about 1 1/4 cups), and mix with 2 tablespoons of the sugar. Set aside.
- Put the bread in the bowl of a food processor and process for a few seconds to make 2 cups of coarse fresh bread crumbs. Set aside.
- Put the remaining berries and the sugar in the processor bowl and process until smooth. Transfer to a bowl and lightly fold in the bread crumbs. Divide the pudding among six 1-cup containers and refrigerate for 2 to 3 hours or longer.
- To serve, spoon reserved berry slices onto six dessert dishes. Unmold pudding on top of the berries; serve with sour cream, if desired.

Nutrition Information

- 170: calories;
- 4 grams: protein;
- 145 milligrams: sodium;
- 1 gram: polyunsaturated fat;
- 0 grams: monounsaturated fat;
- 38 grams: carbohydrates;
- 3 grams: dietary fiber;
- 23 grams: sugars;

306.   String Beans Vinaigrette

Serving: Four servings | Prep: | Cook: |Ready in: 15mins

Ingredients

- 1 pound green beans, washed, ends snipped off and sliced on the diagonal
- ½ medium onion, chopped fine
- 1 small clove garlic, chopped fine
- ⅓ cup freshly grated Parmesan cheese
- 6 tablespoons olive oil
- 2 tablespoons tarragon vinegar
- ½ teaspoon salt
- Freshly ground pepper
- 2 medium tomatoes, sliced in wedges
- ⅓ cup black olive

Direction

- Fill a large saucepan with water and bring to a boil. Add salt to taste and the beans. Cook until tender but still firm, about 4 minutes. Drain and set aside.
- Place beans in a bowl with the remaining ingredients except the tomatoes and olives. Mix well and chill. Serve with the tomatoes and olives.

Nutrition Information

- 283: calories;
- 13 grams: carbohydrates;
- 6 grams: protein;
- 505 milligrams: sodium;
- 24 grams: fat;
- 5 grams: dietary fiber;
- 16 grams: monounsaturated fat;
- 2 grams: polyunsaturated fat;

307.   Stuffed Peppers With Red Rice, Chard And Feta

Serving: Serves 4 | Prep: | Cook: |Ready in: 1hours

Ingredients

- 4 medium peppers, preferably red
- 1 bunch Swiss chard, 12 ounces to 1 pound, stemmed and washed
- Salt to taste
- 3 tablespoons extra virgin olive oil
- 2 garlic cloves, minced
- 2 cups cooked red rice
- ¼ cup chopped mint
- 2 ounces feta, crumbed
- ½ cup water
- 2 tablespoons fresh lemon juice
- 1 tablespoon tomato paste (optional)

Direction

- Cut the tops away from the peppers and gently remove the seeds and membranes. Set aside.
- Bring a large pot of water to a boil, salt generously and add the chard leaves. Blanch 1 minute, until just tender, and transfer to a bowl of cold water. Drain, squeeze out water and chop medium-fine. You should have about 1 cup.
- Heat 1 tablespoon of the olive oil in a large skillet or saucepan and add the garlic. Cook, stirring, until fragrant, about 30 seconds, and stir in the chard. Stir for about 30 seconds, until coated with oil and garlic, and season with salt and pepper. Stir in the rice, toss, together, and remove from the heat.
- Transfer the rice mixture to a bowl and stir in the mint, feta and 1 tablespoon olive oil. Season to taste with salt and pepper.
- Spoon the rice and chard mixture into the peppers and place the peppers upright in a lidded saucepan or skillet. Mix together the water, lemon juice, salt to taste, optional tomato paste and remaining olive oil and add to the pan. Bring to a simmer, reduce the heat,

cover and simmer 40 minutes, until the peppers are tender. Remove the lid and allow to cool in the pan. Transfer to plates or a platter, spoon any liquid remaining in the pan over the peppers if desired, and serve.

Nutrition Information

- 288: calories;
- 2 grams: polyunsaturated fat;
- 6 grams: dietary fiber;
- 14 grams: fat;
- 4 grams: saturated fat;
- 8 grams: protein;
- 35 grams: carbohydrates;
- 5 grams: sugars;
- 925 milligrams: sodium;

308.   Sugar Cookies

Serving: 24 cookies | Prep: | Cook: |Ready in: 30mins

Ingredients

- ½ cup flour
- ⅛ teaspoon salt
- ⅛ teaspoon baking powder
- 4 tablespoons unsalted butter, plus 1 tablespoon for greasing cookie sheets, softened
- ⅓ cup sugar
- 1 egg
- ½ teaspoon vanilla extract
- 1 tablespoon grated lemon rind
- 1 tablespoon milk

Direction

- Preheat oven to 325 degrees. Mix the flour, salt and baking powder. Set aside. Grease 2 cookie sheets with 1 tablespoon of the butter or line sheets with parchment paper. Cream the remaining butter. Gradually add the sugar and continue beating until blended. Add the egg, vanilla, lemon rind and milk. Add the flour mixture all at once and beat until smooth.

- Drop teaspoonfuls of dough onto the cookie sheets, spaced 1 inch apart. Bake until golden brown, about 10 to 15 minutes. Set aside to cool.

Nutrition Information

- 45: calories;
- 3 grams: sugars;
- 2 grams: saturated fat;
- 0 grams: dietary fiber;
- 1 gram: protein;
- 5 grams: carbohydrates;
- 17 milligrams: sodium;

---

309. Summer Ratatouille With Farro

Serving: Serves 6 | Prep: | Cook: | Ready in: 1hours30mins

Ingredients

- For the ratatouille
- 1 ½ pounds eggplant, cut into 1/2-inch cubes
- 3 tablespoons extra-virgin olive oil
- Salt
- ¾ pound (2 medium) onions, thinly sliced
- ¾ pound mixed sweet peppers (red, yellow, green), cut into slices about 3/4 inch wide by 1 1/2 inches long
- 4 to 6 large garlic cloves, thinly sliced
- 1 ¼ pounds zucchini, sliced about 1/2 inch thick (if very thick, cut in half lengthwise first)
- 1 pound tomatoes, peeled, seeded and coarsely chopped
- 1 bay leaf
- 1 to 2 teaspoons fresh thyme leaves or 1/2 to 1 teaspoon dried thyme
- ½ teaspoon dried oregano
- Freshly ground pepper
- For the vinaigrette

- 2 tablespoons sherry vinegar or 1 tablespoon sherry vinegar and 1 tablespoon fresh lemon juice
- Salt to taste
- 1 very small garlic clove, pureéd
- 1 teaspoon Dijon mustard
- 6 tablespoons extra-virgin olive oil
- For the big bowl
- 3 to 4 cups cooked farro or spelt
- 2 to 4 tablespoons slivered or chopped fresh basil, to taste
- 6 eggs, poached
- 2 ounces crumbled feta or freshly grated Parmesan

Direction

-
-

Nutrition Information

- 522: calories;
- 28 grams: fat;
- 6 grams: saturated fat;
- 3 grams: polyunsaturated fat;
- 55 grams: carbohydrates;
- 0 grams: trans fat;
- 17 grams: monounsaturated fat;
- 13 grams: dietary fiber;
- 14 grams: sugars;
- 18 grams: protein;
- 1393 milligrams: sodium;

---

310. Summer Tomato Soup With Basil Cream

Serving: Six servings | Prep: | Cook: | Ready in: 30mins

Ingredients

- 2 tablespoons unsalted butter
- 4 large shallots or 1 medium onion, peeled and thinly sliced

- 2 ½ teaspoons salt, or to taste
- 3 pounds juicy, ripe tomatoes, peeled, seeded and coarsely chopped
- 1 pint rich chicken stock (see note)
- 1 pint milk
- White pepper to taste
- ½ cup heavy cream, chilled
- ½ cup loosely packed fresh basil leaves, finely chopped
- Small basil leaves, for garnish

Direction

- In a heavy, medium-size saucepan, melt the butter just until it foams. Add the shallots or onion and saute over medium heat just until wilted and very lightly colored, about seven to eight minutes.
- Stir in two teaspoons of the salt and the tomatoes, cover tightly and cook slowly for about 12 minutes until the tomatoes are soft.
- Transfer the mixture to the bowl of a food processor fitted with a steel chopping blade and puree until smooth. Or pass the mixture through a food mill. Return the puree to the saucepan, stir in the chicken stock and milk, season with white pepper and heat gently for a few minutes.
- In a chilled bowl, beat the heavy cream just until it forms soft peaks. Stir in the remaining salt and the basil. Ladle the soup into bowls, add a good-size dollop of the basil cream in the middle of each bowl and place a couple of basil leaves in the center. To make a decorative design, swirl the cream outwards in a circular or sunburst pattern, using the tip of a knife or spoon handle.

Nutrition Information

- 264: calories;
- 15 grams: fat;
- 9 grams: protein;
- 0 grams: trans fat;
- 4 grams: monounsaturated fat;
- 1 gram: polyunsaturated fat;
- 26 grams: carbohydrates;

- 5 grams: dietary fiber;
- 1092 milligrams: sodium;
- 16 grams: sugars;

311.   Sunday Beans

Serving: Serves 8 | Prep: | Cook: |Ready in: 30mins

Ingredients

- 2 tablespoons olive oil
- 4 ounces slab bacon, diced
- 1 medium yellow onion, peeled and diced
- 3 cloves garlic, peeled and minced
- 1 medium red pepper, seeded and diced
- 2 tablespoons ground cumin
- 1 tablespoon ground coriander
- 1 cup orange juice
- ½ cup pineapple juice
- 3 (151/2-ounce) cans red kidney beans, drained
- Kosher salt
- freshly ground black pepper

Direction

- Heat a large saucepan over medium-high heat. Add the olive oil and, a few moments later, the bacon. Cook, stirring occasionally, until the fat has begun to render out of the bacon and the meat is beginning to crisp, about 5 minutes.
- Lower the heat to medium and add the onion, garlic and pepper. Cook, stirring occasionally, until the vegetables have softened, 5 to 7 minutes.
- Add the cumin and coriander. They will absorb the heated oil in the pan and grow fragrant. Stir for 1 to 2 minutes and then add the juices. Raise the heat to high until the mixture begins to simmer, then lower the heat and reduce to one half of its volume. Taste and adjust the seasonings.
- Stir in the beans. After 5 minutes stir again, then taste and adjust the seasonings. (The mixture can keep, softly bubbling on the stove,

for hours. Add a little juice or water if necessary. Stir occasionally.) Serve with white rice.

Nutrition Information

- 1132: calories;
- 0 grams: trans fat;
- 183 grams: carbohydrates;
- 36 grams: sugars;
- 2096 milligrams: sodium;
- 18 grams: fat;
- 4 grams: saturated fat;
- 5 grams: monounsaturated fat;
- 3 grams: polyunsaturated fat;
- 46 grams: dietary fiber;
- 67 grams: protein;

312. Sweet Potato Soup With Ginger, Leek And Apple

Serving: 6 to 8 servings. | Prep: | Cook: | Ready in: 1hours10mins

Ingredients

- 2 tablespoons canola oil or butter
- 2 leeks, white and light green parts only, cleaned and sliced
- 4 teaspoons minced fresh ginger
- 2 ¼ pounds orange sweet potatoes (like jewel yams or garnet yams), peeled and diced
- ½ pound Yukon gold or russet potatoes, peeled and diced
- 1 to 1 ¼ pounds tart apples, like Braeburn or Granny Smith, peeled, cored and diced
- 2 quarts water
- Salt to taste
- Fresh lime juice and medium-hot chili powder or chipotle chili powder for garnish

Direction

- Heat the oil or butter in a heavy soup pot or Dutch oven over medium heat. Add the leek and cook, stirring, until it is tender, about 5 minutes. Add the ginger and stir together until fragrant, about 1 minute. Add the sweet potatoes, regular potato, apples and water and bring to a simmer. Add salt to taste, reduce the heat, cover and simmer 45 minutes to an hour, until all of the ingredients are thoroughly tender.
- Using an immersion blender, purée the soup (or you can use a regular blender, working in batches and placing a kitchen towel over the top to avoid splashing) until very smooth. Return to the pot, heat through and adjust salt. Ladle into bowls, squeeze a little lime juice and sprinkle a little chili powder over each serving and serve.

Nutrition Information

- 214: calories;
- 2 grams: monounsaturated fat;
- 43 grams: carbohydrates;
- 7 grams: dietary fiber;
- 3 grams: protein;
- 13 grams: sugars;
- 1123 milligrams: sodium;
- 4 grams: fat;
- 0 grams: trans fat;
- 1 gram: polyunsaturated fat;

313. Sweet Potato, Quinoa, Spinach And Red Lentil Burger

Serving: 10 patties | Prep: | Cook: | Ready in: 1hours

Ingredients

- ⅓ cup quinoa (blond or black), rinsed
- ⅓ cup red lentils, rinsed
- 1 ⅔ cups water
- Salt to taste
- 1 ½ pounds sweet potatoes, baked

- 3 cups, tightly packed, chopped fresh spinach
- 3 ounces feta, crumbled (about 3/4 cup)
- 3 tablespoons chopped fresh mint
- ¼ cup minced chives
- 2 teaspoons fresh lemon juice
- Freshly ground pepper to taste
- 1 cup panko or chickpea flour (you will not use all of it)
- ¼ cup grape seed oil

Direction

- Combine quinoa, red lentils, water and salt to taste (I used a rounded 1/2 teaspoon) in a saucepan and bring to a boil. Reduce heat, cover and simmer 15 to 20 minutes, until quinoa is tender and blond quinoa displays a thread, and lentils are just tender. Drain off any water remaining in the pot through a strainer, tapping strainer against the sink to remove excess water, then return quinoa and lentils to the pot. Cover pot with a towel, then return the lid and let sit undisturbed for 15 minutes.
- Skin sweet potatoes and place in a large bowl. Mash with a fork. Add spinach and mash together (I use my hands for this). Add quinoa and lentils, feta, mint, chives, lemon juice, and salt and pepper to taste. Mix together well. Mixture will be moist.
- Take up about 1/3 cup of the mixture and form into a ball (you can wet your hands to reduce sticking). Roll the ball in the panko or chickpea flour, then gently flatten into a patty. Set on a plate and continue with the rest of the mixture. Refrigerate uncovered for 1 hour or longer (the longer the better).
- When you're ready to cook, place a rack over a sheet pan. Heat 2 tablespoons oil in a 12-inch, heavy nonstick frying pan over high heat. Swirl the pan to coat with the hot oil. Lower heat to medium. Place 4 to 5 patties in the pan (do not crowd), and cook until well browned on one side, about 4 minutes. Turn and brown for about 4 more minutes. Remove to rack. Heat remaining oil in the pan and cook remaining patties. Keep patties warm in a low

oven until ready to serve. Serve with a salad and your choice of toppings, such as the usual (ketchup, mustard, relish), or yogurt raita, garlic yogurt, or chutney.

Nutrition Information

- 275: calories;
- 11 grams: fat;
- 3 grams: saturated fat;
- 2 grams: monounsaturated fat;
- 6 grams: sugars;
- 35 grams: carbohydrates;
- 9 grams: protein;
- 462 milligrams: sodium;

---

314. Sweet And Hot Green Beans

Serving: 2 servings | Prep: | Cook: | Ready in: 10mins

Ingredients

- ½ pound green beans
- 1 tablespoon honey mustard
- Dash of salt

Direction

- Wash and trim the green beans; steam about 7 minutes.
- Drain, and put in a serving dish. Toss with mustard, then add salt.

Nutrition Information

- 40: calories;
- 167 milligrams: sodium;
- 0 grams: polyunsaturated fat;
- 8 grams: carbohydrates;
- 3 grams: dietary fiber;
- 4 grams: sugars;
- 2 grams: protein;

315. Sweet And Sour Peppers Stuffed With Rice Or Bulgur And Fennel

Serving: Serves 6 | Prep: | Cook: | Ready in: 1hours

Ingredients

- 3 cups water
- ⅓ cup sugar
- ⅓ cup sherry vinegar
- 1 onion, sliced
- 6 garlic cloves, sliced
- Salt to taste
- 1 bay leaf
- 4 sprigs fresh thyme
- 4 medium or 3 large red peppers, cut in half, seeds and membranes removed
- 2 tablespoons extra virgin olive oil
- 2 medium-size fennel bulbs (about 3/4 pound), finely chopped
- 2 garlic cloves, minced
- 2 cups cooked red, brown or black rice, or bulgur
- Freshly ground pepper to taste
- ½ cup chopped fresh mint, parsley, dill or chervil, or a mix
- 1 to 2 ounces feta, crumbled (optional)

Direction

- Simmer the peppers. Combine the water, sugar, vinegar, sliced onion, sliced garlic, salt, bay leaf and thyme in a large saucepan and bring to a simmer. Add the peppers, turn the heat to medium and boil gently for 15 minutes, checking and spooning liquid over the peppers from time to time if they are not submerged. Remove from the heat, allow to cool, cover and refrigerate until cold.
- Heat the olive oil over medium heat in a large skillet and add the fennel and a pinch of salt. Cook, stirring often, until the fennel is tender and fragrant, about 5 minutes. Add the garlic and continue to cook, stirring, for another 30 seconds to a minute, until fragrant, then stir in the rice or bulgur and mix together. Season to taste with salt and pepper and remove from the heat. Stir in the herbs.
- Set a strainer over a bowl and drain the peppers. Blot them dry with paper towels and arrange on a platter or on plates if serving cold. Arrange in a lightly oiled baking dish if serving hot, and preheat the oven to 350 degrees. Fill with the rice mixture and spoon 2 teaspoons of the marinade over the filling of each serving. Sprinkle on the feta. Serve or chill if serving cold. If serving warm place in the oven for 15 minutes, until the cheese softens.

Nutrition Information

- 389: calories;
- 8 grams: protein;
- 19 grams: sugars;
- 959 milligrams: sodium;
- 7 grams: fat;
- 1 gram: polyunsaturated fat;
- 4 grams: monounsaturated fat;
- 75 grams: carbohydrates;

316. Sweet And Sour Cherries With Bay Leaves

Serving: | Prep: | Cook: | Ready in: P3DT10mins

Ingredients

- ½ pound sour cherries
- 20 black peppercorns, crushed
- 2 bay leaves
- ½ cup white-wine vinegar
- ½ cup sugar

Direction

- Wash the cherries and lay them on a dry cloth. Snip off the nubby ends of the stems with scissors. Using a needle, prick each cherry two or three times and drop it into a one-pint canning jar. Toss in the crushed peppercorns and tuck the bay leaves among the cherries.

- Bring the vinegar, sugar and 1/3 cup water to a boil in a small pan, stirring to dissolve the sugar. Cover the cherries with the liquid, close the jar and let cool before refrigerating. The cherries will be ready to eat in two or three days. Serve with chicken-liver mousse, duck, salami or other charcuterie.

---

317. Sweetbread And Spinach Sausage

Serving: about 20 links | Prep: | Cook: | Ready in: 2hours40mins

Ingredients

- 1 pound sweetbreads
- 1 pound fresh loose spinach
- ¾ pound lean veal, cut into 1-inch cubes
- ¾ pound lean pork, cut into 1-inch cubes
- ½ pound fatback, cut into 1-inch cubes
- ½ cup shallots
- ½ teaspoon white pepper
- ½ teaspoon ground nutmeg
- ½ teaspoon ground coriander
- ¼ teaspoon ground allspice
- ⅛ teaspoon cayenne
- Salt to taste
- 2 eggs
- 1 ½ cups heavy cream

Direction

- Remove all outer membranes, blood and connecting tissues from sweetbreads. Soak them overnight in cool water.
- Drain and cook the sweetbreads in water to cover with salt to taste. Bring to a boil and simmer for 5 minutes. Drain and arrange on a rack with a weight to extract the moisture for one hour. Chill. Cut into 1-inch cubes.

- Clean spinach, removing all tough stems, and wash well. Drain. Cook spinach in the moisture that clings to the leaves over low heat until it is wilted. Drain; cool and then extract as much moisture as possible by squeezing in tea towel or cheesecloth. Chop coarsely.
- Combine sweetbreads, veal, pork, fat, shallots, seasonings and eggs in several batches in food processor and process each batch about 20 seconds with metal blade, until mixture is in very small pieces. After all the batches are processed, return each one to processor, slowly pouring in a portion of the cream while processing for about 15 seconds. The mixture should be smooth but not too fine.
- Combine the meats with the spinach and blend well.
- Using sausage stuffer, stuff casings, twist and tie into 4- to 6-inch links.
- Place sausages in pot of boiling salted water. Return slowly to a boil; reduce heat and simmer slowly for about 10 minutes. Remove from heat and allow to stand for 15 minutes. Drain well and cool.
- To serve, grill or pan-fry sausages in butter. If desired, serve with beurre blanc.

Nutrition Information

- 245: calories;
- 9 grams: saturated fat;
- 13 grams: protein;
- 272 milligrams: sodium;
- 21 grams: fat;
- 0 grams: trans fat;
- 7 grams: monounsaturated fat;
- 3 grams: polyunsaturated fat;
- 2 grams: carbohydrates;
- 1 gram: sugars;

318. Swiss Chard Stalk And Tahini Dip

Serving: About two cups | Prep: | Cook: |Ready in: 20mins

Ingredients

- 1 pound Swiss chard stalks, coarsely chopped (about 4 cups)
- Salt to taste
- 2 to 4 garlic cloves (to taste), peeled, green shoots removed
- ½ cup sesame tahini, stirred if the oil has separated
- ¼ to ½ cup freshly squeezed lemon juice, to taste
- 1 tablespoon extra-virgin olive oil

Direction

- Steam the chard stalks about 15 minutes or until tender when pierced with a fork. Drain well, and allow to cool. Place in a food processor fitted with the steel blade. Puree, stopping the machine from time to time to scrape down the sides.
- In a mortar, mash the garlic with 1/2 teaspoon salt until you have a smooth paste. Add to the chard stalks. Process until smooth. Add the tahini, and again process until smooth. With the machine running, add the lemon juice and salt to taste. Stop the machine, taste and adjust seasonings.
- Transfer the dip to a wide bowl. It will be a little runny (unless the tahini you used was thick) but will stiffen up. Drizzle on the olive oil and serve.

Nutrition Information

- 224: calories;
- 10 grams: carbohydrates;
- 1 gram: sugars;
- 6 grams: protein;
- 220 milligrams: sodium;
- 3 grams: dietary fiber;
- 9 grams: monounsaturated fat;
- 7 grams: polyunsaturated fat;
- 20 grams: fat;

319. Tabbouleh

Serving: 4 servings | Prep: | Cook: | Ready in: 30mins

Ingredients

- ½ cup fine bulgur wheat
- ¾ cup finely chopped onions
- ¾ cup finely chopped fresh coriander or Italian parsley
- ¾ cup seeded and chopped ripe plum tomatoes
- 1 teaspoon minced garlic
- ¼ cup lemon juice
- Salt and freshly ground pepper to taste
- ⅛ teaspoon red hot pepper flakes
- 2 tablespoons olive oil
- 2 tablespoons chopped fresh mint or 1 tablespoon dried

Direction

- Place bulgur wheat in a bowl and cover with cold water. Let soak for the period of time indicated on the package. Drain and place the bulgur in a piece of cheesecloth and vigorously squeeze out extra water.
- Put bulgur in a bowl and add all remaining ingredients except oil and mint. Toss mixture gently but thoroughly with a fork. Stir in oil and mint and serve.

Nutrition Information

- 147: calories;
- 7 grams: fat;
- 1 gram: polyunsaturated fat;
- 5 grams: monounsaturated fat;
- 20 grams: carbohydrates;
- 4 grams: dietary fiber;

- 3 grams: protein;
- 262 milligrams: sodium;

320.   Tangerine Vanilla Floats

Serving: 6 servings | Prep: | Cook: | Ready in:

Ingredients

- 6 large scoops vanilla ice cream
- 3 cups freshly squeezed tangerine juice (from about 12 tangerines) or orange juice (see note)
- Seltzer

Direction

- Divide ice cream among 6 medium-size glasses or cups. Add 1/2 cup tangerine juice to each cup and top off with seltzer. Serve with a straw.

321.   Tarragon Cucumber Pickles

Serving: 2 quarts | Prep: | Cook: | Ready in: 30mins

Ingredients

- 2 large cucumbers (about 1 1/2 pounds)
- 4 large tarragon sprigs, cut into 2-inch pieces
- 2 tablespoons mustard seeds
- 2 tablespoons whole black peppercorns
- 1 tablespoon coriander seeds
- 2 bay leaves
- 4 cups plain rice wine vinegar
- ¾ cup sugar

Direction

- Slice cucumbers crosswise 1/4 inch thick, and pack into 2 quart-size jars. Divide tarragon, mustard seeds, peppercorns, coriander seeds

and bay leaves between 2 double layers of cheesecloth. Tie into bundles with string.

- In a medium saucepan, combine vinegar with sugar and bundles of pickling spices, and bring to a boil, stirring to dissolve sugar. Pour brine over cucumbers, pack bundles of pickling spices on top and let cool. Discard spices, close jars and refrigerate at least 1 hour, preferably 3. Serve cold.

Nutrition Information

- 55: calories;
- 0 grams: polyunsaturated fat;
- 11 grams: carbohydrates;
- 1 gram: protein;
- 9 grams: sugars;
- 3 milligrams: sodium;

322.   Tarragon Potato Salad

Serving: 2 servings | Prep: | Cook: | Ready in: 25mins

Ingredients

- 12 ounces tiny new potatoes
- 1 sprig fresh dill to yield 1 tablespoon chopped
- 1 sprig fresh parsley to yield 1 tablespoon chopped
- 2 teaspoons chopped capers
- 3 tablespoons low-fat sour cream
- 2 tablespoons nonfat yogurt
- 2 teaspoons tarragon vinegar
- Few dashes cayenne pepper
- Dash salt
- Freshly ground black pepper

Direction

- Scrub potatoes, but do not peel. Bring to a boil in water to cover and cook until they are tender but firm, 10 to 20 minutes, depending on size.

- Meanwhile, wash, dry and chop the dill and parsley; rinse capers, and chop. In bowl large enough to hold the potatoes, mix the dill, parsley and capers with the sour cream, yogurt, vinegar and cayenne pepper.
- When potatoes are cooked, drain and cut into quarters and mix with the dressing. Season with salt and pepper, and serve.

Nutrition Information

- 176: calories;
- 0 grams: polyunsaturated fat;
- 4 grams: dietary fiber;
- 2 grams: saturated fat;
- 3 grams: sugars;
- 1 gram: monounsaturated fat;
- 33 grams: carbohydrates;
- 6 grams: protein;
- 168 milligrams: sodium;

323. Tarragon Sauce

Serving: About one and three-quarters cups | Prep: | Cook: | Ready in: 5mins

Ingredients

- 1 cup mayonnaise, preferably homemade
- ½ cup yogurt
- 2 tablespoons finely chopped fresh tarragon or 1 teaspoon dried
- 2 tablespoons finely chopped fresh parsley
- 2 tablespoons finely chopped chives
- 1 tablespoon Dijon-style mustard
- Salt to taste, if desired
- Freshly ground pepper to taste

Direction

- Put the mayonnaise in a bowl and add the yogurt, tarragon, parsley, chives, mustard, salt and pepper. Blend thoroughly.

324. Tart Crust

Serving: 1 tart crust | Prep: | Cook: | Ready in: 10mins

Ingredients

- ¼ pound unsalted butter, chilled or frozen
- 1 ½ cups flour
- Pinch salt
- 3 to 4 tablespoons gewurztraminer, chilled

Direction

- With sharp knife, cut butter into small pieces. Combine with flour and salt in food processor and process with steel blade until butter is cut into tiny flecks and mixture is mealy.
- With food processor running, add 3 tablespoons of wine. Test dough by squeezing a little with finger tips. It should hold together and be moist. If dry and crumbly, add more wine.
- Turn dough onto a board and compress into a ball. Flatten slightly to make a round, flat patty. Put in bowl, cover with towel or wax paper and chill at least an hour.
- Roll out dough on a lightly floured board and fit into 11-inch false-bottom tart tin. Trim off excess dough and prick bottom all over with a fork. If possible chill shell at least 30 minutes. This gives a lighter crust with less shrinkage. Shell can be made ahead and refrigerated two days before using or frozen for future use.

Nutrition Information

- 769: calories;
- 3 grams: dietary fiber;
- 0 grams: sugars;
- 10 grams: protein;
- 153 milligrams: sodium;
- 47 grams: fat;
- 2 grams: polyunsaturated fat;
- 72 grams: carbohydrates;
- 29 grams: saturated fat;

- 12 grams: monounsaturated fat;

---

325. Thanksgiving Mixed Bean Chili With Corn And Pumpkin

Serving: Yield: Serves 6 generously | Prep: | Cook: | Ready in: 2hours15mins

Ingredients

- 1 pound mixed dried beans, such as pintos and black beans, pintos and red beans, or heirloom beans such as San Franciscano, Good Mother Stallards, and Sangre de Toros (see note), washed, picked over, and soaked for at least 4 hours or overnight in 2 quart
- 2 onions, 1 halved, 1 finely chopped
- 4 garlic cloves, 2 crushed and peeled, 2 minced
- 1 bay leaf
- 2 tablespoons grapeseed or sunflower oil
- 3 tablespoons mild ground chili (or use hot, or use more)
- 1 tablespoon cumin seeds, ground
- 1 14-ounce can chopped tomatoes
- Pinch of sugar
- 2 tablespoons tomato paste dissolved in 1 cup water
- 2 cups diced winter squash (about 3/4 pound)
- 1 cup corn kernels (fresh or frozen)
- Salt to taste
- ½ cup chopped cilantro
- Grated or crumbled cheese for serving (optional)

Direction

- Place beans and soaking water in a large, heavy pot. Add halved onion and bring to a gentle boil. Skim off any foam that rises, then add crushed garlic and bay leaf, reduce heat, cover and simmer 30 minutes. Add salt and continue to simmer another 45 minutes to an hour. Using tongs or a slotted spoon, remove and discard onion and bay leaf.
- . Meanwhile, heat oil over medium heat in a heavy skillet and add chopped onion. Cook, stirring often, until tender, about 5 minutes. Add a generous pinch of salt, stir in chopped garlic, stir together for 30 seconds to a minute, until fragrant, and add ground chili and cumin. Cook, stirring, for 2 to 3 minutes, until mixture begins to stick to pan. Add chopped tomatoes with juice, pinch of sugar, and salt to taste. Bring to a simmer and cook, stirring often, until tomatoes have cooked down and mixture is beginning to stick to the pan, about 10 minutes. Stir in tomato paste dissolved in water and bring back to a simmer. Simmer, stirring often, for 10 minutes, until mixture is thick and fragrant.
- Stir tomato mixture into beans. Add winter squash and bring to a simmer. Taste and adjust salt. Simmer, stirring often so that the chili mixture doesn't settle and stick to the bottom of the pot, for 45 minutes. Add more water if chili seems too thick. Stir in corn and simmer for another 10 minutes. The beans should be very soft and the chili thick and fragrant. Taste and adjust seasonings.
- Shortly before serving stir in cilantro. Simmer for 5 minutes. Spoon into bowls. If you wish, top with grated cheddar, Monterey jack, or crumbled queso fresco. Serve with biscuits or cornbread.

Nutrition Information

- 155: calories;
- 2 grams: polyunsaturated fat;
- 25 grams: carbohydrates;
- 9 grams: sugars;
- 4 grams: protein;
- 657 milligrams: sodium;
- 6 grams: dietary fiber;
- 1 gram: saturated fat;

326. The Comme Ça Burger

Serving: 4 to 8 servings | Prep: | Cook: |Ready in: 20mins

Ingredients

- 2 pounds ground beef chuck, 80 percent lean
- Kosher salt
- freshly ground black pepper
- 2 tablespoons mayonnaise
- ½ tablespoon ketchup
- Pinch of cayenne pepper
- Pinch of chili powder
- 1 cup finely shredded iceberg lettuce
- 4 light brioche buns (see recipe) or other large hamburger buns, split
- ¼ pound thinly sliced medium-sharp Cheddar cheese
- 4 thin onion slices

Direction

- Lightly shape meat into 4 4-by-1-inch patties, and refrigerate 1 to 2 hours.
- Heat oven to 375 degrees. Prepare a hot fire on a grill, or heat a large cast-iron skillet over high heat for 3 to 4 minutes. Sprinkle each burger all over with 1/2 teaspoon kosher salt and season generously with black pepper. Sear burgers on grill or in skillet for 2 minutes on each side. Transfer burgers to a broiler pan and bake for 4 minutes for medium-rare. Remove pan from oven. Position an oven rack closest to broiler element, and heat broiler to high.
- In a bowl, whisk mayonnaise with ketchup, cayenne and chili powder, and season with salt and black pepper. Add lettuce and stir to coat. Toast buns. Top burgers with Cheddar and broil until cheese melts, about 30 seconds. Set burgers on bottom buns and top with lettuce and onion slices. Cover with top bun and serve, whole or cut in half.

Nutrition Information

- 412: calories;
- 19 grams: fat;
- 8 grams: saturated fat;
- 1 gram: dietary fiber;
- 7 grams: monounsaturated fat;
- 20 grams: carbohydrates;
- 3 grams: sugars;
- 4 grams: polyunsaturated fat;
- 41 grams: protein;
- 535 milligrams: sodium;

327. Three Greens Gratin

Serving: Serves 6 generously | Prep: | Cook: |Ready in: 1hours15mins

Ingredients

- 2 generous bunches Swiss chard (about 2 to 2 1/4 pounds), stemmed and washed in 2 changes of water
- Salt
- 1 pound beet greens or spinach, stemmed and washed in 2 changes of water
- 3 tablespoons extra virgin olive oil, plus additional for oiling baking dish
- 1 onion, chopped
- ½ pound leeks (1 large or 2 smaller), white and light green parts only, cleaned and chopped
- 3 garlic cloves, minced
- 1 teaspoon chopped fresh thyme leaves
- 1 pound cabbage (1/2 medium), cored and chopped
- 4 eggs
- 1 cup cooked rice or farro
- Nutmeg
- Freshly ground pepper
- 2 ounces Gruyère, grated (1/2 cup)
- 1 ounce Parmesan, grated (1/4 cup)
- ¼ cup breadcrumbs (optional)

Direction

- Bring a large pot of water to a boil while you stem and wash the greens. When the water comes to a boil salt generously and add chard. Blanch for 1 minute, until just wilted, and using a skimmer or a slotted spoon, transfer to a bowl of cold water. Drain and squeeze out excess water, taking the chard up by the handful. Chop medium-fine and set aside. You should have about 2 cups.

- Bring the water back to a boil and blanch beet greens for 1 minute; if using spinach, blanch for 20 seconds only. Transfer to a bowl of cold water, drain and squeeze out excess water. Chop medium-fine. You should have about 1 cup (less for spinach).
- Preheat oven to 375 degrees. Oil a 2-quart baking dish with olive oil.
- Heat 2 tablespoons olive oil over medium heat in a large, heavy skillet and add onion. Cook, stirring often, until tender, about 5 minutes, and add leeks. Cook, stirring, until leeks begin to soften, 2 to 3 minutes, and add garlic and a generous pinch of salt. Cook, stirring, until garlic is fragrant, 30 seconds to a minute, and add cabbage and thyme. Cook, stirring often, until cabbage collapses in pan, about 5 minutes, and add another generous pinch of salt. Continue to cook the mixture until the cabbage is tender, sweet, and beginning to color, about 10 minutes. Stir in chopped blanched greens and season to taste with salt and pepper. Stir together for about a minute and remove from the heat.
- Beat eggs in a large bowl and add a pinch of nutmeg and salt and pepper to taste. Stir in rice or farro, vegetable mixture and cheeses. Scrape into prepared baking dish. If using breadcrumbs, toss with remaining tablespoon olive oil and sprinkle over the top. If not using breadcrumbs drizzle remaining oil over the top.
- Bake 40 to 45 minutes, until top is lightly browned. Remove from heat and allow to sit for at least 10 minutes before serving. Serve hot, warm or room temperature.

Nutrition Information

- 302: calories;
- 0 grams: trans fat;
- 8 grams: monounsaturated fat;
- 30 grams: carbohydrates;
- 16 grams: protein;
- 15 grams: fat;
- 5 grams: saturated fat;
- 2 grams: polyunsaturated fat;
- 9 grams: dietary fiber;
- 7 grams: sugars;
- 1049 milligrams: sodium;

328. Tijoe's Fungi

Serving: Six servings | Prep: | Cook: | Ready in: 1hours40mins

Ingredients

- 3 tablespoons butter
- ½ cup minced onion
- 2 ½ cups water
- ¼ teaspoon salt
- 1 ¼ cups yellow stone ground cornmeal
- ⅓ cup diced tomato, seeded and drained
- ½ cup frozen cut okra, thawed and coarsely chopped and well drained

Direction

- Melt the butter in a small frying pan and cook the onion over medium heat for five minutes, stirring often. Remove from the heat.
- Bring the water to a boil in a three-and-a-half-quart heavy saucepan, preferably a nonstick one. Stir in the salt and slowly pour in the cornmeal, stirring constantly with a wooden spoon. Reduce the heat to low and stir constantly for 10 minutes.
- Stir in the onion and butter, tomatoes and okra. Continue stirring for five minutes until the mixture rolls off the side of the pan and no longer sticks to the bottom.
- Turn the mixture onto a baking sheet and smooth the top evenly with a spatula into a 10-

inch circle, three-quarters of an inch thick. Cool for 15 minutes. Cover loosely with plastic wrap and let rest for one hour.
- Cut the fungi into about one-and-a-half-inch squares and serve at room temperature.

Nutrition Information

- 153: calories;
- 1 gram: sugars;
- 22 grams: carbohydrates;
- 7 grams: fat;
- 0 grams: trans fat;
- 2 grams: monounsaturated fat;
- 127 milligrams: sodium;
- 4 grams: saturated fat;
- 3 grams: protein;

---

329.   Tofu Scramble

Serving: 2 servings | Prep: | Cook: | Ready in: 55mins

Ingredients

- 1 large baked potato
- 2 teaspoons margarine
- 10 ounces firm tofu, drained and crumbled
- Pinch of turmeric
- ¼ cup chopped green onion
- ¾ cup chopped red pepper
- 1 cup slice fresh mushrooms
- 3 tablespoons salsa

Direction

- Peel potato and cut into small cubes.
- Melt margarine in a nonstick skillet and add tofu. Add turmeric and cook over high heat 5 minutes. Add vegetables and cook 5 minutes, or until vegetables are tender but crisp. Stir in salsa and serve.

Nutrition Information

- 421: calories;
- 17 grams: fat;
- 1 gram: trans fat;
- 5 grams: monounsaturated fat;
- 8 grams: polyunsaturated fat;
- 45 grams: carbohydrates;
- 29 grams: protein;
- 268 milligrams: sodium;
- 3 grams: saturated fat;
- 9 grams: dietary fiber;
- 6 grams: sugars;

---

330.   Tomates A La Provencale (Baked Tomatoes)

Serving: Eight servings | Prep: | Cook: | Ready in: 1hours10mins

Ingredients

- 8 (about 2 pounds) ripe, round tomatoes, cored and halved
- Salt and freshly ground black pepper to taste
- 8 cloves garlic, peeled
- ¾ cup freshly ground bread crumbs
- A handful fresh, flat-leaf parsley, finely minced
- 3 tablespoons extra-virgin olive oil

Direction

- Preheat the oven to 400 degrees.
- Arrange the tomatoes, cut side up, in a large baking dish. (Unless the tomatoes are exceptionally watery, do not seed or drain them; they will better hold their shape and the natural juices will mingle nicely with the garlic and herbs.) Season generously with salt and pepper. Slice the garlic into thin chips and sprinkle over the tomatoes. Combine the bread crumbs and parsley, and scatter the mixture over the tomatoes. Drizzle them with oil.
- Bake, uncovered, for one hour, or until the tomatoes are soft, browned and sizzling. Serve immediately.

Nutrition Information

- 260: calories;
- 12 grams: dietary fiber;
- 10 grams: protein;
- 8 grams: fat;
- 1 gram: saturated fat;
- 2 grams: polyunsaturated fat;
- 45 grams: carbohydrates;
- 4 grams: monounsaturated fat;
- 25 grams: sugars;
- 2163 milligrams: sodium;

---

331.   Tomato Salad

Serving: 2 servings | Prep: | Cook: | Ready in: 5mins

Ingredients

- ¾ pound ripe tomatoes
- 1 teaspoon olive oil
- 1 teaspoon balsamic vinegar

Direction

- Wash, trim and slice tomatoes.
- Whisk oil and vinegar in serving bowl; stir in tomatoes to coat well with dressing.

Nutrition Information

- 53: calories;
- 7 grams: carbohydrates;
- 5 grams: sugars;
- 9 milligrams: sodium;
- 3 grams: fat;
- 0 grams: polyunsaturated fat;
- 2 grams: protein;

---

332.   Tomato, Cucumber And Corn Salad

Serving: 6 servings | Prep: | Cook: | Ready in: 20mins

Ingredients

- 1 to 1 ¼ pounds ripe tomatoes, cut in small dice
- ½ European cucumber, 2 Persian cucumbers or 1 regular cucumber, peeled if waxy, seeded if the seeds are large, and cut in small dice
- 2 ears corn, steamed for 4 minutes and kernels removed from the cob
- 1 to 2 serranos or jalapeño pepper, minced (seeded for a milder salad), or 1/2 teaspoon Aleppo pepper
- Salt to taste
- ¼ cup chopped cilantro
- 2 tablespoons rice vinegar
- 1 tablespoon fresh lime juice or lemon juice
- 2 tablespoons extra virgin olive oil
- Optional: 1 ounce feta, crumbled (about 1/4 cup)

Direction

- Mix together all of the ingredients. Let sit in or out of the refrigerator for 15 minutes before serving, then toss again.

---

333.   Tomato, Zucchini And Avocado Salad

Serving: 6 servings | Prep: | Cook: | Ready in: 25mins

Ingredients

- 1 medium zucchini
- Salt to taste
- 5 medium tomatoes, finely chopped
- 1 or 2 jalapeño or serrano peppers, seeded if desired and finely chopped
- ¼ to ½ cup chopped cilantro, to taste

- 1 Haas avocado, ripe but not too soft, cut into tiny dice
- 3 tablespoons freshly squeezed lemon or lime juice
- 2 tablespoons extra virgin olive oil
- Boston lettuce or romaine lettuce leaves for serving

Direction

- Sprinkle the zucchini with salt, and drain in a colander for 15 minutes. Rinse if the zucchini tastes very salty, and drain on paper towels.
- Combine the tomatoes, chiles and cilantro in an attractive bowl. Combine the zucchini, avocado and lemon or lime juice and olive oil in another bowl. Taste and add salt if desired. Add to the tomatoes, and toss together gently. Taste and adjust seasonings. Serve on lettuce leaves as a salad, or serve over rice.

Nutrition Information

- 120: calories;
- 10 grams: fat;
- 1 gram: polyunsaturated fat;
- 7 grams: monounsaturated fat;
- 9 grams: carbohydrates;
- 4 grams: sugars;
- 2 grams: protein;
- 426 milligrams: sodium;

334. Tonics And Teas From My Pantry

Serving: Serves 2 | Prep: | Cook: | Ready in: 30mins

Ingredients

- 4 slices Meyer lemon
- 1 tablespoon minced ginger
- 2 cloves
- ⅛ teaspoon turmeric
- 2 ½ cups boiling water

- 2 to 3 teaspoons honey (to taste)
- Pinch of cayenne

Direction

- Place the lemon slices, ginger, cloves, and turmeric in a large measuring cup or teapot and pour on the boiling water. Stir in the honey, cover and let steep for 30 minutes. Strain and reheat if desired but do not boil. Just before serving add a tiny pinch of cayenne.

Nutrition Information

- 65: calories;
- 0 grams: polyunsaturated fat;
- 19 grams: carbohydrates;
- 3 grams: dietary fiber;
- 10 grams: sugars;
- 1 gram: protein;
- 15 milligrams: sodium;

335. Tuna, Cauliflower And White Bean Salad

Serving: Serves 4 generously | Prep: | Cook: | Ready in: 20mins

Ingredients

- ¾ pound cauliflower, broken into small florets (about 1/2 medium to large head)
- 2 tablespoons sherry vinegar or red wine vinegar
- 1 tablespoon fresh lemon juice
- Salt to taste
- 1 garlic clove, minced or puréed
- ½ to 1 teaspoon Dijon mustard, to taste
- 2 tablespoons plain yogurt or bean broth if using dried beans
- 6 tablespoons extra virgin olive oil
- 1 small red onion, cut in half and sliced in half-moons (optional)

- 1 5-ounce can tuna (packed in water or olive oil), drained
- 1 ½ cups cooked large white beans, or 1 can cannellinis, drained and rinsed
- 2 tablespoons chopped fresh parsley or a combination of parsley and marjoram

Direction

- Steam cauliflower for 5 to 6 minutes, until just tender.
- Place sliced onion, if using, in a bowl and cover with cold water. Soak 5 minutes. Drain, rinse and drain again on paper towels.
- Meanwhile in a small bowl or measuring cup, whisk together vinegar, lemon juice, salt, garlic, mustard and yogurt or bean broth. Whisk in olive oil.
- When cauliflower is tender remove from heat and toss with half the dressing in a large salad bowl. Drain tuna and add to bowl with cauliflower. Break up with a fork. Add cooked beans, onion and herbs. Toss together. Add remaining salad dressing and pepper, taste and adjust seasoning.

Nutrition Information

- 576: calories;
- 22 grams: fat;
- 0 grams: trans fat;
- 18 grams: dietary fiber;
- 33 grams: protein;
- 642 milligrams: sodium;
- 3 grams: polyunsaturated fat;
- 15 grams: monounsaturated fat;
- 67 grams: carbohydrates;
- 4 grams: sugars;

336.   Tuscan White Bean Salad

Serving: 8 servings | Prep: | Cook: | Ready in: 55mins

Ingredients

- 1 pound navy beans
- 4 to 5 large tomatoes, seeded and chopped
- 1 clove garlic, minced (green part removed)
- ½ cup chopped basil leaves
- ¼ cup extra-virgin olive oil
- Coarse salt and freshly ground pepper to taste

Direction

- Soak the beans in water to cover overnight.
- Drain the beans and simmer in water to cover until tender (about 30 minutes).
- Combine the remaining ingredients and toss with the warm beans. Correct seasoning and add more olive oil if necessary. Serve at room temperature.

Nutrition Information

- 268: calories;
- 8 grams: fat;
- 5 grams: monounsaturated fat;
- 38 grams: carbohydrates;
- 10 grams: dietary fiber;
- 14 grams: protein;
- 354 milligrams: sodium;
- 4 grams: sugars;
- 1 gram: polyunsaturated fat;

337.   Vanilla Custard With Prunes Poached In Lemon Verbena And Maple Caramel

Serving: Six servings | Prep: | Cook: | Ready in: 3hours

Ingredients

- 2 tablespoons dried lemon verbena leaves (or substitute 2 chamomile or verbena tea bags)
- 18 pitted prunes
- 5 ounces maple syrup
- 1 ounce heavy cream
- ½ ounce (1 tablespoon) butter
- 2 cups milk

- 1 vanilla bean or 1 teaspoon vanilla extract
- 4 eggs
- ½ cup sugar

Direction

- Prepare an infusion with the lemon verbena or tea bags and 2 cups boiling water. Add the prunes and let soak overnight. Drain the prunes thoroughly and pat dry. Set aside.
- In a small, heavy saucepan, heat the maple syrup to 275 degree, watching carefully to make sure the sugar does not boil over. Remove from heat and whisk in cream and butter. Pour into 6 3-inch ramekins.
- Preheat the oven to 275 degrees.
- If using vanilla bean, bring milk and bean to a simmer in a heavy saucepan; remove from heat and let steep 10 minutes. Strain, and discard the vanilla bean. If using vanilla extract, heat the milk and stir in the vanilla.
- Meanwhile, in a separate bowl, beat together the eggs and sugar and pour in the infused milk. Mix gently. Place 3 prunes in each ramekin and divide the custard among them. Place in a hot-water bath and bake for 45 minutes, or until custard is set. Chill 2 hours. Unmold onto individual serving plates and serve.

Nutrition Information

- 320: calories;
- 1 gram: polyunsaturated fat;
- 9 grams: fat;
- 5 grams: saturated fat;
- 0 grams: trans fat;
- 2 grams: dietary fiber;
- 46 grams: sugars;
- 7 grams: protein;
- 82 milligrams: sodium;
- 3 grams: monounsaturated fat;
- 55 grams: carbohydrates;

338.   Vegan Chocolate Chip Banana Cake

Serving: 1 bundt or 5- by 10-inch loaf | Prep: | Cook: | Ready in: 1hours15mins

Ingredients

- 2 cups all-purpose flour (or gluten-free all-purpose flour plus 1 teaspoon xanthan gum)
- 1 cup sugar
- 1 teaspoon baking powder
- ½ teaspoon baking soda
- 1 teaspoon salt
- ½ teaspoon ground cinnamon
- ½ teaspoon ground nutmeg
- ½ teaspoon ground cloves
- ½ teaspoon ground ginger
- 1 cup mashed bananas (approximately 2 very ripe bananas, mashed on a plate using the back of a fork)
- 1 cup canned coconut milk, mixed well before measuring
- ½ cup canola oil
- 2 teaspoons white or apple cider vinegar
- 1 tablespoon pure vanilla extract
- 1 ½ cups semisweet chocolate chips (dairy free)
- Powdered sugar for garnish

Direction

- Heat oven to 350 degrees. Lightly grease a Bundt pan or a 5- by 10-inch loaf pan.
- In a large bowl, whisk together flour, sugar, baking powder, baking soda, salt, cinnamon, nutmeg, cloves and ginger. In a separate bowl, whisk together bananas, coconut milk, oil, vinegar and vanilla. Pour the wet mixture into the dry mixture and whisk until just combined. Fold in the chocolate chips; do not over-mix.
- Spread the batter evenly into the prepared pan. Bake for about 40 to 45 minutes in a Bundt pan or 50 to 60 minutes in a loaf pan until a toothpick inserted in the center of the cake comes out with a few crumbs clinging to

it. Check the cake often and if it gets too brown on top, cover with foil and continue to bake. Rotate the pan halfway through baking time. Let cool, then sift powdered sugar over top.

339. Vegan Pumpkin Soup

Serving: None | Prep: | Cook: | Ready in:

Ingredients

- 1 (4- to 5-pound) pumpkin (reserve the seeds) or 2 (14-ounce) cans pumpkin purée (plain, not the pumpkin pie purée)
- 2 tablespoons extra virgin olive oil
- 1 tablespoon toasted sesame oil
- ½ cup finely chopped shallots
- 5 cups vegetable stock
- 1 medium russet potato, peeled and chopped into 1/2-inch chunks
- 1 large carrot, peeled and sliced crosswise into 1/2-inch pieces
- 1 tablespoon dark brown sugar
- 2 teaspoons molasses
- Finely minced zest of 1 orange
- 2 teaspoons curry powder
- 1 cup soy milk or other nondairy milk
- ½ cup dark rum
- Dash of Tabasco sauce
- Salt and freshly ground black pepper to taste
- ½ teaspoon freshly grated nutmeg
- 1 ½ cups grated vegan sharp cheddar cheese, or nutritional yeast (optional)

Direction

- To prepare the pumpkin: Cut the pumpkin in half through the center and scoop out the seeds and strings. Reserve the seeds. Carefully cut away the hard peel with a paring knife — or, better, a vegetable peeler — and chop the flesh. You should have about 6 cups of pumpkin flesh.

- In a large saucepan over medium-low heat, warm the olive oil with the sesame oil. Add the shallots and sauté them, stirring occasionally, until they are translucent, 3 to 4 minutes. Add the stock, pumpkin, potato and carrot, raise the heat to high, and bring the mixture to a boil. Reduce the heat to low, cover and simmer until the vegetables are tender, about 25 minutes.

- Using an immersion blender, purée the soup until very smooth, or (carefully!) purée in batches in a blender with a towel placed over the lid. Stir in the brown sugar, molasses, orange zest and curry powder. Over low heat, stir in the soy milk, dark rum and Tabasco sauce. Taste carefully. Season with salt and pepper and add the nutmeg.

- Toast the pumpkin seeds. Preheat oven to 250 degrees. In a roomy bowl, stir the seeds with peanut oil or canola oil — about a half cup of oil for every four cups of seeds. Add a nominal amount of kosher salt. Try adding a bit of thyme, oregano, cumin, coriander, cardamom and/or cayenne pepper, if you like.

- Line baking sheet(s) with parchment paper. Spread the seeds in one layer on the sheets. Toast slowly for about an hour, checking them every 10 to 15 minutes and stirring if they are browning unevenly. Store the toasted seeds in tightly sealed containers lined with paper towels.

- Serve soup in warmed bowls, and pass the toasted pumpkin seeds and vegan cheddar cheese for sprinkling.

Nutrition Information

- 316: calories;
- 9 grams: fat;
- 2 grams: polyunsaturated fat;
- 1593 milligrams: sodium;
- 5 grams: monounsaturated fat;
- 48 grams: carbohydrates;
- 13 grams: dietary fiber;
- 20 grams: sugars;
- 7 grams: protein;

340.   Vegetable Cakes

Serving: 6 servings | Prep: | Cook: |Ready in: 20mins

Ingredients

- 1 cup diced celery
- 1 cup diced carrots
- 1 cup diced onion
- 1 medium-size tomato, seeded and diced
- 1 cup fresh peas
- 3 tablespoons chopped fresh basil
- 1 teaspoon ground cumin
- ½ teaspoon turmeric
- ⅛ teaspoon red pepper flakes
- 1 pound baking potatoes, baked until tender and peeled
- 3 large egg whites
- 3 tablespoons nonfat milk
- 1 cup dried bread crumbs
- Spray of olive oil
- Red pepper coulis (see recipe)

Direction

- In a large nonstick skillet, slowly saute celery, carrots, onion and tomato until they are tender. Partly cover the pan and, if the tomatoes are not sufficiently juicy, add a dash of water to keep from burning. Transfer to a large mixing bowl and add the peas, basil, cumin, turmeric and red pepper flakes. Stir and set aside to cool.
- In another bowl, mash the potatoes.
- In small bowl, whisk together egg whites and milk. Stir into mashed potatoes until smooth. Add remaining vegetable mixture and combine well. Form into 12 two-ounce patties. Put bread crumbs in shallow pan and lightly coat both sides of patties.
- Spray a large skillet with olive oil spray and saute the patties over medium heat until brown, about 5 minutes each side. Serve with red pepper coulis.

Nutrition Information

- 196: calories;
- 1 gram: polyunsaturated fat;
- 37 grams: carbohydrates;
- 6 grams: sugars;
- 8 grams: protein;
- 198 milligrams: sodium;
- 2 grams: fat;
- 0 grams: trans fat;
- 5 grams: dietary fiber;

341.   Vegetable Tostadas With Dark Chili Garlic Sauce

Serving: 4 servings. | Prep: | Cook: |Ready in: 1hours

Ingredients

- For the salsa:
- 2 ancho chilies, stemmed, seeded and deveined (wear rubber gloves to do this)
- 4 garlic cloves, peels on
- 1 canned chipotle chili in adobo, rinsed, stemmed and seeded (wear rubber gloves to do this)
- 1 cup water, more as needed
- 1 tablespoon canola oil
- 1 tablespoon cider vinegar or rice vinegar
- 1 teaspoon sugar
- Salt to taste
- For the tostadas:
- 1 small sweet potato (about 6 ounces), baked
- 1 large carrot (about 6 ounces), peeled and cut in 1/2-inch dice
- 1 medium turnip (about 5 ounces), peeled and cut in 1/2-inch dice
- ¼ pound green beans, cut in 1/2-inch pieces
- ⅔ cup fresh or thawed frozen corn kernels
- 6 corn tortillas, cut in half and toasted in the microwave
- 2 ounces feta cheese or queso fresco, crumbled

- 1 cup thinly shredded cabbage (green or red) or romaine lettuce
- ½ small red or white onion, thinly sliced across the grain (optional)

Direction

- Make the salsa. Place the ancho chilies in a bowl and cover with boiling water. Place a plate on top so that chilies stay submerged. Soak for 30 minutes.
- Meanwhile, toast the garlic cloves in their skins in a dry skillet, stirring, until there are black spots here and there on the skin, the flesh has softened somewhat, and your kitchen smells like toasted garlic. Remove from the heat, allow to cool and remove the skins. Cut away the root end of each clove.
- Drain the soaked chili. Transfer to a blender and add the garlic and chipotle, along with .5 cup of the water. Blend until smooth. Place a strainer over a bowl and strain the sauce.
- Heat a heavy medium saucepan or skillet over medium-high heat and add the oil. Add a spoonful of the purée to see if the pan is hot enough. If it sizzles loudly on contact, pour all of the purée into the pan; if it doesn't, wait a couple of minutes and try again. Cook, stirring, until the sauce thickens and begins to stick to the pan. Add the remaining water, the vinegar, sugar, and salt to taste, and bring to a simmer. Cook, stirring, until the sauce has the consistency of ketchup. Add more water if necessary. Taste, adjust salt, and remove from the heat.
- Steam the carrots, turnips and green beans until tender, about 5 minutes. Add to the sauce along with the sweet potatoes and corn, and stir gently until the vegetables are coated. Heat through in the saucepan and spoon onto the toasted tortillas. Sprinkle with the cheese, cabbage or lettuce, and optional onions, and serve.

Nutrition Information

- 275: calories;
- 9 grams: sugars;
- 3 grams: monounsaturated fat;
- 0 grams: trans fat;
- 2 grams: polyunsaturated fat;
- 44 grams: carbohydrates;
- 8 grams: protein;
- 771 milligrams: sodium;

---

342.   Vegetables À La Grecque

Serving: 6 servings | Prep: | Cook: | Ready in: 1hours

Ingredients

- 6 tablespoons white wine vinegar, champagne vinegar or sherry vinegar
- ½ cup dry white wine
- ½ cup extra-virgin olive oil
- 4 or 5 plump garlic cloves, smashed and peeled
- 1 good-size shallot, coarsely chopped
- Bouquet garni made with 4 sprigs parsley, 2 bay leaves and large sprig of thyme
- 4 teaspoons coriander seeds, lightly crushed
- 1 teaspoon fennel seeds
- 12 black peppercorns
- ½ to 1 teaspoon kosher or fine sea salt, to taste
- ¾ pound carrots, peeled, quartered at fat ends, halved at narrow ends, and cut in 2-inch lengths
- 1 small cauliflower, cut into florets
- ½ pound cremini or white mushrooms, trimmed and quartered if large, or halved if small
- Trimmed hearts from 4 medium-size artichokes, halved or quartered (plus leaves for garnish, optional)
- Juice of 1 large lemon
- Coarse sea salt or fleur de sel
- ¼ cup finely chopped fresh parsley, or use a mix of herbs such as chervil, tarragon, parsley, marjoram, thyme and chives

Direction

- In a 3- or 4-quart saucepan combine vinegar, wine, olive oil, garlic cloves, shallot, bouquet garni, coriander seeds, fennel seeds, peppercorns, kosher salt and 3 cups water. Bring to a simmer over medium heat and cook 15 to 30 minutes while you prepare vegetables.
- Add carrots to the broth and simmer 5 minutes. Add cauliflower, bring back to a simmer, and cook another 15 minutes, until carrots and cauliflower are tender but not mushy. Using a slotted spoon, remove vegetables to a bowl. Some of the broth and seeds can come along with them.
- Add mushrooms to broth and simmer 5 minutes. Remove to bowl with carrots and cauliflower.
- Stir broth and ladle 11/2 cups plus some of the coriander seeds into a small saucepan. Set aside.
- Add artichoke hearts to the pot in which you cooked the other vegetables and simmer 25 to 30 minutes, until tender. Transfer to bowl with other cooked vegetables. If using artichoke leaves, steam them now. When finished, discard this broth.
- Bring reserved broth in the small saucepan to a boil and cook until liquid reduces to 1/2 cup. Pour over the vegetables, add lemon juice and fleur de sel and toss. Taste and adjust seasoning. Leave at room temperature until ready to serve (for best flavor, let vegetables marinate for a few hours), or refrigerate for up to 3 days. Just before serving, garnish with herbs and, if you wish, with steamed artichoke leaves, which can be dipped into the marinade. Serve on small plates with the reduced marinade spooned on top.

343. Vegetarian Apple Parsnip Soup

Serving: 6 to 8 servings | Prep: | Cook: | Ready in: 2 hours

Ingredients

- Homemade Vegetarian broth
- 2 tablespoons olive oil
- 1 onion, peeled and diced
- 4 carrots, peeled and diced
- ½ celery stalk, diced
- 2 leeks, cleaned and diced
- 2 bay leaves
- 2 branches thyme
- 3 tomatoes, diced, or 6 ounces canned San Marzano plum tomatoes
- A few sprigs of parsley
- A few sprigs of chervil
- Salt to taste
- Freshly ground pepper to taste
- Soup
- 1 pound parsnips, peeled and diced
- Juice of 1 lemon
- 2 tablespoons olive oil
- 2 tablespoons butter or pareve margarine
- 6 shallots, diced
- 4 tart apples, peeled and diced
- 1 cup cider
- 8 cups vegetable broth (see above)
- Salt to taste
- White pepper to taste
- A few gratings of nutmeg
- 1 teaspoon cider vinegar (optional)

Direction

- To make the broth: heat the olive oil very slowly in a large pot. Add the onion, carrots, celery and leeks and sauté until the onions are transparent.
- Add 10 cups of water along with the bay leaves, thyme and tomatoes. Bring to a boil and simmer over low heat, half covered, for 45 minutes. During the last few minutes of cooking, add the parsley and chervil, and season with salt and freshly ground pepper to taste. Put everything through a sieve and set the broth aside.
- For the soup: put the parsnips and the lemon juice in a large bowl. Cover with water and let sit until you are ready to make the soup. Drain and dry the parsnips.

- Heat the olive oil and the butter in a heavy soup pot. Add the shallots, parsnips and apples and sauté for about 10 minutes, or until the onions are clear but not golden. Add the cider and cook uncovered for 5 minutes. Then add the broth, bring to a boil, cover, and simmer slowly for 40 minutes. Add salt, white pepper and nutmeg.
- Purée the soup in a blender or food processor, and, if you want more acidity, add the cider vinegar. Serve immediately.

344.   Veloute De Poisson (A Thick White Fish Sauce)

Serving: about 1 3/4 cups | Prep: | Cook: | Ready in: 15mins

Ingredients

- ¼ cup butter
- 6 tablespoons flour
- 2 cups fish broth
- Salt to taste if desired

Direction

- Melt the butter in a saucepan and add the flour, stirring with a wire whisk.
- When blended and smooth, add the broth, stirring rapidly with the whisk. Add salt. Cook, stirring often from the bottom, about 10 minutes.

Nutrition Information

- 187: calories;
- 9 grams: saturated fat;
- 1 gram: polyunsaturated fat;
- 4 grams: protein;
- 11 grams: carbohydrates;
- 0 grams: sugars;
- 445 milligrams: sodium;
- 14 grams: fat;

345.   Veracruzana Chicken Stew With Winter Squash

Serving: 4 to 6 servings. | Prep: | Cook: | Ready in: 1hours45mins

Ingredients

- 1 medium onion, peeled and quartered
- 4 garlic cloves, unpeeled
- 1 28-ounce can tomatoes in juice
- 2 tablespoons extra virgin olive oil
- 6 to 8 skinned chicken legs and/or thighs (can use boneless thighs)
- Salt and freshly ground pepper
- 1 ½ cups chicken stock
- 10 medium green olives, pitted and finely chopped
- 1 tablespoon capers, rinsed and finely chopped
- ¼ cup raisins (optional)
- 1 sprig fresh rosemary
- 1 teaspoon dried oregano, preferably Mexican
- 1 2-inch cinnamon stick
- 1 bay leaf
- ¼ teaspoon cayenne
- 1 pound butternut squash, peeled and cut in small dice
- 2 tablespoons dry sherry (optional)

Direction

- Preheat the broiler. Line a small baking sheet or a pie tin with foil and place the onion and garlic on it. Place under the broiler, close to the heat. Broil for 2 minutes and check. As soon as the garlic skin is charred, remove the cloves and set aside. Turn the onion, using tongs, and continue to broil, turning often, until it is charred and softened, 5 to 10 minutes. Remove from the heat.
- Peel the garlic and transfer to a blender with the onion and tomatoes (do this in 2 batches if your blender is small). Blend until smooth.

- Heat 1 tablespoon of the oil over medium-high heat in a deep lidded frying pan or a heavy casserole. Season the chicken with salt and pepper and brown for 5 minutes on each side, in batches if necessary. Transfer to a bowl. Pour off the fat from the pan.
- Keep the heat high and add the remaining olive oil. Add the blended tomato mixture to the pan all at once. It should sear and splutter. Cook, stirring, for a couple of minutes, until the mixture thickens noticeably, then add 1/2 cup of the stock and salt to taste. Turn the heat down to low and simmer, stirring from time to time, for 15 minutes. Stir in the remaining chicken broth.
- Return the chicken pieces to the sauce, along with any liquid that has accumulated in the bowl. Add the olives, capers, raisins, rosemary, oregano, cinnamon stick, bay leaf, cayenne and squash and bring back to a simmer. Season to taste with salt and pepper, cover and simmer over low heat for 30 minutes, or until the chicken and squash are tender. Stir in the sherry, if desired, and continue to simmer for another 5 minutes. Taste and adjust seasoning. Serve with rice or other grains.

Nutrition Information

- 140: calories;
- 20 grams: carbohydrates;
- 5 grams: dietary fiber;
- 702 milligrams: sodium;
- 7 grams: sugars;
- 1 gram: polyunsaturated fat;
- 4 grams: protein;

346.   Vietnamese Pancakes

Serving: 4 servings | Prep: | Cook: |Ready in: 30mins

Ingredients

- 2 eggs
- ⅓ cup rice flour, available at Asian specialty stores
- Pinch salt
- 1 teaspoon sugar, preferably superfine
- 2 tablespoons plus 2 teaspoons vegetable oil
- 6 shiitake mushrooms, stems removed and finely sliced
- ¼ pound cooked, peeled small shrimp
- 3 pieces thinly sliced lean cooked ham, julienned
- ½ cup bean sprouts
- ¼ cup thinly sliced scallions
- 2 tablespoons finely sliced basil leaves
- 2 tablespoons finely sliced mint leaves

Direction

- In a medium-size bowl, lightly whisk the eggs. Then whisk in the rice flour, 3/4 cup of water, salt and sugar. Set aside for 10 minutes. Strain the batter through a fine mesh sieve to remove any lumps.
- In a 10-inch skillet, heat 2 teaspoons of the oil over medium-high heat. Add the mushrooms, and cook, stirring, until just softened, about 3 minutes. Remove from the pan, and set aside.
- Return the skillet to the stove, and raise the heat to high. Add 1 tablespoon of oil, and heat until very hot. Pour in half the rice-flour batter, and swirl it quickly around to coat the pan evenly. Add half of the mushrooms, and cook, covered, for 1 minute. Remove lid and add half the shrimp, ham, bean sprouts and scallions. Cook, uncovered, until pancake is golden brown and crispy, about 4 to 5 minutes more.
- Use a spatula to loosen the edge of the pancake, and carefully slide it out onto a serving plate. Return the pan to the heat, and add the remaining tablespoon of oil. Pour in the remaining batter, and cook the second pancake in the same manner, using the remaining mushrooms, shrimp, ham, bean sprouts and scallions. Transfer the pancake to another plate. Garnish the pancakes with the

basil and mint, cut into wedges and serve immediately with soy sauce dip (see recipe).

Nutrition Information

- 245: calories;
- 14 grams: fat;
- 9 grams: monounsaturated fat;
- 17 grams: carbohydrates;
- 3 grams: sugars;
- 416 milligrams: sodium;
- 2 grams: dietary fiber;
- 0 grams: trans fat;
- 12 grams: protein;

---

347. Warm Chickpeas And Greens With Vinaigrette

Serving: Serves four | Prep: | Cook: | Ready in: 1hours30mins

Ingredients

- 1 pound spinach or Swiss chard (1 bunch), stemmed and thoroughly cleaned
- ½ pound (1 1/8 cups) chickpeas, soaked for at least six hours in 2 quarts water
- A bouquet garni made with a bay leaf, a couple of sprigs each of parsley and thyme, and a Parmesan rind
- Salt
- freshly ground pepper
- 2 tablespoons fresh lemon juice
- 1 tablespoon red wine vinegar or sherry vinegar
- 1 garlic clove, minced or pureed
- ⅓ cup extra virgin olive oil
- ¼ cup finely chopped flat-leaf parsley
- 1 small red onion, chopped, soaked in cold water for five minutes and drained (optional)

Direction

- Bring a large pot of water to a boil while you stem and wash the spinach or chard. Fill a bowl with ice water. When the water in the pot comes to a boil, add the greens. Cook spinach no longer than one minute. Cook chard one to two minutes. Remove from the pot with a skimmer, and transfer to the ice water. Do not drain the water. Cool the greens for a couple of minutes in the ice water, and then drain and squeeze out excess water. Chop coarsely and set aside. Allow the pot of water to cool for about 15 minutes.
- Drain the soaked chickpeas, and add to the pot along with the bouquet garni. Bring to a boil, reduce the heat to low, cover and simmer for one hour. Add salt to taste, and continue to simmer until the beans are tender, 30 minutes to an hour.
- Drain the chickpeas through a strainer or colander set over a bowl. Return the broth to the pot if you wish to serve it as a light soup. Whisk together the lemon juice, vinegar, minced garlic, salt and pepper to taste, and the olive oil. Combine the cooked chickpeas, greens, parsley and red onion in a bowl, and toss with the dressing. Serve warm.

Nutrition Information

- 401: calories;
- 3 grams: saturated fat;
- 14 grams: protein;
- 4 grams: polyunsaturated fat;
- 8 grams: sugars;
- 474 milligrams: sodium;
- 22 grams: fat;
- 41 grams: carbohydrates;
- 9 grams: dietary fiber;

---

348. Warm Potato Broccoli Salad

Serving: 2 servings | Prep: | Cook: | Ready in: 15mins

Ingredients

- 12 ounces new potatoes
- 16 ounces whole broccoli or 8 ounces ready-cut broccoli florets (3 1/2 to 4 cups)
- 1 large scallion
- 2 teaspoons toasted sesame oil
- 2 tablespoons rice vinegar
- ⅛ teaspoon salt
- Freshly ground pepper to taste

Direction

- Scrub potatoes; do not peel. Cut into half-inch chunks. Cover with water, and cook about 5 minutes.
- Cut up whole broccoli into bite-size florets. Add to potatoes, and cook about 5 minutes.
- Wash, trim and cut scallion into small pieces.
- As soon as potatoes and broccoli are cooked, drain and set aside.
- In serving bowl, mix oil and vinegar. Add potatoes, broccoli and scallions, and stir well. Season with salt and pepper.

Nutrition Information

- 217: calories;
- 38 grams: carbohydrates;
- 4 grams: dietary fiber;
- 8 grams: protein;
- 194 milligrams: sodium;
- 5 grams: fat;
- 1 gram: saturated fat;
- 2 grams: sugars;

349.   Warm Shrimp And Beans

Serving: 4 servings | Prep: | Cook: | Ready in: 1hours15mins

Ingredients

- ½ pound dried cannellini beans
- Salt and freshly ground black pepper
- 7 tablespoons extra-virgin olive oil
- 20 jumbo shrimp, shelled and deveined
- 2 large garlic cloves, chopped
- 1 tablespoon chopped fresh rosemary leaves
- 1 cup diced ripe tomatoes

Direction

- Cover beans with cold water to a depth of 2 inches above the beans. Soak for 4 hours or overnight.
- Drain the beans and place in a saucepan. Cover with cold water to a depth of 2 inches above the beans, bring to a boil, skim the surface, then lower the heat to medium. Cook the beans until they are tender, about 45 minutes. Drain, reserving 1/3 cup of the cooking liquid. Season the beans with salt and pepper to taste.
- Have four plates ready. Heat 2 tablespoons of the oil in a large skillet, add the shrimp and stir in the oil until golden on both sides, approximately 2 to 3 minutes. Add the garlic, rosemary, tomatoes, beans, reserved 1/3 cup of liquid from the beans and salt and pepper to taste. Cook, stirring gently for 2 minutes. Remove from heat and add remaining oil.
- Divide among the plates, arranging five shrimp on each like spokes of a wheel and mounding the bean mixture in the center. Serve.

Nutrition Information

- 438: calories;
- 17 grams: monounsaturated fat;
- 3 grams: polyunsaturated fat;
- 9 grams: dietary fiber;
- 2 grams: sugars;
- 19 grams: protein;
- 374 milligrams: sodium;
- 0 grams: trans fat;
- 25 grams: fat;
- 4 grams: saturated fat;
- 37 grams: carbohydrates;

350.   Warm Vanilla Cakes

Serving: 12 cakes | Prep: | Cook: | Ready in: 1hours

Ingredients

- 7 tablespoons butter; more for molds
- 10 ounces top-quality white chocolate
- 5 eggs at room temperature, separated
- 3 vanilla beans, split in half lengthwise and seeds scraped
- ¼ cup plus 2 tablespoons bread flour, sifted
- Pinch cream of tartar
- ¼ cup plus 2 tablespoons sugar
- Vanilla ice cream

Direction

- Melt butter and 7 ounces white chocolate in a double boiler over water that is hot but not boiling. When mixture is melted, remove from heat and stir until smooth. Whisk in egg yolks and half the vanilla-bean seeds. Sift flour over mixture. Whisk until smooth.
- In an electric mixer fitted with a whisk, combine egg whites and cream of tartar. Whisk until fluffy. Slowly add sugar a little at a time, until meringue is shiny and tight. Fold a little of the chocolate mixture into meringue; then fold meringue into remaining chocolate mixture, until mixture is smooth. Cover with plastic wrap, and refrigerate about 8 hours.
- Heat oven to 375 degrees. Line a baking sheet with parchment paper. Butter 12 metal rings 2 1/2 inches in diameter and 1 1/4 inches high. Place them on parchment paper. Using a spatula, spoon cool batter into a pastry bag with a tip opening of about 1/2 inch. Fill molds 1/3 full. Break remaining chocolate into pieces about 1 inch square and 1/8 inch thick. Drop a piece in each mold. Sprinkle a little cluster of vanilla seeds from remaining beans. Cover chocolate with more batter so molds are barely 2/3 full.
- Bake 12 to 14 minutes, until risen and still a bit jiggly in center. Remove from oven. Have 12 plates ready. Slip tip of a knife under cake, and lift it a little; then slide a spatula underneath, and transfer to a serving plate. Holding mold in place with tongs, run a sharp knife around top edge of mold; then lift mold off cake with tongs. Repeat with other cakes. Serve immediately with ice cream.

351.   Watercress And Red Onion Salad

Serving: 4 servings | Prep: | Cook: | Ready in: 10mins

Ingredients

- 2 bunches watercress
- 2 tablespoons red-wine vinegar
- Salt and freshly ground pepper to taste
- 4 tablespoons olive oil
- ½ cup sliced red onion rings
- ¼ cup finely chopped parsley

Direction

- Cut off and discard the tough stems of the watercress. Rinse and spin dry.
- Place the vinegar in a salad bowl and add salt and pepper. Beat with a wire whisk while adding the oil. Add the watercress, onion rings and parsley and toss well to blend. Serve.

Nutrition Information

- 134: calories;
- 14 grams: fat;
- 2 grams: carbohydrates;
- 10 grams: monounsaturated fat;
- 1 gram: protein;
- 208 milligrams: sodium;

352. White Bean And Shrimp Salad

Serving: Four servings | Prep: | Cook: | Ready in: 3hours40mins

Ingredients

- ½ pound white beans
- 1 teaspoon salt, plus more to taste
- 1 bay leaf
- 1 pound medium-size shrimp, shelled and cleaned
- ½ teaspoon cayenne pepper
- ¼ cup fresh lemon juice
- 2 tablespoons olive oil
- 1 clove garlic, peeled and minced
- 1 white onion, peeled and minced
- ¼ cup minced parsley
- 1 tomato, seeded and cut into 1/2-inch dice
- 1 teaspoon freshly ground pepper, plus more to taste

Direction

- Cover the beans with cold water. Set aside to soak overnight. Drain, rinse under cold water and place in a heavy-bottomed pot. Add 2 cups cold water, 1/2 teaspoon salt and the bay leaf. Simmer until tender, about 1 1/2 hours.
- Place the shrimp in a large nonstick skillet. Add the cayenne and cook over medium-low heat until the shrimp is cooked through, about 5 minutes. Set aside to cool.
- Combine the lemon juice and olive oil in a large glass or ceramic bowl. Add the garlic, onion and parsley. Add the beans, shrimp and tomato. Toss to combine. Season to taste with the remaining 1/2 teaspoon of salt and the pepper. Cover and refrigerate for at least 2 hours, and up to 6, before serving.

Nutrition Information

- 356: calories;
- 0 grams: trans fat;
- 5 grams: monounsaturated fat;
- 4 grams: sugars;
- 30 grams: protein;
- 656 milligrams: sodium;
- 9 grams: fat;
- 1 gram: polyunsaturated fat;
- 42 grams: carbohydrates;
- 10 grams: dietary fiber;

353. White Beans With Chicory

Serving: Serves 4 as a main dish, 6 as a starter | Prep: | Cook: | Ready in: 2hours30mins

Ingredients

- 1 pound dried cannellini beans, washed and picked over, soaked for 4 to 6 hours in 2 quarts water and drained
- 1 medium onion, peeled, cut in half
- 4 garlic cloves, crushed
- 1 bay leaf
- Salt to taste
- 1 pound escarole, chicory or Batavia lettuce, leaves separated and washed
- 3 tablespoons olive oil
- 2 garlic cloves, minced

Direction

- Combine the beans with 2 quarts water in a 4-quart pot and bring to a boil. Skim any foam, then add the onion, crushed garlic, bay leaf and salt to taste. Reduce the heat, cover and simmer for 2 hours, until the beans are very tender. Taste and adjust seasoning. Remove and discard the onion, garlic cloves if desired, and bay leaf. Drain through a colander or strainer set over a bowl. Mash the beans with a potato masher and moisten with some of the cooking liquid. Stir in 2 tablespoons of the olive oil. The purée should be loose.
- Bring a large pot of generously salted water to a boil and add the lettuce. Cook until just tender, about 2 minutes. Transfer to a bowl of

cold water and drain. Squeeze out water and chop coarsely.

- Heat the remaining olive oil in a large, heavy skillet over medium heat. Add the garlic, cook for 30 seconds, and stir in the lettuce. Cook for about 1 minute, stirring, until the lettuce is nicely coated. Season with salt and pepper. Serve with the mashed beans.

Nutrition Information

- 500: calories;
- 11 grams: fat;
- 2 grams: polyunsaturated fat;
- 5 grams: sugars;
- 29 grams: protein;
- 7 grams: monounsaturated fat;
- 75 grams: carbohydrates;
- 19 grams: dietary fiber;
- 626 milligrams: sodium;

---

354.   White Or Pink Beans With Beet Greens And Parmesan

Serving: 4 servings | Prep: | Cook: | Ready in: 2hours15mins

Ingredients

- 2 tablespoons extra virgin olive oil
- 1 large red onion, finely chopped
- 2 to 4 garlic cloves (to taste), minced
- ½ pound white or pink beans (1 1/8 cups), soaked in 1 quart water for 4 hours or overnight
- 6 cups water
- A bouquet garni made with a bay leaf, a few sprigs each parsley and thyme, and 2 good-size Parmesan rinds
- Salt to taste
- 1 generous bunch beet greens (about 3/4 pound), stemmed, washed well in 2 changes of water and coarsely chopped

- Freshly ground pepper
- Freshly grated Parmesan for serving

Direction

- Heat the olive oil over medium heat in a large, heavy soup pot or Dutch oven and add the onion. Cook, stirring often, until the onion is tender, about 5 minutes, and add the garlic. Cook, stirring, until it is fragrant, 30 seconds to a minute. Drain the beans and add to the pot, along with 6 cups water (or enough to cover the beans by at least an inch) and the bouquet garni. Bring to a gentle boil, add salt to taste, cover and simmer 1 1/2 to 2 hours, until the beans are soft and fragrant. Taste, adjust salt, and add pepper. Remove the bouquet garni.
- Stir in the beet greens and simmer 5 to 10 minutes. Serve in wide bowls and pass freshly grated Parmesan for sprinkling.

Nutrition Information

- 101: calories;
- 7 grams: fat;
- 1 gram: polyunsaturated fat;
- 9 grams: carbohydrates;
- 2 grams: sugars;
- 3 grams: protein;
- 5 grams: monounsaturated fat;
- 4 grams: dietary fiber;
- 1268 milligrams: sodium;

---

355.   Whole Roast Salmon

Serving: 6 servings | Prep: | Cook: | Ready in: 45mins

Ingredients

- 1 4-pound Atlantic salmon (2 1/4 inches at thickest point), scaled and cleaned, gills removed, head and tail on, interior cavity well washed
- 2 tablespoons olive oil

226

- 2 tablespoons fresh lemon juice
- 2 tablespoons kosher salt
- Freshly ground black pepper to taste
- ½ to ¾ cup white wine

Direction

- Remove fish from refrigerator. With a large kitchen knife cut 3 deep parallel diagonal slashes in each side. Put the fish on a diagonal into a roasting pan 18 by 13 by 2 inches.
- Rub the olive oil and the lemon juice into both sides of the fish, including the slits, and into the internal cavities. Sprinkle both sides with salt and pepper. Marinate about 1 hour at room temperature.
- Fifteen to 20 minutes before cooking the fish, put rack in center of oven. Heat oven to 500 degrees. Cook fish 22 minutes. Using two very large spatulas, transfer fish to serving platter.
- Put the roasting pan on top of the stove over medium-high heat. Add the white wine to the pan. As it begins to bubble, scrape the bottom of the pan with a wooden spoon. Scrape up all the crispy bits. Reduce liquid by half. Use as a sauce with the fish.

Nutrition Information

- 692: calories;
- 2 grams: carbohydrates;
- 782 milligrams: sodium;
- 45 grams: fat;
- 15 grams: monounsaturated fat;
- 12 grams: polyunsaturated fat;
- 62 grams: protein;
- 10 grams: saturated fat;
- 0 grams: sugars;

---

356. Whole Wheat Seeded Loaves

Serving: | Prep: | Cook: | Ready in: 5hours15mins

Ingredients

- 25 grams sunflower seeds (approximately 2 tablespoons plus 1 teaspoon)
- 25 grams sesame seeds (approximately 2 1/2 tablespoons)
- 25 grams flax seeds (approximately 2 1/2 tablespoons)
- 25 grams rolled oats (approximately 1/4 cup)
- 25 grams pumpkin seeds (approximately 2 tablespoons)
- 180 grams water (approximately 3/4 cup) plus about 60 grams additional water
- 170 grams bread flour or unbleached all-purpose flour (approximately 1 1/3 cups)
- 170 grams lukewarm water (approximately 3/4 cup less 2 teaspoons)
- 4 grams dry yeast (approximately 1 teaspoon)
- 250 grams whole-wheat flour (approximately 2 cups) or 125 grams bread flour and 125 grams whole-wheat flour
- 12 grams sea salt (approximately 1 1/2 teaspoons)

Direction

- Mix seeds and oats together with 180 grams of water in a medium mixing bowl; cover with plastic wrap and and let soak overnight in the refrigerator.
- Combine 170 grams bread flour or all-purpose flour, 170 grams lukewarm water, and yeast in bowl of a standing mixer and mix together until well combined. Cover with plastic and leave to ferment at room temperature for two hours or until it doubles in volume. Meanwhile, remove bowl with nuts and seeds from the refrigerator, drain and bring to room temperature.
- Add drained seeds, 250 grams whole-wheat flour and sea salt to the starter. Start mixing on medium speed. The dough should come together in the first minute. If it does not and you see dry ingredients in the bottom of the bowl, add about 1/4 cup of water. Mix dough for 5 minutes on medium speed, then turn the

speed up to medium-high and mix 5 to 7 minutes more, or until dough is elastic.

- Cover bowl with plastic wrap and set in a warm spot to rise for 1 hour.
- Dust work surface lightly with flour and scrape out dough. Weigh dough and divide into 2 equal pieces. Shape each piece into a ball or into oblong pointed loaves. (For oblong loaves, first shape into balls, cover with a towel or lightly with plastic and let rest for 15 minutes. Then press the dough out to a rectangle about 3/4 inch thick. Take the side closest to you and fold lengthwise halfway to the center of the loaf. Lightly press down to seal. Take the top flap and bring it toward you over the first fold to the middle of the loaf and lightly press down to seal. Flip over so seam is on the bottom and roll back and forth with both hands to form an oblong loaf with pointy ends. Place on a sheet pan lined with parchment paper and repeat with the remaining dough. Cover with a towel and place in a warm spot for one hour.)
- Preheat oven to 450 degrees with a pizza stone on the middle rack and a small sheet pan on bottom of the oven for 30 to 45 minutes. Have 1 cup water ready in a small cup or a glass. (If you have a large pizza stone, you can bake both loaves at once. If you have a standard home pizza stone, bake one loaf at a time and place the other loaf in the refrigerator to slow down the fermentation.) Dust a pizza peel or flat baking sheet lightly with flour, semolina or cornmeal and place one loaf on top. Using a razor blade or a moistened bread knife, make a 1/2-inch deep horizontal cut down the middle of loaf from one end to the other, or if the loaves are round make 2 slashes across top. Slide loaf onto pizza stone and close oven door. Wait 30 seconds, then open oven door quickly and pour water onto the sheet pan on the bottom of the oven to create steam. After 5 minutes take the sheet pan out of the oven. Bake for a total of 30 to 35 minutes, until loaf is dark brown and sounds hollow when you tap the bottom. Transfer loaf to a wire rack to cool

completely for 45 minutes. Repeat with other loaf.

Nutrition Information

- 266: calories;
- 4 grams: polyunsaturated fat;
- 43 grams: carbohydrates;
- 6 grams: dietary fiber;
- 10 grams: protein;
- 7 grams: fat;
- 1 gram: saturated fat;
- 0 grams: sugars;
- 2 grams: monounsaturated fat;
- 279 milligrams: sodium;

---

357.   Whoopie Pies

Serving: 6 pies | Prep: | Cook: | Ready in: 1hours

Ingredients

- For the cakes
- ¼ pound (1 stick) butter, at room temperature
- 1 cup light brown sugar
- 1 large egg
- 1 teaspoon vanilla extract
- 1 ¼ teaspoons baking soda
- 1 teaspoon sea salt
- 2 cups all-purpose flour
- ½ cup cocoa
- 1 cup buttermilk
- For the buttercream filling
- 3 large egg whites
- ¾ cup sugar
- ½ pound butter (2 sticks), at room temperature
- ¾ teaspoon vanilla
- ¼ teaspoon sea salt

Direction

- For the cakes: Preheat oven to 350 degrees. In a mixing bowl, cream together the butter and brown sugar. Add the egg and vanilla extract and beat until light and creamy. In a separate bowl, whisk together the baking soda, salt, flour and cocoa. Add dry ingredients to butter mixture in three parts, alternating with buttermilk, and combining well after each addition.

- Using an ice cream scoop or a spoon, scoop out 12 1/4-cup mounds of batter and place about 6 inches apart on a parchment-lined baking sheet. Bake until tops are puffed and cakes spring back when touched, 12 to 14 minutes. Remove from oven and cool completely before filling.

- For the buttercream filling: For best results, follow directions carefully, paying attention to required temperatures. Fill bottom half of a double boiler (or a medium saucepan) with an inch or two of water, and bring to a boil over high heat. In top half of double boiler (or a metal bowl), combine egg whites and sugar. Place over simmering water and whisk just until sugar is dissolved and temperature reaches 180 degrees on an instant-read thermometer.

- Using a whisk attachment on a heavy-duty mixer, whisk egg whites and sugar on high until they double in volume and become thick and shiny. Continue to whisk until cool. Reduce speed to medium and begin to add butter about 1/2 tablespoon at a time, until all the butter is incorporated. Add vanilla and salt. If mixture looks curdled, continue to whisk until it is smooth. Increase speed to high and whisk for 1 more minute. Use immediately or place in an airtight container and chill for up to 3 days, whisking buttercream again before using.

- For assembly: Using an ice cream scoop or spoon, place 1/4 cup buttercream on flat side of each of 6 cakes, spreading it to edges. Top filled half with another cake to sandwich the buttercream. Store in an airtight container at room temperature for up to 3 days, or wrap individually and freeze for up to 3 months.

Nutrition Information

- 602: calories;
- 23 grams: saturated fat;
- 9 grams: monounsaturated fat;
- 38 grams: sugars;
- 388 milligrams: sodium;
- 8 grams: protein;
- 36 grams: fat;
- 1 gram: trans fat;
- 2 grams: polyunsaturated fat;
- 65 grams: carbohydrates;
- 3 grams: dietary fiber;

358. Wild Mushroom Soup

Serving: Six servings | Prep: | Cook: | Ready in: 45mins

Ingredients

- 1 ½ pounds meaty wild mushrooms, like shiitake, cremini and portobello, or a combination of cultivated and wild mushrooms
- 6 cups chicken or beef stock
- 1 tablespoon curry powder
- 1 tablespoon light soy sauce
- Salt and freshly ground pepper to taste
- 3 tablespoons plain yogurt, lightly stirred
- 1 tablespoon minced coriander leaves

Direction

- Rinse the mushrooms and trim off any tough stems. Chop them fairly fine and place in a heavy 4-quart saucepan with 1/2 cup of the stock. Cook over very low heat for about 25 minutes, until the mushrooms have wilted.
- Stir in the curry powder, cook for 1 or 2 minutes longer and then add the remaining stock and the soy sauce. Simmer for 10 minutes, then remove from the heat and allow to cool briefly.
- Puree the mixture in a blender in several batches. (The results will be much smoother than can be obtained with a food processor.) The soup may be prepared up to this point 2

days in advance and refrigerated, or frozen for later use.

- When ready to serve, reheat the soup and season with salt and pepper.
- Spoon the soup into warmed bowls and float 1/2 tablespoon of the yogurt on top of each portion or gently swirl it to make a pattern. Sprinkle with the coriander and serve.

Nutrition Information

- 98: calories;
- 3 grams: fat;
- 1 gram: dietary fiber;
- 2 grams: monounsaturated fat;
- 10 grams: carbohydrates;
- 4 grams: sugars;
- 7 grams: protein;
- 592 milligrams: sodium;

359. Winter Squash With Anchovies, Capers, Olives And Ricotta Salata

Serving: Serves 6 | Prep: | Cook: | Ready in: 45mins

Ingredients

- 3 tablespoons extra virgin olive oil
- 1 medium onion, chopped
- 1 large garlic clove, peeled and crushed
- 3 anchovy fillets, preferably salted fillets, rinsed, soaked for 5 minutes in cold water, drained and chopped
- 2 tablespoons capers, rinsed, chopped if large
- 2 pounds peeled winter squash, cut in 3/4-inch chunks about 7 cups
- ½ cup imported black olives, pitted
- ¼ ounce (1 tablespoon) freshly grated ricotta salata
- Salt
- freshly ground pepper

Direction

- Heat the oil over medium heat in a large, lidded skillet and add the onion, garlic clove, anchovy fillets and capers. Cook, stirring, until the onion is tender, about 5 minutes. Remove the garlic clove and discard.
- Add the squash, stir together, add about 1/4 cup of water if the pan is dry, and cover the pan. Cook, stirring often, for about 30 minutes, until the squash is tender. Add the olives and continue to cook, stirring, for another 5 to 10 minutes. Season to taste with salt and pepper (you probably won't need much salt).
- Transfer to a serving dish, sprinkle on the ricotta salata and serve.

Nutrition Information

- 140: calories;
- 4 grams: sugars;
- 451 milligrams: sodium;
- 8 grams: fat;
- 1 gram: polyunsaturated fat;
- 6 grams: monounsaturated fat;
- 16 grams: carbohydrates;
- 3 grams: protein;

360. Winter Vegetable Stew

Serving: 4 to 6 servings | Prep: | Cook: | Ready in: 3hours

Ingredients

- ⅓ cup raz al hanout spice mixture (available at specialty markets)
- 2 tablespoons raw cane sugar
- ½ tablespoon kosher or coarse sea salt
- ¾ teaspoon freshly ground black pepper
- 1 6 to 8 pound Hubbard squash
- 10 cipolini
- 10 red pearl onions
- ½ peeled butternut squash, cut into bite-size pieces (about 4 cups)

- 4 tablespoons extra virgin olive oil
- ½ peeled rutabaga, cut into bite-size pieces (about a cup)
- 1 medium peeled turnip, cut into bite-size pieces (about a cup)
- 2 large Peruvian potatoes, peeled and cut into 1-inch chunks
- 3 to 4 large Yukon Gold potatoes, peeled and cut into 1-inch chunks
- ½ leek, thinly sliced (white part and one inch of green)
- 3 toasted cinnamon sticks
- ½ jalapeno pepper, seeded and minced
- ½ teaspoon freshly grated nutmeg
- Squash sauce (see recipe)
- ¼ cup coarsely chopped fresh herbs
- 4 to 6 slices Russian black bread or walnut raisin bread

Direction

- Heat oven to 350 degrees. In a bowl, combine raz al hanout, sugar, coarse salt and pepper. Set aside.
- Cut top off Hubbard squash as a lid. Seed and scrape inside of squash clean. Wash, and reserve seeds. Rub lid and inside of squash with half of spice mixture. Place lid and squash, cut side down, on baking sheet. Cover with foil. Bake for 45 minutes. Remove lid. Return squash to oven, and bake for 45 minutes more, until tender.
- Meanwhile, place cipolini and pearl onions on a baking sheet, and roast for 15 minutes. Spread butternut squash cubes on a separate baking sheet, sprinkle lightly with 1 tablespoon olive oil and roast for 20 minutes. On another baking sheet, arrange rutabaga and turnip cubes in two separate piles. Sprinkle each lightly with 1/2 tablespoon olive oil, and roast, taking turnips out after 15 minutes and leaving rutabaga to continue for 10 minutes more. Peel roasted pearl onions, and cut cipolini onions in half.
- Put potatoes in a steamer basket over simmering water, and steam for 10 minutes, until slightly softened.

- In a large pot over medium heat, warm remaining olive oil. Add onions, leeks, cinnamon sticks, jalapeno and nutmeg, and saute until leeks start to soften. Add squash, rutabaga and turnip, and heat through. Add all of the squash sauce and potatoes, and bring to a simmer. Cook for 20 minutes, until all vegetables are tender.
- Meanwhile, spread Hubbard squash on a baking sheet, sprinkle with olive oil and salt, and toast in oven until they start to pop, about 10 minutes. Set aside to cool.
- When vegetables are done, turn off heat, and add fresh herbs. To serve, ladle stew into cavity of Hubbard squash. Toast bread, and place a slice in each warmed bowl. Ladle stew into bowl. Sprinkle spice mix on rim of squash. With carving knife, cut a thin slice of squash horizontally across rim. Place slice on stew in bowl. Sprinkle rim with more spice mix, and the stew with more fresh herbs. Repeat with remaining bowls. Garnish with seeds.

---

361. Wolfgang Puck's Salmon With Celery Root Puree

Serving: Four servings | Prep: | Cook: |Ready in: 50mins

Ingredients

- The sauce:
- 6 tablespoons unsalted butter
- 1 shallot, chopped
- 1 clove garlic, minced
- 1 tomato, peeled, seeded and chopped
- ½ bottle cabernet sauvignon
- 2 tablespoons balsamic vinegar
- 1 cup chicken stock
- Salt and freshly ground pepper to taste
- The celery-root puree:
- 1 medium-sized baking potato, peeled
- 1 celery root, peeled
- ½ cup heavy cream
- 2 tablespoons butter

- Salt and freshly ground pepper to taste
- The salmon:
- 1 ½ tablespoons fresh ginger, finely minced
- 1 ½ tablespoons black pepper, chopped or roughly cracked
- 4 salmon fillets, Alaskan King or other, each about 6 ounces
- Olive oil for grilling or sauteing

Direction

- To make the sauce, heat two tablespoons of the butter in a large saute pan until the butter is foamy. Add the shallot, garlic and tomato and saute at medium-low heat for about five minutes, or until the shallot is translucent.
- Add the wine and vinegar and cook over medium-high heat until reduced by half. Add the chicken stock and reduce again by half. Finish the sauce by stirring in the remaining four tablespoons of butter, one tablespoon at a time. Season with salt and freshly round pepper to taste. Keep warm.
- Prepare the celery-root puree by chopping the potato and celery root into one-inch cubes. Put in a medium-sized pot and cover with lightly salted cold water. When the water comes to a boil, cook for 15 to 20 minutes, or until soft. Drain and return the potato and celery root to the pot. Heat briefly until the excess moisture evaporates.
- Pass the celery Root-potato mixture through the small disk of a food mill or a ricer. (Do not use a food processor; it will make a gluey puree.) Return to the pot.
- Stir in the cream and cook, stirring, over medium heat for about three minutes, or until thickened.
- Remove from the heat. Stir in the butter and the salt and pepper to taste.
- In a small bowl, combine the ginger and black pepper. Season the salmon with salt and coat with the ginger-pepper mixture. If grilling or broiling the salmon, sprinkle the fillets with olive oil and cook two minutes on each side. If sauteing the salmon, heat one tablespoon of olive oil in a large saute pan. When the pan is

very hot, add the salmon and cook two minutes on each side.
- Divide the sauce among four warm dinner plates. Spoon equal amounts of celery-root puree on the center of each plate. Place salmon on top.

---

362.   Zhug

Serving: About 8 servings (1 generous cup) | Prep: | Cook: | Ready in: 40mins

Ingredients

- 2 teaspoons whole black peppercorns
- 2 teaspoons coriander seeds
- 1 teaspoon cumin seeds
- ½ teaspoon cardamom seeds, extracted from about 10 cardamom pods
- 6 garlic cloves, smashed
- 4 serrano chiles, cut into very thin coins
- 1 to 3 teaspoons kosher salt, to taste
- 3 tightly packed cups roughly chopped cilantro leaves and stems
- 1 ½ tightly packed cups roughly chopped parsley leaves
- ½ cup extra-virgin olive oil

Direction

- In a small, dry pan, toast the peppercorns, coriander seeds, cumin seeds and cardamom seeds over medium heat, shaking the pan occasionally, until slightly toasted and fragrant, about 2 minutes.
- Transfer the seeds to a large mortar and pestle, and pulverize into a coarse powder.
- Add the garlic and chiles, and season evenly with kosher salt. Grind the mixture together until a tight paste forms, 4 to 5 minutes.
- Add about 1/3 of the cilantro and parsley, and continue to pound together into a rough paste, another 4 to 5 minutes. Repeat two more times, adding the remaining cilantro and

parsley in two batches, until the mixture is a slightly pulpy paste, 4 to 5 minutes.

- Drizzle in the olive oil while constantly pounding and grinding together the herb mixture until you achieve a loose, homogeneous paste. Continue to mix until it has the consistency of applesauce, about 2 minutes. Let it stand 10 minutes before serving.

363. Zrazy Zawijane (Stuffed Rolls Of Beef)

Serving: 6 servings | Prep: | Cook: | Ready in: 2hours55mins

Ingredients

- 1 four-inch piece of stale French bread, crust removed
- 1 Polish-style dill pickle
- 3 thick slices of slab bacon
- 6 thin slices rump or round steak, about 4 ounces each
- 2 medium-size onions, peeled, halved and very thinly sliced
- Salt and freshly ground black pepper to taste
- 1 ½ cups chicken or beef broth
- 2 Polish dried mushrooms, or 1/2 ounce Italian dried porcini
- ¼ cup or more all-purpose flour
- 2 tablespoons cooking oil
- 2 tablespoons unsalted butter

Direction

- Preheat oven to 350 degrees.
- Slice the bread lengthwise into six pieces, each one as thick as an index finger. Slice the pickle lengthwise into six fingers. Cut each bacon slice in half crosswise.
- Place a steak slice between two pieces of plastic wrap or wax paper and pound evenly until it is very thin. Distribute a few onion slices over center of meat, add a finger of

bread, one of pickle and a half slice of bacon. Sprinkle a very little salt (the bacon will add salt) and some pepper over all. Wrap the steak slice around the stuffing and tie or fasten with toothpicks. Repeat with remaining steak slices.

- Bring the chicken or beef stock to a slow simmer and add the dried mushrooms. (If using Italian mushrooms, soak them first in warm water for 20 minutes, then rinse to rid them of sand.) Remove from heat and let mushrooms steep in hot stock for at least 20 minutes.
- Roll beef rolls in the flour.
- Heat one tablespoon of oil and one of butter in a skillet over medium-high heat until butter foam subsides. Add remaining sliced onion and cook, stirring and tossing slices until onion is thoroughly browned; remove to an ovenproof dish. Add remaining butter and oil to the pan and brown the beef rolls evenly on all sides. When rolls are thoroughly browned and crisp on all sides, add to the dish with the onions. Distribute onions over and around beef rolls.
- Add stock and mushrooms, and bring to a gentle simmer on top of the stove. Place in oven and bake about two hours, or until the beef rolls are fork tender and the braising liquid has reduced to a syrupy gravy.

Nutrition Information

- 379: calories;
- 1 gram: dietary fiber;
- 29 grams: protein;
- 24 grams: fat;
- 11 grams: carbohydrates;
- 3 grams: polyunsaturated fat;
- 2 grams: sugars;
- 590 milligrams: sodium;
- 8 grams: saturated fat;
- 0 grams: trans fat;

364. Zucchini Salad

Serving: 6 servings | Prep: | Cook: |Ready in: 12mins

Ingredients

- 2 medium zucchini (about 1 1/2 pounds total)
- ½ teaspoon salt
- ½ teaspoon ground black pepper
- 2 tablespoons white wine vinegar
- 4 tablespoons corn or safflower oil

Direction

- Preheat oven to 400 degrees.
- Wash the zucchini, trim and discard the ends, and cut crosswise into 1/4-inch thick rounds. Arrange the rounds in one layer on a large cookie sheet and sprinkle them with the salt. Place in oven for 5 to 7 minutes, until they soften slightly.
- Transfer the rounds to a bowl and toss them lightly with the pepper, vinegar and oil. Serve immediately.

Nutrition Information

- 93: calories;
- 9 grams: fat;
- 1 gram: protein;
- 7 grams: polyunsaturated fat;
- 2 grams: sugars;
- 185 milligrams: sodium;

- 8 flat anchovy fillets
- Salt and freshly ground pepper to taste
- 1 tablespoon red wine vinegar
- 3 tablespoons olive oil
- 2 tablespoons chopped fresh parsley or basil

Direction

- Trim the ends of the zucchini and cut them slightly on the bias into 1/4-inch thick slices. Drop the slices into boiling salted water. Let them simmer half a minute. The zucchini should remain crunchy. Drain and let cool.
- Arrange the zucchini and tomatoes in alternate patterns in a round dish. Sprinkle with the onions and chopped egg. Arrange the anchovy fillets on top. Sprinkle with salt, pepper, vinegar and oil. Add the parsley and serve.

Nutrition Information

- 106: calories;
- 8 grams: fat;
- 1 gram: dietary fiber;
- 5 grams: carbohydrates;
- 3 grams: sugars;
- 4 grams: protein;
- 341 milligrams: sodium;

365. Zucchini Tomato Salad

Serving: 4 to 6 servings | Prep: | Cook: |Ready in: 10mins

Ingredients

- 3 small zucchini, about 1 pound total
- 4 ripe plum tomatoes, sliced
- ¼ cup finely chopped onion
- 1 hard-boiled egg, coarsely chopped

Index

Conclusion

Thank you again for downloading this book!

I hope you enjoyed reading about my book!

If you enjoyed this book, please take the time to share your thoughts and post a review on Amazon. It'd be greatly appreciated!

Write me an honest review about the book – I truly value your opinion and thoughts and I will incorporate them into my next book, which is already underway.

Thank you!

If you have any questions, **feel free to contact at:** _author@thymerecipes.com_

Mary Rosado

thymerecipes.com

Printed in Great Britain
by Amazon